THIRD LANGUAGE ACQUISITION AND LINGUISTIC TRANSFER

Is acquiring a third language the same as acquiring a second? Are all instances of nonnative language acquisition simply one and the same? In this first book-length study of the topic, the authors systematically walk the reader through the evidence to answer these questions. They suggest that acquiring an additional language in bilinguals (of all types) is unique and reveals things about the links between language and mind, brain and cognition, which are otherwise impossible to appreciate. The patterns of linguistic transfer and what motivates it when there are choices (as can only be seen from third language acquisition onwards) underscore a key concept in linguistic and psychological sciences: economy. Overviewing the subfields examining multilingual acquisition and processing, this book offers an expanded systematic review of the field of multilingual morphosyntactic transfer and provides recommendations for the future emerging field.

JASON ROTHMAN is Professor of Linguistics at UiT The Arctic University of Norway and Nebrija University in Madrid, Spain.

JORGE GONZÁLEZ ALONSO is a Postdoctoral Researcher in Linguistics at UiT The Arctic University of Norway.

ELOI PUIG-MAYENCO is an ESRC Postdoctoral Research Fellow at the University of Southampton, United Kingdom.

CAMBRIDGE STUDIES IN LINGUISTICS

General Editors: P. AUSTIN, J. BRESNAN, B. COMRIE, S. CRAIN, W. DRESSLER, C. J. EWEN, R. LASS, D. LIGHTFOOT, K. RICE, I. ROBERTS, S. ROMAINE, N. V. SMITH

Third Language Acquisition and Linguistic Transfer

In this series

Earlier issues not listed are also available

THIRD LANGUAGE
ACQUISITION AND
LINGUISTIC TRANSFER

JASON ROTHMAN

UiT The Arctic University of Norway & Nebrija University

JORGE GONZÁLEZ ALONSO

UiT The Arctic University of Norway

ELOI PUIG-MAYENCO

University of Southampton

CAMBRIDGE
UNIVERSITY PRESS

CAMBRIDGE
UNIVERSITY PRESS

University Printing House, Cambridge CB2 8BS, United Kingdom

One Liberty Plaza, 20th Floor, New York, NY 10006, USA

477 Williamstown Road, Port Melbourne, VIC 3207, Australia

314–321, 3rd Floor, Plot 3, Splendor Forum, Jasola District Centre,
New Delhi – 110025, India

79 Anson Road, #06–04/06, Singapore 079906

Cambridge University Press is part of the University of Cambridge.

It furthers the University's mission by disseminating knowledge in the pursuit of
education, learning, and research at the highest international levels of excellence.

www.cambridge.org
Information on this title: www.cambridge.org/9781107082885
DOI: 10.1017/9781316014660

First published 2019

Printed and bound in Great Britain by Clays Ltd, Elcograf S.p.A.

A catalogue record for this publication is available from the British Library.

Library of Congress Cataloging-in-Publication Data
Names: Rothman, Jason, author. | Gonzalez Alonso, Jorge, 1986– author. | Puig-
Mayenco, Eloi, 1990– author.
Title: Third language acquisition and linguistic transfer / Jason Rothman, Jorge
Gonzalez Alonso, Eloi Puig-Mayenco.
Description: New York, NY : Cambridge University Press, 2019. | Series: Cambridge
studies in linguistics ; 163 | Includes bibliographical references and index.
Identifiers: LCCN 2019018393 | ISBN 9781107082885 (hardback)
Subjects: LCSH: Language transfer (Language learning) | Multilingualism. | Language
acquisition. | Economy (Linguistics) | Language and languages – Study and teaching. |
BISAC: LANGUAGE ARTS & DISCIPLINES / Linguistics / Psycholinguistics.
Classification: LCC P118.25 .R68 2019 | DDC 404/.2–dc23
LC record available at https://lccn.loc.gov/2019018393

ISBN 978-1-107-08288-5 Hardback

To Mom
To Irati and Oihan
To Laura
In memory of David Rothman, Albert Puig-Mayenco and
Blueberry

Contents

Figures

Tables

Acknowledgments

It is said that it takes a village to raise a child. It seems to us that this is even more true when your child is a research monograph. This book reflects the input – direct and indirect alike – of a long list of people. Imperfect as such an attempt is destined to be, we would be remiss not to try to thank everyone explicitly here.

First, to our beloved families – wonderful partners, children (human and pet alike), parents, siblings, friends and lab members/mates, whom we count as members of our families – this book would have been impossible without your support, understanding and generosity on so many levels. It is a testament to what you all bring to our lives in general, particularly to the indulgence with which you permit us to work crazy hours and deal with our ever-changing priorities and moods to accomplish this arduous task. This book would not have been possible had it not been for you, and so it stands most directly in your honor. We love you and thank you from the bottom of our hearts.

To our many colleagues in the field who have directly and indirectly shaped the content of this book, we are forever in your debt. We are especially grateful to all the researchers who have contributed to the emerging field of L3/ L*n* morphosyntax; without them, we could not have written this book, and the field would not be as promising. A special note to our colleagues who have offered competing models: thank you for your ideas, argumentation, dedication to finding empirical answers to difficult questions and, most sincerely, for the many conversations (and critiques) we have had over the years. Although we do not see eye-to-eye on all the merits, we are proud to consider you all as cherished and respected colleagues, and even as our friends. Our nascent field is potentially special – or at least small – enough that mutual respect and, when necessary, collegial disagreement not only abound but are also the default. Although there will be statements and/or interpretations of ours with which you disagree, we hope that you find our treatment of your work and that of others accurate and handled with the respect we intended.

We wish to acknowledge our gratitude to several colleagues who took the time to read parts of the book and offered very helpful comments: Terje Lohndal, Ellen Bialystok, David Green, Judith Kroll, Viorica Marian, Rex Sprouse, Tanja Kupisch, Bonnie Schwartz, Roumyana Slabakova, Fatih Bayram, Jennifer Cabrelli Amaro, Marit Westergaard, Tom Rankin, Itziar Laka, Elena Valenzuela, Mike Iverson, Tanja Angelovska, Rosalinde Stadt, Aafke Hulk, Laurent Dekydtspotter, Jeanne McGill, Kathleen Bardovi-Harlig, Becky Halloran, Theres Grüter, Francesco Saldarini, Isabel Jensen, Bror Strand and Stela Leticia Krevelj, as well as the anonymous reviewers of the manuscript. There is no doubt that your comments have improved this book enormously. If you should reread parts of it, we hope you will appreciate how very earnestly we took your suggestions and criticisms.

The team at CUP has been wonderful throughout the long process of writing this book. In particular, we wish to thank Helen Barton for her keen editorial eye, her encouragement and her relentless support. Most of all, we thank her for her patience with us. We also wish to thank the series editorial board for their support of the book, particularly Suzanne Romaine, whose rapid and exceedingly positive response to including the book in this series was extremely humbling.

Of course, we could not have taken on such a project without the support of our colleagues, institutions/centers, laboratories and students. In this regard, we wish to thank the School of Psychology and Clinical Language Sciences, the Centre for Literacy and Multilingualism (CeLM) and the Centre for Integrative Neuroscience and Neurodynamics (CINN) at the University of Reading, as well as the University of Reading's Psycho-/Neurolinguistics Lab. In addition, we thank the Department of Language and Culture and the Language Acquisition, Variation and Attrition (LAVA) research group at UiT The Arctic University of Norway as well as the Acquisition, Variation, and Attrition (AcqVA) cross-university research group in Norway (UiT and NTNU).

1 *Setting the Context*

1.0   General Introduction

This book is about the acquisition of a third language (or more additional languages) in adulthood; that is, when a bilingual – a child who is a simultaneous (2L1) bilingual, a child who has sequentially acquired a second language (L2) or an adult who is a sequential L2 bilingual – acquires yet another language later in life. Is learning a third (L3) or more (L*n*) language different from learning an L2 or just more of the same? If the process is different or similar, what are the implications for important questions related to linguistics, psychology, cognitive science and other fields? Addressing and providing some answers to the aforementioned is the overarching goal of this book.

For a very long time, it was taken for granted that all instances of nonnative, sequential language acquisition were fundamentally equivalent. Such a claim was never stated explicitly; however, standard empirical practice in the study of adult L2 acquisition across virtually all paradigms suggested that few people were preoccupied with the heterogeneous groups in so-called L2 studies before the turn of the millennium. In fact, it was not until the mid-2000s that researchers, at least those studying the acquisition of morphosyntax, began to contemplate in earnest the effect of knowing more than one previous language and thus to differentiate true L2 from multilingual learners systematically, at least with regard to L3 learners. Consequently, new questions began to emerge organically, such as the role that having more than one previously acquired system has on subsequent acquisition/processing or how this influence is selected among choices. At the time of writing this book in 2017–2018, gone are the days in which no one questioned linguistic-experience inclusion criteria in L2 acquisition. We now know that whether or not a target nonnative language is chronologically a second or later language matters a great deal for morphosyntax in the L3 initial stages and throughout L3 development. While we do not yet

1

understand all the variables that contribute to the following statement's veracity, the datasets available from over 15 years of dedicated L3 research – which we will review during the course of this book – clearly show that variables conspire such that the course of learning L3 morphosyntax is altered by the cumulative experience of having acquired not one but at least two previous languages.

As this book is primarily concerned with understanding the selection and subsequent effects of morphosyntactic transfer in the earliest stages of L3 acquisition, it is prudent to highlight from the outset that we take linguistic transfer to be at the level of mental representation of the developing grammar (that is, in terms of competence). This means that transfer differs in nontrivial ways from other subcases of crosslinguistic influence, which sit at the level of performance – real-time language use – even if true transfer and nonrepresentational instances of crosslinguistic influence can show exactly the same surface effect at times. Crosslinguistic influence is thus taken to include both representational (transfer) and nonrepresentational influence that manifests as in-the-moment bleeding over from another language at the level of performance/production. Thus, while transfer is a subtype of crosslinguistic influence, it should be distinguished from other types that map onto more superficial influences. The importance of this distinction is discussed and defended in much greater detail in Section 1.4. Moreover, this book will contextualize all the variables that pertain to research of this type by reviewing as much formal linguistic empirical work as is available on the topic of morphosyntactic L3/L*n* transfer.

The writing of this book is timely precisely because we have achieved a critical mass of data across an impressive cohort of L1→L2→L3 language pairings in recent years. Indeed, it is time to combine all this research in order to understand what a bird's-eye view of the available data tells us, while the relative youth of the field makes it possible for us to address all or a majority thereof. As homage to this nascent field, this book attempts to accomplish the following:

(a)   to contextualize, situate and provide a critical review of the study of adult L3 morphosyntax as it exists;

(b)   to challenge some of the current theorizing while making suggestions for standardizing terms and empirical practices;

(c)   to provide a research synthesis of as many studies as were available at the time of writing this book; and

(d)   to make some suggestions regarding where we think the field is going and/or should go.

1.1   Setting the Stage

What does it mean to be multilingual? *Multi-* derives from the Latin word *multus*, meaning much or many. For some, *multi-* refers to any number greater than one. Under such a view, anyone who speaks more than a single language is multilingual, including all types of native and sequential (nonnative) bilinguals. For others, *multi-* minimally denotes more than two. According to this view, one can only be considered multilingual if one is at least a native or sequential trilingual. This book will argue that – despite the same qualitative underlying (mental) mechanisms driving language acquisition and processing in all scenarios irrespective of age (see de Bot & Jaensch, 2015; Rothman, 2013, 2015) – the acquisition of a second and a third language are, on the whole, destined to present differently by the very nature of differences in the variables that contribute to them.

For the moment, however, to drive home an important point from the beginning, let us (over)simplify the world by defining people according to two macro-linguistic categories of monolinguals and nonmonolinguals, whereby the latter – anyone who is not a monolingual – is a subtype of multilingual. Based on this definition, what do you suppose the incidence of multilingualism in the world to be? The answer to this question might well surprise you. If you were to stop a random person on the streets of Cedar Rapids (Iowa, USA), Taiki (Japan), Henley-on-Thames (UK) or Jaén (Spain), it is highly likely that this person's guess would undershoot the reality of global multilingualism significantly. Were you to ask this same question to someone in Luxembourg City (Luxembourg), Barcelona (Spain), New Delhi (India), Tromsø (Norway) or Nairobi (Kenya), the answer might overshoot reality significantly. Why might it be the case that a typical British and Luxembourgish response would differ in this way?

Most estimates place global monolingualism at around 40%, which means that roughly 60% of the world's population consists of people who can be qualified as speakers of at least two languages (e.g., Ansaldo, Marcotte, Scherer, & Raboyeau, 2008; Grosjean, 1989; Potowski & Rothman, 2008; Romaine, 1995). Despite there being a verifiably accurate answer to the above question, the context/environment in which the people who are asked live is likely to influence the response. Although multilinguals outnumber monolinguals worldwide, there are few places in which the actual global distribution is true of local or even national contexts. Global percentages are averaged across groups of people; the actual incidence of monolingualism and multilingualism is not distributed evenly at most local levels. Therefore, it is not usually the case that 60% of any given subset population is multilingual, despite it being true that roughly 60% of the superset (the world's) population is multilingual. Let us take the European Union (EU) as an example, bearing in mind the generally positive view of bi-/multilingualism that thrives in this region. In fact, according to the 2012 *Eurobarometer Survey on Europeans and their Languages*:

(a)   88% think that knowing languages other than their mother tongue is very useful.

(b)   98% say mastering foreign languages will benefit their children.

(c)   72% agree with the EU goal of at least two foreign languages for everyone.

(d)   77% say that improving language skills should be a policy priority.

As discussed by Marian and Shook (2012), the EU reported having 56% bilingualism in 2006 across its member states.[1] However, countries such as the UK are reported to have less than 20%, whereas countries such as Luxembourg, the Netherlands and Sweden report over 90%. While it can be said, then, that the arbitrary borders that encompass the EU as a whole more or less reflect what is believed to be the global distribution of multilingualism and monolingualism, this is only true for the average, not for the majority of individual member states. Nevertheless, what is true of the world as a whole and increasingly of more subset populations is that multilingualism dominates as the default case for linguistic knowledge.

Although much of the world has been multilingual for centuries, if not millennia, multilingualism in what have been functionally monolingual environments in contemporary terms, such as the United States, is sharply on the rise. Of course, multilingualism is clearly not a new phenomenon in such environments, where monolingualism is, in some sense, induced artificially by educational policies, the introduction of national languages, the status quo of default hegemonies (financial and others) and so on. Nevertheless, what is true of these societies compared to bona fide bi-/multilingualism is that the landscape of language distribution and function is de facto monolingual in a majority of policies, allowing for pockets of difference from this default state of affairs. A 2013 United States census report indicated that the number of people over the age of five who spoke a language other than English at home increased from 23,060,040 to 59,542,596, or by 158.2%, between 1980 and 2010. To put this increase into perspective, it is useful to know that, during the same period, the number of people over the age of five who spoke only English at home increased from 187,187,415 to 229,673,150, or only by 22.7%. In a subsequent United States census report focusing on the largest 15 metro-politan areas (by population) in 2015, 10 cities reported that at least a quarter of people aged five or older spoke a language other than English at home, while six cities reported that this was the case for at least a third of the population, and two reported that more than half of the demographic did so (New York 38%, Los Angeles 54%, Chicago 29%, Dallas 30%, Houston 37%, Washington DC 26%, Miami 51%, San Francisco 40%, Riverside 40% and Phoenix 26%). Although a handful of languages, such as Spanish and Vietnamese, constitute the vast majority of the "other" language category, roughly 350 languages contribute to this category of a language other than English. In New York City alone, for example, 192 different languages are reported as heritage languages that are spoken at home. The growth in bilingualism in the United States since only the 1980s is just one example of the consequences of increased globalization that has defined the greater part of the past 50 years or so. The distribution of the roughly 20% of natural bilinguals in the United States as a whole also reflects the global reality of actual distribution, at least in societies that were traditionally considered to be monolingual, whereas metro-politan areas have tended to be more linguistically diverse and thus dispropor-tionate epicenters of multilingualism.

Even in traditionally monolingual environments, the economic, social, linguistic, and cognitive values of bilingualism are reinforced by global migration patterns and the changing faces of internationalization and global markets. In all environments, particularly in those that are traditionally monolingual, multilingualism is often an additive process. That is, more people today are learners of second, third or more additional foreign languages than ever before. For decades, English has been the default second language of much of Europe and beyond (Jenkins, 2009; 2015). Since a mere fraction of Europe can claim English as a native language, this means that much of Europe's population that speaks English has learned it as a nonnative foreign language. Because compe-tence in English is becoming a default expectation for younger European citizens, it is less often the case that studying English alone as an additional language is deemed sufficient. Increasingly, young people are studying two or more additional languages, both in and outside of environments that are themselves multilingual. Although native English-speaking countries have traditionally lagged behind in terms of promoting learning a foreign language, and particularly with regard to learning multiple foreign languages, in 2014 Scotland legislated its 1+2 language policy, which will be fully implemented in 2021. In its essence, the 1+2 language policy will result in Scottish children taking two foreign languages throughout the course of their child-hood education through, at least, the third year of secondary schooling (roughly 14–15 years old). As can be seen, whether as the byproduct of naturalistic multilingualism or due to the purposeful study of foreign languages in monolingual environments, more people today have competencies in more than one language, sometimes in many more than one.

Linguistics and psychology, to name but two disciplines, have been investigating bilingualism for decades, with a notable increase in the past 20 years (Kroll & Bialystok, 2013), seeking – among other related questions – to understand the extent to which native and nonnative language acquisition and processing are similar and/or different. Understanding this more fully might be one of the best ways to reveal some processes of the mind, particularly how language is mentally represented. Over the past 40 years or so, much research on nonnative, second language acquisition (SLA) has focused on the question of whether an adult mind can acquire and represent language qualitatively in the same way that a child's mind can. Is there a fundamental difference between child and adult language acquisition? The answer to this question is a complex one and will be the subject of the next section of this chapter. Suffice it to say, for now, that there is plenty of evidence – even mere lay observation – to suggest that the processes are different on some level. However, it is not clear that differences in the routes of learning (such as developmental sequences) and ultimate success mean that the mechanisms underlying child native and adult nonnative acquisition are fundamentally distinct. What is clear, however, is that language acquisition is determined partly by previous linguistic experience. In the case of the young monolingual child learning her native language, there is no previous language-specific experience with other languages that can intercede to shape the path of acquisition. Whenever there are opportunities from experience with other languages, there seems to universally be influence from that other language, even in young children. Research has revealed that simultaneous bilingual children (see, e.g., Nicoladis, 2018; Serratrice, 2013) and child second language learners (see Chondrogianni, 2018; Haznedar, 2013) show evidence of crosslinguistic influence from the other language they already know or are in the process of acquiring, depending on age. The fact that adults show more crosslinguistic influence is perhaps not surprising since they have spent more time being monolingual than have children who are learning second languages. In any case, what is clear is that previous linguistic experience is deterministic for the acquisition of subsequent languages, irrespective of age.

It is only very recently that researchers have begun to ask whether or not one should predict differences between second and third language acquisition a priori, or if the divide is best kept as a difference between native versus nonnative acquisition and/or child versus adult acquisition. In either position, there would be no need to separate the acquisition of a second from a third (or more) language(s), since the second and the third would be equally nonnative and the age of acquisition can be controlled irrespective of the number of languages. As alluded to above, whether by design or not, until the past decade or so, most researchers in L2 acquisition focusing on morphosyntax did not distinguish systematically between true L2 and L3 acquisition, as many so-called L2 studies have included a combination of true L2 learners and multi-lingual participants. Over the past decade, however, much research has argued and shown that L2 and L3/L*n* acquisition are significantly different processes, particularly with regard to how previous linguistic experience unfolds at the beginning stages and the ensuing impact this has on development over time (see, for discussion, Cenoz, Hufeisen, & Jessner, 2001; De Angelis & Dewaele, 2011; González Alonso & Rothman, 2017a; González Alonso, Rothman, Berndt, Castro, & Westergaard, 2017; Rothman, Cabrelli Amaro, & de Bot, 2013). It is now relatively uncontroversial to claim that L2 and L3/L*n* acquisition are unique processes that are worthy of serious study in their own right. It is important to emphasize from the outset that claiming the processes are distinct at some level merely reflects observation from empirical studies, in that L2 and L3 acquisition under controlled conditions can present differently. The claim, however, is definitely not an evaluative statement regarding any possible extent to which underlying mechanisms involved in one language, say the L2, are distinct from those involved in another, such as the L3. As discussed in Rothman (2013), the null hypothesis is that all acquisition is underlyingly the same and makes use of the same mechanisms. Rothman argued that what appears to be different between L1 and L2 compared to L3/L*n* acquisition would, then, be a reflection not of the internal mechanisms at play but rather of how they interact with external elements which, by definition, are different across all groups. For example, a child L1 learner likely has a hardwired predisposition to avoid redundancies in grammar formation to the same extent as adult nonnative speakers; however, due to the fact that she has not yet had the language-specific experience that an L2 learner has had, and an L3/L*n* learner even more, each of these cases presents differently on the surface in terms of the paths and even the outcomes of development. In fact, there is no shortage of evidence that child L1 acquisition displays hardwired constraints (domain-general and/or domain-specific ones) that delimit the course of language acquisition (Ambridge & Lieven, 2011; Guasti, 2002; Snyder, 2007). Accordingly, observable differences might very well sit at a superficial level, which is partially explained by the amount and nature of linguistic (and other) experiences that apply to various types of acquisition scenarios in different ways.

For various reasons that will be discussed in detail throughout this book, it is no longer optional or merely cautiously prudent to treat adult L2 and L3 acquisition differently as it relates to scientific inquiry. Moreover, only in multilingualism can one really begin to disentangle the dynamics of previous linguistic influence on subsequent language acquisition/learning/processing, precisely because multilingualism provides the opportunity for influence to come from multiple sources. Determining what is selected and why, specifically in multilingualism, has the potential to tell us much more about the mind and about how language is represented than merely describing the initial interlanguage grammars for L3/Ln learners.[2] However, the importance of describing and understanding the nature of initial-stage grammars is not to be understated, precisely because describing the initial L3/Ln interlanguage grammars accurately and effectively delimits the success of developmental and ultimate attainment theories (González Alonso & Rothman, 2017a). The strength of any building is inherently related to the strength of its foundation; similarly, the relative success of developmental theories is partly dependent on their accuracy in describing the initial points of departure of that which they seek to explain.

1.2   Adult Second Language Acquisition: Acquisition Potential and L1 Effects

Before honing in exclusively on L3/Ln acquisition, it is important that we explain briefly what has been done over the past 40-plus years of research into adult nonnative L2 acquisition. This is crucial for several reasons. There is no denying that the study of L3 acquisition and its theoretical basis emerges from the study of adult L2 acquisition. Moreover, certain facts that originated in the literature on L2 acquisition and have been imported into L3 acquisition studies need to be established to justify how and why the L3 acquisition of morphosyntax is studied the way it is today. Thus, this section provides a nonexhaustive review of the main questions in L2 acquisition studies of morphosyntax as well as the tendencies that can be identified after more than four decades of dedicated research in light of what they bring to bear on L3/Ln acquisition.

With the exception of children who grow up learning more than two languages from the beginning of their lives, multilingual acquisition occurs after a period of bilingualism; that is, either simultaneous (2L1) or sequential (child L2 or adult L2) bilinguals acquiring yet another language in childhood or adulthood. Many sequential L3/Ln learners – in fact, the robust majority of the subjects used in the available L3/Ln studies to date – were previously adult second language (L2) learners; that is, individuals who were initially monolingual and who then (successfully) acquired an L2 starting after the onset of puberty. Given that we are particularly interested in how previous linguistic systems affect/contribute to the initial mental representations of L3/Ln interlanguage grammars, what determines the selection of a source (the L1, L2 or both), the timing of transfer (one complete system transfer at the beginning, partial transfer throughout development or somewhere in between) and what the knock-on effects thereof are for L3/Ln development, it is quite important that we engage with what is known regarding adult L2 acquisition. This is true for several reasons, to which we now turn.

First, although there is still much to investigate and to be revealed, adult L2 acquisition is much more widely studied and better understood than is sequential multilingual acquisition. Since sequential L3 acquisition shares more contextually defining characteristics with adult L2 acquisition than it does with child L1 acquisition in some obvious and not so obvious ways (see Bardel & Falk, 2012; Falk & Bardel, 2011), understanding what is known in the larger, better investigated subfield of adult nonnative acquisition can allow us to consolidate the implications of decades of work and to capitalize on them to avoid pitfalls as this nascent field grows. Crucially, doing so permits us to have an informed point of departure for the creation and testing of L3/Ln hypotheses. As some insights from decades of studying L2 acquisition/processing are more or less uncontroversial, such insights can be used a priori to shape our initial L3/Ln predictions. Methodologically, the collective experience of SLA has already highlighted some constraints for testing and/or which methodologies work best for probing adults' initial grammatical hypotheses, interlanguage development and ultimate attainment. Thus, engaging with the L2 literature affords us the opportunity to not have to reinvent the wheel. Observations of differences between the two subcases of language acquisition, however, do not necessarily mean that they are accomplished using or sustained by distinct underlying cognitive mechanisms. In fact, L3/Ln studies need designed-for-purpose methodologies and independent theories, a point we will stress repeatedly in this book. Nevertheless, it is also likely that there will be behavioral crossover among all instances of adult language acquisition, if reflective of nothing more than the commonality of variables they share as compared to instances of child L1 (such as fully developed domain-general cognition at the onset of learning, knowledge of a completely developed native system, differences in quantity and quality of input exposure, individual personality traits that affect and/or delimit how we seek out input and what we do with it and so forth).

Knowing what is possible and impossible in terms of grammatical acquisition in adulthood is part and parcel of being able to develop sound theories of multilingual acquisition and processing, particularly with regard to offering meaningful predictions for transfer. If it were truly the case, as some have claimed, that adult L2 learners cannot acquire new morphosyntactic representations for domains in the L2 that differ underlyingly from those in their L1 or do not exist in their L1 (e.g., Bley-Vroman, 1989, 2009; Clahsen & Felser, 2006a, b; Long, 2005, 2007; Meisel, 2011), then one could not expect to see unambiguous transfer of grammatical representations that could only have been acquired during the course of L2 acquisition.

Let us consider the following scenario to drive the above point home. Albert and Vincent met two years ago at university. Albert is from rural Catalonia in the northeastern part of Spain. He speaks Catalan and Spanish as his native languages (exposed to both by native-speaking parents from birth). Vincent is from Seattle, Washington. English is his sole native language. As was the case for Albert with regard to English, Vincent was an exceptionally successful second language learner of Spanish during his teenage years. The new best friends have decided that learning yet another language is important for their future success as businessmen and, since they speak the same languages well, they decide they will enroll in Portuguese classes together. No one would deny that Catalan, Spanish and Portuguese are closely related languages, as all are direct descendants from Latin and are known as modern Romance languages. Accordingly, these languages share many grammatical commonalities that English lacks. One such property is known as grammatical gender. Grammatical gender is an overt classification or a morphological attribution observed in lexical nouns, and must appear in the agreeing elements within a determiner phrase (DP). Gender as an inherent property of the noun is known as *assignment*, and is part of the entry a noun will have in the mental lexicon. The morphological reflection of gender in determiners (articles, demonstratives, quantifiers and so on) is known as *agreement*, which makes sense considering that it denotes agreement with the inherent, lexical gender of the noun they modify. Therefore, while nouns such as *el cuchillo* 'the knife' and *la cuchara* 'the spoon' are arbitrarily assigned masculine and feminine gender respectively,[3] adjectives such as *sucio* 'dirty' have no gender per se, but do change their forms to reflect the gender of the noun they modify, as can be seen in *El cuchillo está sucio* versus *La cuchara está sucia* 'the knife/spoon is dirty'. By contrast, English does not have grammatical gender, and so articles such as 'the' and adjectives such as 'dirty' take the same form irrespective of the noun(s) they modify. There are many additional properties that correlate with whether or not representations for gender exist in the grammar, such as restrictions on the types of nominal ellipsis. Should it be the case that both Albert and Vincent show evidence of transfer of grammatical gender at the very beginning stages of learning Portuguese? Could they possibly do so in principle? The answer to this depends heavily on whether or not novel grammatical properties (that is, properties not instantiated in the L1) can be acquired in an L2, such that a mental representation from an L2 is available for transfer. If Albert and Vincent both show evidence of transfer of gender at the earliest stages of acquiring Portuguese, it must be the case that L2 learners can acquire representations for properties that are not acquired during the course of L1 acquisition in childhood – otherwise, Albert would be the only one able to show such effects from Spanish/Catalan. Therefore, to be able to make meaningful predictions for transfer in L3 acquisition, one must first know what is available in principle, which relates strongly to research on adult L2 acquisition over the past four decades.

Claims that no new grammatical representations can be acquired past puberty extend their scope tacitly to the case of adult L3 acquisition, not only with regard to the domains of grammar that can be acquired in L3 acquisition but also and, particularly interestingly, with regard to transfer potential. Simply put, one cannot transfer something for which one does not have an underlying representation. With all of the above in mind, a few things seem clear. It is logical to build L3/Ln theories based on what we believe we know about L2 acquisition, testing the waters to begin with and allowing sound empirical experimentation to inform us as to what is the same, similar or indeed different between adult L2 and L3/Ln scenarios. Furthermore, there is a mutually beneficial relationship between L2 and L3 studies, whereby each can provide the other with important evidence to adjudicate between competing proposals. Given that this book is primarily interested in transfer at the initial stages of L3 acquisition, it is crucial for us to know – to the extent that is possible – what is, in principle, available for transfer from the L1 and the L2 at the level of the underlying representation. We now turn to the relevant literature on adult L2 acquisition to attempt to justify the expectation that distinct L2 representations are available for initial-stage transfer into L3 acquisition, at least for sufficiently proficient L2 learners, which implies that new grammatical representations can, in fact, be acquired in adulthood.

*1.2.1   Can Grammatical Representations Distinct from One's Native
Language Be Acquired in Adulthood?*

An implication of claiming that adult L2 acquisition is destined to be fundamentally different from native L1 acquisition (e.g., Bley-Vroman, 1989, 2009; Long, 2005, 2007; Meisel, 2011; among many others) is that seemingly good L2 performances for domains of grammar where the L1 and L2 differ in formal representation must derive from something other than native-like representations, such as explicit training and taught knowledge in the L2, rote learning and/ or local adjustments to underlyingly L1 representations. If this is so, it would not be the case that L3 learners have access to distinct underlying L1 and L2 mental representations for the purpose of L3/L*n* transfer. Such a scenario would not necessarily mean that there is nothing distinct in one's L2 knowledge that could influence L3 development, such as metalinguistic knowledge, memorized (proceduralized) knowledge of language-specific forms, processing strategies, communicative strategies and more. It would, however, mean that the actual underlying grammatical representations are the same in the L1 and the L2. If one is specifically interested in modeling that which determines/predicts which language's mental representations, the L1 or the L2 or both, are transferred to the target L3/L*n*, determining that a learner actually has the potential for having competing mental representations for selection in the first place is a crucial preliminary step. In fact, from an extreme viewpoint, if it is impossible to acquire distinct L2 underlying representations, examining selectivity in the transfer source is potentially a prima facie example of chasing after fool's gold, or is a moot endeavor. After all, as in the real-world scenario of transferring monies from one bank account to another without sufficient funds to do so, one cannot transfer an L2 linguistic representation that one could not possibly have acquired. Thus, if it is truly the case that adults cannot acquire L2 representations distinct from the underlying L1 representations, one would never be able to disentangle the transfer source meaningfully, as transferring L2 mental representations of the morphosyntactic system is essentially the same as transferring those from the L1.

In fact, in light of the above logic, one could use initial stages L3/L*n* transfer data regressively to inform us regarding what can and cannot be acquired in adult L2 acquisition. This was first suggested and shown tenable by Iverson (2009b, 2010) via a study of nominal ellipsis (also called noun drop; see, e.g., White, Valenzuela, Kozlowska-Macgregor, & Leung, 2004, as well as Example 1 from Spanish below) in L3 Brazilian Portuguese by native L1 English speakers who were highly successful L2 Spanish learners, compared to monolingual speakers of English who were learning Portuguese as an L2. In most analyses (e.g., Bernstein, 1993; White et al., 2004), nominal ellipsis is typically licensed by the presence of gender and number morphology on agreeing elements within the DP (that is, determiners and adjectives), which allow the interlocutor to recover the relevant noun from a series of referents that are already constrained by the real-world context. In Iverson (2009b, 2010), the bilinguals learning an L3 performed significantly better in the experiments than did the monolingual L2 learners. In fact, the latter group showed no significant difference from the Brazilian controls after only a few months of exposure and learning (the same amount and type as the monolinguals learning Portuguese as an L2). Iverson concluded that such differences were related to the experience that the bilingual L2 group had with Spanish and, therefore, their performance also reflected acquisition of Spanish nominal ellipsis, a secondary effect of instantiating formal gender features as described above for the case of Albert and Vincent. Since the advantage for the bilinguals can only be attributed to transfer from Spanish, he concluded that underlying representations for grammatical gender must have been acquired in L2 Spanish, contrary to the predictions of L2 representation deficit approaches, and were thus available for transfer.

(1) A: *¿Qué*   *gafas*   *quieres ?*
         Which   glasses$_{FEMPL}$ want$_{2SG.PRES}$?
         Which glasses do you want?
     B: *¿Puedes*   *pasarme*   *las* _____ *rojas ?*
         Can$_{2SG.PRES}$ pass-me   the$_{FEM-PL}$ red$_{FEM-PL}$?
         Can you pass me the red [ones]?

Typically the byproduct of considerable and conscious effort and/or significant access to a native community, as in the case of prolonged naturalistic L2 immersion, advanced proficiency in adults acquiring a second language is actually relatively common. What is not common is for an adult L2 learner to be so successful across all domains of L2 grammar (lexis, morphosyntax, phonology and so on) that she passes as a native speaker; that is, she is indistinguishable from monolinguals of the target L2 grammar. The extent to which the rarity of L2 learners who achieve a truly native-like level of ultimate attainment reflects anything more than individual opportunity for success is not yet clear (e.g., Rothman, 2008c; Rothman & Guijarro-Fuentes, 2010). In other words, when one claims that roughly 5% or fewer L2 learners achieve the highest levels of native-like ultimate attainment, does this really mean that the remaining (overwhelming) majority of 95% are unable to do so? Conversely, is it possible that the opportunity for success is what best explains the low incidence of native-like ultimate attainment overall? Perhaps the vast majority of L2 learners simply do not acquire/learn an L2 under the optimal conditions that would enable them to achieve such an outcome. In other words, is it really specific talent for learning languages as an adult that explains the anomalous 5% or so, or is the reason simpler – they, unlike most adult language learners, enjoyed optimal conditions for L2 learning? Alternatively, is it possible that some individuals are simply more likely to be successful language learners in adulthood because they are somehow less susceptible to variables that conspire to explain the lack of overall success in L2 acquisition (less prone to L1 influence, better able to disregard extraneous noise, higher domain-general cognitive abilities that prove advantageous to language learning and thus proverbially dig an individual out of L1 entrenchment)? In both scenarios, individual differences can be explored without jumping to the conclusion that, since most do not attain native-like competence, none can, specifically due to purported loss in the brain's neurological plasticity.

1.2.2   Is There a Critical Period for Adult Nonnative Language?

The question thus becomes what underlies the "opportunity for success" in this context. This parallels the long-standing debate surrounding the application of the Critical Period Hypothesis (Lenneberg, 1967; Penfield & Roberts, 1959) to adult SLA. Do ubiquitous differences that characterize child first language versus adult L2 development and ultimate attainment – which no one denies – follow from a biologically based critical period,[4] after which adults are prevented from acquiring L2 competence in the same way that L1 native speakers do? Is there a biologically induced age effect – in whole or in part – for accessing/using cognitive and/or domain-specific linguistic mechanisms that guide language acquisition in children? Conversely, is it possible that both children and adults make use of exactly the same mental (internal) mechanisms to acquire language, and that differences merely obtain as a result of extraneous factors that distinguish the learning tasks of the two sets of acquirers?

When considering the questions above juxtaposed, it is important to bear in mind the extraneous factors that could be relevant and deterministic. Virtually all monolingual children

(i)   find themselves in an environment that inundates them with significant quantities of rich input from native speakers;

(ii) will not have to deal with crosslinguistic influence/transfer from previously acquired languages affecting the path of development; and

(iii) have a primordial need to acquire at least one language to help them encode the world around them and to use it to communicate their thoughts, needs, and desires.

By contrast, the typical adult acquiring an L2

(i) is not surrounded by quantities of native input anywhere near that of a child learning her L1;

(ii) receives and must filter significant amounts of nonnative input (such as from classmates);

(iii) has to deal with crosslinguistic influence/transfer from her L1 that can hinder as much as it facilitates; and

(iv) does not have the same inherent need/intrinsic motivation for acquiring an L2 because her world is already completely encoded in linguistic terms and she can express herself fully in the L1.

It has been suggested that the above and/or other extraneous factors combine in various ways to explain specific subtypes of observable differences between children and adults. Such a view circumvents the need to claim that child versus adult acquisition processes are fundamentally different (e.g., Alemán Bañón, Fiorentino, & Gabriele, 2014; Bialystok & Hakuta, 1994; Birdsong, 1992; Birdsong & Molis, 2001; Epstein, Flynn, & Martohardjono, 1996; Hakuta, Bialystok, & Wiley, 2003; Rothman, 2008b; Schwartz & Sprouse, 1996, 2013; Slabakova, 2006; White, 2003a). In Bialystok and Hakuta's (1994: 86) words, morphosyntax "remains accessible throughout life, even though the circumstances of our lives may muddy that access." This claim is substantiated by three distinct types of evidence, the first corresponding to the aging brain in general, and the second and third to language acquisition/processing evidence from adults. To begin, the entire notion of a critical period was originally predicated on the strong belief that the modular mind was deeply affected by the loss of neurological plasticity after puberty; that is, non-pathological, morphological changes to the structure of the adult brain affecting its ability to reorganize or redistribute functions as needed. However, we know now that the brain remains much more malleable throughout the lifespan than was previously claimed, meaning that there is no sharp decline in neurological plasticity culminating around puberty (see Fuchs & Flügge, 2014, for review). Evidence against (a strong version of) a critical period affecting sequential adult language acquisition comes from research showing that there are (i) highly successful older learner exceptions to the general L2 acquisition outcome and (ii) significant behavioral and neurolinguistic/processing data that fail to show qualitative differences in the acquisition outcomes and/or real-time processing between adult native and nonnative speakers, particularly in domains of the L2 grammar for which measurable critical period effects are predicted.

It is possible, however, that adults simply no longer have the same abilities for language acquisition as children; that is, the linguistic and/or cognitive learning mechanisms that guide child acquisition are no longer available – at all or to the same degree – after a specific time window in early adulthood (e.g., Abrahamsson & Hyltenstam, 2009; Bley-Vroman, 1989, 2009; Bylund, Abrahamsson, & Hyltenstam, 2012; Bylund, Hyltenstam, & Abrahamsson, 2013; Graena & Long, 2013; Hawkins & Casillas, 2008; Hawkins & Chan, 1997; Long, 2005; Meisel, 2011; Tsimpli & Dimitrakopoulou, 2007). Successes in adult L2 performance are acknowledged by researchers advocating a biologically induced age-related explanation for some L1 versus L2 differences. However, performance successes within L2 domains of grammar that are predicted not to be acquirable in adulthood – for example, a property that has no equivalent counterpart in the L1 – are understood as byproducts of adults' generally high ability to learn patterns and/or their metalinguistic knowledge about the L2. In such cases, the underlying mental representations in child and adult learners would be different. Such a view is based on at least two factors: (i) the finding that there is, in general, an inverse correlation between increasing L2 age of onset and incidences of native-like acquisition overall (e.g., Abrahamsson & Hyltenstam, 2009) and (ii) the idea that any and all evidence of differences in L1 versus L2 competence/performance outcomes provide unassailable evidence for some type of critical/sensitive period. From such a perspective, the relatively few older L2 speakers who are indistinguishable from natives are considered anomalies or insignificant exceptions to an otherwise generalizable rule.

If evidence of any difference between children and adults is to be equated to a critical period effect, there should be no debate on the matter, since nobody denies the robustness of such evidence. However, we are all interested in the qualitative nature of *why* these differences obtain. In fact, investigating the *why* will ultimately determine whether or not the differences we observe reflect a true critical period for adult L2 acquisition, whereby 'true' is defined as an a priori impossibility to acquire grammatical properties of the L2 that cannot be transferred or somehow reassembled from features of the L1. As pointed out by Rothman (2008c), claims about critical/sensitive periods map onto a *can* versus *cannot* as opposed to a *do* versus *do not* dichotomy. Furthermore, they make both global (general) and more fine-grained predictions. The fact that most adult L2 learners *do not* become indistinguishable from native monolinguals or that one can find some differences in at least some domains of knowledge (for example, fine-grained features of phonology) in those who seemingly do, does not necessarily imply that they *cannot* acquire an L2 in qualitatively the same way as do native monolingual children.

If the underlying cause of child L1 versus adult L2 differences is truly an outcome of biological (neurological) maturation – as opposed to the gamut of potential permutations of other factors that might be more explanatory in placing individuals on a continuum of success, such as L1 influence, the quality and quantity of available input, patterns of language use and opportunities for use, among many other factors – we could reasonably expect no exceptions. In fact, if the claim is one of (im)possibility (neurological maturation makes it "*cannot*") as opposed to predicting very low occurrences (as in "typically *do not*'"), then exceptions complicate the picture. This is compounded by the fact that, although exceptions are seemingly rare, when one considers the actual incidences of opportunities for L2 learners to achieve native-likeness, the rarity becomes less impressive. How many L2 learners are actually engaged sufficiently with the L2 for it to be reasonable that they would achieve proficiency levels that are indistinguishable from those of natives?

Global-level predictions whereby any L1 versus L2 difference alone constitutes proper evidence in favor of critical/sensitive period(s) are well attested in the literature. At the more fine-grained level, however, things begin to break down. For example, hundreds of studies showing that L2 learners acquire to native-like levels various grammatical properties that should be impossible or exceedingly rare under a critical or even sensitive period approach exist. Successes in the acquisition of such discrete domains/properties of L2 grammar pose significant challenges, such as complete target acquisition of domains of L2 morphosyntax, particularly when accompanied by subtle, native-like semantic entailments that cannot be transferred from the L1 (Schwartz & Sprouse, 2013; Slabakova, 2006, 2016). Although there is no shortage of studies that show the opposite, the problem of explanation still rests in the hands of those who advocate critical/sensitive period(s) applications to L2 learning. This is true because, while no theory/approach precludes difficulties and/or the lack of acquisition of some L2 properties as a result of other factors, critical period approaches predict that some things should simply be impossible. When one shows the impossible to be possible, it is reasonable to assume that there is something askew in the original claim.

1.3   Who Is a Multilingual?

If you are sufficiently interested to be reading this book, it is likely that you already have a good idea of what a multilingual is, at least in the most obvious sense. In fact, as the very term suggests, a multilingual is an individual who has knowledge of multiple languages. As discussed in Section 1.1, it is reasonably defensible to argue that bilinguals are multilinguals, having, by definition, competence in more than one language. For the purposes of this book and in light of the argument alluded to above, we consider multilingualism to involve at least three languages. Thus, a multilingual learner would by definition need to be bilingual – either a simultaneous or a sequential bilingual – at the onset of L3/Ln learning. Even if we agree to the previous stipulation, it is not necessarily the case that we would all agree unanimously regarding who would qualify as a multilingual and who would not. Thus, while having knowledge of at least three languages is a necessary condition to be considered multilingual, it is itself potentially not a sufficient condition.

To illustrate the above point, let us consider a few scenarios concerning potential multilinguals. We might suggest that you read the scenarios as if doing so were an exercise with a friend or small group in the following manner:

(a) have a piece of paper and pen to hand;

(b) write the numbers 1–10 vertically, whereby each corresponds to a separate line on the page;

(c) inform all participants that they will be read 10 scenarios concerning individuals who may or may not be multilinguals, and that their job will be to listen carefully and determine which are indeed multilinguals;

(d) instruct everyone listening (including yourself) to place a checkmark next to **all** and, crucially, **only** those scenarios that one accepts as a multilingual, with the numbers written on the page corresponding to one of ten scenarios; and

(e) when everyone is poised to pay careful attention, read each scenario out loud. Once you have your paper ready, let us consider the ten scenarios below with the following question in mind: *Is _____ a multilingual?*

1. **Max** is from the USA and so is his father, but his mother is from Germany. Max has been a naturalistic bilingual in German and English (seemingly balanced) from childhood. Since the age of seven, he has been exposed to Spanish at school but is now, at the age of 16, studying it intensively and has achieved relatively good proficiency. As he lives in a part of the USA in which there are large Hispanic communities, he is able to use this language on a daily basis, as well as English and German.

    *Is **Max** a multilingual?*

2. **Juanita** was born and raised in Los Angeles, California, USA. Both her parents are from Mexico and only speak Spanish. Juanita's first language is Spanish, but she started learning English at the age of five when she first went to school and is now, at the age of 20, dominant in English. She recently began to learn Portuguese in college.

   *Is **Juanita** a multilingual?* not yet

3. **Paulina** is from a small town in rural Pennsylvania. Her native language is English. She started learning French at the age of 14 and was very successful. Later, she majored in French in college, where she also began to take Italian courses and became quite proficient. She now teaches both French and Italian at high school in the town in which she was raised.

   *Is **Paulina** a multilingual?* yes

4. **Oihan** was born in Tromsø, Norway, of Spanish parents. His mother is from Vitoria in the Spanish Basque Country, and his father is from Asturias. His mother spoke to him exclusively in Basque from the time he was born, although the primary language spoken among others in his home (such as between Oihan and his dad and between his dad and mom) was Spanish. Of course, Norwegian was imparted by the larger society and was the language in which he was formally educated. As a young adult, Oihan is incredibly fluent, and even literate, in all three languages.

   *Is **Oihan** a multilingual?* Yes

5. **Dieter** was raised in Geneva, but his parents were originally from Zurich. His parents came to speak French very well, albeit as a nonnative language, and decided to speak to **Dieter** primarily in French as a first language although he was exposed to Swiss German in his home at a very early age. He understands Swiss German well and can get by when speaking it but with significant difficulty. As a teenager, he is currently continuing his studies of English in school, which he began roughly seven years ago.

   *Is **Dieter** a multilingual?* No

6. **Ana Lúcia** is from Portugal. She studied English from the second grade and became very successful. In fact, she taught English for over

a decade in Lisbon as a young adult. At the age of 40, she moved to Brazil and is being confronted with what seems to her like a new language: Although she already understands Brazilian Portuguese for the most part, it is also clear that it is sufficiently different that it causes receptive and especially productive communication problems for her.

*Is **Ana Lúcia** a multilingual?* no

7. **Laura** is from Barcelona. In her particular community, virtually everyone speaks Catalan and Spanish. Now, at the age of 16, she is at the end of a year's study exchange program in London where she was able to be immersed in English. It was an extremely useful start to what will continue to be several years of English study.

   *Is **Laura** a multilingual?* maybe

8. **Harun** is from Malaysia. One of his parents is ethnically Tamil and the other is a native speaker of Malay. Harun learned both of these languages at home in early childhood and, because he lives in a Cantonese-majority community, he also learned Cantonese at an early age. Now in his mid-fifties, Harun no longer feels too comfortable speaking Tamil as he has not used it in over 15 years since his mother passed away.

   *Is **Harun** a multilingual?* don't know

9. **Jenna** is from Cape Town, South Africa. Her native language is Afrikaans. Born in the 1970s, Jenna was partially raised by a caregiver who taught her fluent isiXhosa as a child. In her early teens, Jenna was first exposed to English and, today, she uses English more for work and in her daily life than she does the other languages, although she maintains all three at a high level.

   *Is **Jenna** a multilingual?* yes

10. **Su Young** is a native speaker of Korean. At the age of nine, she was adopted by a French couple and moved from Korea to France. As her foreign-language requirement at school, she has studied English for a very long time. She has not used or spoken Korean since leaving Korea, which was over 20 years ago.

   *Is **Su Young** a multilingual?* maybe

Now that you have read and considered the 10 scenarios above, how many did you check off as being multilingual? If you were to convert the checks to a numeric value, what would your score be out of 10? If you did this alone, were you equally confident about each check you assigned; that is, were some scenarios more straightforward than were others? Did some scenarios make you pause and equivocate? How confident are you that everyone would arrive at the same score? If you did this with a friend, are your scores the same? Better still, if you did this in a group, are all the scores the same?

The chances are that, even in a group of two, the scores will vary. In fact, in presentations on multilingualism that we have given over the years, in which we have presented very similar scenarios and asked the audience to do this exercise, there is generally an incredible range of scores, irrespective of the makeup of the audience – that is, even (and perhaps particularly) when everyone in the room is a linguist who works on multilingualism. You might ask, how can this be? Should it not be clear who is and thus who is not a multilingual? Again, if you are doing the exercise in a group you will have immediate evidence that things are not black and white. For some scenarios, there is no question that the person depicted qualifies as a multilingual, but not all cases are as cut and dried as those of Oihan and Jenna.

What you might have noticed is that the above scenarios actually involve covarying factors that could prove deterministic for inclusion for some and not for others. For example, many people will include Harun. After all, he clearly acquired three languages. However, some will hesitate or not include him because he no longer uses one language – Tamil – often or ever; therefore, he is presently more akin to a bilingual than to a multilingual. More severe or clear cut, for similar reasons, would be the case of Su Young. The fact that she has seemingly lost Korean completely might be taken to mean that, at best, she is now bilingual. The variable of active use of more than two languages could be a deterministic criterion (subconsciously) used to judge inclusion as a multilingual.

As another example, let us consider the case of Ana Lúcia. Accepting that she is multilingual requires that you are willing to consider Brazilian Portuguese and European Portuguese as distinct languages, as argued on linguistic categorization and acquisition grounds by several independent scholars (e.g., Azevedo, 2005; Castro, Rothman, & Westergaard, 2017; Galves, 2001). Nevertheless, some (perhaps many or most) would not accept these as distinct languages as opposed to dialects of a single language. In the former case, Ana Lúcia should unquestionably qualify as a multilingual; based on the latter perspective, she would not.

Current language proficiency matters for some more than it does for others. In a liberal interpretation of multilingualism, Juanita might be included because she is clearly a proficient bilingual who is now starting the process of acquiring a third language. Minimally, she is an emerging multilingual but, from a more conservative perspective that might require one to have full communicative competence in all three languages, for example, the fact that she is not yet an advanced speaker of Portuguese would disqualify her from inclusion. It might also be the case that, for some, a multilingual can only be considered as such if s/he has native or near-native proficiency in all three languages across all linguistic domains. If such a criterion were applied, the ensuing score would be very low indeed.

These three factors are mere examples of variables that could be used differently by individuals – without any pretense or agenda – and thus explain the discrepancies in scores provided in any given cohort. At the same time, these and other variables echo the fact that determining who qualifies as a multilingual is – and likely should be to an extent – a fluid process. The fact is that all and exceedingly few of the scenarios above would rightly qualify as multilingual depending on the contextualized purpose of the label, especially in light of the particular research questions in specific studies. If a research question is asking about what happens at the initial stages of multilingualism (first exposure period to a third or more language), then Juanita becomes an ideal candidate. In reality, Juanita is the only person who should be considered appropriate for such a study. Thus, while all the scenarios above involve people speaking three or more languages, not all would qualify as the type of multi-lingual suitable for all multilingual studies. The fact that individuals no longer or do not yet have specific competencies in all the languages in some cases renders them nontraditional multilinguals, and this reality makes it difficult to achieve unanimous consensus. Most importantly for our purposes, a multilingual is a person who is having/has/has had access to more than two languages and is having/has/has had the opportunity to develop mental grammars for more than two languages. Anything beyond this minimal defining characteristic is important, if not crucial to be considered on balance for inclusionary and exclusionary criteria for particular multilingual studies; however, the question of suitability for particular research questions does not change that fact that, at some level, all the scenarios involved relate to multilingualism.

As unsatisfying as this might be, we will not provide you with a correct numeric score because (alas!) there is no correct score. In closing, we simply highlight that, beyond the essential inclusion criteria for multilingualism, the rest is a matter of subjective opinion that is ideally made more objective by supporting it with tenable motivations, on scientific grounds, for why some are included and others are not. Simply put, from a research perspective, the choice of who qualifies as a multilingual for any given study needs to be commensurate with the needs and goals of the said study; depending on the questions, this inevitably means that some will qualify and others will not, even when all scenarios involve exposure to three or more languages at some level.

1.4   Linguistic Transfer as a Construct

Acquisitionists often need to consider variables that are extralinguistic, such as the impact of motivation, socioeconomic status or attitudes toward the target language, to name a few. They (we) also take into account that what a learner shows in speech or writing is rarely all there is to her linguistic knowledge. Eventually, however, it is precisely this relatively stable, consolidated knowledge of the language that we are interested in: linguistic representations. In simple terms, one can think of mental linguistic representations as cognitive blueprints for the multiple different elements that make up a language: vocabulary, morphological and syntactic structure, semantic fields, pragmatic conventions and so on. These blueprints are created and strengthened through use, and they are modified if they consistently fail to help the speaker parse the target language.

Although there can be more than one way to understand the relationship between linguistic representation and language processing (see, e.g., Cunnings, 2017; Lewis & Phillips, 2015, for discussion), we assume that both comprehension and production operate over the same system of symbols – linguistic representations – in the mind of the speaker: the grammar. Language is thus parsed in real time through the grammar, and the interactions that take place at the level of on-line language processing can and do eventually reconfigure that underlying knowledge. However, this is not the only way in which a grammar can be modified. As we will see, linguistic representations can be changed by, or even copied from, other representations in the same or in other languages, without the *direct* mediation of language processing. This means that, although changes in a speaker's mental grammar are always motivated by some kind of (recurrent) inconsistency between the input and the grammar, there are cognitive mechanisms at play that allow those blueprints to be modified or replaced by others without the constant trial-and-error stream of information from input parsing it generally takes to make this kind of change – a shortcut of sorts, with regard to how grammar restructuring generally works. Before we can discuss how these two types of change interact in a multilingual context, it is useful to explain some terminology.

Crosslinguistic influence can be broadly defined as the interaction between two, three, or more languages that are part of a speaker's linguistic competence. It has long been a central theme in the literature on bi-/multilingual language acquisition – both simultaneous and sequential – irrespective of the theoretical approach (see, e.g., Alonso Alonso, 2016; De Angelis, Jessner, & Kresic, 2015; Jarvis & Pavlenko, 2008; Odlin, 1989, 2008, 2012, among others). Throughout this book, we deal primarily with a particular instantiation of crosslinguistic influence; namely, that which affects linguistic representations above and beyond their use in (receptive or productive) language processing. As we understand it, the construct of linguistic transfer refers to reduplication of a representation from previously acquired linguistic representations, as an initial hypothesis for a given domain (literally, a copy) while acquiring a new target language (Schwartz & Sprouse, 1994, 1996, 2013; White, 2003b). This definition has two corollary assumptions. The first is that nontarget language influence cannot be considered to be transfer unless it is shown to obtain relatively consistently for a given item or across items within the same paradigm; that is, when it is clearly not a mere slip of the tongue, suggesting that the mental representation for a certain linguistic property, structure or lexical item is actually affected. The second assumption is that transfer and processing-related crosslinguistic influence (that which corresponds to momentary slips and therefore presents inconsistently) can and will indeed cooccur. The terms crosslinguistic influence and transfer are often used interchangeably, both as a convention for those who agree functionally with the intuitive difference between representational transfer and other things that conspire to show cross-language effects, and for those who do not find the distinction to be convincing or necessary. To avoid potential confusion, we will use the term 'transfer' when referring to representation, and cross-language effects (CLE) when referring to crosslinguistic influence at other levels.

Although some researchers have adopted this position (see, e.g., González Alonso & Rothman, 2017a; Herdina & Jessner, 2002; Paradis, 2004), the distinction between transfer and CLE is not always clear in the literature. In our view, any avoidance – conscious or otherwise – of engaging in an unambiguous definition of both terms has nontrivial consequences at all levels of scientific inquiry, from experimental design to the interpretation of results and theory building. In the context of sequential bi-/multilingualism, in which not all the languages are acquired simultaneously, the transfer of linguistic knowledge from previously acquired languages is generally motivated by not yet having the target linguistic representations necessary to parse the target input that the learner is receiving. This state of the target grammar, which we refer to in this context as 'underspecification,' gives rise to difficulties in parsing the input. Depending on one's theoretical position and/or the stage of interlanguage development under consideration, this underspecification can be of two kinds. The first is the lack of an interlanguage representation for a given grammatical property. This gap in the interlanguage system may prompt the emergence of a new representation that is copied from that of a previously acquired language. The second kind of deficit affects the entire nascent interlanguage system which, upon initial exposure to the L2 or the L3, is in a general state of underspecification. According to Rothman (2013), for reasons of cognitive economy, this unstable situation triggers a proverbial search for support from previously acquired languages in the form of *wholesale* transfer (that is, one involving a complete grammar) in an effort to use whatever previous resources are available to parse the incoming data while avoiding redundancy in the creation and development of linguistic representations (see Section 4.3.1 in Chapter 4). In the case of L2 acquisition, it has been proposed that this transfer comes from the only possible source: the L1 (see Schwartz & Sprouse, 1996). Given the more complex nature of previous linguistic experience in an L3/Ln acquisition scenario, we propose that a mechanism is activated within the learner's internal linguistic parser whereby every instance of structural similarity between each previously acquired language and the parsed L3 input increases activation of the corresponding language. When this activation reaches a certain threshold, the grammar of this previously acquired language is transferred in its entirety in order to provide an initial interlanguage for the L3 (Rothman, 2015), which will eventually change and develop through further L3 input exposure. Although, as we will see in subsequent chapters by reviewing various models, the aforementioned claims regarding how transfer actually occurs in L3 acquisition are not without controversy or dissenting opinions; in our view, what should be relatively uncontroversial is that transfer itself sits at the level of representation proper.

CLE (also called 'interference'; see, e.g., Herdina & Jessner, 2002), by contrast, encompasses influence on the *processing* of any given property among linguistic systems that have stable representations for that property. These instances of crosslinguistic influence do not concern linguistic representations directly and are thus circumscribed to the domain of language processing. Examples of CLE include the production of false cognates (such as the English word 'embarrassed' instead of 'pregnant' due to the influence of the Spanish word 'embarazada' [pregnant]), tip-of-the-tongue (TOT) states (e.g., Brown, 1991; see especially Ecke, 2004, and Ecke & Hall, 2013 for TOT in the context of multilingualism),[5] and variability in how certain structures, such as relative clauses, are interpreted – in particular, whether a relative clause (RC) such as *who owns a Mercedes* is understood as referring to the first or the second noun phrase (NP) of the main clause in the sentence *The sister*$_{NP1}$ *of the lawyer*$_{NP2}$ *who owns a Mercedes came by the office yesterday.* At the level of morphological production, CLE can also pertain to the seemingly random or patently inconsistent use of inappropriate morphology (errors of commission) or the lack of using obligatory morphology (errors of omission) that (a) seemingly correspond to influence from another known system and (b) "pop up" intermittently alongside evidence that otherwise suggests mastery of the target system (see Lardiere, 1998a, 1998b, 2007). This does not mean that CLE cannot have an indirect, long-term effect on representation (see, e.g., Dussias & Sagarra, 2007) but rather that both the causes and the consequences of this influence are, in principle, external to linguistic competence in the target language.

From the above argumentation, it would be fair to interpret that we assume a dynamic model of underlying representation, which, to a large extent, we do. Following on from this, one might then ask how a dynamic representation allows for variability, as it must in real language in the real world, either in its architecture or in terms of output/behavior. A subsequent question would also follow: How can one distinguish this variation between representation and processing (that is, non-transfer in the sense we mean for CLE), and do so predictably? We have already alluded to a proverbial litmus test, which also reflects the type of variation we are discussing – that is, nonnative variation as opposed to native types. Variation in native dialects typically reflects consistency (as the difference is consistent, variation is assessed by considering consistent differences across varieties) and seldom reflects intermittent errors of commission. Nonnative language variation, in addition to being (mostly) systematic when described in its own terms – that which we would label transfer – often reflects seemingly unconstrained, in-the-moment variability. This can potentially be best exemplified via errors of commission that are (a) virtually unattested in native speakers, and (b) are distributed in two ways; when consistent, we would consider them as transfer and, in the more common case, when they are inconsistent, we would consider them to be CLE. When errors of commission, rare as they are, occur in native-speaker production, they have a well-attested and logical processing reason; for example, number agreement attraction: 'the **key** to the cabinets **are** on the table' (e.g., Bock & Miller, 1991; Lago, Gračanin-Yuksek et al., 2018; Quirk, Greenbaum, Leech, & Scartvik, 1972; Tanner, Nicol, & Brehm, 2014). The consistency proxy to which we have appealed as a form of litmus test is a way to isolate behavior that can reasonably be associated with a representation. In principle, there should also be other ways, such as psycholinguistic indices of qualitatively consistent and native-like processing; for example, eye movements that reveal specific processing patterns or electrophysiological brain wave components in response to qualitatively different types of violations, such as the N400 and the P600 (see Section 6.5 in Chapter 6).

Although not exactly relevant for the present discussions in this book as we see them, we take native-speaker variation very seriously – within the individual and across individuals – particularly as it relates to multiple dialects of what is commonly referred to as a single language in the mind of the same speaker. We also take models of multi-competence (Cook 1991, 2003a; see Section 2.1.3 in Chapter 2) and Multiple Grammar Theory (Amaral & Roeper, 2014; Roeper, 1999; Yang, 2018; Yang & Montrul, 2017) applied to nonnative language acquisition equally seriously. However, in the spirit of the distinction we are attempting to make here, we see these insights as running in parallel, not in opposition, to the main claim. Intuitively, there seems to be a difference between transfer as we have defined it and crosslinguistic influence that is not representational in nature (CLE). In fact, there are important considerations that are debated and relevant, such as whether representations are shared across subsystems or distinct grammars – even those that pertain to so-called monolinguals with knowledge of multiple registers or dialects – for how one interprets or applies the distinction we wish to make. Nevertheless, it seems practical and thus useful to have a distinct label for capturing that which is representational versus what is not. Doing so is, after all, our main point and goal here.

1.5   Previous Language Experience ≠ Metalinguistic Knowledge

Although there are discrepancies regarding how they interact and the extent to which they interface, language acquisitionists of all schools agree that a speaker may possess, simultaneously, knowledge *of* a language (that is, of its grammar) and knowledge *about* the language, as well as a subtype of the latter: knowledge about her knowledge of a language – if the reader will excuse the tongue twister (e.g., N. C. Ellis, 1993; R. Ellis, 2005; Felix, 1985; Krashen, 1981; Paradis, 2004, 2009; Rothman, 2008a, among others). Knowledge of language is, roughly speaking, what allows us to produce and understand well-formed sentences in a given language. Again, most acquisitionists would agree that this knowledge is implicit or tacit; that is, the speaker is not consciously aware of it. In parallel, most speakers develop knowledge about the grammar, which we generally refer to as *metalinguistic knowledge,* explicit linguistic knowledge and the like. As the name suggests, this knowledge is explicit, and is consciously stored in memory – in other words, the speaker is aware of its existence. It can have a number of different sources, including a conscious effort by the speaker to infer the mechanics of the language, the memorization of pedagogical rules learned in a classroom setting, and the analogical extension of these rules to attempt to figure out examples that have not been taught explicitly. Note that, as a result of its origin, this type of knowledge comprises generalizations of different granularities and is, therefore, not necessarily *on target*; that is, it does not necessarily lead to the creation or deciphering of well-formed sentences as spoken by native speakers of the language.

A common misunderstanding in the L3 literature is that prior language-learning experience automatically entails metalinguistic knowledge of the grammar(s) learned past puberty. Crucially, this claim is not always made for the first or native language; that is, a monolingual will not necessarily have metalinguistic knowledge of her native language despite ample experience with it. While any language-learning process most likely spawns some amount of conscious reflection on, for example, the morphological, lexical and syntactic characteristics of the target language – perhaps described more accurately as metalinguistic *awareness* – whether this is equally true of all instances of nonnative language acquisition is unclear, as is whether it can be claimed to display even relative uniformity across learners, instances of acquisition, and language combinations. This elusiveness of an otherwise intuitive concept makes metalinguistic knowledge/awareness a poor candidate to use as a reliable predictor in models of L3/L*n* acquisition at present. In this book we will argue that, to be incorporated within an explanatorily adequate theory of L3/L*n* acquisition, this construct needs a careful operationalization that includes, but is not limited to,

(i)   a committed, unambiguous definition of what metalinguistic knowledge is, inclusive of various subtypes if they exist;
(ii)   a description of its involvement in language processing; and
(iii) hypotheses about its interface with implicit linguistic knowledge (see, e.g., N. C. Ellis, 2005; Krashen, 1981; Paradis, 2004, 2009; Schwartz, 1993; Slabakova, 2015).

In using the term 'metalinguistic knowledge' within an L3 setting, one must be aware that naturalistic learning and classroom instruction generate largely different amounts of explicit knowledge of grammatical rules for an L2 (e.g., Felix, 1985; Rothman, 2008a). Even if both learning contexts produce some amount of metalinguistic knowledge, at least part of it is destined to be qualitatively different. For example, it is possible that a natural nonnative learner notices apparent differences between her L1 and the target nonnative language and, as a result, creates some conscious, idiosyncratic meta-rule to explicate the noticed difference. By contrast, a classroom learner is literally taught metalinguistic rules of a pedagogically descriptive nature in very explicit terms. As a result, the system of metalinguistic knowledge that a classroom nonnative speaker has is destined to be more uniform across L2 learners of language X who share the same L1, and much more exhaustive in nature. For these reasons, studies focusing on the role of metalinguistic knowledge in L3 acquisition must minimally control for – or systematically manipulate – this aspect of their learner groups' prior linguistic experience. Moreover, it is not clear whether, when one asks a person to be reflective about so-called metalinguistic knowledge, all learner types (or indeed all individuals within the same type) will be able to articulate equally what they possess in terms of metalinguistic knowledge. This is true because metalinguistic knowledge itself can be implicit or explicit.

Explicit metalinguistic knowledge is precisely that which can be articulated and, in the case of a classroom learner, tends to come from explicit instruction. Implicit metalinguistic knowledge, by contrast, is something that cannot be articulated easily; nor does it sit at a level of immediate consciousness. However, unlike something that is acquired – comes to be known passively – in the truest sense, it is knowledge that has been deduced based on an implicit comparison of the L1 and the target language, and appears in the form of seeming intuition. By definition, then, such knowledge could only apply to things that are noticeably different among the languages involved at some level. Good candidates for implicit metalinguistic knowledge would be so-called compensatory strategies in nonnative acquisition that give rise, according to theories that advocate fundamental differences in native versus nonnative acquisition past a critical age, to seemingly native-like behavior for domains of grammar that learners are predicted not to be able to acquire given maturational constraints.

To provide a tangible example of both explicit and implicit metalinguistic knowledge in the sense we mean here, let us consider the cases of both naturalistic and classroom learners of nonnative English whose L1 is Mandarin Chinese. In the former case, the naturalistic learner might *notice* that English verbs tend to have certain obligatory morphological markings for tense – third person singular *-s* for present and *-ed* for past – and develop some type of unconscious rule that relates to a high rate of producing the corresponding morphology, either in addition to acquiring new nonnative abstract features or in lieu of acquiring the nonnative underlying syntax due to a maturationally conditioned inability to acquire the formal properties of present and past tense in English, since the relevant syntactic features are missing in their L1. Such knowledge would be metalinguistic because it corresponds to a rule of sorts in the minds of individual learners related to language, but it is not a linguistic rule in itself. It is interesting to note that native speakers can also have this type of metalinguistic knowledge of their L1 – particularly those trained in their L1 for the purpose of teaching it or those who acquire a nonnative language in adulthood and apply an implicit comparison to their L1 in reverse. However, in this case, it would surely exist in parallel to actual linguistic rules (see Felix, 1985; Rothman, 2008a, for why this might also be the case for naturalistic L2).

Linguistic rules, for lack of a better term, relate to the acquisition/representation of abstract features of grammar. In this sense, a linguistic rule for tense simply means that the grammar has a representation for the abstract feature of [*u*present] and [*u*past], inclusive of all entailments related to the specification of a formal tense feature in the grammar. In the case of classroom learning, students are taught specifically about the obligatory nature of tense morphology and the function thereof. Students are given tangible rules regarding how this is distributed across the language and what (some of) the form-to-meaning mappings are. Thus, a Chinese student of classroom English quite literally *knows* that verbs in the third person singular must be marked with -s obligatorily; whether or not the student does this consistently is a different question, and what variability in production indicates is a matter of debate that is not immediately relevant here (see, e.g., Hawkins & Liszka, 2003; Haznedar & Schwartz, 1997; Lardiere, 2009; Prévost & White, 2000; Rothman, 2007b). Such pedagogically descriptive rules are good candidates for explicit metalinguistic knowledge since they are accessed and articulated easily by classroom learners, they have been taught to nonnative speakers purposefully and they remain consciously accessible over time.

If, given certain theoretical assumptions, explicit knowledge of the grammar of previously acquired languages – and the purported subsequent ability to make meaningful cross-language comparisons – is predicted to change, if not enhance, subsequent language acquisition (Cenoz, 2001), then increased explicit metalinguistic knowledge should provide those L3 learners whose L2 learning experience involves (more) explicit instruction with an advantage in comparison to those who learned their L2(s) in a naturalistic setting. Based on the same general logic, but where previous explicit metalinguistic knowledge is simply taken to alter subsequent processes, it should follow that degrees of explicit metalinguistic knowledge/awareness in both previously acquired languages will affect L3 acquisition differently. For example, an L3 learner who has explicit metalinguistic awareness in only the L2 versus one who has it for both the L1 and the L2 might show very different (and predictable) patterns of crosslinguistic influence (see, e.g., Falk, Lindqvist, & Bardel, 2015). If, on the other hand, what is intended by a 'metalinguistic knowledge' advantage is some kind of gain in enhanced sensitivity to linguistic cues resulting from the cumulative experience of bilingualism, even and especially if this is not necessarily explicit, then one should expect no difference or fewer differences between both types of learners. In fact, the claim that accumulated language-learning experience translates into higher sensitivity to subtle linguistic cues in the input is one that transcends paradigms and has been favored since early L3 studies (e.g., Cenoz, 2003; Cenoz & Valencia, 1994; Flynn, Foley, & Vinnitskaya, 2004; Hammarberg, 2001; Sanz, 2000; Swain, Lapkin, Rowen, & Hart, 1990; Westergaard, Mitrofanova, Mykhaylyk, & Rodina, 2017, among others). Unlike increased *metalinguistic* awareness/knowledge, however, enhanced *linguistic* sensitivity need not be, to any degree, a function of the type of learning experience (that is, naturalistic learning versus classroom instruction), but rather a byproduct of language acquisition more generally. One important assumption that follows from this is that the role of this factor is incremental from the very first stages of L1 acquisition, and might be most clearly observable when comparing learners with greater (e.g., L2 versus L3) or lesser (e.g., child versus adult L2A) amounts of prior acquisition experience (see, e.g., Rothman, 2015). With regard to the main focus of this book, the potential effects of metalinguistic knowledge and enhanced linguistic sensitivity are expected to interact distinctly with the mechanisms underlying linguistic transfer and are, therefore, present to different degrees in a number of models of morphosyntactic transfer in L3 acquisition. As we will argue repeatedly when examining these proposals, it is important that both theoretical and empirical assessments of factors related to linguistic experience use working definitions that are as concrete and unambiguous as possible.

1.6 The Scientific Method in L3 Theorizing: Predictions and Falsifiability

A main point we will attempt to make in this book is in fact an epistemological one; that is, it does not only concern our research field but applies to how we do science more generally (Nosek, Ebersole, DeHaven, & Mellor, 2018). The psycholinguist, and our friend, Professor Itziar Laka summarized the main issue poignantly in a recent keynote presentation in which she introduced a new theoretical model entitled Originating Variation from Order (OVO):[6]

> This is my working hypothesis. I'll push it as far as it goes, but I welcome and encourage people testing it: as with any theory, we need to discard it and move on. Which is why I'm putting forward a strong version of it, because theories need to make testable predictions. Otherwise, if we start being vague about things, what are we doing, really?   (Laka, 2018)

As is common in fields that grow so rapidly in such a short period, a large portion of the L3 studies published to date interpret their data post hoc; that is, they formulate new hypotheses from a single dataset instead of using it to confirm or reject a set of predictions made a priori by theories or models that already exist. While this is natural and even necessary when exploring uncharted territory, a useful – that is, externally applicable —understanding of the L3/L*n* acquisition process ultimately depends on our ability to make predictions. For example, there is no way our research can be of use to foreign-language teachers who work within multilingual settings unless we can offer them some insights into how typical multilingual development takes place (e.g., Benati & Schwieter, 2017; González Alonso & Rothman, 2017b; Hahn & Angelovska, 2017) and how this may apply in the specific case(s) of their learners. In Chomsky's (1965) terms, we need theories that are not only observationally and descriptively adequate but which are also explanatorily so; that is, theories that account for both the *what* and the *how* of L3/L*n* acquisition.

At the time of writing this book in 2017–2018, at least six L3/L*n* specific models have been proposed within (pyscho)linguistic approaches to explain (at least some aspects) of L3/L*n* morphosyntax. The abundance of models can be partly explained by different theoretical concerns: L3/L*n* acquisition is a highly complex process, and not everybody is interested in the same aspects or parts of it. However, such a range of theories probably suggests that, at least to some extent, we have some issues of miscommunication – the field keeps expanding sideways faster than it moves forward. In our view, two factors are largely responsible for this. The first is that we have often proposed new hypotheses without first discarding existing ones "safely." The second factor, which contributes to the first, is that a substantial number of models, new and old, are partially or wholly unfalsifiable; that is, they cannot be proven wrong or, by extension, correct either! (We will return to this shortly). Since the second factor seems to lie at the heart of the problem, let us address that first.

As we said at the beginning of this section, it is essential that a model makes clear, testable predictions. Doing so helps us to make the knowledge we are able to obtain via experimentation transferable to other domains; that is, to render it applicable beyond answering our research questions. It is also the only reliable way to determine whether a given model is pointing toward the correct variables. Note that, unless we can observe data that *only one* model can predict beforehand, other explanations cannot be ruled out, even if the model has correctly identified the factors behind the effects we can observe.

To illustrate the above point, let us consider a simplified weather model.[7] Imagine that astronomers discover a planet, Earth 2.0, with a large amount of water. Moreover, this planet has a similar water cycle to the one we have on Earth. As part of our study of Earth 2.0, we need to understand why rain falls when it does. Accordingly, a consortium of governmental space agencies sends a rover to collect relevant data. A first model, let us call it Model A, assumes that the time it will take to rain in any given place depends on the ground temperature (measured in degrees Celsius). Let us call (t) the temperature on the ground – as opposed to at some point in the sky – and (d) the number of days it takes to rain from the moment we measure the temperature. We need to account for the following observations: once, it took one day to rain; on a different occasion, it took four days. Formally, d={1, 4}. Model A claims that the relationship is simple: $d=t^2$. That is, if we take the value for the day's temperature and square it, we will have the number of days it will take to rain. NASA, the authors of the model, rightly pointed out that the observations of one and four days took place after the temperature had been 1° C and 2° C, respectively. Their model thus accurately *describes* the data thus far: for a temperature of t=1, our equation establishes that the number of days will be 1^2; that is, 1. Similarly, for a value of t=2, (d) computes as $2^2=4$, matching the second observation. One might then be tempted to assume that Model A not only describes the data but also *explains* it.

However, this is not necessarily the case. Consider two more models: one, which we will call Model B, claims that Model A has ignored something that also plays an important role: atmospheric pressure (p, for short). According to this model, the days it takes to rain are the sum of the temperature and pressure values, with the latter being measured in atmospheres (atm): d=t+p. Its proponents, the European Space Agency, rightly point out that the pressure was 0 and 2, respectively, when the initial observations of one and four days were made. The other model, which the Russian Federal Space Agency inevitably called Model C, also claims that temperature alone is the key, but the relationship between this and the time it takes to rain is not the one proposed by NASA. For them, d=3t−2. That is, take the temperature, multiply it by three, subtract two, and you will have the number of days. Thus far, Models B and C are just as capable of accommodating the observed data as is Model A (if you do not believe us, you are welcome to do the calculations yourself!). However, these three models are clearly not the same: they just happen to make the same predictions for (d) when (t) and (p) take on these values. The best way to decide among them, then, would be to measure the number of days with temperatures and pressures for which these models predict different things. For example, how long would each model predict it would take to rain on Earth 2.0 if the temperature were 9° C and the pressure were 1 atm? Models A and C do not consider atmospheric pressure, and would predict d=81 (9^2) and d=25 (3×9−2), respectively. Model B, on the other hand, predicts a sum of (t) and (p); that is, 15 days. These predictions are mutually exclusive – if one is right, the others cannot be – and thus constitute the best way for us to determine which model best explains the data. Of course, it could be that what we observe matches none of these predictions. In that case, we can say that all models are falsified (proven wrong) for this observation. When this happens with some consistency to a model, its predictive power is demonstrably low. It is then time for us to refine or to abandon some or all of the existing models altogether.

What we mean to highlight with this example is that, while new data are always welcome and necessary, the collection thereof is more immediately useful when it has been guided by predictions based on specific theories. These two aspects complement each other: Theories and models (must) emerge from the observation of unexplained or poorly understood data; conversely, the ability of well-formed models to anticipate observations is essential so that we do not keep reinterpreting the data we have. If a model is indeed a true model, it will make predictions. If it does not, it simply cannot receive that name, even when the dialog that surrounds the so-called model makes shrewd observations and offers interesting insights. With clear predictions in sight, we can collect new data that allow us to falsify a given model and, eventually, to discard it when a critical mass of data points in the same direction. By extension, this means that one must *choose* the language pairings and the domain of grammar being tested very carefully in combination with what the models' predictions are.[8] If one seeks to compare various models, it is inappropriate to choose a domain of grammar and/or a pairing of languages that would not render different – and therefore falsifiable – predictions across the models. Failing to do so means that we will complicate the intended task unnecessarily. It also means that we will increase the amount of noise – a potential killer for scientific progress. Of course, all domains of grammar and all language pairings are worthy of study; the question is one of appropriateness for the specific questions at hand. One must ask: Will a study examining the acquisition/processing of domain A in the L3 of language X help us to determine the tenability of competing models against one another for learners of L1Y→L2Z and/or L1Z→L2Y? If so, excellent. If not, one should determine what tweaking would make it so and act accordingly, perhaps by changing the language pairing or swapping the domain of grammar tested.

The above, in fact, embodies a vital premise when conducting scientific work more generally because science has its own "presumption of innocence": A well-formed theory is assumed to be right – or, at least, potentially right – until it is proven wrong. Of course, any new theory or model must at least be compatible with as much available data as the literature has to offer. Otherwise, what we call the "burden of proof" (the obligation to provide evidence) rests on the new proposal. Cautious scientific prudence, subsumed under the construct of Occam's razor, also dictates that the least adorned model – that which has the smallest number of caveats and is seemingly the most straightforward – is preferable in the event that any two models cover the data more or less equally well.

The reason we begin with the default assumption that a theory is correct and then attempt to prove it wrong is that, for all we know, the very notion that we could come up with one theory that is correct in absolute terms is highly unlikely, if not somewhat arrogant – as this has never happened before, and it is unlikely that it will occur in the near future. Even some of the most successful and long-lived scientific theories in history, such as the theory of evolution (Darwin, 1859), or the theory of special relativity (Einstein, 1905), have been refined substantially or limited in scope on the basis of an increasingly available macro dataset over time, and the fact that they are nonetheless still in existence today is absolutely exceptional. Because science demands the benefit of the doubt to be given to theories that meet a minimal threshold of reason, it is essential that any and all theories *can* be falsified. If they cannot, it would be extremely unproductive for us to even consider them, since we would never be able to disprove them (which, of course, would not mean they are wrong, just that we simply would have no scientifically acceptable means to determine this). As you can see, then, "right" is a highly relative term in science: Theories are never quite *right*, they are in whole or in part just *not-yet-falsified*. Inherent in the scientific method is the goal of trying to falsify our (own) theories so that we can discard otherwise reasonably logical proposals in a principled way and thus make progress. After all, being wrong in science is sometimes even more important than is being right.

If the above seems at all contradictory, think of the board game *Clue* – or *Cluedo* if you are from outside North America. *Clue* is a classic (and very popular) murder-mystery board game, the goal of which is for each player to find out who murdered the host (with what and where in the house) at a party before any other player does so. The game begins with the revelation of the murder of Mr. Boddy/Dr. Black (location depending). There are, in principle, quite a few possible answers (324, to be exact) considering all the combinations of *who* (six characters), *where* (nine rooms) and *what with* (six potential weapons). Round after round, the players propose a number of hypotheses: 'I think/say it was Mrs. Peacock, in the kitchen, with the candlestick!' a given player might proclaim when it is her first turn. Once the cards show that this first player was partly or completely wrong, we are down to just somewhere between 323 and five explanations of our host's murder – the latter only if the player was extremely lucky. After a few rounds of testing various hypotheses, we will have reduced the range of possible answers significantly, and we will be a little closer to the truth. This is precisely how science makes progress: by eliminating reasonable possibilities.

Now, even the simplest phenomenon in the natural world has many more than 324 possible explanations if we want to understand every detail of it. This does not mean, however, that the intermediate steps are useless. The closer we come to understanding something, the easier it will be for us to put that knowledge into practice. We do not yet know everything there is to know about how birds fly – for one thing, we do not quite fully understand how gravity works, at least not on all scales; for example, the tried-and-true theory of gravity does not usually hold at the subatomic scale level (e.g., Dirac, 1930; Feynman, 1965) – but we certainly know enough to build planes that fly, satellites that stay in orbit and rockets that can land on Mars. All of this was possible because, at some point in the process, we discovered – not without pain – that birds did not fly (just) by flapping their wings. Although we now know that it is mainly a bird's ability to glide and create lift force by stretching out its wings that results in the apparent miracle of flight, wing flapping was certainly a reasonable hypothesis to explain flight and was thus ripe for testing. Once the evidence showed that flapping wings is (potentially necessary but) not sufficient to explain flight, we were able to discard the proposal that birds fly only because they move their wings up and down. Alternatively, if someone had proposed that the main factor behind bird flight was that these animals were chosen by God, we would have had no way to prove this wrong – or to offer meaningful support for it being right, for that matter. Here, we simply have a difference between faith and the scientific burden of proof. The former requires no indexical evidence per se; that is, belief and anecdotal evidence suffice, while the latter obligatorily thrives on it. As we are a science proper, of course we require much more than mere anecdotes.

In principle, there is nothing inherently wrong with proposing a new model or theory even when there is not yet a critical mass of data that seems to point in its direction – although ideally there would be – provided that the new theory is (i) not in contradiction with the available data within the literature and, crucially, (ii) is testable. In this sense, a proposal that claimed birds fly because they have beaks would be just as likely to be wrong or right as would the God argument, but at least we would be able to validate it empirically. To make hypothesis testing an easier task, when proposing a model a researcher must be able to offer what Jacobs (2000: 730) called the *"strongest falsificator"*; that is, "an effect that the model excludes under all initial conditions." In simpler terms, this is what cannot happen if the model is right. In our latest example, what would be the strongest falsificator within a theory of flight that proposed beaks as the ultimate factor behind birds' success? Because this hypothesis is so straightforward, the question has an easy answer: If the theory is right, no bird without a beak should be able to fly. However, it is not entirely uncommon for some birds not to have beaks, be it as a result of a mutation or after being attacked by a predator. These animals have serious difficulties eating and their chances of survival are therefore rather slim, but they are certainly able to fly. Thus, we can say that the theory has been falsified because its strongest falsificator has been shown to obtain.

Admittedly, developing models that are fully testable is not always easy: It requires more than just the commitment of the scientist when it comes to details. We sometimes have a hunch that something happens in a certain way (for example, birds fly mainly because stretching out their wings allows them to glide in the air and avoid plummeting to the ground), but we are unsure about the specifics (Is it a matter of surface? Is it related to how their feathers interact with the air? Possibly both?). Committing to the strongest possible version of our model – one that makes predictions for even the smallest details – is the most productive way to proceed because it will allow us to determine which parts of the model are on the right track and which need to be changed or discarded. This is the ideal way to move forward in terms of theory building (growing in a linear way as opposed to having a sideways trajectory as a field), precisely because – as we acknowledged from the outset – no current theory in any science is absolutely correct in its current form. However, being logical from the start, all theories worthy of serious consideration surely have some insights that are best kept, even when major tenets are proven wrong as the result of empiricism. By building new theories on the basis of what works and what does not from older ones, the baby is not thrown out with the bathwater, so to speak. We will keep referring to commitments and the concept of the strongest falsificator in further chapters, as these will be useful when we discuss and evaluate current models of transfer in L3/L*n* morphosyntax.

To return to our two original factors (the premature offerings of new models – sideways growth – and the fact that some models are by their very nature simply unfalsifiable; see González Alonso & Rothman, 2017a), once we have established what makes a model falsifiable (and thus a model, strictly speaking), a pressing question remains: When is it then necessary to propose a new model? If we examine the intense debate surrounding L3/L*n* models in recent years, we will find that not all of the arguments claimed by some to be incompatibilities are actually so. In fact, while some proposals have directed our attention toward new variables, such insights/directives in and of themselves do not (necessarily) constitute a justification for proposing new models unless they offer predictions that are mutually exclusive of those of existing theories and meet the criteria of Occam's razor; that is, they explain all of the existing data sets better or equally well but are improved by being less adorned and thus more elegant. Remember Earth 2.0? If the European Space Agency had limited itself to pointing out that pressure matters, we would still be no wiser about the new planet's water cycle. Instead, it articulated this argument in Model B, which states specifically *how* it is that pressure matters and, more importantly, generates predictions that can be tested against those of NASA's Model A. Unless authors commit to a set of unique predictions and how to apply these predictions a priori – before data are collected – new (and old) models cannot be falsified. When one begins the task of constructing a new study that tests models, what each model would predict should follow immediately without major angst or disagreement. If one finds it relatively difficult to determine what the predictions are for any given model, this can only mean one of two things: (a) the researcher does not quite understand the main tenets of the models as well as s/he should, or (b) there is something not quite right about the model itself. There are many positive and negative things we could say about literally all of the current models of transfer in L3/L*n* acquisition, including our own, as we will in Chapter 4. However, even when we believe the data point in the direction of falsification of a given model, the mere fact that the model avails itself to such scrutiny means it was a well-formed theory from the start. From a scientific point of view, far worse than actually being wrong is the inability of something to be proven wrong in the first place.

Let us take the fact that most proposals have intellectual merit as a given and that dismissing an entire proposal outright because it falls victim to the cautionary tale above – it cannot be wholly or partially falsified – might also be premature because doing so could constitute a missed opportunity to heed some new insights that are offered. It is often the case that newer proposals are better at determining the specifics of a process than was the original model, and can thus be seen as refinements or newer versions of the same model. On other occasions, they will not make new predictions themselves, but will help us to understand parts of a previous model or theory; for example, how it is that the stretching out of wings allows birds to glide. One of our aims in this book will be to re-examine old and new proposals, and to ask ourselves when it is strictly true that we are looking at competing models. To the extent that some of them can be combined with or incorporated in previous theories, we will attempt to define a set of models of L3/L*n* acquisition that is smaller in number but which contains stronger, better-articulated hypotheses that we can really test against each other (see Chapter 4).

Ultimately, when we do have a proposal that represents a separate, competing model, it is a shared responsibility to ensure that it is understood as such. By shared, we are referring to the burden that both the authors and the readers have. An author has the ultimate responsibility of making the claims and predictions of her model as clear and applicable as possible. The reader's responsibility is to understand what any given model claims, nothing more nor less, while resisting the temptation to adorn it or ascribe to it things that its authors did not claim. In this regard, it is vital that two things about a model are clear. The first is which phenomenon, process or subprocess it is designed to explain; that is, what exactly are we trying to understand through the model? This helps to ensure that its predictions can be tested adequately within the limits of the object of study, since a theory is only truly testable to the extent that it is understood within the exact parameters for which it claims to make predictions. For example, a theory regarding bird flight cannot be falsified on the basis of evidence from rocket propulsion experiments although both clearly overlap in propelling an object through the air in seeming defiance of gravity. This allows precision at both ends of reasoning: Deductively, the model's proponents are encouraged to define the scope of their theory, which can only be falsified or supported by data that fall within such empirical scope; inductively, fellow researchers are fully aware of what models they should consider when evaluating potential accounts of their data. Once the scope of a theory or model is defined appropriately, the second thing that should be clear about it is precisely what predictions it makes. These must be laid out unambiguously, particularly highlighting where they diverge from the predictions of competing proposals when these exist. We strongly believe that this kind of consideration can contribute to channeling research efforts in the most productive direction possible, focusing the debate on what are indeed fundamental – and empirically testable – differences in the models in terms of their descriptions and explanations of the data.

1.7   Theory Building and the Importance of Solid Foundations

Recall that a central claim of this book is that research on transfer-related phenomena during the first few months of L3 acquisition is essential if we are ever to characterize the role of transfer in L3 as a whole. In itself, this is hardly controversial: Everyone should agree that a developmental process needs to be modeled from beginning to end; thus, informative data from all stages are vital. However, the point we are trying to make here is that it might be wise to adjust our theory building according to a similar developmental pattern; that is, moving on to intermediate and advanced stages only after we have achieved a good understanding of how L3/Ln acquisition begins. There are at least three reasons we think this is a good idea – one admittedly follows from our own theoretical position, which is itself empirically testable; the other two, however, apply more widely and involve how one may approach the task of modeling the role of linguistic transfer over the course of L3 acquisition. The first reason is that, if the grammar of one (or both) of the previous languages is transferred in whole or even in part soon after the learner is first exposed to the L3, this will have obvious consequences for how the rest of the process (L3 development itself) unfolds over time. The second is that any theory of dynamic transfer in multilingualism, regardless of whether it assigns a special status to the beginning, generates predictions for that period that have enduring implications for the L3 interlanguage and can, therefore, be followed into more advanced stages.

The third and final reason has to do with the nature of transfer and is itself multifaceted. Since its output can (partly) match or mismatch the target language property, linguistic transfer can have nonfacilitative or facilitative results – or can present a slightly more complex pattern that leads to (at least partially) off-target performance. The first scenario is of course the one in which transfer is most apparent, and is the most useful in terms of tracing crosslinguistic influence to its source: Not only are learners making errors but these can be seen to match the grammatical configuration of a previously learned language. Often, however (perhaps more often than not), transfer effectively serves the cognitive purpose that arguably gives rise to it, and a targetlike representation is copied from one of the learner's previously acquired languages. When this happens, the underlying mechanisms of grammar building become essentially opaque to us: There is virtually no way to determine whether targetlike performance is the reflection of a linguistic representation that was transferred from a previous language (L1 or L2) or of one that was acquired along the developmental path in much the same way as someone with no previous (or applicable) linguistic experience, such as a monolingual child, would have acquired it. Of course, there may be certain indications that transfer has played a role in the acquisition of a given grammatical property (early acquisition of typically late-acquired properties, acquisition of a complex property without previous knowledge of properties or structures that commonly precede it in L1 acquisition and so on), but this is, at best, indirect evidence. As discussed in Section 1.4 above, linguistic transfer is generally triggered and/or permitted by a state of (general or particular) underspecification in the target grammar. With regard to the learning task of acquiring the L3 grammar, this state becomes less frequent as proficiency increases: Representations become more stable and targetlike, reinforced by input and use, and interlanguage gradually progresses toward a state of full identity with the target grammar. In other words, there are fewer reasons for previous language properties to be transferred into the L3 because – there are progressively fewer cases of underspecification or parsing failure – that is, the absence or inadequacy of representations in the learner's current interlanguage – that make it necessary or sufficient for transfer to take place. Conversely, the initial stages are a time at which the L3 interlanguage is at an obvious state of underspecification; thus, by definition, there will be more instances of transfer for us to examine. It seems logical, then, to assume that *any* model put forward to explain the role of transfer in L3 acquisition will find more unambiguous occurrences of its object of study at earlier stages of acquisition.

With the above in mind, it is perhaps easier to see why we consider that following predictions from the beginning into further stages of L3 acquisition is the best way to proceed, irrespective of the theory to which one subscribes. While most models have proposed a single factor as determining the source of transfer – for individual properties or for the entire grammar – as well as some other potentially intervening variables, they all agree on what triggers linguistic transfer: underspecification in the L3 interlanguage grammar. Without an estimate of which grammatical representations might be weak or missing at any given point, it is impossible for these models to predict when transfer can occur and thus when we are most likely to observe its effects. As stated above, a theory is useless if it cannot make predictions; thus, the very nature of linguistic transfer places strong constraints on the predictive power of any model that is proposed to account for it. Observations made toward the start of the L3 developmental process alleviate this uncertainty by providing a context in which interlanguage grammars are less targetlike by definition and may thus potentially reveal more instances of nonfacilitative transfer – and where the predictions of all the models are compatible. Note that, unless one seeks to argue that the source of transfer is ultimately determined by different variables at different stages of development (one of many logical possibilities), models that are proposed to account for linguistic transfer in L3/Ln acquisition as a whole should find the initial stages to be an equally suitable testing ground as any other point in the developmental sequence.

1.8   Taking Stock: The What, When, How and Why of Transfer in L3 Acquisition

The title of this section is indeed the million-dollar question – however, much to our regret, it will not be answered here! Nonetheless, our hope is that this chapter has convinced you of why these questions are important to us linguists, acquisitionists, psychologists and cognitive scientists, and particularly how we might best go about the task of finding some answers to them. In the remainder of the book we will unpack many of these aspects related to linguistic transfer in multilingual language acquisition and processing.

Since this is a monograph that we hope can and will also be used as a teaching tool, we would be remiss to not take advantage of the opportunity to present – in a nonexhaustive fashion – the larger field of multilingualism for several reasons. We believe that doing so will help the reader to understand the specificity of the main focus of this book for what it is, a piece of a much larger puzzle that is multilingualism. At the same time, we hope to present scholars who are new to the L3 field with a virtual smorgasbord of information, such that the interested reader will know where to start to investigate other equally interesting aspects of studies on multilingualism. Thus, the next chapter presents a brief overview of related subdisciplines of linguistic inquiry focusing on multilingualism. Chapter 3 will continue to hone in on the central topic of this book by presenting research conducted on lexical access and acquisition, as well as phonology, all with a specific focus on multilingualism. Chapter 4 is dedicated entirely to a comprehensive – exhaustive to the extent possible – discussion of transfer in L3/Ln morphosyntax. Once we are situated and have defined where we are and where we want to be clearly, we will present a systematic review of the empirical studies conducted thus far on the role of linguistic transfer in L3/L*n* acquisition in Chapter 5. This review will weigh in on the debates introduced in the previous chapter and will highlight the variables that have been revealed by the aggregate of the available data as being the most explanatory overall. Finally, we will dedicate some space and time to addressing some loose ends and future directions for the field, which has only started to break into the tip of the iceberg: the dynamics of transfer/CLE in multilingual systems.

Notes

1. Other estimates that suggest a slightly lower percentage exist. For example, the *Eurobarometer Survey on Europeans and their Languages* estimates the number to be 54%. Regardless of the precise number, the points made herein remain the same, particularly since all estimates provide a number in the ballpark of the mid-50s range.
2. The term interlanguage, as coined by Selinker (1972), refers to the different grammars through which a given second language learner progresses in transition from an initial hypothesis (which, most authors would agree, will be heavily based on the L1 for second language learners) to the target grammar; that is, the most accurate possible grammar that can ideally be inferred from the input provided to the learner. While interlanguage is, by definition, idiosyncratic and therefore unique to each learner, it is generally assumed that some general patterns can be observed across larger groups of nonnative speakers, as determined by factors such as L1, learning context (for example, naturalistic versus instructed learning), amount of exposure, differing complexity of the target linguistic structures and so on.
3. Determining whether a noun is or is not highly likely to be feminine or masculine is not arbitrary at all in Spanish, which is regarded as having a (relatively) transparent gender system (particularly compared to other languages, such as German, Norwegian or Dutch). Nouns that end in -o are overwhelmingly masculine, and nouns ending in -a are overwhelmingly feminine. Thus, by 'arbitrary' we are referring to the fact that a spoon is randomly assigned the feminine gender and a knife the masculine gender at the level of the syntax in a way that is unrelated to the inherent semantics of either noun. That this is seemingly not random in its phonological ending is a completely different matter.
4. For ease of exposition and given the limited space, we use the term 'critical period' in a catchall way. That is, 'critical period' is used herein as a proxy for either a singular absolute critical period for all domains of grammar, multiple critical periods applying at different times to distinct domains of grammar (such as an earlier one for phonology as compared to syntax) or even to sensitive periods that apply gradually over time as opposed to a sharp critical period effect. This is because explaining the differences and the literature that debates them is peripheral to the points in question, although we acknowledge that distinguishing between them for other important issues matters a great deal.

5. Tip-of-the-tongue (TOT) states are occasional and momentary failures in lexical retrieval, characterized by a feeling of knowing the intended word and being able to produce it imminently. TOT states in the speaker's native language have traditionally been thought of as an indicator of moderate L1 attrition, but recent work suggests that they might be better explained by dynamic interference (e.g., Ecke & Hall, 2013; Gollan, Bonanni, & Montoya, 2005).

6. Originating Variation from Order (OVO) is a generative-based processing attempt at explaining constituency order preferences crosslinguistically. OVO is informed by decades of work with bilinguals of O(bject)V(erb)–V(erb)-O(bject) languages (such as Basque–Spanish and Japanese–English bilinguals) in Laka's laboratory, and assumes the minimalist claim that Merge generates an unordered set, which means that, at the level of syntactic computation, there are hierarchies and dependencies but no order per se. OVO claims that language-specific linearization preferences (particularly in terms of the OV/VO divide) emerge only at the level of processing when the speaker is faced with the need to 'flatten out' and express the computation along a time dimension. OVO seems to imply that the factor behind this is a universal tendency to reduce the distance of dependencies, which is resolved differently for different languages – for example, Basque compromises to verb medial order when the first constituent is long.

7. A meteorologist would surely be horrified by the amount of simplification that follows since numerical weather prediction is based on extremely complex mathematical models. Please remember, though, that this is just meant to be an illustrative example!

8. Our emphasis on the word "choose" is not unmotivated: As researchers, we are able to decide beforehand the *what* and the *how* of our investigations, which means that our choices in focus and methodology must be guided by precise theoretical questions.

2 *Theoretical Approaches to Sequential Multilingualism*

2.0 General Introduction

In this chapter, we aim to summarize the range of work that has been and continues to be conducted on multilingual populations from various theoretical paradigms and/or distinct subareas of theoretical and applied linguistics. Any attempt to be exhaustive in this regard would be doomed from the start, as space – and likely the attention of the reader – would surely be an obstacle. Moreover, and of equal importance, doing so would distract us from the main goal of this book, which is to understand the dynamic nature of representational morphosyntactic transfer in adult multilingualism and the manifold theoretical implications that derive from revealing this. That being said, it is important to understand the larger context in which our choice of focus is situated and thus appreciate the piece of the larger puzzle that it is. Therefore, this chapter serves to provide a cursory snapshot of the puzzle itself.

As is to be expected, different paradigms that focus on various pieces of this larger puzzle have their own sets of interests and questions on which they tend to focus; however, this does not preclude an overlap among approaches, regardless of whether this is immediately clear to the neophyte and/or to the established researcher studying L3/L*n* acquisition. In order to better equip the reader to evaluate the data discussed in these studies, it is important to highlight the theoretical and empirical questions that have taken center stage in each approach. Most of the core issues that we address in this book – introduced in the first chapter – can be approached from different theoretical standpoints. Of course, this is not to say that all major debates take place at the dividing lines between these schools. As we will see, some debates are specific to one theoretical approach and irrelevant to others, whereas two seemingly irreconcilable paradigms might (partially or wholly) share the same or similar views on a particular subject, potentially unbeknownst to themselves (Rothman & Slabakova, 2018). Since the research interests of different theoretical approaches only ever partially overlap, dialog between them is thus most meaningful when we identify these common areas and understand the differences in their proper contexts. Thus, while most of the discussion in this book will be framed within generative approaches to/understandings of language acquisition, we will naturally refer to some of the research on crosslinguistic influence conducted within functional, sociolinguistic, and educational approaches to L3 acquisition when relevant to the discussion in subsequent chapters. For this reason, it is prudent to introduce all such approaches, and the major findings therein, from the outset, not least because they bring much to bear on work done in formal linguistic approaches to L3/L*n* acquisition. This is necessary because the entirety of the literature that examines L3/L*n* is interrelated at some basic level: To be an L3/L*n* scholar, generally speaking, one needs to be aware of the various subareas in the field, inclusive of all questions asked and the evidence base that provides current attempts at answers.

2.1   Cognitive Approaches

Our species-specific capacity to acquire any given human language has prompted questions crucial to our understanding of the role of human cognition in the developmental trajectory of language acquisition for more than a century (e.g., Darwin, 1859; Saussure, 1916). For example, scientists have long been interested in the nature of human language, how and why it is acquired effortlessly by any child (barring impairment) and why it shares universal characteristics across distinct language systems. Irrespective of differences in terms of theoretical backgrounds, most approaches to first, second and third language acquisition with roots in any paradigm of theoretical linguistics share an interest in language as a cognitive phenomenon, above and beyond its social dimension. From this perspective, and to provide a broad definition, language acquisition is the process of creation and consolidation of mental representations (grammar) that allows a speaker to produce and understand utterances in a given natural language. Differences across paradigms, when reduced to their core (that is, to those aspects in which they are truly mutually exclusive), often concern the role of input in the acquisition process and the necessity of postulating domain-specific (innate) linguistic knowledge (see, e.g., Rothman & Slabakova, 2018; Rothman & VanPatten, 2013). The question is not whether input is deterministic for language acquisition – be it a first, second, third or tenth language – as no theory denies the necessity of high-quality input (ideally with high quantity as well). The question is whether or not the combination of input and whatever domain-general cognitive mechanisms contribute to language learning is not only necessary but indeed *sufficient* to explain the complexity and specificity of resulting multilingual grammars.

2.1.1   Generative Approaches

UG is based on Gen. Appoa.

Both children and adults – but least controversially the former – are remarkably efficient language learners: We can acquire languages in the face of scarce and inconsistent input, which is only a subset of what could be produced by combining the same "linguistic tools" (that is, the same structures and words). In other words, linguistic input often underrepresents the ensuing system arrived at in ultimate attainment.[1] The term 'poverty of the stimulus' (henceforth POS) is used to capture the aforementioned situation with regard to how developing child grammars as well as adult grammars in a state of ultimate attainment project well beyond that which they could have acquired from the input itself (see, e.g., Berwick, Pietroski, Yankama, & Chomsky, 2011; Hauser, Chomsky, & Fitch, 2002; Lasnik & Lidz, 2016; Pinker, 1994; Rothman, 2008b; Rothman & Iverson, 2008; Schwartz & Sprouse, 2013; Valian, 2014; Yang, 2016; Yang, Crain, Berwick, Chomsky, & Bolhuis, 2017). Innatist approaches to language, fueled by the POS observation/argument, maintain that innate universal knowledge (that is, domain-specific to language) imposes constraints on the nature and number of hypotheses a learner can develop about the language(s) to which she is exposed, and thus delimits the shape that natural human grammars can take in the mind. Simply put, this means that natural languages represent only a fraction of all logically possible grammars (there are certain properties that no known languages have, yet which should be possible in principle), and we humans are innately equipped with the set of universally applicable principles that impose those limits. This "genetically endowed blueprint" permitting children to reduce the hypothesis space to a manageable level is traditionally referred to as Universal Grammar (UG). *Universal Grammar*

From its earliest conceptualizations, UG proposed answers to the above quandaries, offering itself as the gap filler to account for how grammars, or languages, in the mind come to project beyond exposure and experience, outlining what has since been termed the Basic Property of Language (BPL). The BPL is the observation that a human language is composed of a finite computational system that generates an infinite number of expressions, each having a categorical interpretation in thought and sound (see Berwick & Chomsky, 2017, for discussion). Initially, linguists struggled to construct grammars that accounted for the subtle intricacies of language and its variations across language systems, relying largely on highly ordered, complex, transformational rules to describe it, such as those found in Chomsky's (1957)

Syntactic Structures. Notwithstanding, it was recognized as early as the mid-1960s that, while such rule systems accounted for a great deal of crosslinguistic variation, they did little to explain the ease with which children acquired their native language. Therefore, it was proposed that the rule system predicated by UG be minimized into specific constraints on UG itself. A need for such simplification was evident, at least in the observation that specific linguistic rules are often restricted to certain domains (e.g., Chomsky, 1975). Over the next decade or so, linguists observed an impressive host of systematic constraints on UG, which came to be known as Principles and Parameters (P&P) within the framework bearing the same name, the aim of which was to combine the complex rules into a single transformational operation that would be parameterized by certain admissible alterations that could, in turn, capture and explain crosslinguistic variation in the narrowest terms possible. Eventually, the goal of the general program shifted to uncovering a single operation that was responsible for building the structure underlying human language syntax. Out of these efforts the Minimalist Program (Chomsky, 1995) was born.

In the 60 years that followed the earliest instantiations of UG, it was duly noted that human language syntax displays at least three basic properties that can be explained within a minimalist framework:

(i)   human language syntax is non-linear (except in production and parsing, including morphology and phonology/phonetics) when compared to non-human primates;

(ii) hierarchical structure affects meaning and interpretation; and

(iii) hierarchical structure is seemingly infinite (that is, recursive) (Berwick & Chomsky, 2015, 2017; Fitch & Hauser, 2004; Fitch, Hauser, & Chomsky, 2005; Hauser et al., 2002).

It has been assumed that these three properties together comprised the fewest explanatory, but necessary, variables of language and, therefore, are the best candidates for a single operation for the building of syntactic structures, which later became formalized as Merge (e.g., Chomsky, 2001). Merge, simplistically speaking, is responsible for forming and structuring syntactic objects hierarchically (that is, sets). For example, syntactic object A and another syntactic object B are merged to form a new but hierarchically structured object such as the set $\{A,B\}$, which itself is labeled by an algorithm charged with satisfying the conditions of minimal computation. For example, Merge would combine the objects *eat* and *apple* into the set $\{eat, apple\}$. The features of the combination head are then labeled by a minimal search. According to the traditional idea that *eat apples* is, by virtue of its constituent structure, a verb phrase, the head is *eat*. The new set, or verb phrase headed by *eat*, is then able to progress through further computations (that is, recursion; see Berwick & Chomsky, 2015, 2017, for discussion).

Returning to how UG accounts for BPL, this can be summarized very simply as follows: UG is an internal computational system responsible for the hierarchical building of human language syntactic sets (i.e., Merge) and which interfaces with both external components such as production (phonology/phonetics), parsing and morphology (word building), as well as with conceptual systems (i.e., cognition) for appropriate inference making and interpretation. Whatever the actual architecture of UG is, whether it is indeed only Merge and other formal features of grammar, a literal blueprint of linguistic principles restricting the hypothesis space of all logical possibilities of human language or some combination thereof, generative scholars argue that it must be the minimally required biological guide to language learning that can explain the outcomes of linguistic competence that are not explained on the basis of principles of domain-general cognition alone.

Whether UG is still accessible after puberty – that is, in what is called sequential adult nonnative or second language acquisition – has been at the core of a long-standing debate within generative approaches to second language acquisition (GenSLA; see Rothman & Slabakova, 2018; Schwartz & Sprouse, 2013; White, 2018, for review) because partial or complete inaccessibility to UG might explain at least some differences between children and adults in their developmental trajectories and ultimate success as language learners (e.g., Bley-Vroman, 1989, 2009; Clahsen & Felser, 2006a; Clahsen & Muysken, 1986, 1989; Hawkins & Casillas, 2008; Hawkins & Chan, 1997; Meisel, 1997; Tsimpli & Dimitrakopoulou, 2007). It is fair to say, however, that theories advocating full accessibility of UG have been favored in recent years. This is true in part because observable differences between child and adult learners can also be accounted for by (a combination of) influence from the first language (e.g., Foley & Flynn, 2013; Jarvis, 2000; Schwartz & Sprouse, 1994, 1996; White, 2003b) and factors related to language processing (e.g., Cunnings, 2017; Grüter & Rohde, 2013; Herschensohn, 2000; Hopp, 2006, 2014; Kaan, 2014; McDonald, 2006; Prévost & White, 2000; Sagarra, 2012, among others). Such factors offer explanatory adequacy without necessarily assuming that the mental machinery involved in the creation of L1 and L2 linguistic representations differs in any fundamental way.

Within the past 15 years, researchers in the generative tradition have turned their attention to the multilingual context, in which a sequential third or further language (L3/L*n*) is acquired in adulthood. As we have claimed throughout, the jump from two to three languages is not a trivial one. Research on L3/L*n* acquisition can contribute in unique ways to the two main themes in generative approaches to SLA: the role of previous linguistic knowledge (transfer) and ultimate attainment potential (see Cabrelli Amaro, Flynn, & Rothman, 2012; Flynn, 2009; García Mayo, 2015; García Mayo & Rothman, 2012; González Alonso et al., 2017; Leung, 2007b; Rothman, Iverson, & Judy, 2011). The first, transfer, as we know well by now, is the primary focus of this book. The second, ultimate attainment in an L2, can be explored using the initial stages of L3 acquisition as indirect evidence of what can (and what, if anything, cannot) be acquired in an L2 (e.g., Cabrelli Amaro, Iverson, & Judy, 2009; Iverson, 2009b, 2010): Transfer from the L2 into the L3 can reveal the state of representation achieved in the then-current version of the L2 grammar. It is not surprising, then, that most early work on L3 morphosyntax was focused on a comparison between L2 and L3 learners of the same target language (e.g., Bohnacker, 2006; Klein, 1995; Leung, 1998, 2001, 2002, 2003, 2005a, 2005b, 2006, 2007a, 2008; Rothman & Cabrelli Amaro, 2010), in an effort to understand how the presence or absence of additional languages could affect language acquisition in different ways, even for learners who had the same L1 and were acquiring the same target language. Needless to say, the pedagogical implications of this distinction cannot be overstated: In brief, it means that teaching L2 and L3 learners in the same way, even if they are native speakers of the same language, can be a fundamental mistake. That is, the learning tasks of an L2 learner of French and an L3 learner of French, even when both are native speakers of English, can be quite different depending on what the L2 of the L3 French learners is, as well as the level of proficiency they have in the L2. The L2/L3 distinction has been one of the strongest links between the empirical study of L3/L*n* acquisition from a generative perspective and the practice of foreign-language instruction (e.g., González Alonso & Rothman, 2017b).

Most recent generative work on L3/L*n* acquisition has focused on modeling the influence of previously acquired languages on L3/L*n* grammatical development, both in terms of initial hypotheses (initial-stages transfer) and of implications for the learnability of the target language (e.g., Bardel & Falk, 2007; Falk & Bardel, 2011; Falk et al., 2015; Flynn et al., 2004; Flynn, Vinnitskaya, & Foley, 2008; González Alonso & Rothman, 2017a; Rothman, 2010, 2015; Slabakova, 2017; Westergaard et al., 2017; see also Håkansson, Pienemann, & Sayehli, 2002; Pienemann, Lenzing, & Keßler, 2016, for research within Processability Theory; a different, yet nativist theory). Simply put, these studies have proposed a series of models to account for

[handwritten: generature - applying rules to generate output]

how transfer from prior languages interacts with UG to constrain development of the L3/L*n* grammar. More specifically, these models have addressed how the first component of this interaction (transfer) is selected systematically among multiple available sources; that is, what leads the learner's grammar-building mechanisms to transfer (copy) linguistic properties from the L1 instead of the L2 into the L3, or vice versa. This being said, generative L3/L*n* scholars have also discussed issues of development that follow from or are covered directly by these models, particularly regarding the L3/L*n* learning task (e.g., Berkes & Flynn, 2012b, 2017; González Alonso & Rothman, 2017a). Since this book is particularly concerned with the larger topic of morphosyntactic transfer in L3/L*n* acquisition, we will leave an in-depth discussion of these models and their implications for Chapter 4 and elaborate here on other frameworks that will not receive focused attention in the core of the volume.

2.1.2 Usage-Based Approaches

For the past 20 years, extensive work has been conducted on (sequential) multilingualism from functional perspectives on linguistics and language acquisition – broadly (and henceforth) referred to as usage-based theories (see, e.g., Bates & MacWhinney, 1982, 1989, Bybee, 1985, 1995, 2010; Croft, 2000; N. C. Ellis, 1998; N. C. Ellis & Wulff, 2015; Givón, 1979; Goldberg, 2003, 2006; Hopper, 1987; Langacker, 1987; O'Grady, 2008, 2013; Tomasello, 2003; Wulff & N. C. Ellis, 2018). These approaches share a view of language as a cognitive instrument. Usage-based linguists agree that humans are ideally and biologically equipped to acquire/use language, but only insofar as they possess the domain-general cognitive, motor and social skills that make it possible: In other words, usage-based theories of language reject the notion of a genetically endowed language faculty, maintaining that language is learned (and learnable) without the need to resort to preexisting, domain-specific knowledge. *[handwritten: they don't believe in Universal Grammar]* According to this view, language learning proceeds from exemplars (concrete, context-specific pairings of form and meaning) all the way to more abstract patterns and structures as the learner gathers sufficient information to extend form-meaning relationships confidently from the particular to the general. In other words, contingencies related to input frequency are argued to lead to generalizations, whereas statistical preemption is claimed to give rise to hard linguistic constraints (Perek & Goldberg, 2017).

A key concept underlies usage-based approaches to language and linguistic development, namely that linguistic symbols (for example, words and sentence structure) map onto preexisting, nonlinguistic categories, which are themselves our way of structuring the human perception of the world. Cognitive development depends greatly on our ability to categorize objects; that is, to recognize that the objects we have encountered on different occasions are in fact the same, or at least should be considered within the same category, despite varying degrees of difference across the external (context or ground) and internal (figure) properties of the object (Bornstein, 1984; Bornstein, Arterberry, & Mash, 2010; Harnad, 1987). When we see an apple on a table in the kitchen, for example, we will notice some of its physical characteristics, which will help us recognize the same fruit if we then stumble upon an apple tree with some apples hanging from it or lying on the ground. The more frequently we are presented with apples, and the more varied the context is, the stronger our category representation will be for that object. Usage-based approaches assume that linguistic symbols are abstracted and categorized in very much the same way as nonlinguistic objects: With sufficient repetition in sufficiently meaningful contexts, an abstract category will eventually be created in the mind of the speaker. This parallel with non-linguistic cognitive activity is a fundamental claim of the paradigm. In other words, usage-based theorists contend that language is built upon cognitive (domain-general) not linguistic (domain-specific) universals (Greenberg, 1963; see, e.g., MacWhinney, 2001).

Different languages map their linguistic symbols onto cognitive categories in different ways depending on the real-world context in which a given language has developed – that is, the physical environment in which the speech community could be found. Rice is likely to be categorized perceptually as rice in very similar ways by any human, but it features much more prominently and prototypically within the category 'food' in South East Asia than it does in Scandinavia. Inevitably, these differences translate to language, such that the words for 'food' and 'rice' are more strongly connected in Thai than they are in Norwegian. A more extreme but equally valid example is that of grasshoppers, which are considered a delicacy in certain areas of Mexico but would not be likely to be eaten by Mexican Americans living in California. It is likely that the mental lexicon of some Mexican Spanish speakers has associations between the words for 'grasshopper' and 'food' that are not to be found in Mexican Americans in Los Angeles. Categorization preferences extend beyond vocabulary: According to a usage-based approach, the canonical word order (for example, subject-verb-object, SVO, or object-verb-subject, OVS) in a given language simply reflects how that language typically structures information within a sentence. For example, in SVO languages such as English or Italian, the first noun in an N(oun)-V(erb)-N(oun) sequence will most likely be the subject of the sentence. On the other hand, OVS languages (admittedly a rare group) such as Apalaí, Huarijio or Hixkaryana tend to express the object of the sentence first, and so the first noun in an N-V-N sequence should usually have the object function. Of course, things are not quite this simple: Even languages that are typically SVO, such as Italian, Norwegian, Spanish or Russian, allow for an OVS order on certain occasions, and often under different linguistic pressures; for example, OVS might arise in Norwegian for object emphasis, related to its V(erb) second (2) rule, and this order also arises in the case of Italian and Spanish for discourse salience (focus) reasons. This is not a problem for a listener who is proficient in these languages because grammatical functions such as 'subject' or 'object' will be signaled through means other than word order, such as case marking, prosody (stress and intonation) and the like. These different means of conveying grammatical information, known in usage-based theory as *linguistic cues* (e.g., Bates & MacWhinney, 1987), have different degrees of importance in different languages; for example, word order and prosody are particularly important in languages in which inflectional morphology is poor and thus not particularly informative, such as English, but they are less relevant in languages such as Turkish or Basque, which are agglutinative languages that express most grammatical functions through morphology.

Since the linguistic cues that signal the relationship between the form and the meaning of an utterance are weighted differently in each language, some of the most prominent models of language learning within the usage-based paradigm maintain that learning a language primarily entails determining the set of cues that operate in that language and, most importantly, the hierarchies that are established among them. In the Competition Model (henceforth CM; Bates & MacWhinney, 1987, 1989; MacWhinney, 1987, 2005), linguistic cues compete with each other to guide the interpretation of an utterance toward one meaning or another. The learning task will then always be to determine the availability and reliability of these cues in the specific language at hand. Importantly, this is as true for the child acquiring her L1(s) as it is for the nonnative learner who acquires a second, third or successive language. This is indeed a notable point of convergence between usage-based and generative approaches: What makes the learning task different for the latter type of learner is the undeniable influence of prior linguistic knowledge. From the perspective of the CM, a nonnative learner needs to overcome and reconfigure previous assumptions – retreating from L1 entrenchment – developed in the course of L1 learning with regard to the linguistic cues that are available and how they relate to and interact with each other (e.g., MacWhinney, 2005, 2012). Returning to our previous examples, an L1 Basque learner of L2 English will have to become aware that case marking is rarely available in this language (save for the pronominal system in which case is marked overtly – for example, I/me/my for first person singular depending on its grammatical function) – and that word order is a much stronger, reliable cue to meaning and grammatical functions in English than it is in Basque.

The above scenario evidently becomes more complex when several previous languages are part of the speaker's communicative competence. While the learning task remains unchanged in this view, most work dedicated to an empirical assessment of the CM in multilingual contexts has focused on the question of how the different and often conflicting cues operating in previously learned languages affect the establishment of a targetlike set of cues in the L2/L3/Ln differently (e.g., Marijuan, Lago, & Sanz, 2016; Sanz, Park, & Lado, 2015). In a study that tracked L3 learners ab initio – that is, from the very first exposure – using Latin as the target language, Sanz, Park, and Lado (2015) investigated the interaction of cue hierarchies for thematic role assignment in the L1, L2 and L3 for two groups of English native speakers, who were intermediate to advanced learners of L2 Japanese (n=10) and Spanish (n=15). Participants were exposed to L3 Latin vocabulary and sentences in which case marking (nominative/accusative), subject-verb agreement and multiple variations of word order were exemplified, both in isolation and in combination with each other – in other words, case marking in combination with SVO word order and distinctive subject-verb agreement, case marking with subject-verb agreement or case marking alone (without SVO and with uninformative agreement). Pretest, immediate posttest, and delayed posttest measures were collected over a period of four weeks in three different sessions. Participants showed signs of resorting to L1 cue hierarchies before training – in the pretest session – by relying mainly on SVO word order, the predominant cue in English, and disregarding subject-verb agreement and case marking. This was assumed to be a result of the relative imbalance in these speakers' L1-L2 competence, which was strongly in favor of their first and dominant language (English). In further sessions, the participants' performances began to reflect some reliance on cues other than SVO word order, which Sanz et al. interpreted as an indication that their L3 cue hierarchy was slowly overcoming the entrenched processing patterns of the L1, possibly with some help from targetlike cue configurations in their (respective) L2s.

Sanz et al. (2015) took their results to suggest that both languages remain active forces in the development of an L3-specific cue hierarchy, although L1 entrenchment is likely to minimally constrain the initial stages of L3/Ln processing and acquisition – at least in the case of unbalanced sequential multilinguals. This latter proviso is nontrivial, and is a point to which we will return in greater detail in various chapters, such as sections of Chapter 4 (see Sections 4.2.1.1 and 4.3.4.1) and throughout Chapter 5. A major bonus of this study is the truly ab initio design, whereby all L3 input (and its shape) can be controlled. As a result, we are assured of examining transfer effects at bona fide initial stages, where such effects can reliably be teased apart from L3 learning itself. That being said, if it is the case that, for the properties under investigation, we are not completely sure that the L2 had reached a state of proficiency that would indeed allow it to compete with the L1 (that is, a truly distinct L2 cue hierarchy or one in which L1 influence can be disentangled), showing L1 influence in the initial stages of the L3 may not be generalizable in the ways we would hope. Would the same results be found for L2 speakers who have reached such a level of competence in the L2? If so, what is shown is truly generalizable. If not, the value is in no way diminished. We would simply have a better understanding of what its coverage entails; that is, is the influence of the L1 at the initial stages really an inevitable default, or is it more indicative of what happens when dealing with lower levels of L2 proficiency?

The CM is not the only usage-based proposal that has been explored in the context of multilingualism. Recent work has focused on addressing traditionally important issues within the framework, such as the impact of input frequency and distribution on native and nonnative language production (e.g., Linford, Long, Solon, & Geeslin, 2016; Morgenstern, Beaupoil-Hourdel, Blondel, & Boutet, 2016), the direct, unmediated interpretation of metaphoric and performative language, such as speech acts (in other words, without first processing the literal meaning of a sentence such as 'Why don't you open the window?'; Kania, 2016), exemplar-based development (e.g., Hochmann, Azadpour, & Mehler, 2008; Tammelin-Laine & Martin, 2016), the use of specific bi-/multilingual discourse units ('blended units,' Fauconnier & Turner, 2003) that become disengaged from their original source languages (Achard & Lee, 2016) and the role of cognitive universals, or functional pressures, in constraining the number of possible grammars found in natural languages (e.g., Fedzechkina, Jaeger, & Newport, 2012, 2013; Fedzechkina, Newport, & Jaeger, 2016; Hudson Kam & Newport, 2005; Tily, Frank, & Jaeger, 2011), among other topics (see chapters in Ortega, Tyler, Park, & Uno, 2016, for a recent compilation). It should be noted that usage-based researchers do not always assign a special status to L3/L*n* as opposed to previous instances of nonnative language acquisition, developing models of L2/L*n* acquisition instead (e.g., Pajak, Fine, Kleinschmidt, & Jaeger, 2016). Under such an account, it is assumed that previous linguistic knowledge does not impact on the process of learning the target language in a significantly

[handwritten annotation: priori - Knowledge that requires no evidence "all bachelors are unmarried"]

different way in L2 versus L3/L*n* acquisition (but see Sanz et al., 2015, for arguments in favor of considering these processes separately), despite a demonstration on empirical grounds – that is, the sum total of evidence to the contrary – that influence from both languages is possible a priori, which must mean that, at some level, this influence affects acquisition/learning differently in L2 and L3/L*n* contexts (e.g., De Angelis, 2007; De Angelis & Dewaele, 2011; Rothman et al., 2013).

2.1.3   Multi-competence

Over the past 25 years, cognitive approaches to multilingualism have gradually shifted toward a perspective in which the linguistic competence of multilinguals is not made up of a series of discrete, monolingual-like grammars and lexicons but rather constitutes a unitary language system integrating several subsystems, namely multi-competence (e.g., Cook, 1991, 1992, 2003a, 2016; see, e.g., Berkes & Flynn, 2016; de Bot, 2016; Ortega, 2016, for integration of the framework within different theoretical approaches; see also Herdina & Jessner, 2002, and Jessner, 2008, for compatible models within Dynamic Systems Theory; Paradis, 2004, for a similar approach from neurolinguistics; Paradis, 1981, for a notable precedent of the idea). This view has implications for the way in which we conceptualize language learners, particularly those acquiring a nonnative language: The L2 subsystem in the multi-competence of an L2 learner of English is a completely different entity from that of an L1 English monolingual; thus, there is no reason for us to expect that they will function in identical ways.[2] It follows from this assumption that using L1 monolinguals as our standard of comparison for nonnative learners – as well as simultaneous bilingual and multilingual speakers – is misguided and thus scientifically unproductive. The claim of a comparative fallacy between monolingual and multilingual speakers has been a recurrent argument in SLA (e.g., Bley-Vroman, 1983; Klein, 1998; Ortega, 2013; Rothman, 2008b), simultaneous bilingualism (e.g., Grosjean, 1989), heritage language acquisition (e.g., Kupisch & Rothman, 2018; Pascual y Cabo & Rothman, 2012; Putnam & Sánchez, 2013) and neurolinguistics (e.g., Paradis, 2004) but has only become widely accepted in recent times (Ortega, 2013).

A second premise of multi-competence that has proved highly influential is the idea that both growth *and* decay are a part of language development and that multi-competence is, by its very nature, a dynamic system: Languages become larger and stronger (that is, more activated) over time if there is sufficient use – in comprehension, production, or both – but they also decay and deteriorate when the speaker is not sufficiently exposed to them for a certain amount of time. Similarly, the addition of a new language induces fundamental changes in the system for two main reasons: (i) the organization of the multi-competence system will likely change to accommodate the new linguistic material, and (ii) crosslinguistic influence will take place between the new language and the previous ones in all directions – in other words, the new language will also affect preexisting ones. These two exponents of dynamicity (the simultaneous occurrence of growth and decay, and the multidirectionality of crosslinguistic influence) have contributed to a better integration of work conducted on different but interrelated aspects of language development and from a vast range of theoretical perspectives. In other words, these tenets that can be likened to multi-competence have had a direct influence on or are compatible with work done in both usage-based and generative research.

The above can be appreciated nicely in the generally accepted importance of understanding language attrition (e.g., Schmid, 2013a, 2013b; Schmid & Köpke, 2017) – the loss or deterioration of a language – in its own right, and as the key to providing more ecologically valid explanations for some linguistic behavior that seems to reflect deficits in linguistic representation. For example, Rothman and colleagues (e.g., Kupisch & Rothman, 2018; Pires & Rothman, 2009; Rothman, 2007a, 2009b; Rothman & Treffers-Daller, 2014) have shown that at least some of the differences between monolingual native speakers and heritage bilinguals of the same language can be explained by examining the input to which each group is typically exposed:[3] It is often the case that the parents of heritage speakers, as well as the larger community in which they acquire their L1, show signs of attrition, which means that their grammars no longer resemble those of monolingual speakers of the same language (Bayram, Pascual y Cabo, & Rothman, 2018). In other words, as the target grammars for heritage and nonheritage native speakers are different, the outcome of acquisition will also be different by necessity. From this perspective, terms such as 'incomplete acquisition' or 'arrested development' (e.g., Montrul, 2008) are woefully inaccurate because such acquisition is actually complete with regard to its actual target; the fact that this target (the grammar of attrited L1 speakers) differs from an idealized version thereof (the grammar of monolingual L1 speakers) is, or should be, irrelevant to any consideration of ultimate attainment on the part of heritage speakers.

Finally, the multidirectionality of crosslinguistic influence has been studied extensively in the SLA context, with studies that have focused on the (potential) influence of the L2 on the L1, at representational (e.g., Fernández, 2003; Jegerski, VanPatten, & Keating, 2016; Kecskés & Papp, 2000; see also chapters in Cook, 2003a) and processing (e.g., Dussias, 2003, 2004; Dussias & Sagarra,

2007; Jegerski, Keating, & VanPatten, 2016) levels alike (see also Flege, 1987; Flege & Port, 1981, for early findings in phonology). This line of inquiry has been adopted by researchers in L3/Ln acquisition, most notably Cabrelli Amaro and colleagues (Cabrelli Amaro, 2017b; Cabrelli Amaro, Amaro, & Rothman, 2015; Cabrelli Amaro, Iverson, Giancaspro, & Halloran, 2018; Cabrelli Amaro & Rothman, 2010; see also Fung & Murphy, 2016, and Wrembel, 2011, for similar findings), who have investigated how regressive transfer from the L3/Ln into prior languages may affect early and late-acquired languages differently. Other researchers (e.g., Cheung, Matthews, & Tsang, 2011; Hui, 2010; Yang, Matthews, & Crosthwaite, 2016) have suggested that L3 influence on the L2 might counter previous L1-on-L2 effects, both facilitative and nonfacilitative, in what Matthews, Cheung, and Tsang (2014) have termed "anti-transfer."

2.1.4   Dynamic Systems Theory

Over the last 15 years, various studies have endeavored to model multilingual development from the perspective of what has been variably called Complexity, Dynamical, or Dynamic Systems Theory (DST), depending on the scientific field. DST, which is best understood as an epistemological approach rather than as a theory per se, is based on a nonreductionist view of the subject of study – be it a weather system, a cell, an ecosystem, language development or the movement of a double pendulum – with an emphasis on the immense number of variables and interactions among those variables that conspire to give rise to the general behavior of the system. One of the core aspects of DST is the nonlinear nature of these interactions, which means that one can rarely identify factors that change in a manner that is directly or inversely proportional to that of other factors. In other words, cause-effect relationships are hardly ever straightforward from a DST perspective.

Over the past two decades, DST has also been applied to the study of L2 acquisition (e.g., Kramsch, 2002; Larsen-Freeman, 1997, 2002; in particular, see de Bot, Lowie, & Verspoor, 2007, and papers in the 2008 special issue of *The Modern Language Journal* [92(2)], for an overview) and multilingual development (e.g., de Bot, 2016; de Bot, Lowie, Thorne, & Verspoor, 2013; Herdina & Jessner, 2002; Jessner, 2008; Lowie, 2012). The Dynamic Model of Multilingualism (DMM) proposed by Herdina and Jessner (2002) highlights – and seeks to capture – the ever-changing nature of multilingual development. This dynamicity is most apparent in two defining aspects of multilingualism. The first is that, very much as in L2 acquisition but quantitatively more so, the course of multilingual acquisition/development is constrained by the interaction of variables that are psychoaffective (such as motivation and self-esteem), cognitive (such as working memory capacity and metalinguistic awareness), linguistic and sociocultural (such as socioeconomic status [SES] and attitudes toward a minority language) in nature. The second is that language decay and attrition are not only common but are also intrinsically related to language acquisition – recall that this is also a central tenet of multi-competence approaches (see de Bot, 2016, for a discussion of the compatibility between multi-competence and DST). One of the main goals behind the advancement of the DMM was to develop a theoretical basis that is independent of L1 and L2 acquisition research, which by definition cannot capture the complex dynamics of multilingual development (Jessner, 2008).

For the reasons we have just discussed, the DMM and other DST approaches reject the notion of individual 'language' in a traditional sense, emphasizing the existence of 'individual language systems' that are themselves part of a larger psycholinguistic system. While this might seem to be a trivial terminological distinction, some authors (e.g., de Bot, 2016; Larsen-Freeman & Cameron, 2008, among others) have argued that thinking of languages as individual entities within the mind of a multilingual speaker is reductionist at best, and that a speaker's language repertoire can be better understood if we characterize it as an interconnected network of linguistic behaviors associated with particular social contexts. While the DMM's approach does not completely do away with what Larsen-Freeman and Cameron (2008) called the "simplifying metaphor" of self-contained language systems, it does constitute a middle ground that emphasizes dynamicity and interconnectedness over the individual identity (that is, the autonomy) of one language or another. In other words, it highlights crosslinguistic influence instead of idealized, monolingual-like development. As a result, the DMM considers that language choice depends on the particular communicative context of the speaker at any given time, and that even this choice may be more or less flexible – that is, the speaker may be more or less likely to switch between languages as a function of the interlocutor, the social environment and so on. We will return to this when we discuss Grosjean's *language modes* in Section 3.1 in Chapter 3.

The best way to think about nonlinearity, a DST feature implemented in the DMM, is perhaps that change – assumed by definition in all theories of development – is itself subject to constant change. That is, we cannot assume a stable relationship between the variables whereby x+y always equals z. In our meteorological example from Section 1.6 in Chapter 1, one cannot simply assume that the number of days ('d') until the next storm will always be d=t+p (to use Model B). While the result could still be dependent on the same variables, namely temperature and pressure, the relationship between them might change; in other words, the right formula to predict 'd' could be $d=6t-1/p$ at some point. The idea behind DST, then, is that we should (i) consider as many fundamental variables as possible, and (ii) model not only the relationship of those variables with the outcome but also the changes in that relationship. In line with this, the DMM assumes that the stability of the language (super)system, in which the dynamics of interrelatedness among the different language subsystems are complex and ever-changing, depends greatly on 'language maintenance' (that is, the amount of time and effort that a learner can dedicate to using a given language) because the system is subject to limited cognitive resources. Note that this is not only related to decay – if the learner does not use a language often, it will start to decline – but also to growth – if the learner starts dedicating more time to one language or another, these will become stronger at the expense of other language subsystems. In either case, the stability of the system is compromised; thus, even the smallest changes in the communicative habits of the speaker will have consequences for the dynamics of the multilingual system.

In light of the above, it is easy to understand one of the main tenets of the DMM, which is also shared by other DST approaches to language (e.g., de Bot, 2000, 2016; de Bot et al., 2007), namely that the border between the individual and society is elusive and, in fact, is merely a construct from the perspective of DMM/DST. This is related to the concept of embeddedness, whereby the different subsystems of a complex system are nested and fully interconnected. While traditional approaches to language have separately recognized the multiply embedded character of both human cognition on one hand and sociolinguistic contexts on the other, the argument here is that there is no convincing reason to regard the boundary between the individual and his or her immediate social context any differently from other boundaries in the complex system. This assumption is shared by other influential theories of multilingualism that aim to reconcile cognitive and sociolinguistic perspectives, such as Wei's (2018) *translanguaging*.

The DMM places much emphasis on that which distinguishes multilingual from nonmultilingual speakers. The model uses the term 'M-factor' (short for *multilingualism factor*) to refer to the set of properties in a multilingual system that emerge as a result of contact among the individual psycholinguistic systems; in other words, the 'language systems' or simply 'languages,' in traditional terms. These include a relatively large number of factors, from enhanced monitoring skills to heightened sensitivity to crosslinguistic variation, all of which are related to the awareness of, and operation over, the psycholinguistic system itself in one way or another. In other words, these are fundamentally *metalinguistic* skills (see Thomas, 1988, for an early discussion on the role of metalinguistic knowledge/awareness in L3). Jessner (2008) maintained that the M-factor was precisely what differentiated monolinguals from multilinguals, and accounted for cumulative effects of multilingualism in L*n* acquisition (e.g., Cenoz, 2003). The ability to shift focus between form and meaning, to self-detect and repair errors in speech and to manage interference from contextually nonrelevant language systems dynamically – so that shared resources are accessed while preventing competition from disrupting speech – are all skills associated with the M-factor that purportedly give multilinguals an edge in the learning task.

It should be apparent from this cursory overview that research within cognitive approaches to L3/L*n* acquisition is growing in volume and scope, and that different theoretical perspectives on language and linguistic development regard the multilingual setting as a uniquely informative window into core questions within their paradigms. In our view, this is more than a clever observation of what new variables can contribute to old problems: It is a tacit acknowledgment that multilingualism is, or at least should be, our default view of language competence. In the following two sections, we will see if this is also true of social and educational perspectives, in which sequential multilingualism brings its own set of challenges.

2.2 Sociolinguistic Approaches

Broadly defined, sociolinguistics is the study of the dynamic, multifarious relationships between language and society (see, e.g., Bayley, Cameron, & Lucas, 2013; Coulmas, 1998; Labov, 1966, 1994, 2001; Mesthrie, 2011b; Milroy & Gordon, 2003; Romaine, 1994, 1995, Tagliamonte, 2011, 2006; Wodak, Johnstone, & Kerswill, 2011, among many others). Accordingly, it is concerned with the social dimensions of language, as well as with the linguistic dimensions of society. Sociolinguistic approaches call attention to the social dimensions of language, claiming that they are as important to understanding language (its acquisition and particularly its use) as is the study of abstract linguistic (mental) competence that is typical of cognitive-based approaches to linguistics. According to some scholars, linguistic paradigms devoid of sociolinguistic considerations are unable to provide truly explanatory accounts of many aspects pertaining to 'real language,' or the way language is used in social contexts and changes over time (Mesthrie, 2011a; but see Cornips, 1998, 2018).

Although we do not agree with the above statement, we would concede that sociolinguistic and cognitive-based approaches typically operate under distinct theoretical concerns and motivating questions. We also see, highlighted particularly by the study of multilingualism itself, that neither set of approaches could answer all linguistic questions worthy of serious consideration in utter isolation from each other. In fact, we would advocate that both are needed and should be combined, when appropriate, to obtain the most informative and ecologically valid answers to questions of overlapping interest. Despite differences in focus between sociolinguistic and more cognitive-based approaches, the multifaceted nature of multilingual acquisition highlights how one cannot ignore social dimensions even when focused solely on cognitive questions. For example, sociolinguistic variables have significant weight in issues that are central to the cognitive enterprise (for instance, access to linguistic input as well as qualitative and quantitative issues relating thereto). Conversely, cognitive considerations clearly come to bear on multilingual acquisition above and beyond anything related to the social dimension. Thus, whether or not one is interested in the way that language use interacts with and reflects social structure, it is undeniable that humans acquire and process language within specific social contexts, the related variables of which (what cognitive linguists tend to refer to as 'learner/speaker external' variables) may be crucial for understanding linguistic behavior in more depth than can be achieved by strictly cognitive considerations alone – that is, the representational and processing aspects of language. Returning to our example of heritage speakers in the previous subsection, the nature of the input they received from their families and other members of the heritage speech community seems to be one primary reason for the differences we observe between them and monolingual L1 speakers – or at least speakers who have acquired the same L1 in a majority language context (Kupisch & Rothman, 2018). However, to explain why the input these speakers received appears different, one must ultimately consider the multiple social dimensions behind changes in the grammar of first generation immigrants immersed in a different language context (Bayram et al., 2018; Pascual y Cabo & Rothman, 2012).

One of the features that sets sociolinguistic and educational approaches to multilingualism apart from (at least some) cognitive approaches is the extension of the term's definition to include both individual and societal level multilingualism. According to this view, there is a special emphasis on the simultaneous and intertwined existence of this phenomenon within and among individual citizens, such that speakers (or speech communities) of several languages may exist within largely monolingual societies, and vice versa – in other words, not all monolingual speakers live in monolingual societies and not all multilingual societies consist exclusively of multilingual speakers. In fact, one of the main arguments within sociolinguistics is that the very notion of 'language' is elusive and is subject to political, identity and historical considerations (Deumert, 2011). Mutual intelligibility, for example, is often taken to be a relatively unbiased linguistic criterion. However, Norwegian and Swedish speakers can understand each other easily, yet these are invariably considered different languages. The same occurs with speakers of Urdu and Hindi, at least in informal speech (as these two languages present large lexical differences in their standard varieties). Conversely, Cantonese and Mandarin speakers are virtually unable to understand each other, despite the official use of the term 'Chinese dialects' by the government of the People's Republic of China; a similar thing happens to speakers of, say, Egyptian Arabic when exposed to the Moroccan variety, or to speakers from Milan when exposed to so-called southern Italian dialects such as Calabrese.

The flexibility of these and other criteria in the consideration of different varieties as separate languages thus complicates the definition of societal and individual multilingualism. Take Ana Lúcia, our European Portuguese-born friend from Section 1.3 in Chapter 1 as an example; recall that she was already a highly proficient speaker of L2 English before moving to Brazil at the age of 40, where she also picked up Brazilian Portuguese and used it daily. Did you think of her as a multilingual? If not, why not? In fact, Ana Lúcia's is one prototypical case of how social construal of the notion of language, which is itself grounded in historical and political reasons specific to each linguistic variety, can affect our perception of a speaker's mental linguistic competence. However, whether Ana Lúcia is 'cognitively' a multilingual in the same sense as is a less controversial case (the simultaneous trilingual Oihan, also from Section 1.3, for example), meaning both their brains deal with more than two grammars, is largely independent of whether the European and Brazilian varieties of Portuguese are regarded socially as different languages – although, linguistically, they are substantially different (see, e.g., Castro et al., 2017; Escudero, Boersma, Rauber, & Bion, 2009; Martins, 2006). However, it does matter for the kind of linguistic and educational policies that different governments adopt for populations with a similar profile: For example, should Jamaican children be educated using Standard British English as the language of instruction? This kind of question, which will be the focus of the next subsection, exemplifies the impact of sociolinguistic variables and their interaction with a more abstract, idealized study of language.

In situations of societal multilingualism, in which more than one language is spoken in a given society or within a given territory, it is rare – perhaps even unattested – that all languages have the same status. This imbalance, generally referred to as *diglossia* or *polyglossia*, produces a situation in which the different languages are assigned different functions, often associated with varying degrees of prestige, for which sociolinguists generally use the terms highly valued (H) and less-valued (L) as vague extremes of a continuum (see, e.g., Schiffman, 1998). Seminal work on diglossia (Ferguson, 1959) was in fact set on characterizing the relationship between spoken regional varieties of a language and the written standard, which was often associated with higher SES and more formal situations. It soon became apparent, however, that diglossia was also common in strictly multilingual societies (Fishman, 1967), in which one language assumed the H-functions while others were limited to informal or different types of low-prestige contexts. The dynamics of di- and polyglossia are complex, and the complementary distribution of functions across languages and language varieties is rarely clear cut (Schiffman, 1998). Sociolinguistic approaches to multilingualism have typically been concerned with the impact of language status on factors such as identity and language shift, whereby a more prestigious language might eventually displace the native language of a given speech community (e.g., Fishman, 1964, 1967, 1991; Ostler, 2011). In particular, there has been an emphasis on exploring the global influence of English as a lingua franca, both in Europe (Cenoz & Jessner, 2000) and in a postcolonial setting (Schneider, 2007; see also Schneider, 2011, for review).

SES is one of the most prominent social variables affecting language use, and has thus received attention beyond the scope of sociolinguistic studies, such as in recent debates about cognitive function in bilingual and multilingual speakers (e.g., Calvo & Bialystok, 2014; Morton & Harper, 2007; Nair, Biedermann, & Nickels, 2017). SES represents a clear link between social structure and language use, and is in fact a proxy for several important factors in language and literacy development, as the home environment, access to quality education, the amount of carer-child interaction and the parental education level all typically vary as a function of SES (Ginsborg, 2006; see, e.g., Dodsworth, 2011, for review). This has implications for many fields within the broader study of language development, not least of which is the clinical detection of language disorders. Standardized assessment instruments are often ill-suited to differentiate between linguistic behavior that signals a potential disorder and that which is normal given that the child is familiar only with a low-SES variety (e.g., Campbell, Dollaghan, Needleman, &

Janosky, 1997; Hendricks & Adlof, 2017). In studies focusing specifically on multilingualism, SES has been highlighted as one key determinant in language choice, and is linked to the practice of codeswitching between H- and L-varieties/languages in contexts of polyglossia (e.g., Dewaele, Petrides, & Furnham, 2008; Wolff, 2000). This is in fact unsurprising, and connects a few of the dots that we have already glimpsed in this subsection: High-SES individuals within multilingual societies have better access to quality education, literacy and exposure to varieties or languages that dominate H-functions; thus, it is only natural that they are more adept at switching among different varieties or languages (although see, e.g., Ennaji, 2005, for reports of unfavorable attitudes toward Moroccan Arabic–French codeswitching in Morocco). With regard to sequential multilingualism, however, evidence regarding the role of SES in L3/Ln acquisition is mixed – some studies suggest that it might be an important factor in facilitating linguistic development (e.g., Lasagabaster, 1998; see the review in Sanz & Lado, 2008), while others have found that its effects do not appear to be as prominent when other variables such as amount and frequency of exposure are controlled (Dewaele, 2005). However, note that, as SES is frequently correlated with these factors, an assessment of their independent effects is not always straightforward, or even possible.

The study of the relationship between gender and language use has also been central to the sociolinguistic enterprise from its inception (e.g., Lakoff, 1975; Thorne & Henley, 1975; see also Schilling, 2011; Talbot, 2010; Tannen, 1994; Wodak & Benke, 1998). This concerns both the role of language in the social construction and the perpetuation of gender roles – in connection with biological sex, sexual identity and many other intertwined factors – and the reciprocal impact of these on use and attitudes toward language-related issues (for example, the language status and language choice in multilingual societies) as a function of sex-based gender roles – that is, male versus female. It should be acknowledged that, for reasons of focus, most research on multilingualism and L3/Ln acquisition conducted by linguists has typically dealt with the latter; that is, with male versus female language use/attitudes within multilingual communities and groups of L3/Ln learners. In this sense, the role of language and gender in the economy and the reproduction of gendered identities in multilingual contexts has featured prominently in work by Piller, Pavlenko, Takahashi, and colleagues (e.g., Pavlenko, Blackledge, Piller, & Teutsch-Dwyer, 2001; Piller & Pavlenko, 2004, 2009; Piller & Takahashi, 2006; Takahashi, 2013). In the context of foreign-language learning, for example, Takahashi (2013) investigated Japanese women's high motivation to learn English, which is seen as a symbol of the West and displays a strong connection to the concept of mobility. Similarly, gender is now routinely included in studies on language attitudes within the European context, yielding mixed results and complex patterns of influence (see, e.g., Huguet & Llurda, 2001; Jongbloed-Faber, van de Velde, van der Meer, & Klinkenberg, 2016; Safont Jordà, 2007; Ytsma, 2007).

Finally, it is worth discussing the attention that much research over the course of the past four decades has placed on motivation and attitude in second and third language acquisition (e.g., Dörnyei, 1994, 2001; Dörnyei & Ushioda, 2011; Ushioda, 2016; Ushioda & Dörnyei, 2012). While the role of motivation in language learning poses its own challenges related to the operationalization of the term before we can understand its effects on the learning process, it seems clear from this body of research that several social and psychoaffective factors modulate the disposition of learners and foreign-language users, and that this in turn has an impact on language learning. With regard to second and third language acquisition, studies on motivation have reported mixed results (see, e.g., Bernaus, Masgoret, Gardner, & Reyes, 2004, and the meta-analysis in Masgoret & Gardner, 2003, for favorable evidence; compare results in Lasagabaster, 1998, and Vandergrift, 2005, for a much weaker correlation between motivation and achievement).

Motivation seems to vary with age (e.g., Dewaele, 2005; Lasagabaster & Huguet, 2007), as do general attitudes toward multilingualism (Cenoz, 2003). These may depend on several factors pertaining to language status, with majority languages in multilingual contexts and L3s related to social and economic elites being regarded more favorably (e.g., Bernaus et al., 2004; Mettewie & Janssens, 2007). In this regard, native speakers of a majority language, such as Finnish in Swedish-speaking areas of Finland, seem to have a more positive attitude to learning in L3/Ln acquisition (Lasagabaster, 2001). While multilingualism does not seem to improve learners' attitudes toward language learning when compared to bilingualism (Brohy, 2001), studies on communicative anxiety by Dewaele and colleagues (e.g., Dewaele, 2002, 2007; Dewaele et al., 2008; see also Santos, Gorter, & Cenoz, 2017) found that bilinguals were more affected than were multilinguals. These authors attributed the difference to the apparently positive correlation between the number of languages spoken and variables such as socialization, perceived competence and communication skills (see also Baker, 2006; Wolff, 2000). Multilingualism has also been linked to higher degrees of metalinguistic (e.g., Cenoz, 2003; Jessner, 1999, 2008) and metapragmatic awareness (e.g., Fouser, 1997, 2001; Safont Jordà, 2003, 2005), which some authors argue are notable predictors of achievement in nonnative language acquisition.

In the next section, we will discuss educational approaches to L3/ L*n* acquisition, which are charged with the task of incorporating and instrumentalizing the accumulated knowledge on both the internal and the external factors we have presented thus far.

2.3   Educational Approaches

If you remember the percentages pertaining to the incidence of multilingualism that we mentioned in Chapter 1, you will probably find it hardly surprising that multilingual education models are on the rise all over the world (Rothman et al., 2013). For some countries, moving away from mono- and bilingual programs is simply a natural step in embracing their historical (or recent yet notable) linguistic diversity. For others, it follows from a strong determination to help their citizens keep pace with the demands of globalized trade, job and financial markets, or from efforts to enhance and promote the integration of immigrant communities. Whatever the reasons, the truth is that multilingualism is now a central concern in language planning and language policy (e.g., Berthoud & Lüdi, 2011; Clyne, 1998; Daoust, 1998; Tollefson, 2011), in which education models and language teaching are key components (Cenoz, 2009; García, 1998; C. Leung, 2011; Stroud & Heugh, 2011; in particular, see chapters in Cenoz & Genesee, 1998; Cenoz & Gorter, 2015; Gorter, Zenotz, & Cenoz, 2014, for a focus on multilingual education from different perspectives).

Multilingual education can be defined in a narrow or a broad sense. It depends on whether we consider only those models in which several languages are used as a medium of instruction (e.g., Baker, 2006, 2007; Cummins, 2010) or a range of situations in which the presence of several languages occurs, but not necessarily as part of the school curriculum; for example, when these are home languages of some students but are not taught or used in class (see, e.g., Cenoz, 2009, 2015, for discussion). The latter scenario is not uncommon in territories in which a conscious effort is made to maintain the native language in a situation of diglossia with regard to a majority language, usually that of the broader sovereign state in which the region is located. Multilingual models such as those in Wales, Catalonia or the Basque Country, to mention three European enclaves that fit this profile, include programs in which the minority language is the only language of instruction, while the majority language is taught as a single subject on par with foreign languages (e.g., Gardner, Puigdevall i Serralvo, & Williams, 2000).

Several efforts to provide comprehensive yet flexible typologies of bilingual and multilingual education have been made (e.g., Baetens Beardsmore, 1993;

Baker, 2006; Cummins, 2003; Hornberger, 1991, 2007; W. F. Mackey, 1970; Skutnabb-Kangas, 2000; Ytsma, 2001, among many others; see Edwards, 2007, and chapters in Genesee at al., 2006, for review). However, the socio-linguistic, socioeconomic and political variables are so numerous, and the educational contexts so diverse, that these typologies have often been criticized for being either too rich to be practical or too rigid to be widely applicable. As with any analysis based on discrete variables in which levels are partially or completely opposed to each other (for example, elite versus folk bilingualism, subtractive versus additive bilingualism and so on), typologies of this type allow for an impractical number of possible combinations, few of which actually match real-life educational contexts (Baker, 2006).

In an attempt to overcome these problems in characterizing educational programs in which several languages are involved in some way, Cenoz (2009) proposed the Continua of Multilingual Education, in which different combinations of the linguistic, educational and sociolinguistic variables typi-cally involved in the configuration of multilingual education models yield approaches that are positioned along a continuum, rather than being concep-tually opposed to each other. The model is based on a definition of multilingual education that emphasizes school aims over the sociolinguistic context or the medium of instruction: "teaching more than two languages provided that schools aim at multilingualism and multiliteracy" (Cenoz, 2009: 32; see, e.g., Baker, 2006; Genesee et al., 2006; May, 2008, for similar criteria). A couple of well-known examples should suffice to illustrate Cenoz's (2009) proposal: immersion programs in Canada, where schools aim at a national population that is linguistically competent and literate in (at least) the country's two official languages (French and English), and the Basque Country, where the design of multilingual education programs centers on the revitalization of the region's vernacular language.

The Basque Country is a historical region that falls within present-day Spanish and French territories. As a language isolate, Basque (called *euskara* or *euskera* by its speakers) has somewhat miraculously avoided extinction despite centuries of contact with three of the most politically powerful lan-guages in history: Latin, French and Spanish. While the strong monolingual orientation of republican education programs in France, together with 40 years of dictatorship in Spain, compromised its vitality severely for the past 200 years, Basque now boasts one of the fastest growing communities of speakers and has by far some of the strongest institutional support of all minority languages in Europe. These two aspects, which Giles, Bourhis, and Taylor (1977) considered central to language vitality, have in turn promoted progress in a third supporting leg: social status. Two Spanish territories, the borders of which overlap partially with the historical Basque region, declared Basque co-official with Spanish following the transition to a constitutional monarchy between 1975 and 1978: the Basque Autonomous Community (from 1979) and Navarre (from 1986, although only in its northern half).

A natural consequence of co-officiality is that knowledge of Basque is today an increasingly important – if not inescapable – requisite to work for the civil administration, which is already bilingual on paper and is rapidly becoming so in practice. In the Basque Autonomous Community (BAC), this has boosted the number of children registered in educational programs in which Basque is the language of instruction, which now include over 70% of primary and secondary school students in the region, considering both public and private education centers (Basque Government Department of Education, 2017). The system of models based on the language of instruction was introduced by law in 1983 and has been implemented since 1984 in order to regulate the proportion of Basque and Spanish within the educational system. Model A uses Spanish as the sole language of instruction, with the exception of the Basque language subject, which is taught in Basque. Similarly, teaching in Model D is conducted exclusively in Basque, except in the Spanish language classes. In the more compromising Model B, subjects are divided between Spanish and Basque as languages of instruction. All three models include, in addition to Basque and Spanish, the study of one (primary school) or two (secondary school) foreign languages, one of which is typically English.

The astonishing feat of language revitalization achieved in the BAC is more apparent when we compare the current registration figures for Model A (Spanish only), which were below 10% in 2017–2018, with its initial numbers in 1984–1985, when registration was almost 65%. Despite this steady increase, which includes over 200 thousand more Basque speakers in the past 25 years and a total of 631 thousand overall (33.9% of the population; Basque Government and Government of Navarre, 2017), Spanish is still the dominant language in the BAC territory as a whole, with up to 47% of the population being Spanish monolinguals. Furthermore, many Basque citizens (up to 19%) are only passively bilingual; as they are from Spanish-speaking homes, their contact with Basque is often limited to their school years or to certain work environments. This uneven progress highlights the difference between macro and micro levels within the social dimension of multilingual education (Cenoz, 2009): While the vitality of Basque is undeniably on the increase, the dominance of Spanish in many students' social networks still hinders a true balance in the region's societal bilingualism. Nonetheless, the Basque model is an example of how using the minority language as the language of instruction can contribute to a healthier relationship between two (or more) co-official languages by extending the knowledge and use thereof to monolingual communities of the majority language.

Canadian immersion programs (e.g., Genesee, 1987; Lambert & Tucker, 1972; Swain & Lapkin, 1982) were developed in the 1960s and had a simple yet powerful vision: to ensure that Canadian citizens were at least bilingual and biliterate, being competent in both English and French irrespective of their native language. While Canada has always been a migrant-welcoming country, the model was originally oriented toward achieving some degree of homogenization between Francophone and Anglophone Canadians. This was achieved by immersing English-speaking students – or, rather, students from different English-speaking areas of Canada – in school programs in which French was the sole language of instruction (see, e.g., Genesee, 1987, 2008, for a discussion of bilingual programs for majority language speakers; see also Johnson & Swain, 1997; Johnstone, 2006, for typologies of immersion models). As in the case of the Basque Country, it is understood that exposure to the majority language (these students' L1) is sufficiently provided in out-of-school contexts, including the home. Evaluations of the model seem to suggest that this is a fair assumption, since native speakers of a majority language participating in bilingual immersion programs have been shown to achieve language competence and literacy skills comparable to those attending regular schools (Genesee, 2008).

Notably, the Canadian immersion model originated in Quebec, where English native speakers are a minority, and spread rapidly to other English-speaking areas of the country. Despite its origin, the model has become popular as an example of bilingual education models for speakers of the majority language. Perhaps because the original students were already a minority linguistic community, or perhaps because this was not a low-SES minority, Canadian bilingual immersion did not contemplate the situation of pupils with a home language other than English, such as native speakers of Cree languages or Ojibwe. For these students, the context becomes essentially multilingual – although, by most current definitions, the educational model itself cannot be regarded as such because these students will not have the opportunity to be instructed or acquire literacy skills in their native language (Cenoz, 2009). Genesee (2008: 565) explained that, even when these students attend bilingual immersion programs in which the indigenous language is the medium of instruction (for example, Mohawk schools in Canada; see Jacobs & Cross, 2001), they are at risk of academic underachievement because the linguistic challenge they face is multiplied: Ethnic minorities of different types (that is, both with and without a mother tongue that differs from the majority language, such as African-Americans) usually speak nonstandard varieties of the majority language. Since literacy is aimed at the standard variety, Standard English – or French or Spanish or whatever standard variety applies to a specific context – constitutes a further target language for them to acquire. Similar arguments have been made in recent years by researchers studying heritage speaker acquisition outcomes in adulthood in at least two ways. Polinsky (2015) rightly highlighted how the standard variety of the heritage language, if studied formally as is done at universities in early adulthood by an increasing number of heritage bilinguals, might constitute a case of third language acquisition insofar as the standard is a distinct target language. Moreover, as others have pointed out regularly, heritage language grammars, however different from standard monolingual ones they happen to be, are complete, yet different because heritage bilinguals, unlike typical monolinguals, do not usually have ample access to the standard variety unless they have formal education in the heritage language. When they do, this reduces heritage-to-monolingual comparative differences dramatically (Bayram et al., 2017; see Kupisch & Rothman, 2018, for review).

According to traditional typologies of bilingual and multilingual education, the Canadian model can be classified as an elite bilingualism program, since both English and French are high-status languages and participation is the conscious choice of parents who want their children to become bilingual. In this sense, it is also a straightforward example of an enrichment program (e.g., Baker, 2006) – that is, one that is designed to increase the language repertoire of speakers of a majority language and, by extension, of additive bi-/multilingualism (see, e.g., Aronin & Singleton, 2012; Lambert, 1973). On the other hand, the Basque model could be considered a hybrid of maintenance and enrichment programs,[4] an example of recursive or reconstructive bilingualism (e.g., García, 2008) or even a folk, multilingual version of programs implementing additive bilingualism, which are traditionally associated with elite or upper-middle class social groups (e.g., de Mejía, 2002). It seems evident, just from the brief classification attempted in this paragraph, that discrete variables rarely succeed in accounting for the reality of multilingual education. Cenoz's (2009) model seeks to abandon these di/trichotomous distinctions in favor of a series of continua associated with educational variables (for example, language[s] of instruction, school contexts and teachers), each of which ranges from less to more multilingual. These are inscribed within a sociolinguistic context with macro (language status, media use and the like) and micro (family environment) levels in which each element also varies along a similar continuum. Finally, educational factors also interact with a linguistic variable, namely linguistic distance. For this variable, the continuum refers to the overall structural distance, in linguistic terms, between the different languages involved. Combinations of languages that are more distant from each other (such as Spanish, Basque and English in the Basque Country) are situated toward the 'more multilingual' end of the scale. Cenoz's (2009) model is particularly powerful in that it allows us to capture subtle differences among variations of the same program, and not only among observably distinct programs. For example, teachers from immersion programs in Anglophone Canada have less chance of being naturalistic bilinguals than are those in Quebec. Similarly, there are differences at the micro sociolinguistic level between Basque multilingual schools depending on where they are situated – in other words, whether they are in a traditionally Basque-speaking region or a Spanish-speaking one. While teachers are likely to have the same profile in this case (because the Basque Country is a relatively small region, mobility is more frequent), differences in the home environments of students will have an impact on the overall outcomes of the educational program.

As we can see, multilingual education is a complex universe in which linguistic, sociolinguistic and educational variables interact. For this reason, and when the opportunity arises, it is important that we focus on translating insights from theoretical and experimental L3/L*n* acquisition research, as well as the sociolinguistic study of multilingualism, into informed applications for pedagogy and language planning in multilingual environments. Researchers and practitioners in the field of multilingual education proper are thus in charge of demanding, administering, and coordinating the incorporation of these insights from the privileged vantage point of hands-on engagement with multilingual learners. At present, to highlight one example, increasing attention is being directed toward these kinds of implication/application efforts from theoreticians who recognize the potential practical use of what cognitive-based research in multilingualism can contribute in terms of more cognitive and linguistic evidence-based pedagogies (e.g., Benati & Schwieter, 2017; González Alonso & Rothman, 2017b; Hahn & Angelovska, 2017), following in the footsteps of similar work in SLA (e.g., Whong, Gil, & Marsden, 2014, for a review; see also contributions in Whong, Gil, & Marsden, 2013). This having been acknowledged, more needs to be done in the future to ensure a fruitful, bilateral circulation of knowledge between both ends – and indeed among all the different points – of the theory-practice continuum in (instructed) sequential multilingualism.

2.4 Taking Stock: Multiple Perspectives, Multiple Interactions

When considering research in a field as broad and intrinsically complex as multilingualism, even within a cursory overview of this type, it is difficult to abstract away from the narrow focus of each subarea. However, at least one common thread should have become apparent to the reader as the chapter progressed: Much of the complexity of sequential multilingualism originates in the quantitative and qualitative changes that an additional language introduces. In quantitative terms, the machinery becomes undeniably heavier: The new language requires a redistribution of the available cognitive resources, which need to adapt to incorporate, store and manipulate new representations in real time. Socially, new contexts of use open up for the speaker, who needs to adopt novel strategies and adjust to potentially different interactions with the language's speech community. However, the most impactful changes are not related to relocating resources or managing more linguistic material: It is the way in which the new language interacts with preexisting linguistic knowledge and use that seems to make a larger difference.

The study of linguistic transfer in L3/L*n* acquisition is central to characterizing the precise nature of this interaction. Because linguistic representations are the building blocks of language, sequential multilingualism can never be understood fully until we determine how, why and under what conditions representations are transferred into the L3 from one previous linguistic system or another. The next chapter begins to discuss the basis on which we feel justified in making such a sweeping statement by considering how multilingualism in psycholinguistics (processing proper) has been addressed over the past few decades, particularly with regard to what has proven to be a fruitful ground for testing theoretical proposals: the multilingual lexicon. We will also examine the literature on the role that previous linguistic knowledge plays specifically in L3/L*n* lexical acquisition; that is, the relative role that an L1 and/or an L2 play in building lexical representations when bilinguals acquire additional languages. Finally, we will offer a brief review of the domain of L3/L*n* phonology, in which exciting work in the past few years has begun to launch a truly independent subfield of multilingual phonology in which questions of L1 versus L2 influence have featured prominently. This next chapter thus concludes the portion of the book that provides a general overview of L3/L*n* studies, the purpose of which was both to properly contextualize the piece of the larger puzzle that is the main focus of the book – L3/L*n* morphosyntax and transfer – as well as educate the novice reader about the puzzle itself.

Notes

1. Many scholars have argued that there is no mismatch between available input and ensuing competence or, for those that acknowledge a gap between input and resulting grammars, that the gap is filled without a specifically linguistic language faculty (see, e.g., Ellis & Wulff, 2015; Evans, 2014; Levinson, 2001; O'Grady, 2008, 2013; Perek & Goldberg, 2017; Pullum & Scholz, 2002; Wulff & Ellis, 2018).
2. In fact, it should be clarified here that Cook (2016) himself proposed substituting the term 'L2 learner' for the purportedly more respectful 'L2 user,' which does not characterize L2ers as subordinate to L1 speakers, and restricting the use of the former denotation to those contexts in which an individual is merely learning the language but rarely using it outside of the classroom, such as foreign-language learning.
3. We follow Rothman's (2009b: 156) definition of a heritage language: "[A] language spoken at home or otherwise readily available to young children, and crucially . . . not a dominant language of the larger (national) society."
4. Note that what draws the line between maintenance and enrichment programs is, more often than not, the linguistic profile of the student community. While there are by-province differences in the proportion of Spanish and Basque native speakers within the BAC, any Model D classroom will be likely to have pupils whose L1 is Basque – and who are thus effectively attending a maintenance program – and pupils whose L1 is Spanish, for whom Model D is an example of an enrichment program. A similar claim, although perhaps less frequently, can be made for French native speakers (a social majority in Quebec) who attend French immersion schools in Francophone Canada.

3 Multilingual Lexis (Acquisition and Processing) and Phonology

3.0 General Introduction

In the same spirit as the previous chapter, the present one endeavors to further contextualize the larger puzzle in which L3 morphosyntactic studies are located. In fact, it is important to understand the historical provenance of the theories and related empirical work within L3/Ln morphosyntax on which the remainder of the book will focus. In equal measure, it is important to keep abreast of the trends in the related fields of multilingual acquisition and processing, not only to be a well-rounded L3/Ln scholar but also to understand one's own subarea better and to ensure the continuity of ideas via potential, when appropriate, cross-fertilization. Thus, before traveling down the road of L3/Ln morphosyntax and transfer studies from a formal linguistic perspective, it makes sense to recap what has been or is being done in the related fields of multilingual lexical processing and acquisition, as well as in phonology. As we will see, there is good reason to do so. To begin, key insights from the study of transfer effects, specifically in L3/Ln lexical acquisition, have paved the way for the adjacent field in many ways, to the extent that we seek to explore similar questions in morphosyntax. We will also understand the key role that the psycholinguistic study of L2/L3 lexical processing has played in our understanding of how the mind juggles more than one and particularly more than two languages, providing key insights into methodology and epistemology in L3/Ln morphosyntax. Finally, we will see how there is a younger, similarly nascent subfield of L3/Ln phonology that is emerging in parallel. We will see how, as L3/Ln morphosyntactic studies have used key insights from the comparably older lexical subfield, so too have some researchers in L3/Ln phonology used L3/Ln morphosyntactic theory as a basis to kick-start its own bespoke trajectory toward the future.

3.1   One Brain, Multiple Languages

Review articles, handbook chapters and monographs on bi- and multilingualism – particularly those with an inclination toward cognitive (neuro)science – frequently begin by defending how extraordinary it is that some people can juggle two or more languages within a single brain. In fact, when considering any brain function in some detail – from memory to hearing to motor control – we are inspired by some sense of wonder, even though we rarely dwell on these faculties in everyday life. Simultaneous and early multilinguals (the Oihans, Maxes and Silvias of the world, if you recall our friends from Chapter 1) often take their linguistic abilities for granted, almost as much as they do their vision. Therefore, why do linguists, psychologists, cognitive neuroscientists, anthropologists and others typically portray multilingualism as such a cognitive and social feat? Focusing on the cognitive side for now (the social side is discussed later in this chapter), an honest answer would have two parts, which are somewhat contradictory. The first is, quite simply, because multilingualism *is* impressive from a cognitive point of view: The daily linguistic interactions of a multilingual individual are a remarkable exercise in the regulation and monitoring of vast amounts of noisy, rich and regularly conflicting information. The second is because we are still burdened with a perspective bias: These language-juggling skills are bound to seem all the more impressive if one conceptualizes multilinguals as several monolinguals in one person.

This (implicit) assumption remained mainstream until the late twentieth century and followed, perhaps inevitably, a research tradition in which scientists were often monolinguals from English-speaking countries. As we will see, the 'fractional view' (Grosjean, 1989) of bi-/multilingualism has now been widely challenged (e.g., Amaral & Roeper, 2014; Cook, 1991, 2003b; Grosjean, 1998, 2001; Lüdi & Py, 2009; Paradis, 2004; Rothman, 2008b; among many others; see contributions in Cook & Wei, 2016, in particular). However, this in turn opens up new questions: What *does* the multilingual system look like? How do competent multilingual speakers manage to communicate efficiently in each of those languages separately (that is, why do they sometimes *perform like* several monolinguals in one person)? How does the relative "strength" of languages within the multilingual system change over time?

The question of whether it is more accurate to describe the different languages of a multilingual as separate systems – a discrete set of "monolingual" systems – or as subsystems within a larger, integrated linguistic architecture is not trivial at all. For one thing, making one or the other assumption has implications for the linguistic behavior we come to expect from these speakers. Early research on the psycholinguistics of bilingualism introduced the concept of speech modes (e.g., Grosjean, 1982; Soares & Grosjean, 1984). These are, loosely speaking, the different ways in which bilinguals access their linguistic representations during production and comprehension depending on the interlocutor or the environment; in other words, the situation. Grosjean (1982, 1989) argued that bilinguals must adjust their speech depending on whether their interlocutor is competent in only one or in both of their two languages, or whether the situation encourages or even allows language mixing. These variables generate a "situational continuum" that ranges from a purely monolingual mode (in either of the languages of the bi-/multilingual) to a purely bilingual mode, in which the speaker is free to switch between the languages. Thus, when Oihan (Chapter 1.3) speaks to his friends from Madrid, who are not familiar with Basque or Norwegian, he defaults to a monolingual mode in which Spanish is selected and all other languages must be suppressed to the extent possible. When he goes to the Basque Country to visit his family, however, he is frequently free to use Basque or Spanish, at least with some people, since his interlocutors will understand either. Finally, when at home with his parents, Oihan adopts a fully multilingual mode, in which Basque, Norwegian and Spanish can be used, and even combined when he deems this necessary. Of course, how often and to what extent a multilingual switches between his or her languages depends on many factors, from the interlocutor to the situation to the habits of his/her linguistic community (for an exhaustive overview of linguistic codeswitching, see contributions in Bullock & Toribio, 2009; and papers in Munarriz-Ibarrola, Parafita Couto, & Vanden Wyngaerd, 2018; for a review specifically from the perspective of multilingualism, see Wei, 2013).

Understanding the linguistic behavior of bilinguals within a theory of speech/language modes helped to reconcile the seemingly contradictory results from the literature on lexical access, which spent much of its earlier days attempting to determine whether bilinguals had two separate lexicons or just one larger lexicon in which words from both languages coexisted (e.g., Kroll & Tokowicz, 2005; Paradis, 2004; see also Section 3.2. below). On one hand, researchers found that tasks engaging particular word forms in one language or another (such as having to name the picture of a cow in French (*vache*) while the English word 'cow' was visible on screen) were more challenging for bilinguals than they were for monolinguals, particularly when compared in their L1; that is, when bilinguals and monolinguals shared their native language (e.g., Ivanova & Costa, 2008) – which seemed to indicate the existence of two different lexicons, one for each language, that were in competition. On the other hand, this type of processing cost seemed to disappear in more conceptually oriented tasks, such as the semantic categorization task, in which participants are asked to assign the words with which they are presented to a particular semantic category or to confirm the target word's membership of that category. When considered together, these results suggest that there is, in fact, some degree of crosslinguistic interference, although this seems to take place mainly at the level of lexical entries, somehow sparing conceptual semantics. Conflicting evidence for and against different language lexicons being represented together fueled the debate regarding segregated versus integrated memory systems for much of the 1960s and 1970s (e.g., Kirsner, Smith, Lockhart, King, & Jain, 1984; Meyer & Rudy, 1974; see Kroll & Tokowicz, 2005; Paradis, 2004, for review). Most of the evidence we have accumulated over the past few decades seems to support a partially integrated system (Model type E in Kirsner et al.'s 1984 taxonomy), exemplified in Paradis's Three-Store Hypothesis (Paradis, 1978, 1980; see Paradis, 2004, for an overview).

A core claim of the Three-Store Hypothesis is that the linguistic and conceptual cognitive systems must be separate, thereby ruling out traditional accounts of mental linguistic representation in bilingualism in terms of a one-store (all languages access the same central storage of information) or two-store (information is represented separately for each language) layout; hence the reference to "stores" in the name. Notably, some one- and two-store models failed to dissociate the conceptual from the lexical level: Concepts exist as linguistically encoded units and are thus retrieved via the specific lexicon that verbalizes them in one language or another. Paradis (2004) refers to the clinical literature for examples that refute this idea, principally the literature on various types of aphasia. Generally speaking, aphasia is a loss (or degradation) of the ability to produce and/or comprehend speech as a result of pathological or nonpathological brain damage. Aphasic patients, even those with severe cases of nonfluent aphasia (agrammatism) or jargon aphasia (that is, fluent but unintelligible speech), are usually capable of performing well in tests of nonverbal intelligence, theory of mind, nonverbal memory, causal reasoning and, more importantly, picture classification (Varley & Siegal, 2000). These results are indicative of a dissociation between linguistic and other cognitive functions, including the manipulation of strictly conceptual information. The Three-Store Hypothesis posits a language-independent storage of conceptual-experiential information, which is accessed separately by the different language subsystems (that is, languages) present in the multilingual mind.[1] The architecture proposed by Paradis explains the (neuro)functional separation of conceptual and linguistic information, as well as the difference between conceptual and lexical semantics. Given that the encoding of conceptual information is unique for every language, word pairs that we conventionally understand as translation equivalents may evoke perceptually different prototypes because the bundles of conceptual features that constitute their lexical semantics differ in a number of (variably subtle) ways. We will return to this below when discussing a number of lexical organization models.

Although the psycholinguistic literature eventually abandoned a focus on physical representation in favor of function (in other words, it stopped being concerned with how languages are stored and focused on how they are *used* separately), the increasingly widespread adoption of neuroimaging techniques such as positron emission tomography (PET) and structural and functional magnetic resonance imaging ([f]MRI) in the late 1990s reversed this tendency somewhat, bringing attention back to the issue of whether native and nonnative languages were subserved by the same or by different neural networks (e.g., Kim, Relkin, Lee, & Hirsch, 1997). In connection with fundamental differences in cortical representation between the L1 and the L2, researchers focused on the immediately related question of whether the age of acquisition of the L2 (that is, early versus late bilingualism) would play a role in the distribution of these neural networks and, if so, how. Contrary to early claims (e.g., Albert & Obler, 1978; see Paradis, 2004: 97ff., for an extensive review and critique), there seems to be no convincing evidence today of different brain lateralization in bilinguals as compared to monolinguals (e.g., DeLuca, Miller, Pliatsikas, & Rothman, 2019; Liu & Cao, 2016; Solin, 1989): In both populations, language is processed primarily in the left hemisphere. Similarly, there seems to be no evidence to sustain the claim that the L1 and the L2/L*n* are localized differently in the brain (Paradis, 2004; Perani & Abutalebi, 2005); i.e., that similar functions may be subserved by different neural networks depending on the language. Instead, L1/L2 differences, in parallel with early versus late L2 processing, seem to be of a quantitative nature: In comparison to the L1, L2 processing – both in early and in late bilinguals – involves an increased volume of activation (e.g., Rüschemeyer, Zysset, & Friederici, 2006), a difference that is replicated when comparing early and late L2ers (Hernandez, Hofmann, & Kotz, 2007). In fact, structural MRI research into the brain of simultaneous and sequential bilingual individuals has revealed that the amount of L2 use is correlated positively with the reshaping of certain cortical areas, and that "use" is best operationalized here as continuous or frequent activation – as a result of L2 immersion, for example – instead of related but less influential proxies such as proficiency or age of acquisition (Pliatsikas, DeLuca, Moschopoulou, & Saddy, 2017; see Pliatsikas, 2019, for an extensive review of brain changes associated with multilingualism).

Irrespective of what the actual neural substrate of the multilingual language system is eventually determined to be, most of the work in recent and current approaches to the topic of language processing in multilingual individuals is now focused on how the different languages interact in real-time use, as well as the conditions and mechanisms that allow for this to happen. We will see this in the following section, which addresses what is, by far, the best studied aspect of multilingual cognition: the lexicon (see Bobb & Kroll, 2018, for review).

3.2   Processing and the Multilingual Lexicon

That L2 processing is, generally speaking, slower than is processing in the L1 is one of the earliest findings in psycholinguistics. Toward the end of the nineteenth century, Cattell (1887) conducted a series of seminal experiments in which he found, among other things, that it took his participants longer to name pictures in their nonnative language. This (nowadays) relatively uncontroversial observation raises the question of whether such delays stem from a differential representation or use of native and nonnative languages or are more generally a consequence of bi-/multilingual systems being cognitively "heavier" – in other words, of managing more with the same resources. While the answer might lie somewhere in between the two accounts, they have largely been explored independently of each other. Here, we report some findings from the past few decades, placing special attention on the scarcity of work conducted specifically on multilingualism as compared to mono- and bilingualism.[2]

Crosslinguistic influence, understood in the broad sense of interference among different languages, is particularly salient in the realm of individual words (see Weinreich, 1953, for an early account). For this reason, much of the work conducted to investigate the interaction between the languages of a multilingual individual has focused on developing models of word recognition and production that would account for several well-established effects – longer response latencies in picture naming and different processing costs in L1→L2 versus L2→L1 translation, among others. In what follows, Sections 3.2.1 and 3.2.2 introduce two of the main research areas in the field, each of which deals with one pivotal (and complementary) aspect of lexical representation: lexical access, and lexical incorporation and organization. Just as the architecture and distribution of a warehouse is relevant for the way in which goods are stored and retrieved, lexical access and lexical organization are two sides of the same coin, and therefore their insights must inevitably be understood in connection with each other. Finally, in Section 3.2.3, we will discuss some of the issues related to speed of processing in multilingualism, which inevitably relate to theories of lexical access and organization, in an attempt to determine how many of these processing differences can be accounted for in terms of a multilingualism effect, and how many are an L1 versus L2/L*n* issue instead.

3.2.1 Language (Non)Selectivity in Lexical Access

Much of the scientific discussion about the architecture of bi-/multilingual language systems over the past three decades has revolved around a simple question with a predictably complex answer: Is the multilingual lexicon partitioned in several language-specific sublexicons, or is it all essentially contained in one store? In more technical terms, do multilinguals have functionally separate lexicons for each of their languages, or do translation equivalents – as well as semantic, phonological and orthographic neighbors – compete for selection even when only one language is appropriate in a certain context? When stripped down to the fundamental cognitive arguments at stake, the language-selective versus nonselective debate asks the question of whether choosing context-appropriate words engages attentional or inhibitory control mechanisms in order to choose the correct word from all the lexicons available to a multilingual and, in particular, from the various lexical alternatives to roughly similar concepts, such as the selection of *perro* instead of *dog* when a Spanish–English bilingual names the domestic animal in a Spanish monolingual context.

The vast majority of the data collected in pursuit of this question stems from two experimental methods. The first is the lexical decision task (LDT), in which participants are asked to distinguish between words and nonwords in a given language, with target items – most commonly written, but also in auditory form – presented in isolation. Targets can be primed or unprimed; that is, other stimuli (primes) may be presented immediately before the target, potentially conditioning the participant's response. Within primed LDTs, one may further distinguish between masked priming, whereby prime presentation is made subliminal through subconsciously short display time and visual masking procedures, and overt priming, in which both the prime and target are consciously (though not always equally) perceivable. The second experimental method that has provided important evidence for and against language selectivity in lexical access is

PWI = Picture Word Interference

the picture-word interference (PWI) task. In this design, a variation of the well-known Stroop task (Stroop, 1935), participants are asked to name pictures in the presence of written or spoken word distractors, the presentation timing of which may be manipulated so that they appear before, simultaneously with or after the onset of the picture's display.

LDT = Lexical Decision Task

When considering and attempting to integrate results from LDT and PWI experiments, we should not lose sight of the fact that each of these paradigms has typically informed the modeling of only one of the two sides of bilingual lexical access: As a comprehension methodology, LDTs have been used to test theories about lexical access in bi-/multilingual word recognition (and speech comprehension), while results from PWI tasks are normally discussed in the context of bi-/multilingual speech production models. Of course, both top-down and bottom-up processes are involved in both types of tasks to some extent, which means that, in a way, all data are eventually relevant for individual theories on both sides of the question. In any event, the models we develop to account for receptive and productive multilingual lexical processing must ultimately be compatible in that they must assume the same architecture of the mental lexicon however different their specific access and retrieval mechanisms are considered to be. Bearing this in mind, let us now discuss some of the results from these two methods that have contributed to our understanding of the problem.

Different types of LDTs have been employed to determine the extent to which lexical items from a nonrelevant language – that is, a language that is not appropriate for the task or conversational context in which the multilingual finds herself – remain active and indeed compete for selection. The most reliable of all cross-language interference phenomena, with experimental evidence dating back almost 40 years (Caramazza & Brones, 1979), is the cognate (facilitation) effect.[3] Cognates, broadly defined as etymologically related words in different languages that retain some degree of semantic, orthographic and/or phonological overlap, constitute a particularly important piece of the multilingual lexical representation puzzle, since most of their information can be considered redundant across languages, and therefore are good candidates for partially shared or at least strongly interconnected representations (e.g., Sánchez-Casas & García-Albea, 2005). The observation Caramazza and Brones (1979) made in their seminal study, namely that L2 words were identified more quickly when they were cognates of L1 words, has been replicated and dissected in a long tradition of research that has managed to identify different dimensions of the effect in relation to the various degrees of overlap that cognates may present.

L1 - L2

Seminal Cognate Study

Although the cognate effect seems to be more robust in L2/L*n* word recognition (e.g., Caramazza & Brones, 1979; Dijkstra, Grainger, & van Heuven, 1999; Lemhöfer & Dijkstra, 2004; Lemhöfer, Dijkstra, & Michel, 2004), a number of studies have also found evidence for cognate status facilitating word recognition in a speaker's native language. Van Hell and Dijkstra (2002) reported on a study with L1 Dutch–L2 English–L3 French speakers who were tested exclusively in their native languages using a word association task (Experiment 1), whereby participants were asked to say the first word that came to mind out loud in relation to the target stimulus presented on screen, and an LDT (Experiments 2 and 3). Cognate status was manipulated across all experiments in such a way that the target Dutch words were cognates of their English translation equivalents or of their French counterparts, or were non-cognates altogether. Overall, their findings showed faster responses to L1-L2 cognates than to non-cognates, something that was also true of L1-L3 cognates only when participants were highly proficient in the L3 (French). Testing trilingual cognate effects in the opposite direction (from more to less proficient languages), and partly addressing a gap in van Hell and Dijkstra's study, Lemhöfer et al. (2004) observed that, irrespective of recency of activation, multilinguals (L1 Dutch–L2 English–L3 German) showed a strong cognate effect in an LDT in L3 German. Participants responded fastest to words that overlapped in the three languages (such as *echo*), then to words that were cognates in (L1) Dutch and (L2) German (such as *schuld*, 'guilt'), and slowest to words that were uniquely German (such as *antrag*, 'application'). In a control experiment using the same materials with German monolinguals who had little or no knowledge of English or Dutch, all stimuli yielded approximately the same response times. Comparable results were obtained by Szubko-Sitarek (2011), who observed similar patterns when testing participants in their L3 (German) and their L1 (Polish).

Some of the findings from the PWI literature (e.g., Costa & Caramazza, 1999; Costa, Miozzo, & Caramazza, 1999) have been interpreted in favor of a language-selective view of lexical access in bi-/multilinguals (see Costa, 2005, for an extensive account). This position does not dispute the idea that all languages in the multilingual system are constantly active, nor does it even question whether the activation of certain conceptual features or bundles of features (for example, the concept 'CAT') spreads to all lexicons in parallel, reaching the different lexical items that encode the concept in these languages (such as *cat, gato,* and *chat,* in an English–Spanish–French trilingual). The difference with language-nonselective models of lexical access is that, in this case, the parser *does not consider* candidates from languages other than the response-relevant one, irrespective of their level of activation. This means that the crucial factor for these models is the system's ability to focus and defocus attention on specific subsets of lexical items – that is, the language-specific lexicons – rather than resolving competition among candidates of different languages through inhibition of the non-relevant items.[4]

Costa et al. (1999) employed the PWI paradigm in seven experiments in which Catalan–Spanish bilinguals named pictures in Catalan in the presence of same-language and different-language (written) distractors. Their results included, among others, two important observations. The first is that translation equivalents facilitated, instead of inhibited, the naming of pictures; that is, a table (*taula* in Catalan) was named more quickly when the distractor word was the Spanish *mesa* ('table'). This is contradictory to some of the findings from the LDT paradigm (see below), and undermines the cross-language competition argument. In fact, Costa et al. interpreted this result within a language-selective model: While translation equivalents are comparably activated by the conceptual level (stimulated by the picture) and further activate each other through their semantic links, they do not compete afterwards because the parser only considers one of them for selection. In this way, the net effect of the interaction between the distractor and the target word is one of facilitation. A second interesting finding of their study is that phonological overlap between the target and distractor words produced facilitation, even if there was no semantic overlap, and even if the words belonged to different languages (for example, Spanish *barro*, 'mud,' as a distractor of Catalan *baldufa*, 'spinning top'). It is interesting that this effect disappeared when the distractor was the translation equivalent of the phonologically similar word instead of the word itself (such as the Catalan distractor *fang*, 'mud,' over the picture of a spinning top). Note that, as we have said, *barro* did facilitate the naming of the spinning top when superimposed directly onto the picture as a distractor. Where, then, is the effect lost? Costa et al. suggested that this was due to phonological and orthographic facilitation being fundamentally sublexical in nature: Since, when translating from *fang* to *barro*, activation reaches a lexical entry (Spanish *barro*, 'mud') in a non-relevant language, this item is no longer considered and thus no longer interferes with the response. When *barro* is the distractor, however, its letters and phonemes are able to activate words in either lexicon because these levels are blind to language distinctions.

Hermans, Bongaerts, de Bot, and Schreuder (1998) used a similar manipulation involving translation and phonological similarity in a series of PWI tasks with Dutch–English bilinguals, in which the target language was English. Experiment 1 used English phonological neighbors as distractors, whereas in

Experiment 2, phonologically related Dutch words were used. Importantly, both experiments used auditory distractors and included what the authors referred to as the 'Phono-Dutch' condition, in which the distractor was an English word that was related phonologically to the target's Dutch translation equivalent (for example, *bench*, related to the Dutch word *berg*, 'mountain,' when naming the picture of a mountain). Unlike Costa et al. (1999), the presentation timing of the distractor and the target picture were manipulated in such a way that the stimulus onset asynchrony – in other words, the difference between the presentation of the target and the distractor, usually abbreviated as SOA – could be −300 milliseconds (the distractor appeared 300 milliseconds before the picture), −150 milliseconds, 0 milliseconds (simultaneous presentation) or +150 milliseconds. While phonological facilitation from English distractors obtained at all SOAs, this was only the case at +150 milliseconds with the Dutch distractors (Experiment 2). Furthermore, whereas semantic interference took place in Experiment 1 (with, for example, *valley* as a distractor when naming the picture of a mountain), similar inhibition obtained in the Phono-Dutch condition in Experiment 2, which suggests that Dutch translation equivalents could be activated indirectly and entered into competition at higher representational levels but were eventually abandoned before the stage of phonological encoding. Note that this last result differs from the findings in Costa et al. (1999), for whom translation equivalents did not seem to activate phonological neighbors in the response-relevant language. It is possible that modality effects with regard to the presentation of distractor words, which were written in Costa et al.'s (1999) work and spoken in Hermans et al.'s (1998) study, can explain this discrepancy as a difference in quantity rather than in quality if we were to assume that effect sizes varied across modalities, but this is not entirely clear.

In light of these varied and often contradictory results from both experimental paradigms, it became clear that an accurate characterization of the multilingual lexicon's architecture required a closer inspection of well-established effects. One obvious course of action was to attempt to deconstruct the cognate effect, in order to understand where and when competition (or, in this case, cooperation, but in any case interference) took place between lexical items of different languages. Recall that cognates have varying degrees of overlap in semantic, orthographic and phonological terms; thus, manipulating these dimensions is essential to pinpoint the locus (or loci) of cross-language interaction. In an article that proposed an extension of the Bilingual Interactive Activation (BIA) model (e.g., Dijkstra & van Heuven, 1998; Grainger & Dijkstra, 1992), Dijkstra et al. (1999) systematically tested cognate effects in a series of progressive demasking and lexical decision experiments. The six conditions examined across the three experiments, which employed Dutch–English bilinguals and a control group of English monolinguals, included semantic overlap in combination with phonological (SP), orthographic (SO) and phonological + orthographic overlap (SOP), as well as word pairs in which the overlap was strictly formal, in turn subdivided into orthographic (O), phonological (P) or both (OP). The combined pattern of results from these experiments suggests that what underlies cognate facilitation effects is the semantic and orthographic dimensions, whereas phonological similarity between the target word and its counterpart has the opposite effect; namely, it produces inhibition and delays processing. The authors concluded that interlingual homographs, words that are identical in form but have no meaning relation across languages (such as *room*, the Dutch word for 'cream'), must be represented twice in the multilingual lexicon in order to account for seemingly contradictory competition and facilitation effects among these word pairs (see, e.g., Dijkstra, van Jaarsveld, & ten Brinke, 1998). The study and subsequent discussion in Dijkstra et al. (1999) highlight the complexity of crosslinguistic interactions in the multilingual lexicon, whereby shared characteristics at one or more levels of representation (for example, phonology, orthography and lexical semantics) do not necessarily justify an assumption of shared representations for the sake of nonredundancy. For a further, more recent discussion of the representation of partially overlapping, as well as identical cognates, we direct the reader to Peeters, Dijkstra, and Grainger (2013).

Further work on cognates and interlingual homophones/homographs within the LDT paradigm (e.g., de Groot, Delmaar, & Lupker, 2000; Duyck, 2005), as well as experiments manipulating within- and between-language orthographic and phonological neighborhood densities of target words – that is, the number of existing words that differ in only one letter or sound from the target (e.g., Jared & Kroll, 2001; Van Heuven, Dijkstra, & Grainger, 1998; Van Heuven, Dijkstra, Grainger, & Schriefers, 2001) – continued to lend support to the language-nonselective view of lexical access. This was true of studies of word recognition in isolation as well as of experiments in which these effects were measured in the context of full-sentence reading (e.g., Duyck, van Assche, Drieghe, & Hartsuiker, 2007; Van Assche, Duyck, Hartsuiker, & Diependaele, 2009). While recent work has emphasized the speed at which initially nonselective lexical access becomes constrained by semantic and discourse factors (e.g., Libben & Titone, 2009; Schwartz & Kroll, 2006; see Lauro & A. I. Schwartz, 2017, for a meta-analysis), the dominant view today is that the activation of nonrelevant languages is still not completely suppressed and that multilingual processing is fundamentally nonselective at most, if not all, representational levels (Kroll, Bobb, & Wodniecka, 2006; see van Assche, Duyck, & Hartsuiker, 2012, for review).

3.2.2   Lexical Representation and Incorporation in Multilingualism

Much of our discussion in the previous section has taken for granted that translation equivalents are, in one way or another, connected in the multilingual lexicon, regardless of how these connections are then exploited by the parser and what the net effect – facilitation or inhibition – might be in actual processing when activation of one word spreads to its translation equivalent(s). It is nevertheless important to ask ourselves what the precise nature of that connection is, particularly because an integrated theory of the multilingual lexicon must contain models of *what* is accessed in addition to *how* it is accessed – and one might even argue that the first aspect must epistemologically precede the second (e.g., Marslen-Wilson, 2001). This section will provide a brief introduction to lexical organization via the literature on (cognate and noncognate) translation equivalents and will proceed to a discussion of how the multilingual lexicon comes to be; that is, how new words are incorporated into the network.

Similarly to the lexical access debate, two tasks have yielded the vast majority of the evidence for multilingual lexical organization, namely lexical decision (LDT) and semantic categorization tasks (SCTs). Crucially, both tasks have predominantly been used in the context of masked translation priming. This is a specific case of the masked priming paradigm, which we described above as a priming method in which prime stimuli are presented subconsciously by reducing their display time to well under 100 milliseconds and masking their presentation (forward, backward or both) using symbols or nonsensical letter strings. This technique, developed in monolingual studies by Forster and Davis (1984), has been applied to bi-/multilingual tasks by using translation equivalents as prime-target pairs and comparing the effect to a baseline condition in which prime and target words are also from different languages but are unrelated in form or meaning. If target words are responded to faster when preceded by their translation primes, this result is taken as evidence that activation of the prime spreads to the target within the multilingual lexicon. As we have seen, for LDTs, this response has to do, primarily, with the lexicality (word status) of the target stimulus. SCTs are similar in their approach but differ critically in the representational levels they potentially tap – which, some have argued, might make SCTs superior for testing the theoretical questions at hand; see, e.g., de Groot (2010) and Lupker and Pexman (2010).

Categorizing "food" is conceptual

The participant's task in semantic categorization experiments is to decide whether or not the target word belongs to a given semantic category (such as 'food'). While the final responses in an LDT and an SCT are equally binary, the SCT ensures that participants process the target word all the way "up" to the conceptual level, since evaluating the connection between the word's lexical entry and its conceptual semantics is necessary to make a decision.[5]

While the field is (or should be) equally concerned with coexistence and organization in the lexicon of balanced as well as unbalanced – typically sequential – bi-/multilingual speakers, the latter group has provided some of the most revealing insights. The difference between these two populations is best perceived in the most vulnerable context for translation priming effects: L2 primes with L1 targets. In fact, while L1 primes prime their L2 translation equivalents consistently, irrespective of whether these are cognate pairs (that is, the effect obtains with and without form overlap), most studies comparing L1→L2 and L2→L1 translation priming in LDTs have observed an asymmetry between these two priming directions, whereby L2→L1 translation priming is typically weak and highly unreliable (see Wen & van Heuven, 2017, and Xia & Andrews, 2015, for comprehensive overviews). Two factors seem to attenuate this imbalance to the point of making it disappear, namely linguistic proficiency and cognate status. Highly proficient bilinguals, typically simultaneous or early acquirers, generally display comparable translation priming effects in LDTs for both directions of priming, even with noncognate pairs (e.g., Basnight-Brown & Altarriba, 2007; Duñabeitia, Perea, & Carreiras, 2010; Duyck, 2005). This is typically not the case for unbalanced or low-proficiency bilinguals (e.g., Dimitropoulou, Duñabeitia, & Carreiras, 2011), with some exceptions (e.g., Duyck & Warlop, 2009; Lijewska, Ziegler, & Olko, 2018). Cognate translation priming, on the other hand, has been shown to survive differences in bilingual proficiency; thus, it obtains reliably in both directions, and for both balanced and unbalanced bilinguals (e.g., Davis et al., 2010; Nakayama, Sears, Hino, & Lupker, 2013).

The (masked) translation priming asymmetry in LDTs has a counterpart in SCTs: Translation priming typically occurs in these tasks only for words that are exemplars of the semantic category at stake – in other words, targets for which the expected response is 'yes' (e.g., Finkbeiner, Forster, Nicol, & Nakamura, 2004; Xia & Andrews, 2015; but see Lijewska et al., 2018) – and only if this category is predefined clearly. Wang and Forster (2010, Experiment 4) found that unbalanced Chinese–English bilinguals did not show L2→L1 translation priming effects in an SCT when the categorization required an ad-hoc evaluation (for example, 'Is this object larger than a brick?') instead of

as proficiency ↑ L2 words establish their own direct conceptual links

confirming membership of a given semantic category – as is typical of SCTs. These results suggested that the reduced asymmetry of translation priming effects observed in SCTs with regard to LDTs was not merely a result of the task requiring the activation of semantic features (see Wang & Forster, 2010; Xia & Andrews, 2015, for a discussion).

In summary, we have seen that task type, linguistic proficiency, cognate status and priming direction (L1→L2 or L2→L1) all influence the presence and magnitude of translation priming effects. What does this imply for theories of multilingual lexical organization? In other words, how do models of lexical representation in multilingualism account for these effects? Although a substantial number of proposals would have to accommodate these results (see Lijewska et al., 2018, for an overview), three models have received the most attention in recent years: the Revised Hierarchical Model (RHM; Kroll & Stewart, 1994; Kroll, van Hell, Tokowicz, & Green, 2010), the BIA+ Model (Dijkstra, 2003; Dijkstra & van Heuven, 2002) and the Sense Model (SM; Finkbeiner et al., 2004). While all of these models posit largely similar architectures (for example, they all assume a common conceptual store and non-selective access to lexical representations), differences in the conceptualization of the L1-L2 relationship, as well as in key components of the processing system, yield different predictions and explanations of the observed asymmetries as a function of the type of task and of the priming direction. We will now summarize these briefly before moving on to discussing lexical incorporation.

The RHM originally proposed that the connections between L2 words and the corresponding conceptual features only develop over time, so that, initially, these relationships are mediated by L1 translation equivalents, which are then connected to the L2 words through *lexical* links. Crucially, these are one-way connections (from the L2 to the L1) and are only envisioned as serving an integrating purpose; according to the model, their strength should decrease as L2 words begin to establish their own direct conceptual links, which takes place as a function of proficiency. This accounts nicely for the higher processing cost in L1→L2 as compared to L2→L1 translations, irrespective of proficiency (the original scope of the model), but has a more difficult time dealing with the translation direction asymmetry in masked priming: If L2 representations are connected strongly with their L1 equivalents at the lexical level, L2→L1 translation priming should be robust; all the more so in low-proficiency bilinguals. In addressing the masked translation priming asymmetry, proponents of the model (e.g., Kroll & Tokowicz, 2001; Kroll et al., 2010) have suggested that L2 words may in fact develop conceptual links at an early stage (however weak), which would account for the different size of the effect as a function of

RHM – Revised Hierarchical Model

translation direction, as long as we assume that translation priming in LDTs is mainly achieved through shared conceptual nodes between the L1 and L2 translation equivalents. While this is sufficient to explain the asymmetry in LDTs, the RHM is still somewhat compromised by the task sensitivity of the effect: Under the same account, there is no reason that L2→L1 translation priming should occur reliably in SCTs.

Dijkstra and van Heuven's (2002) BIA+ faces a similar problem. Recall from our discussion above that nonselectivity is at the heart of this model, which means that the constant, simultaneous activation of both languages' lexical representations is assumed. To resolve competition between target and non-target representations, the BIA+ posits a language node, which increases the resting activation of representations from the response-relevant language (for example, the L1) and inhibits those of the nonrelevant one(s).[6] Because the resting activation of L2 representations, particularly in unbalanced or low-proficiency bilinguals, is assumed to be comparatively lower than is that of their L1 counterparts, a brief presentation of an L2 prime may not be sufficient to activate it, thereby preventing any possible priming effect; this is not the case for L1 primes, which need very little stimulation to become active and potentially prime their L2 translation equivalents (Lijewska et al., 2018). This possibly interacts with the regulatory role of the language node, which will be more effective in inhibiting L2 representations when the task focuses on L1 targets than it will when the opposite is the case. These differences in resting activation and perceptual sensitivity between the languages, however, would predict comparable asymmetries in an SCT.

The SM (Finkbeiner et al., 2004) was proposed to address these issues in a unified manner. The SM proposes two different explanations for the phenomena at hand – the translation priming asymmetry and its sensitivity to task demands – which relate to the same basic idea: All words are polysemous to some extent and thus have several meanings or *senses*. It should be noted that the SM, unlike the BIA+ and the RHM, is very much an extension of de Groot's (1992) Distributed Feature Model and, as such, it is considered a *distributed* connectionist model. In simple terms, this means that the semantic features associated with individual words are assumed to be distributed across the network, instead of being bundled together under a given lexical item. As a result, different pairs of translation equivalents have different degrees of semantic overlap (that is, they share a different number of senses), with cognates – as opposed to noncognate translations – being obvious candidates to be positioned at the higher end of the scale. The knowledge a speaker has of a given word's senses typically depends on proficiency: The more proficient

Nonselectivity – constant simultaneous activation of both languages is assumed

a speaker is in a language, the greater the number of senses of a word she will be aware of. It follows from this that L2 lexical representations in unbalanced, and particularly in low-proficiency, bilinguals are normally underspecified to a greater or lesser degree. Based on this account, the senses of which a speaker is aware for an L2 word will always be a subset of those she knows for its L1 translation equivalent. Because the SM sees translation priming as a fundamentally semantic phenomenon, the proportion of shared senses between the L1 and L2 members of a pair is crucial for the effect to obtain. This would explain the asymmetry in LDTs: Because the L2 prime activates only a relatively small number of the total senses for the L1 target, priming will be weak or nonexistent. In the other direction, however, the L1 prime will activate most, if not all, of the L2 target's currently represented senses, thus maximizing the magnitude of the semantic priming effect. Note that this also accounts nicely for the amelioration of the asymmetry as a function of proficiency: Greater competence in the L2 will lead to more specified, semantically richer representations that will reduce the gap with their L1 translation equivalents progressively.

To explain the task sensitivity effect, the SM proposes a filtering mechanism whereby only those senses that are relevant to the category the SCT is tapping are considered, the rest being "filtered out." Because category-defining senses are the most common, these are likely to make up most of the group of senses shared between the L1 and the L2 representations. In essence, the filtering mechanism cancels out the asymmetry generated by the disproportion of senses by reducing the number of relevant L1 senses to very much the same as those connected to the L2 word. In turn, this explains a secondary asymmetry, namely that task sensitivity only applies to exemplars (that is, words that belong to the semantic category at hand). When the target word – and therefore its prime – does not belong to the category, there is no opportunity for filtering to take place. However, recent studies that have made a direct comparison of L1→L2 to L2→L1 masked translation priming across tasks have failed to confirm the SM's prediction that the asymmetry observed in the LDT should always be reduced significantly (or disappear) in the SCT (Lijewska et al., 2018; Xia & Andrews, 2015), which undermines the filtering component of the model.

Considering all of the above results together, the evidence suggests overwhelmingly that words in the multilingual lexicon are only functionally segregated and that complex connections are established at several representational levels. Coupled with essentially nonselective processing mechanisms – which might be entirely blind to language membership at certain levels in reading and speech comprehension, such as orthography and phonology – this high

Major Point

interconnectivity must engage different types of monitoring, attentional and inhibitory control mechanisms to accomplish the (only seemingly simple) task of allowing multilinguals to express themselves in their language of choice, a demand which, in contexts such as codeswitching, can change rapidly.[7] With the exception of some considerations of the role of proficiency, however, the studies above do not provide a developmental perspective on the multilingual lexicon. In essence, we need to ask ourselves how these complex and often ephemeral connections come to be. In addressing this question, we will also return to the bilingual/multilingual distinction: While much of the literature presented above is ambivalent, if not agnostic with regard to differences between bilingual and multilingual speakers, lexical incorporation theories are concerned more directly with the specific dynamics of the multilingual system in similar ways to other domains of grammar such as phonology and morphosyntax, as discussed in the remainder of this chapter and in the next.

The Parasitic Model (Hall, 1992, 2002; see also Ecke, 2015; Ecke & Hall, 2014; Hall & Ecke, 2003) proposes that new representations enter the multilingual lexicon by attaching to well-established lexical items from previously acquired languages. In Hall and Ecke's (2003) terms, new L3/L*n* words are parasitic upon L1 and L2 hosts, which provide the anchor points via which the new representation can be accessed. Note that one fundamental assumption underlying this model is shared with the RHM: Initially, conceptual links to L2 words are too weak to guarantee reliable retrieval of these items, which demands some type of mediation by more easily accessible lexical entries (see Herwig, 2001, for a similar account). According to the model, and similarly to the RHM, crosslinguistic links of this type are used to access the new lexical items via their L1/L2 hosts until sufficiently strong conceptual links that permit the direct retrieval of these representations through the activation of the relevant conceptual features are established. Subsequently, parasitic connections are gradually abandoned, and the L3 representations become independent from their initial hosts – except in the case of translation equivalents, which obviously retain some degree of (conceptually mediated) connection.

Unlike the RHM, and other proposals such as Weinreich's (1953) seminal work, the Parasitic Model contends that the similarities exploited between the L3 parasite and its L1/L2 host(s) need not be restricted to conceptual semantics but can be established at different levels of representation instead, including form (orthographic or phonological), frame (for example, syntactic context, word category and argument structure) and concept. In doing so, the Parasitic Model adopts a three-level structure of lexical entries in which a morphophonological form is associated with a particular grammatical specification and

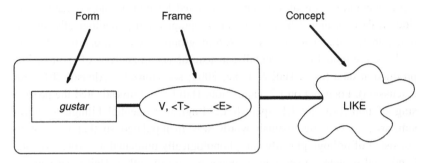

Figure 3.1 *Lexical triad for the Spanish word* gustar, *'like' (adapted from González Alonso, 2012)*

a bundle of conceptual features (see Jackendoff, 1997; Levelt, 1989; Levelt, Roelofs, & Meyer, 1999, for similar proposals), the latter of which are external to the language proper – that is, they are nonverbal knowledge (see Figure 3.1 for a schematic representation). While any of the three levels of these *lexical triads* may serve as the basis for the parasitic connection, the model is particularly strong in predicting the less obvious cases of form- and frame-based incorporation (see, e.g., Hall et al., 2009).

Hall and Ecke (2003) referred to the incorporation of new L3 representations via form- or frame-related L1/L2 hosts as *acquisition crosslinguistic influence*. Until independent conceptual links for the new lexical item can be established, temporary connections to the L1 or L2 hosts will be necessary in order to retrieve the parasite word. This means that, in some cases, the host will be produced instead, even when there is no meaning connection between the host and the parasite; that is, even when the L1/L2 and the L3 word are not translation equivalents. This phenomenon, which Hall and Ecke (2003) called *competence crosslinguistic influence* (CCLI), is perhaps most common when the parasitic link has been established on the basis of frame similarities (for example, when the L3 word is a verb with a similar argument structure – although a different meaning – to that of an L1/L2 verb). Note that, in some cases, it is also possible that the host is a well-established L3 representation, in which case frame-based CCLI is particularly common.

While it is not easy to predict which level of similarity will be exploited by a given L3 representation, since this may be subject to individual differences, some types of words are more likely candidates to establish connections at one or more levels of representation. We have already seen that much work in lexical access and representation has investigated the processing and representation of cognates in the multilingual lexicon. Pseudocognates, both (identical) interlingual homophones/homographs and phonologically similar noncognates, are a particularly interesting group of words if one is seeking to evaluate the model experimentally, instead of via an analysis of spontaneous production data (as in Hall & Ecke, 2003; see González Alonso, 2012, for discussion). Focusing on L2 acquisition, Hall (2002) investigated the processing of nonwords by L1 Spanish–L2 English sequential bilinguals. Form similarity to existing Spanish words was manipulated so that the stimuli consisted of orthographically and phonologically unrelated nonwords, on one hand, and pseudocognate nonce sequences, on the other. Hall's participants claimed to be more familiar with the latter group and, when asked to provide a meaning for these pseudocognates, proposed definitions that were often in line with the existing Spanish words (the perceived cognates). Hall concluded that, in the absence of cues to the meaning of the new forms, these learners assumed cognate status for the L1-L2 pairs, which helped them incorporate the new form into the network by assigning it a highly specified, if only provisional, lexical representation.

In a different use of pseudocognates, González Alonso (2012) presented L1 Polish–L2 English–L3 Russian speakers with pictures to name in one or another of their three languages, which were varied pseudo-randomly during the experiment. These pictures were preceded by an auditory prime in one of the other two languages, followed by a visual cue to indicate the response-relevant language for the upcoming picture stimulus. Primes were either pseudocognates; for example, the English word *fabric* heard before naming the picture of a factory (фабрика, *fabrika*) in Russian, or unrelated noncognates. Consistently, participants were faster at naming pictures in L3 Russian when these were preceded by pseudocognate L1/L2 words. This suggests that the L3 lexical representations were still attached to formally similar L1/L2 hosts through parasitic links – particularly considering that full processing of the prime (note that priming was overt here) would have activated its conceptual semantics, which in turn should cancel out the potential sublexical priming effects of hearing phonologically similar forms. Notably, the effect was less prominent for the more advanced learners.

The research reviewed in this section suggests that lexical organization and incorporation are highly dependent, at least initially, on crosslinguistic lexical links, which are established through the use of cognitively economical acquisition mechanisms. However, the tendency for multilingual systems is to develop language-specific relationships between the different lexicons and the speaker's conceptual-experiential knowledge, which eventually substitute, bypass or outgrow these original lexical-level "shortcuts." The following section will provide a brief review of some issues related to the impact of the bi-/multilingual experience on language processing in comparison to its monolingual counterpart, and what this can tell us about the models of lexical organization and access we have just discussed.

3.2.3 Verbal Fluency and Processing Speed

The consequences of the bi-/multilingual experience for (nonverbal) executive functions – that is, the mind's ability to control, monitor and regulate several sources of conflicting information through selective attention and the inhibition of nonrelevant stimuli – have been studied extensively for the past three decades, with a majority of the available data supporting a multilingual advantage (see, e.g., Bialystok, 2009, 2011, 2016, 2018; Bialystok, Craik, & Luk, 2012; Kroll & Bialystok, 2013, for review; cf. Antón et al., 2014; Duñabeitia et al., 2014; Paap, Johnson, & Sawi, 2015). In parallel, a different line of research has focused on characterizing what has come to be known as the *bilingual disadvantage* (in contrast to the *bilingual advantage* in executive function). As mentioned briefly in our introduction to Section 3.2, it is a well-known fact that bi-/multilinguals are generally slower at retrieving words, particularly in their weaker languages, than are monolingual speakers of these languages. Some of the pioneering work considering the additive effect of multilingualism on lexical retrieval was conducted by Mägiste (1979, 1986). In a cross-sectional study comparing monolingual (German and Swedish), bilingual (L1 German–L2 Swedish) and trilingual speakers (various L1s–L2 German–L3 Swedish), Mägiste (1979) found that trilingual and bilingual speakers displayed longer latencies in various comprehension and production tasks (see Mägiste, 1986, for similar results), with the latter lagging behind in terms of proficiency development. Unsurprisingly, given the literature we have reviewed, proficiency in the L2 and the L3 ameliorated this effect. Even though the focus of Lemhöfer et al.'s (2004) study mentioned before was on the cumulative cognate effect across three languages, the authors did show a similar cost – although they did not comment on it – when one compares the different participant groups: The monolingual group displayed systematically shorter response times than did the multilinguals (the smallest difference was 18 milliseconds in the triple-cognate condition, the largest difference was 112 milliseconds in the German control condition and the median was 73 milliseconds in the nonword condition). While no statistical analysis is available to determine whether these differences are significant, they are striking in numerical terms, particularly when considering that, in the multilingual experiment, a 22-millisecond difference between triple and double cognates was significant.

Although, as we can see, data from (visual or auditory) comprehension paradigms can also be used to shed light on the bi-/multilingual disadvantage, most of the work conducted to address this issue specifically has focused on speech production (see Sandoval, Gollan, Ferreira, & Salmon, 2010, for review). In comparison to monolinguals, it is generally accepted that multilinguals have smaller vocabulary sizes – in both comprehension and production (e.g., Bialystok, 2001) – in all of their languages; however, when considered together, the cumulative vocabulary tends to be considerably larger than is that of monolinguals on average (e.g., Bialystok, 1988; Doyle, Champagne, & Segalowitz, 1978; Nicoladis & Genesee, 1997; Pearson, Fernández, & Oller, 1993). For example, Portocarrero, Burright, and Donovick (2007) tested monolingual and bilingual college students in a number of tasks measuring vocabulary size and verbal fluency in English. They found that, on average, bilingual students had smaller vocabularies than did their monolingual peers and that this effect was correlated mildly with age of arrival (which, in their study, effectively equaled age of acquisition): the younger their bilingual participants when entering the country, the larger and more diverse their vocabulary size.

Besides sheer vocabulary size, experimental results in two more production measures have generally shown bi- and multilinguals at a disadvantage: picture-naming latencies and verbal fluency. In a study investigating both picture naming and picture classification in English, Gollan, Montoya, Fennema-Notestine, and Morris (2005) observed that bilinguals presented inflated naming latencies relative to monolinguals, even though English was their dominant language. Importantly, this result was not replicated in the classification task, in which participants were asked to classify pictures as natural or human made and where both groups displayed comparable response times. While the studies we have reviewed thus far make a solid case for the bilingual disadvantage, it is important to note that the most compelling evidence in this sense – and the best way to adjudicate between an L2 or a bilingualism effect as the ultimate factor behind this phenomenon – must come from tasks in which bi- and multilinguals are compared to monolinguals in their first and dominant language. Ivanova and Costa's (2008) study was the first to conflate the L1 factor in terms of dominance and order of acquisition; thus, their bilingual groups, Spanish- and Catalan-dominant bilinguals, had acquired their dominant language first, whereas previous studies such as that by Gollan et al. (2005) had examined speakers with switched dominance. In a picture-naming task with Spanish as a target language, Ivanova and Costa

(2008) found that Spanish monolinguals were faster than were Spanish-dominant bilinguals, who in turn were faster than their Catalan-dominant peers. This effect was maintained through several repetitions of the stimuli but was significantly smaller for high-frequency words. Taken together, this last finding and the picture classification results in Gollan et al. (2005) are in line with the lexical access literature in suggesting that the differences between bilinguals and monolinguals are not located at the level of conceptual representation but rather emerge within the lexical domain.

The second source of evidence is verbal fluency tasks, which typically examine one of two dimensions of this skill: semantic or letter fluency. In semantic fluency assessments, participants are asked to produce as many exemplars as possible of a given semantic category within one minute – 'animals' is a classic example. Letter fluency, on the other hand, is measured by asking participants to name as many words as possible starting with a particular letter or sound, the most common being *f, a* and *s*. In these verbal fluency tasks, bilinguals have been shown to produce fewer exemplars than have monolinguals, both by younger (e.g., Gollan, Montoya, & Werner, 2002) and healthy older adults (e.g., Rosselli et al., 2000). However, this seems to be true mainly of semantic fluency, whereas letter fluency tasks have often failed to show a difference between the groups (e.g., Bialystok, Craik, & Luk, 2008; Gollan et al., 2002; Portocarrero et al., 2007). This suggests that some specific aspect of bilingualism may compensate for the general effect in the letter fluency task. Bialystok et al. (2008) suggested that this may be related to the different brain areas involved in the semantic and letter fluency tasks: While semantic fluency depends on temporal regions, the letter fluency task recruits the frontal cortex more specifically, which is the locus of executive functions and an area that much research has shown to be enhanced in younger and older bilinguals.

The question that remains, however, is what exactly causes the generally slower lexical retrieval observed in multilinguals, both in their dominant and nondominant languages? Two possibilities have been discussed, namely

(i) that lexical access is delayed by the activation of competing words from the other language; for example, *cow* would interfere with and delay the retrieval of *vaca* when a Spanish–English bilingual names a picture of a cow in Spanish, and

(ii) that words in the bilingual lexicon are of relatively lower frequency compared to the same lexical items in a monolingual lexicon.

The position summarized in (ii), formalized as the weaker-links hypothesis (Gollan, Montoya, Cera, & Sandoval, 2008; later renamed the frequency-lag hypothesis, Gollan et al., 2011), elaborates on a simple but powerful idea, which is that bi-/multilinguals have, on the whole, less experience with the same words than do monolinguals because their overall linguistic experience is distributed across several languages. The frequency-lag hypothesis can account for the bi-/multilingual disadvantage in lexical access across all ranges of proficiency. Just as even high-frequency words have weak representations in the mental lexicon of novice L2 learners, attenuation of the effect by increased proficiency is ultimately limited: Even highly proficient bilinguals use their languages to a (frequently much) smaller degree than do monolinguals. Recent research comparing trilinguals and bilinguals of different age groups – the crucial dimensions along which the competition and frequency-lag accounts differ in their predictions – have obtained mixed results, suggesting that multilingual lexical retrieval is affected both by cognitive load and by factors related to differences in linguistic experience (Sullivan, Poarch, & Bialystok, 2018).

One might argue that cognate facilitation effects, which studies such as Lemhöfer et al. (2004) have shown to be cumulative, do much to counteract the multilingual disadvantage in lexical retrieval. However, this can hardly be generalized to a sufficiently large effect: For many, if not most, language combinations – except in very closely related language pairs – the number of cognates across lexicons is smaller than is the number of noncognates. In any event, both the competition account and the weaker-links hypothesis highlight the same problem: In most cases of lexical retrieval, bi-/multilinguals will be at a disadvantage, be it because the word has a weaker representation – or, rather, weaker conceptual links – or because it has to compete crosslinguistically with phonological neighbors and translation equivalents. It follows that true multilinguals, as opposed to bilinguals, might have increased difficulties precisely because competition, as well as overall experience, is dispersed across more linguistic systems (multiple sets of phonological neighbors, cognates and so on). It is relevant to mention here that a combination of both accounts had already been proposed by Mägiste (1979) as the most likely explanation for her data. In a sense, proposals such as the weaker-links hypothesis contribute to reconciling the findings from studies supporting both language-selective (e.g., Costa et al., 1999) and language-nonselective (e.g., Dijkstra & van Heuven, 2002) models, as they explain the relatively lower activation of lexical representations in the multilingual lexicon – particularly for the weaker languages – and therefore account for processing lags without necessarily invoking inhibitory mechanisms or ruling out cooperation – as opposed to competition – between translation equivalents (as in Costa et al., 1999).

Thus far, we have discussed several aspects of the multilingual lexicon that are directly related to the cohabitation of lexical items from different languages, both in on-line (real-time) language use and in the processes of lexical incorporation that often rely on prior knowledge to consolidate memory traces for new form-meaning pairings. The following section will introduce the literature that focuses on L3/L*n* lexis from a purely acquisitional perspective, which implies considering learner-external factors – situational contexts, linguistic and educational environments/backgrounds and so on – as well as other learner-internal variables that have not yet been the focus of this chapter; for example, motivation, self-monitoring and metalinguistic awareness, among others.

3.3 Lexical Acquisition in a Third or Further Language

The perceptual saliency of words in connected speech over other elements; for example, word and sentence structure, makes lexical items an obvious window into differences and similarities across languages, particularly – and most relevantly for our discussion – in the context of a speaker who is exposed to a language that is (at least partially) unknown to her. This fact, to which we will return in further chapters (particularly in Section 4.3.3.1 in Chapter 4), was noted in early work on bi-/multilingualism (e.g., Weinreich, 1953) and explains why much of the research that has focused on the role of previous languages in L3/L*n* acquisition has considered vocabulary somewhat independently of grammar (morphosyntax) – if considering the latter at all. This section will provide an overview of the topics that have been considered in the study of vocabulary acquisition in sequential multilingualism, which has been dominated by research on learners in formal (instructed) contexts. A terminological word of caution is in order before we proceed. As a general rule, these authors have not made a distinction between transfer and CLE in the sense that we established in Section 1.4 in Chapter 1 and – when the distinction matters – to which we adhere throughout the book. In fact, and perhaps as an inherited term from 1950s behaviorist psychology (which discussed the *transfer of skills* in several learning contexts extensively), *transfer* is pervasively used in the literature to refer to episodic and systematic cases of crosslinguistic influence alike. Note, however, that occasional instances of nontargetlike word production, particularly when not adapted to the target language (that is, when using the source language's original phonology and morphology), are most likely examples of what Hall and Ecke (2003:72) called *performance crosslinguistic influence*; that is, "the production of non-target language items that are in competition with existing target language entries." Of course, the most obvious candidates for this type of nontargetlike production are translation equivalents, which seem to be the default case in the literature into which we are about to delve. Irrespective of the level at which crosslinguistic influence is taking place, the following studies provide important insights into the relative influence that different previous languages have in the acquisition and use of a third or further language, suggesting that this influence might indeed be constrained by the adoption of different roles by each language or group of languages.

Frequently cited as one of the most important early treatments of multilingualism, the work by Vildomec (1963) provides analyses of phenomena that have become commonplace knowledge in the field. One example of this is his observation that the presence of nontarget words in L3/L*n* speech has some systematicity to its sourcing, in that function words are more commonly borrowed from an L2 (that is, another nonnative language) than they are from the speaker's native language. This finding has been replicated in much if not most of the literature since then, including Stedje's (1977) study of L1 Finnish L2 Swedish L3 German speakers. In her study, Stedje found that L2 Swedish function words were often inserted into L3 speech, which she attributed partially to typological similarity between Swedish and German. However, note that, as typological similarity and nonnativeness (L2 status) are confounded here, it is difficult to say which of the factors could underlie the effect. Williams and Hammarberg (1998: 303) cited a personal communication with Stedje that sheds some light in this regard, as a second group of L1 Swedish–L2 English–L3 German speakers was also tested. Function words in this group of learners, when nontargetlike, seemed to come predominantly from L2 English. While Williams and Hammarberg (1998) viewed this fact as tipping the balance in favor of L2 status, the close typological similarity between Swedish, English and German means that this case is perhaps less informative than would be an ideal comparison with, say, an L1 Swedish–L2 Finnish–L3 German group. In other words, it would be necessary to operationalize and articulate the effect of typological similarity theoretically in order to determine whether Swedish would still be the predominant source of influence on German in the presence of English.

Much of the current literature on L3/L*n* vocabulary acquisition refers back to two seminal studies. The first is Ringbom's (1987) research on Swedish-speaking Finns as L3 English learners (see also Jarvis, 1998, 2002; Odlin & Jarvis, 2004; Sjöholm, 1976, 1979, for other studies within the same population). The second is the aforementioned longitudinal case study by Williams and Hammarberg (1998), following the progress in L3 Swedish of the first author, an L1 English–L2 German sequential bilingual. The relevance and impact of these studies (together with much subsequent work by the authors, see Ringbom, 2007, and Hammarberg, 2009, respectively, for overviews) rests on the fact that they were among the first systematic attempts to define a variable set to quantify and model the role of previously acquired languages in L3/L*n* acquisition, at least with regard to the lexical domain. Let us now discuss these and other related studies.

Ringbom (1987) reported on a large-scale study based on a battery of English entrance tests employed during the 1970s and 80s at the English Department at Åbo Akademi, the Swedish-speaking university in Finland. These represented over a decade of data from L1 Finnish–L2 English and L1 Swedish–L2 Finnish–L3 English learners, the latter group being the most common profile at Åbo Akademi. While Ringbom (1987) did not consider now-relevant variables and concepts in L3/L*n* acquisition explicitly, the data are invaluable, both in number and in kind, for the study of sequential multilingualism. The overall picture shows a clear advantage of the L1 Swedish participants, which Ringbom attributed to the similarity between Swedish and English enhancing the acquisition of the latter as a target language by native speakers of the former. Note – and this is something to bear in mind in anticipation of our discussion of current morphosyntactic models in Chapter 4 – that Ringbom considered native-language influence and typological similarity to be conspiring factors. In fact, very much in line with the general assumptions made at the time, typological/structural similarity is regarded implicitly as being subordinate to L1 status/nativeness. In other words, what Ringbom suggested was that L1 influence would be greater and more positive, the more closely related the L1 and the L2/L3 were. The emphasis on facilitation over inhibition is explicit and deliberate in the book, perhaps as a reaction to the focus on *negative transfer* that some studies had inherited from the field of psychology in the previous decades (e.g., Postman, 1962). The proverbial other side of the coin is thus ignored: The advantage of Swedish-speaking Finns over their peers is attributed exclusively to the facilitative role of their L1, rather than to the combined effects of Swedish-induced facilitation in that group and Finnish-induced nonfacilitation in the other.

L1 Swed
L2 Finn
L3 Eng

One of Ringbom's (1987) most important contributions was his proposal of a typology of crosslinguistic influence, in particular of the type he called overt – that is, following from consciously perceived similarities between the source and target languages. He identified two categories. The first consists of lexical transfer, in which Ringbom included

(i)   loan translations or calques (such as *child wagon* instead of *pram*, from the Swedish *barnvagn*),

(ii)   semantic extensions (such as 'He bit his *language*,' from the Finnish *kieli*, meaning both *tongue* and *language*), and

(iii) [partially false] cognates (such as *fabric* instead of *factory*, from the Swedish *fabrik*; 'The *hound* is the best friend of man,' from the Swedish *hund*, meaning *dog* in all contexts).

The second category consists of borrowings of nontarget items and their insertion in L2/L3 discourse. These include

(i)   unmodified insertions (for example, 'I was *pigg* after the shower,' from the Swedish *pigg*, meaning *refreshed*), called "complete language shifts" by Ringbom, in which the nontarget item is used phonologically and morphologically intact with regard to the source, and

(ii)   hybrids, blends and relexifications, in which the inserted item under-goes some adaptation to the target phonological or morphological system (for example, 'I'm tired in the morning, but in the evening I feel *piggy* '). This last distinction – and all of Ringbom's typology, by and large – has been taken up in later studies of L3/L*n* vocabulary acquisition.

While further work by the same author (e.g., Ringbom, 2001, 2007; Ringbom & Jarvis, 2009) continued to explore the role of crosslinguistic similarity, dissociating it more clearly from variables related to order of acquisition, the 1987 book was not the only early study to propose a deterministic role of typological similarity in L3/L*n* vocabulary acquisition. Around the same time, an article by Singleton (1987) reported on data from a case study investigating the oral production of an L1 English learner of L*n* French, who had previously acquired some knowledge of Irish Gaelic, Latin and Spanish. Across several conversations with native speakers of French, the learner consistently showed influence from Spanish, particularly at the lexical level. Similarly to Ringbom (1987), Singleton was careful to distinguish between cases in which the produced forms were somewhat adapted to the specific constraints of French morphology and phonotactics – which he saw as true instances of transfer – and those in which the Spanish form seemed to have been produced intact, which he associated more directly with codeswitching. However, his discussion of the learner's use of the (seeming) Spanish *es que* ([ɛs ke], 'is that') instead of the target French *c'est que* ([sɛ kə], '(it) is that') suggests that the correlation between morpho-phonologically adapted borrowings and representational transfer is far from straightforward.

In another study with French as a target L3, Dewaele (1998) analyzed the production of 31 Dutch native speakers who were speakers of English and French as their second and third languages, although in different orders for different groups (L2 French, n=32; L3 French, n=7). Dewaele focused on these speakers' *lexical inventions*, a concept akin to what Ringbom (1987) called hybrids or adapted language switches. These were essentially non-target lexemes adapted to the target morphology/phonology (for example, **règer* [rɛʒe], presumably from the Dutch *regeren*, 'to govern,' when targeting the French *gouvernent*, '[they] govern'). Dewaele (1998) found that these lexical inventions were based on English significantly more often for those speakers who had this language as their L2 when compared to the L1 Dutch–L2 French speakers, whose lexical inventions were sourced predominantly from Dutch. In terms of the factors behind the quantity and quality (source) of CLE, Dewaele argued that more formal contexts seemed to correlate with a greater number of lexical inventions, perhaps because the learners were less proficient in these registers, and that formal similarity between the target language's lexicon and that of prior languages was a key predictor of the source of influence (see also Ringbom, 1986; Singleton & Little, 1991, for similar arguments in earlier research).

Williams and Hammarberg (1998) presented a detailed analysis of two years' worth of conversations in Swedish between the authors, beginning in the year that Sarah Williams arrived in Sweden. Besides spontaneous conversations, the data also contained semiguided interviews and a fair amount of elicited production, mainly from narratives. The main goal of the study was to determine the relative contribution of S. Williams's L1 (English) and highly proficient L2 (German) in the acquisition of L3 Swedish. While these data have been examined in the context of other linguistic domains (see Hammarberg & Hammarberg, 1993, for an analysis of phonological aspects) and certainly more in-depth in further work by Björn Hammarberg (see Hammarberg, 2009, for an overview), the original study was particularly focused on what the authors called *unadapted language switches*, which correspond to complete language shifts in Ringbom's (1987) typology and to codeswitches in Singleton (1987). A consideration of these phenomena in S. Williams's speech led to the observation that insertions of this type were most frequently German words, and that English lexical items were rarely produced in this way. Instead, English made frequent appearances to comment on, clarify and self-monitor utterances, as well as to request assistance from the interlocutor. These facts were interpreted by Williams and Hammarberg (1998) as indicating that the background languages adopted different and complementary roles in L3 acquisition: While the L1 played an *instrumental* role, the L2 had a *supplier* role, becoming the default source of transfer/CLE in contexts in which the underspecification of the target form triggered the production of a nontarget translation equivalent or some kind of approximation in meaning. Whether these roles can indeed be generalized to background languages in terms of order of acquisition independent of other factors, such as typological proximity, which had been highlighted by previous studies, is something that cannot be fully disentangled in Williams and Hammarberg's data. A considerable amount of subsequent (and current) work on vocabulary acquisition in L3/L*n* has been dedicated to answering this question, as we will see below.

Since the instrumental and the supplier role are fundamentally distinct, Williams and Hammarberg assumed that different factors might underlie the assignment of one or another function to the speaker's background languages. Thus, an instrumental role is likely to be assigned to languages that both speakers have in common because *instrumental* interactions are fundamentally destined to negotiate meaning and to comment on production; thus, they need to be understood by the interlocutor (see Hammarberg, 2006, for a more fine-grained articulation of these factors). The *supplier* role, in this account, is due to variables that are internal to the learner, such as recency of activation, typological similarity, proficiency (in the L3 and in prior languages) and L2 status, the latter referring to the shared status of the L3 and the L2(s) as nonnative languages.[8] Bardel and Lindqvist (2007) investigated the interaction of these variables in the L3 Italian of an L1 Swedish speaker who was also variably proficient in English, French, and Spanish. They discovered that lexical insertions, which they called codeswitches in line with Hammarberg and colleagues' terminology, were mainly sourced from Spanish, and that certain attempts at word building were based on French. It is interesting that Spanish was neither the most proficient nor the most recently activated of the speaker's L2s, which suggests that these factors are secondary to typological similarity and L2 status in constraining lexical crosslinguistic influence in L3/L*n* acquisition. Bardel and Lindqvist proposed the interaction of proficiency, typology and L2 status, whereby the *least* proficient L2 has the greatest chance of influencing the L3, provided that it is also typologically similar (see De Angelis & Selinker, 2001, for similar results). The fact that French lexical roots were most commonly used in the speaker's attempts to guess targetlike, morphologically complex (for example, derived) words can perhaps be explained by the nature of these processes and by the fact that the speaker was a linguist who worked with French. Since these are, for the most part, explicit and consciously monitored efforts, it seems reasonable to think that the speaker would have sought to build on knowledge that was most readily accessible to her in this manner.

Language production in the case studies of six learners of L3 French analyzed by Lindqvist (2009) suggested that the typological similarity factor may extend beyond nonnative status. These learners, who had English, Spanish, Swedish and Irish Gaelic in different combinations as their native and nonnative languages, all showed influences that came predominantly from Spanish – where available – or English, which were the typologically closest languages to French in their respective cases. In Williams and Hammarberg's (1998) terms, Spanish and English took on the *supplier* role for these learners, whereas Swedish and English, which were shared with the researcher, were most often used in an *instrumental* role. By contrast, Lindqvist and Falk (2014) argued for a stronger role of L2 status in a study of 11 L1 German–L2 English–L3 Swedish learners, some of whom also had some knowledge of French. An analysis of these learners' production revealed that 85% of their function words showed influence from English, their strongest L2, whereas transfer/CLE was more balanced in the case of content words, with up to 67% being traceable to L1 German. Lindqvist and Falk attributed this mismatch to claimed differences in memory storage between the two types of words, an issue to which we will return in Section 4.2.2 in Chapter 4. What is important for the present discussion is that sole reliance on typological similarity between the L3 and the background languages would predict a greater amount of lexical transfer/CLE from German for these learners, which was not the case in at least half of the analyzed instances. Similarly, even within the L2s, English was clearly preferred over French as a source of function words, which Lindqvist and Falk conceded may have been an effect of typological similarity – although proficiency and recency of activation, two of the factors discussed originally by Williams and Hammarberg (1998), were also aligned with English for these learners.

A similar, albeit not as clear cut, distribution of roles was also reported by Falk and Lindqvist (2018), who examined the L3 Swedish production of four L1 German speakers whose L2 was English. Note that this group is particularly relevant because it addresses the confound that we highlighted in our discussion of Williams and Hammarberg (1998) directly. As it is the mirror image of S. Williams's profile – who, as you may recall, was an L1 English–L2 German speaker – a combined look at the data should shed some light upon the question of whether German took on the supplier role for Williams because it was her L2 or because typological similarity is arguably greater between Swedish and German than it is between Swedish and English.[9] The results presented by Falk and Lindqvist (2018) are interpreted as partially in conflict with Williams and Hammarberg's (1998) model. On one hand, and with some exceptions that might be attributed to methodological factors, the instrumental role seemed to be adopted by English, the language that the interviewers and informants had in common. This is in line with the communicative/common ground factor proposed in the original model. As for the supplier role, this was not exclusively assigned to the L2 (English), as previous studies (e.g., Hammarberg, 2006; Williams & Hammarberg, 1998) would have suggested. Instead, the four learners showed influence from both their L1 and various L2s – English, as well as Spanish or French, when available – in unadapted switches and lexical insertions of different kinds. Taken together, these results suggest that unmonitored or implicit CLE – the type that unadapted switches most likely reflect – is not as predictable from the original factors proposed in Williams and Hammarberg's model, and that complex interactions of variables are seemingly in place for different types of learners (Falk & Lindqvist, 2018).

It is worth noting that not all research of transfer/CLE in L3/L*n* vocabulary acquisition has focused on quantifying and classifying the relative contribution of previously acquired languages. Another line of enquiry, most notably pursued by Jarvis and colleagues, is concerned with the scope and impact of *conceptual transfer* (see, e.g., Jarvis, 2016; Jarvis et al., 2013, for reviews). This construct is related to Slobin's (1991) *thinking for speaking* theory and, in part, to Levelt's (1989) *micro-planning* at the stage of utterance conceptualization. In other words, conceptualizing involves selecting, encoding and assembling a number of conceptual features in order to semantically "build" a certain event that is expressed through language-specific lexical items and syntactic structures. Importantly, different languages focus on – and therefore verbally encode – different aspects of the same reality. A good example is the classification of languages as verb-framed and satellite-framed, depending on whether they encode the manner and the path of motion events together in the verb (verb-framed languages) or separately combine a verb – for manner – and a particle – for path (satellite-framed languages). The contrast between Spanish and English is useful to illustrate this. While Spanish, a verb-framed language, uses verbs such as *subir* ('go up') or *entrar* ('go in') in which manner and path of motion are encoded jointly, English – as can already be gleaned from our glosses – tends to verbalize these two aspects separately, as in *go down, roll up, run through* and so on. A considerable body of literature has been dedicated to determining the extent to which these automatized, language-specific ways of conceptualizing can and do indeed transfer into newly acquired languages. While much of this research has focused on L2 acquisition (e.g., Alonso Alonso, Cadierno, & Jarvis, 2016; Bylund & Jarvis, 2011; Munnich & Landau, 2010; Schmiedtová, von Stutterheim, & Carroll, 2011), some of it also applies to the L3/Ln context (see Jarvis, 2016, for review).

When considered together, the studies that we have reviewed in this section – as well as those we will discuss in the next – foreshadow the complex issue of the selection of the transfer source in L3/Ln acquisition, in which several previously acquired languages are available in principle, which will take center stage from Chapter 4 onwards. While we will not yet go into detail, it is apparent from an overview of the literature on lexical L3/Ln acquisition that several factors seem to conspire in the creation of different dynamics favoring crosslinguistic influence to occur from one previous language or another. With regard to the most implicit/automatic instances of crosslinguistic influence, those exemplified by what Hammarberg and others call 'unadapted language switches,' internal factors such as nonnative/L2 status and (perceived) typological proximity, have received the most attention and support from the empirical evidence we have accumulated thus far. As we will see in Chapter 4, different variations of (some of) these factors are at the heart of the debate regarding the source(s) of transfer in L3/Ln morphosyntax.

Before we move in this direction, however, there is one more domain worth considering. Some of the research that we discussed in Section 3.2 above (the lexicon from a psycholinguistic perspective), and particularly research on lexical access, has stressed the importance and relative autonomy of sublexical levels of representation, such as phonology and orthography (recall, e.g., Costa et al., 1999; Xia & Andrews, 2015). The following section will introduce an under-studied but rapidly rising subarea of L3/Ln research, namely the study of phonological acquisition in sequential multilingualism. In the case of phonology, somewhat different from the psycholinguistic study of lexical processing reviewed in Section 3.2, and progressing toward the more developed distinction in multilingual morphosyntax we will discuss in subsequent chapters, we see the emergence of a research program/tradition that delineates strictly between bilingualism on one hand and multilingualism on the other.

3.4 Phonology in L3/Ln Acquisition

In parallel to the recent interest in the acquisition of L3/Ln morphosyntax, there has been a surge of research into phonology in sequential multilingualism, which is now considered a nascent subfield in its own right (Cabrelli Amaro &

Wrembel, 2016; for reviews, see Cabrelli Amaro, 2012; Wrembel, 2015; for state-of-the-science research, see contributions in Wrembel & Cabrelli Amaro, 2016). As was the case with its counterpart in morphosyntax, the field developed partly from studies in the acquisition of L2/foreign-language phonology when it became apparent that considering L2 and L3/Ln acquisition separately was not only methodologically prudent but was also theoretically relevant. While there are notable precedents in recognizing the complexity of multilingual phonology as distinct from regular L2 phonology (e.g., Chamot, 1973; Llisterri & Poch-Olivé, 1987; Rivers, 1979; Singh & Carroll, 1979), specific and robust interest was not revived until the 1990s (e.g., Hammarberg & Hammarberg, 1993; Williams & Hammarberg, 1998).

The field has inherited, perhaps inevitably, the limitations or asymmetries in scope that are also typical of studies in L2 phonological acquisition (Cabrelli Amaro & Wrembel, 2016). The majority of currently available data has focused on production by L3 learners and/or perception of that production (for example, foreign accentedness; see Cabrelli Amaro, 2017b; Hammarberg & Hammarberg, 2005; Kamiyama, 2007; Lloyd-Smith, Gyllstad, & Kupisch, 2017; Onishi, 2016; Wrembel, 2012ab, among others). Prosodic features, such as stress or intonation, have not received as much attention as have well-known segmental features such as voice onset time (VOT; e.g., Llama & López-Morelos, 2016; Tremblay, 2007; Wunder, 2010), although there are some exceptions (see Cabrelli Amaro, 2017b; Gut, 2010; Louriz, 2007; Wrembel, 2009).

On the subject of vowels (e.g., Cabrelli Amaro, 2017b; Kopečková, 2015; Lechner & Kohlberger, 2014; Missaglia, 2010, among others), most of the research has focused on how vowel production in multilinguals reflects the multidirectionality of crosslinguistic influence within the phonological system. Sypiańska (2016) studied two groups of L1 Polish speakers living in Denmark. The bilingual group consisted of 10 L1 Polish–L2 Danish speakers, whereas the second, larger multilingual group had English as an L3 in addition to L1 Polish and L2 Danish. Compared to native-speaker baselines obtained from spontaneous speech, the vowels of Sypiańska's bilingual and multilingual participants showed influence from various sources (for example, L2 Danish vowels were articulated further back in both groups, possibly as a result of crosslinguistic influence from Polish), including L1 Polish vowels that differed – in particular, they were fronter and higher – both from the monolingual baseline and between bilingual and multilingual speakers. This last finding is particularly important because it exemplifies the way in which the multilingual system is subject to change with each additional language, even if previous language experience is shared by a bilingual and a multilingual group. Interestingly, L3 English vowels were targetlike, which Sypiańska attributed to combined L1-L2 influence rather than to an absence of crosslinguistic influence. Given that L2 Danish vowels retract in both groups, the author assumed that only L1 Polish, and not L3 English, had an influence on the vowel system of the L2. This does not mean that regressive transfer did not obtain: As we have said, L1 Polish vowels were affected regressively by L2 and L3 phonology.

In fact, regressive transfer effects, to which we will return briefly in Chapter 6, have also been studied in L3/Ln phonology. Cabrelli Amaro (2017b) examined the phonological perception and production skills of 23 English–Spanish bilinguals (with different orders of acquisition) who were learners of L3 Brazilian Portuguese (BP). Word-final vowel reduction, present in English and BP but absent in Spanish, was examined in the participants' perception (via a forced-choice preference task) and production (via a delayed repetition task) of the participants' L3 BP as well as in L1/L2 Spanish – the latter only for those participants who showed evidence of having already acquired the property in BP. The rationale of the study was the following: Given that acquiring the property in L3 BP can influence the phonological systems of the L1 and the L2, which was the first empirical question, which one will it affect the most? This question is of course pointless in the case of English, which already has vowel reduction in unstressed word-final position. In the case of L1/L2 Spanish, which retains full vowels even in this context, the consequences of acquiring the contrast in the L3 are not as clear. Attempts at answering this question, already addressed in previous work by the author (e.g., Cabrelli Amaro & Rothman, 2010), had led to the Phonological Permeability Hypothesis (PPH), according to which early acquired phonological systems (L1s or child L2s) are more resistant – that is, less permeable – than are late-acquired systems (adult L2/Ln) to the regressive influence of an L3/Ln. Cabrelli Amaro's (2017b) results were mixed in this regard: While she did not find significant differences between the groups in terms of perception, Spanish production differed at least in some aspects from native-speaker controls in the L2 Spanish group only. While the absence of a clear effect in comprehension weakens an interpretation in terms of these learners' phonological representations being affected, it seems clear that at least some aspects of production are more stable in systems that are acquired early.

Part of the research into L3/Ln phonological acquisition has shared the related field of L3/Ln morphosyntax's focus on the preconditions and selection of transfer sources, and has even considered the very models put forward to account for L3/L*n* morphosyntactic transfer that are detailed in Chapter 4 and which are the constant focus in the remainder of this book (e.g., Kopečková, 2014; Lloyd-Smith et al., 2017; Onishi, 2016; Sypiańska, 2016; Wrembel, 2012b). While some of the earlier studies pointed to a dominant influence of the L1 (e.g., García Lecumberri & Gallardo del Puerto, 2003; see also comments in Ringbom, 1987), more recent, controlled studies using mirror-image groups have allowed researchers to disentangle variables that are also prominent in theories of morphosyntactic transfer, such as order of acquisition and (perceived) typological proximity. Llama, Cardoso and Collins (2010), for example, examined the VOT of voiceless stops in the L3 Spanish of two groups of bilinguals with the same background languages (French and English) but with different orders of acquisition: One of the groups was L1 English–L2 French and the other L1 French–L2 English. Llama et al. found that the Spanish VOTs of their participants resembled that of their L2, irrespective of whether this was English or Spanish for either group. Kamiyama (2007), Tremblay (2007) and Wrembel (2010) all presented similar results across different phonological properties that are seemingly in support of L2-default influence on L3 phonology.

A number of confounds complicate these findings, however. The first is that, in the three studies just mentioned, only one L3 group was examined, which effectively confounds the order of acquisition with any other variables that are language-dependent (such as typological similarity, as discussed in Section 3.3). In such a situation, as we argued in our discussion of Williams and Hammarberg (1998) above, it is essentially impossible to determine whether the L2 effects observed are a result of L2 status or have more to do with similarity between the second and third languages for that combination in particular. In fact, two further studies by Wrembel (2012a, 2012b) reported on data that were able to shed some light on the confound present in Wrembel (2010), in which the (L2) German influence on the L3 English of Polish native speakers was originally interpreted as indicating a prominent role of the L2. The participants in the 2012 studies were L1 Polish speakers who had French (2012b) or English (2012a) as their L2, and who were acquiring English and French, respectively, as their L3s. Across both studies, Polish was the most notable influence on these speakers' accents in their third languages, although English also had a considerable impact on L3 French in Wrembel's (2012a) work, which severely compromises an account of these results in terms of L2 status.

Llama et al.'s (2010) study used mirror-image groups and could thus potentially disentangle the typology and L2 status variables. At least two methodological aspects of the study should be addressed before suggesting which factor conditioned phonological crosslinguistic influence most prominently. The first is that the comparison between L2 and L1 production was conducted employing published VOT ranges instead of by testing L1 production in the same speakers. In the absence of this information, it is possible that the participants' L1s had changed as a byproduct of L2 acquisition, displaying somewhat hybrid values in between monolingual norms of the L1 and the L2. The second methodological question relates to L3 proficiency: Because these learners were tested at intermediate stages of proficiency – or at least well past initial exposure to Spanish – it is extremely difficult to ascertain whether the observed VOTs are indeed L2-like as a result of direct crosslinguistic influence from that language, or if they result from gradual modifications of originally different transferred values (see Cabrelli Amaro, 2012, for a more detailed critique). This discussion connects the dots among several questions we have introduced in previous chapters/sections nicely – recall the multi-competence view of an ever-changing linguistic system in Section 2.1.3 in Chapter 2, or the monolingual bias we discussed in Section 3.1 above, and some relevant methodological issues we will address in Chapter 5, such as the importance of mirror-image groups and testing the L1 and the L2, as well as the L3.

Overall, the study of phonological acquisition in L3/L*n* contributes important insights into the variables that condition and restrict linguistic transfer in sequential multilingualism, but the field has specific concerns that do not necessarily run parallel to the study of L3/L*n* morphosyntax. In fact, it may very well be the case that these two domains are only loosely interrelated in terms of the factors that motivate transfer versus CLE – a crucial distinction in morphosyntax (see Chapter 4 onwards) that has been less strongly considered in the study of phonology – being distinct in each. As Cabrelli Amaro (2013a; see also Cabrelli Amaro & Wrembel, 2016) argued, it is important that the field expands to test different language combinations and different target languages, which have been mostly limited to Indo-European languages at present. Only in this way will we be able to compare the selection of the transfer source in phonology and morphosyntax, and to ascertain whether the insights from these two related subareas of L3/L*n* acquisition research are indeed complementary or have less to say about one another with regard to linguistic transfer than one might expect. Another path forward would be to test both domains of grammar in a single study, which has been done recently by Llama (2017) and Cabrelli Amaro, Pichan, Rothman, and Serratrice (2018). Such studies can shed the most direct light on comparability across the two modules of grammar.

3.5   Taking Stock

Through the discussions in this chapter, one can appreciate the role that multi-lingualism has played in the development of psycholinguistic theories over time, and in our understanding of the complexity entailed in linguistic, particularly lexical, processing, selection, competition and more. We can also begin to appreciate a recurrent theme in the decades-long progression of specific psycholinguistic questions: What is the role of previous experience in shaping subsequent processes, and how can this question be asked in terms of language? Multilingualism affords a natural laboratory that is unprecedented in this regard. To truly understand the way a system works, it is fair to assume that it has to be taxed sufficiently to reveal its dynamics. Are two languages sufficient to fully tax the system, or can more than two (at least three) begin to unlock secrets we did not even ponder a few decades ago?

Despite the fact that true multilingualism – when researchers have chosen to differentiate bilinguals from bona fide multilinguals – does not feature as prominently in lexical processing studies on the whole, when it has, it has provided invaluable insights into shaping theories moving forward. It might very well be the case that, for some questions, topics, issues and debates in lexical processing, differentiating between bilingualism and multilingualism does not matter; that is, what is true of one will be true of the other. We actually find this doubtful, not least on the coattails of studies that have explored potential differences and that have often found some. It stands to reason that more matters, particularly if one driving force for behavioral cognitive and linguistic effects of bi-/multilingualism relates, at least in part, to competition. Simply put, if competition mechanisms (such as activation and suppression) result in changes/differences in bilinguals, then it is reasonable to assume that when shared across more languages – or subsystems – in a single mind, this would increase the competition and be a primary contributor to a continuum of differences among various types of nonmonolinguals. Thus, we expect to see increasing differentiation of bilinguals from true multilinguals in the processing literature over the coming years. If it turns out that being multilingual does not matter, as we suspect it will not for certain aspects and questions then, at a minimum, we will know this on sound empirical grounds as opposed to making an educated assumption.

The recurrent theme of attempting to model and understand the influence of previous experience is increasingly obvious in the L3/L*n* fields of lexical acquisition and phonology that were reviewed in this chapter. In fact, the influence of previous experience is largely understood almost exclusively in linguistic terms in both of these domains. As we saw, there is a healthy tradition of examining and questioning the role that previous linguistic experience – grammatical competence in one's native L1 and/or other subsequently acquired languages L2(s) – plays in L3/L*n* lexical acquisition. Although it is admittedly a small field, it has been an active one for several decades. As we will see, it would be fair to say that the specific interest in L3/L*n* lexis, and the idea of examining L3/L*n* separately from L2 acquisition, originated with this research, and proposals concerning the different influences of previous languages on the L3/L*n* lexicon form the basis of the theories to which we will shift our focus in the remaining chapters. L3 phonology is a fledgling field in its own right, and it is not surprising that it shares a preoccupation with the recurrent theme that we have been discussing. In recent years, it has attempted to apply to phonology, with some success, theories proposed to capture the selection of multilingual transfer sources in morphosyntax. However, such attempts have also made it clear, at least to some researchers, that the near future for L3/L*n* phonology will include the creation of bespoke theories more conducive to the realities of phonology proper.

We are now well equipped to turn toward the main focus of the book, L3/L*n* morphosyntax, with which the next chapter commences. Unsurprisingly, our recurrent theme will take center stage there. Ultimately, we are interested in understanding everything there is to know about how bilinguals acquire more languages over time; that is, from start to finish. However, we are specifically preoccupied with understanding the beginning as best we can. Just as the integrity of any building is only as strong as its foundations precisely because each floor, as the whole is erected, rests on the stability the foundation provides, developmental theories of multilingualism are beholden to the accuracy of descriptions of the initial stages, in order to be able to model transitional trajectories meaningfully from that point. To the extent that previous linguistic knowledge matters, it is crucial to understand what influences L3/L*n* and why, in order to have the best chance of being successful in the field's collective quest to crack the proverbial code and to reveal how multilingual acquisition and processing unfold.

Notes

1. 'Language-independent' refers here, simultaneously, to independence from a particular language subsystem and to independence from the linguistic system altogether: In this sense, conceptual representations occupy a different place within cognition, which explains why both (linguistic) semantics and conceptual-experiential cognitive

function can be affected independently by lesions, pathology or the temporal disconti-
nuation of normal function (Paradis, 2004). This does not mean, however, that no
interaction exists between the two levels such that one may modify the nature of the
other. Concepts, for example, are often constrained linguistically and respond to
language-specific bundlings of otherwise entirely conceptual (nonlinguistic) features.
Once formed, these concepts are accessible and operative beyond their lexical-
semantic encoding and may be retrieved for tasks involving nonverbal activity.

2. Although most of the studies presented in this section focused on bilinguals, we
believe that most of their findings can be applied to multilingualism without controversy (e.g., de Bot, 2004). As pointed out by de Bot and Jaensch (2015), and
parallel to much of the literature on the acquisition of nonnative morphosyntax,
researchers have often ignored the distinction between bi- and multilingualism,
which makes it highly likely that some of the findings reviewed here are, in fact,
from multilinguals.

3. As Duyck, van Assche, Drieghe, and Hartsuiker (2007) rightly pointed out,
Caramazza and Brones (1979) were not targeting the question of language selectivity, nor did they interpret the cognate effect in those terms: Their study focused on
evaluating serial versus parallel orthography-to-phonology conversion in reading.
However, it is frequently cited as the first study showing clear cognate facilitation
effects and should be acknowledged here as such.

4. This position is also in line with a more profound questioning of the idea that lexical
selection, even in monolingual contexts, is resolved via competition and differential
levels of activation; for a critique, see Mahon, Costa, Peterson, Vargas, and Caramazza
(2007).

5. As Grainger and Frenck-Mestre (1998) and de Groot (2010) have pointed out, this is
not necessarily true of the lexical decision task, as lexicality (word status) can already
be evaluated at lower levels of representation – lemma or lexeme – and can even be
guessed sublexically on the basis of phonotactic constraints. Because translation
equivalents are presumably connected at the lexical level, as well as through their
links to largely overlapping sets of conceptual features, we might be missing half of
the picture if the LDT is indeed unreliable in terms of tapping into higher representational levels.

6. In the mechanics of Interactive Activation (IA) models (e.g., Collins & Loftus, 1975;
McClelland & Rumelhart, 1981), of which the BIA+ is a prime example, the lexicon
is conceptualized as an interconnected network across which activation (which
enters the system from conceptual or perceptual input) spreads unevenly and is
regulated by excitatory and inhibitory links between the nodes. For
a representation to become active – and for it to have the potential to be selected –
a threshold of activation has to be reached. All representations are assumed to have at
least some level of resting activation (that is, the activation level at which they
remain once an episode of excitation or inhibition has expired). Weighting is adjusted
in the system by lowering or increasing threshold/resting activation levels selectively, which allows for certain representations to be activated more (or less) easily.

7. We will not be discussing those control mechanisms here although they are by far one
of the most extensively studied aspects of multilingual cognition and are a central

piece of the puzzle that connects the bi-/multilingual experience with well-documented differences in nonlinguistic behavior between monolingual and multilingual individuals (see Bialystok, 2009, 2016, for review). For an overview of the topic and different extensions and revisions of its most influential theory, Green's (1986, 1998) Inhibitory Control (IC) model, we refer the reader to Abutalebi and Green (2007, 2016), Green and Abutalebi (2013), Green and Wei (2014) and Meuter (2005), as well as to the many references therein.

8. Other authors have also argued for this factor, which De Angelis (2005) called *association of foreignness*, often in conjunction or interaction with (perceived) typological similarity (e.g., De Angelis, 2007; Hammarberg, 2009).

9. It should be said here that Björn Hammarberg himself had already reported on a case study focusing on a learner who had the mirror-image profile of that in the original study: L1 German–L2 English–L3 Swedish. His results seemed to confirm the initial intuition of the model, since English (now the L2) also played the instrumental role here, as well as the supplier role. While the results are less clear cut than were those in the original 1998 study (there are also numerous instances of German acting as the supplier language), these seemed to lend support to the L2 status variable as deterministic for transfer sourcing, above and beyond the effects of other factors assumed to play a role, such as typological similarity, recency of activation, and the like.

4 Transfer in Multilingual Morphosyntax

4.0 General Introduction

The aim of this chapter is to offer the reader a panoramic yet comprehensive view of the theoretical issues and models that have attracted the most attention within generative approaches to L3/L*n* morphosyntactic acquisition, with a particular emphasis on how transfer selection from previously acquired languages is hypothesized to apply. To the best of our ability, all models will be treated in an equal fashion. This does not mean that the description of each model will have or could possibly have the same level of detail, for justifiable reasons. To begin, models have appeared at different times, which correlates with more or less temporal opportunity to have been tested and to have gathered a critical mass of evidence. Moreover, not all models have had an equal amount of support from the published literature – a detailed analysis of which is the focus of Chapter 5 – and/or have had the same level of updating by their authors over time. Finally, we are naturally inclined toward a particular model for obvious reasons. Having direct knowledge of the history and epistemology of this model in particular, we are in a unique if not privileged position to offer greater depth of coverage of the Typological Primacy Model (TPM: Rothman, 2010, 2015, see Section 4.3 below). Accordingly, there will be an independent section for the TPM, as well as commentary in the sections related to the other models from our vantage point; in other words, with the TPM in mind. Since the section on the TPM is by far the longest and requires some information found in the explanations of the other models to be contextualized properly, it makes the most sense to us for it to be the final model presented. Thus, when referring to specific arguments from the TPM throughout this chapter before it is presented in full detail in Section 4.3, we refer the reader to the precise subsections within Section 4.3 in which the relative arguments are explained in detail and are justified.

Notwithstanding the above caveats, each model, as we understand it, will be fully explained. To help the reader to grasp the fundamentals of each theory, we

[handwritten: generative approaches are based on innate lang acquist device when kids develop the]

offer a detailed explanation of its tenets and highlight the seminal work – inclusive of one exemplary study for each model – that best illustrates, or in some cases originally motivated, the theory at hand. We walk the reader through studies that have provided further evidence for some of the given theories over time, indicating how later datasets contributed to the reshaping or refinement of the original/preceding proposal when applicable.

Throughout the book, we have made reference to the fact that we would focus on generative approaches to L3/L*n* morphosyntax. However, since such theories and this book primarily address transfer, one could easily ask why or even how this is indeed a "generative" approach/treatment. After all, and although conceived of differently in other paradigms, transfer is not a concept owned by generative grammar; quite the contrary, in fact. What makes the subfield of L3/L*n* morphosyntax into which we are about to delve generative is at least threefold, all of which will be reinforced throughout the next chapters: (a) as is the case in generative approaches to L2 acquisition (GenSLA), the formalities of generative grammar are taken as the point of departure, inclusive of the formal description of the properties being examined and the learning tasks that follow from them; (b) the provenance of the foregrounding ideas, for example the specificity of how we understand differences between transfer (representation) and CLE,[1] the distinction between acquisition and learning, imports from GenSLA theorizing, and so on; and (c) the methods used and what they are accepted to show – of course, methods do not belong to any single paradigm, but their utility and interpretations do reflect paradigmatic preferences.

This book is definitely not just for generative researchers (nor do we ignore relevant work done in complementary paradigms), not least because we are focusing on a domain that does not require acceptance or always great knowledge of generative theory and, when it does, we fill in the blanks. This book is thus for all who are inquisitive about the dynamic nature of how previous linguistic representations influence subsequent language acquisition. If our theoretical swing is not to your liking, that is of course perfectly fine. Whatever you take transfer to be – although we might fervently disagree – can be better understood, we hope, by the evidence and discussion we are about to present.

Obviously, all theories discussed here are predicated on evidence from empirical data; there is seeming support for all positions. However, as mentioned above, given that theories/models have emerged at different times as critical masses of data become available, it is not always the case that specific data sets support only one model or even continue to support models (unambiguously) as they were first claimed to do (and did). Thus, after presenting this emerging field as completely as possible and highlighting where the aforementioned caveats may apply in this chapter, we will return to a more detailed analysis of a large amount (all, to the extent possible) of available data from the relevant published – or otherwise publicly available – literature in aggregate in the following chapter.

4.1   Transfer in L2 Acquisition

Toward the end of the twentieth century, much of the theoretical and experimental work in GenSLA examined the question of what role, if any, previous linguistic knowledge played in the acquisition of a second language (L2). Two logical possibilities with regard to transfer at the onset of L2 acquisition were initially explored, namely that it originated from the L1, or that there was no transfer at all (e.g., Bley-Vroman, 1989, 2009; Epstein, Flynn, & Martohardjono, 1996; Flynn, 1987; Odlin, 1989; White, 2003b). As the then nascent field of GenSLA began to expand in the 1990s, the notion of transfer became more nuanced. Although, logically speaking, whenever one referred to previous specific linguistic transfer, it implicitly (and rightly) would come from the L1, various proposals of partial transfer were offered from the 1990s onwards. The Minimal Trees Hypothesis (MT; Vainikka & Young-Scholten, 1996) essentially claimed that only L1 lexical categories (such as verb phrase [VP] and noun phrase [NP]) were transferred to the initial state of L2, but not functional categories (such as aspect phrase [AspP], mood phrase [MoodP] and complementizer phrase [CP]). L2 learner behavior was thus predicted to show evidence of L1 influence, yet in a restricted cohort of properties, essentially those that related to lexical categories.

Similar theories, such as Valueless Features (VF; Eubank, 1994), also claimed transfer to be partial. The proposal was that syntactic features from the L1 were indeed transferred into the initial state of L2; however, the values of these features were left inert (unspecified). Details aside, a then-current generative theory postulated that grammatical features were parameterized in binary terms; that is, a feature was strong or weak (+ or −). For example, a strong (+) wh-feature in English required the movement of wh-words to a fronted position, whereas the weak (−) wh-feature of Chinese explained why wh-words remained in situ. If features are transferred, yet the value (strong versus weak) is inert, the prediction is that wh-movement will be variable, regardless of what the value of that feature in a particular L1 is since, being inert, it will vacillate until it is fixed for the L2 target during the course of

Majority of linguistics believe in full transfer.

development (if this is possible at all; see Beck, 1998, for a developmental corollary theory to Eubank's 1994 initial-state hypothesis according to which features are argued never to be valued). Thus, it was argued that the grammatical concept that the formalized feature represented would be transferred, but its L1 distribution – which is related to the valuation of the feature – would not be.

It is probably fair to say that pondering the exact nature of L1 transfer has gone out of focus in GenSLA, given that no new positions on the topic have been advanced since the 1990s. Perhaps this is more reflective of the stalemate among the three logical possibilities that have already been offered, namely no representational transfer at all (Epstein et al., 1996), full transfer of the L1 grammar (Schwartz & Sprouse, 1996) and selective or partial transfer of the L1 (Eubank, 1994; Vainikka & Young-Scholten, 1996). Conversely, it might be indicative of the fact that changes in current generative linguistic theory make it more difficult to schematize what partial transfer would be in formal terms. For example, VF might very well capture and thus explain the spirit of observable variation at the beginning of L2 acquisition, which is clearly not random. Nevertheless, since concepts such as binary feature values such as strong/weak have fallen out of favor in mainstream generative theory, this makes it difficult to capture the essence of VF, for example, in contemporary terms.

As Schwartz and Sprouse (2000) discuss, observations based on sound (empirical) data and the data themselves are never truly susceptible to changes in theoretical descriptive apparatus; however, as real changes take place, it can become difficult to capture previous insights formally to the extent that they are dependent on a then-current theory. We would venture to guess that the main reason that L1 transfer is not currently the hot topic it was in the 1980s and 1990s within GenSLA relates to the critical mass of studies over the previous decades that clearly show evidence of L1 transfer above and beyond that which partial transfer approaches advocated. At present, few scholars advocate a *no transfer* position. It is not the case that all GenSLA scholars maintain that full transfer is completely accurate, although it might be fair to say that it is the majority view.

It is interesting to point out that all formalized transfer theories within GenSLA propose systematic transfer that is highly predictable. From the vantage point of testability (theoretical falsifiability), this is a very good thing. By systematic, we mean that each theory envisions what it proposes as a default mechanism that is pervasive across the system. In the case of no transfer positions, the systematicity rests in the fact that, as a default, no representations are transferred at all. In the case of full transfer, which envisions the initial state of the L2 as a copy of the final-state grammar of the L1, it is clear to see systematicity in that the default is the complete transfer of all syntactic representations. Even though partial transfer hypotheses advocate selectivity in what is transferred from the L1, they are highly systematic in what they claim is transferred: only X – lexical categories (MT), lexical and functional categories with an inert feature value (VF) – and always when X is able to transfer to all environments in the L2. Unlike the case of L3/L*n* acquisition, as we will see, there are, at least at present, no formalized theories in GenSLA advocating for property-by-property transfer from the L1 to the L2 (presumably guided by facilitation; transfer only when it helps), potentially because of the difficulty arisng from such a position, given the requirement that theories must make predictions a priori. When would transfer occur if it is indeed property-by-property? Why would it happen in some cases and not others? If it truly is property-by-property, then why do we observe instances of nonfacilitative transfer (in other words, what predicts when it will happen?), which no one denies abound in L2 acquisition (and, as we will see, in L3/L*n*)? Even if one can offer answers to some of these queries that make logical sense – and there certainly are some isolated answers that would – all must be answered adequately to approximate a tenable property-by-property position; that is, making clear, testable predictions. Obviously, it would not be sufficient for a theory to be able to explain an outcome; it must first be able to predict the outcome it can explain. This is not to suggest that property-by-property transfer is impossible, or that it is not actually what happens. There is, in fact, some evidence to suggest that arguing for this might be on the right track. To be theoretically tenable, however, such a position will need to render itself testable and thus explanatorily as opposed to descriptively accurate over time.

As we proposed in the first chapter, modeling transfer (its source, its timing, and its impact on development) is inevitably more complicated in L3/L*n* acquisition, since more factors come into play – the most important and obvious being that the number of potential sources increases. In other words, while only two macro scenarios are relevant in the L2 context – either there is no transfer, or there is at least some (full or partial) transfer, logically coming from the L1 – in L3/L*n* acquisition there are at least four a priori logical possibilities:

    (i)   there is no transfer,

    (ii) transfer comes exclusively from the L1,

    (iii) transfer comes exclusively from the L2, and

    (iv) transfer may come from either language, or from both at the same time (see, e.g., González Alonso & Rothman, 2017a).

Starting in the early 2000s, some of these scenarios have been formalized into models or hypotheses attempting to describe how transfer selection operates in sequential multilingualism. To date, no studies have adopted the claim in (i), namely that there is no transfer from previously acquired languages. This is partly due to the aforementioned, ample evidence from all paradigms of SLA research showing L1 effects in L2 acquisition (e.g., Alonso Alonso, 2016; Foley & Flynn, 2013; Jarvis & Pavlenko, 2008; MacWhinney, 2005; Odlin, 1989, 2008, 2012; Schwartz & Sprouse, 1996); by extension, it is a fair assumption that this will also be the case in L3/Ln acquisition. In what follows, we describe the possible scenarios for transfer in L3/Ln acquisition and how they factor into specific formulations in current L3/Ln models.

4.2   Current L3/Ln Transfer Models

In this section, we describe the current models of morphosyntactic transfer in L3/Ln acquisition – or a logical position without a formalized model to date – by walking the reader through some relevant data sets that have been interpreted in favor of each approach. Each subsection also contains an in-depth review of an exemplary study, which we dissect, summarize and present to the reader in an exemplary box, followed by a detailed discussion. We then provide an overview of the methods and results of additional studies that are often cited in connection with the model at hand. One logical possibility, namely a no transfer position, will not have its own subsection, as mentioned above, due to the absence of theoretical and empirical work contemplating this scenario specifically for L3/Ln acquisition.

4.2.1   The Default L1 Transfer Scenario

The first logical possibility when examining transfer source selectivity in L3/Ln acquisition is that transfer will come exclusively from the L1. Both recent studies (Hermas, 2010, 2015) as well as earlier work (e.g., Jin, 2009; Lozano, 2003; Na Ranong & Leung, 2009) have suggested that the L1 might have a stronger effect on the L3; that is, that the learner's native language might be the default source of transfer. Researchers advocating for this scenario have not yet ventured a detailed explanation; in other words, the mechanisms explaining why this should be so have not been articulated. By analogy with the other default model, discussed in the following section, the main idea is that the cognitive status of the L1 would condition transfer selection, thus assigning it a privileged status. A possible account, which future studies are called to examine, is that seemingly supporting evidence for an L1 default scenario is essentially conflating two (frequently overlapping) factors: order of acquisition, whereby

[handwritten note: priori – Something that can be known without data]

the L1 is the first language to be acquired in chronological terms, and dominance, which relates to differences in competence, amount and type of use, and self-perceived ease when speaking a given language, among others. For most L3 learners who acquired their L2 during adulthood (the typical case of sequential multilingualism), the L1 tends to remain their dominant language. It might be the case that this dominant L1 is somehow more accessible for transfer selection (see Lloyd-Smith et al., 2017). It should be noted that, with the exception of Hermas (2010, 2015), most of the research pointing to an L1 default in morphosyntax predates many of the present models of transfer in L3/L*n* acquisition, which means that the data in these studies (and even Hermas's) could be equally explained by, or compatible with, the currently available formal models, in light of (now) relevant variables not considered at the time; for example, when the L1 is also the typologically most similar language to the L3. We will return to this issue in the following chapter.

To the extent that it may be modeled, the L1 default scenario is a strong hypothesis in that one can easily draw falsifiable predictions for any linguistic triad and any linguistic property that one decides to study. Take, for example, the case of an L1 English–L2 Korean learner of L3 Japanese. Should the L1 default hypothesis make the correct predictions, we should always see evidence of (L1) English transfer to L3 Japanese. Consequently, any indication of transfer from (L2) Korean for this specific learner would constitute counterevidence.

Very few studies claim an L1 default or privileged effect. Lozano's (2003) doctoral dissertation stands out as perhaps the first leading toward this as a potential conclusion. He had already suggested that it was possible to detect traces, in the advanced L3 Spanish of his participants, of what had been instances of transfer from L1 Greek at some point. In addition, pioneering work by Leung and colleagues also contributed some evidence suggesting that a predominant influence of the native language was a possibility worth examining. Na Ranong and Leung (2009) examined the L3 Chinese of 20 L1 Thai–L2 English learners, as well as the L2 Chinese of seven L1 English speakers. In addition to these two groups, Na Ranong and Leung tested 20 native controls. In their study, they examined the distribution of null objects, which are licensed in Chinese and Thai but disallowed in English. To test the participants' knowledge of null objects, the authors devised an off-line interpretation task with biclausal sentences that contained embedded null or overt objects. They administered the task in (L3) Chinese and (L1) Thai. After being presented with the sentences containing null objects, the participants were asked to choose among five possible answers that contained potential referents of these objects. Their results showed that the L3 learners interpreted null objects similarly in Chinese and Thai.

When comparing the responses of the L2 and the L3 group, however, the differences were not statistically significant. While this compromises the L1 transfer account, Na Ranong and Leung (2009) argued that the small-scale nature of the study might be able to account for this lack of difference, particularly considering that there were only seven L1 English–L2 Chinese speakers in the study. They conducted an individual analysis of the responses and suggested that the L1 seemed to have a facilitative effect in their L3 group. Their conclusions were aligned with those of Hermas (2010) in that they also claimed that the data pointed to a privileged status of the L1 for morphosyntactic transfer in L3/Ln acquisition. However, Na Ranong and Leung (2009) also highlighted that, for their specific language triad, the L1 and the L3 happened to be typologically related, a factor that, according to the authors, might have played an important role in the selection of the transfer source. As a result, it could equally be the case that this study lends support to the TPM (Rothman, 2010, 2015). To be fair, as this study predated the TPM, the authors could not have considered the model although, as acknowledged, they did mention the confound between L1 status and typological proximity.

Jin's (2009) work is similar to that of Na Ranong and Leung (2009) in two ways. First, it also examined null objects, and second, Chinese was one of the languages in the triad. This study targeted the L3 Norwegian of L1 Chinese–L2 English speakers. Null objects are licensed only in certain contexts in Norwegian, whereas, as you may recall from our discussion above, English disallows them completely and Chinese allows for them in all contexts. Unlike Na Ranong and Leung (2009), this design sidesteps confounding overall typological proximity of the languages between the L1 and the L3, shifting it instead to the L2 and L3. Jin tested 40 L1 Chinese–L2 English learners of L3 Norwegian in a grammaticality judgment task (GJT) with sentence correction. The author tested this domain in the participants' L2 (English) and predicted that accuracy rates for the English and Norwegian tasks would be similar due to facilitative transfer from English to Norwegian. A 72% accuracy rate in the English task was taken to be indicative of targetlike acquisition of L2 English with regard to the property under investigation. Accuracy in the L3 (34.5%) was reported broken down by proficiency level, with 21.4% for the beginner group, 25%, for the lower intermediate and 57.1% for the higher intermediate group. Jin interpreted these results as evidence against the initial prediction, since transfer from L2 English was not obvious in the L3 of these participants. The author attributed this to the privileged status of the L1 and argued that these data constituted evidence against proposals favoring a predominant role of the L2 and typological similarity between the L3 and previously acquired languages.

[margin handwritten notes: L1 Chinese / L2 Eng / L3 Norway]

Box 4.1 Exemplary study for a default L1 transfer scenario (Hermas, 2010)

Hermas (2010)

Citation: Hermas A. (2010) Language acquisition as computational resetting: Verb movement in L3 initial state. *International Journal of Multilingualism* 7(4): 202–224.

L3	English
Previously acquired languages	Moroccan Arabic (L1), French (L2)
Linguistic domain examined	Verb movement
Participants	Group 1 (n=20): L3 learners of English, L1 Arabic, L2 French
	Group 2 (n=25): Native speakers of French
	Group 3 (n=25): Native speakers of English
Proficiency in the L3	Beginner
Task	Acceptability judgment task (AJT)
	Preference task (PT)

Example AJT: Hermas (2010: 363)	**Example PT: Hermas (2010: 363)**
Lucy plays not chess with her sister	1a) Kamal smokes not cigarettes
	1b) Kamal does not smoke cigarettes
a. 'Completely acceptable'	a. 'Sentence A is better than B'
b. 'It may be acceptable'	b. 'Sentence B is better than A'
c. 'It may be unacceptable'	c. 'Sentence A and B are
d. 'Completely unacceptable'	equally acceptable'

Results

Table 4.1 *Accuracy rates (%) by structure and grammaticality in AJT (adapted from Hermas, 2010: 352)*

Structure	Grammaticality	Group A L2	Group FR	Group A L3	Group EN
Adverb	Target Ok	86.61	94	81.94	94
	Target *	46.11	75.11	17.5	84.66
	Total	67.36	84.55	49.72	89.33
Negation	Target Ok	90.55	92	82.77	94
	Target *	81.11	90.66	63.61	95.11
	Total	85.53	91.33	73.19	94.55

L1 Arabic
L2 French
L3 Eng

4.2.1.1   An Exemplar Study: Hermas (2010)

One of the first studies to commit explicitly to the idea of a possible L1 default scenario was that of Hermas (2010); see Box 4.1 for details.

Hermas (2010) examined the L3 English knowledge of L1 Moroccan Arabic–L2 French speakers with a specific focus on verb movement. English is a language that lacks verb movement, whereas both French and Arabic display this property. Why, then, did Hermas choose a linguistic domain that behaved similarly in the L1 and the L2? The answer is that the specific target of the study was actually a more fine-grained property, in which a three-way distinction among these languages can indeed be found, namely the distribution of frequency adverbs. While adverbs tend to follow the verb in both Arabic and French as a result of verb movement (unlike English – compare (1) to (3)), frequency adverbs in Arabic also have the option of preceding the verb without altering the meaning of the sentence (irrespective of discourse context, apparently; see Fassi Fehri, 1993). This flexibility is not true of French, in which frequency adverbs obligatorily follow the verb.

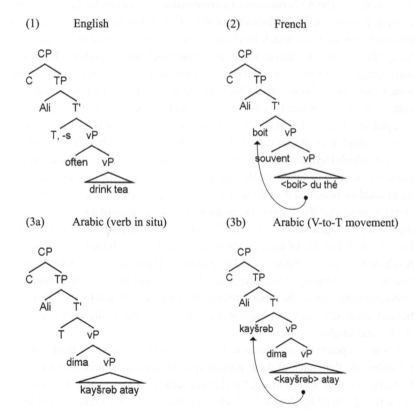

(1)   English

(2)   French

(3a)   Arabic (verb in situ)

(3b)   Arabic (V-to-T movement)

All sentences in the non-English trees are equivalent to the English sentence in (1). As shown in (1) and (2), English does not require V-to-T movement, whereas such movement is required in French, giving rise to obligatory differences in surface word order for adverbs. Arabic allows optionally for V-to-T movement, as seen by comparing (3a) and (3b), and thus allows adverbs to be placed in the English and French positions.

Overall, this means that French and English pattern differently, in that English requires frequency adverbs to be in the preverbal position. The experimental design in Hermas (2010) capitalizes on the fact that Arabic allows for both configurations.

In order to test these structures, an acceptability judgment task (AJT) and a preference task (PT) were employed. Each was administered in both the L2 (French) and the L3 (English) to determine whether each participant had a targetlike distribution in the L2 – see Chapter 5 for potential implications of (not) doing so. The AJT consisted of a combination of grammatical and ungrammatical experimental and distractor items. The participants were given four different options from which to choose ('completely acceptable,' 'it may be acceptable,' 'it may be unacceptable' and 'completely unacceptable'). In the PT, participants were shown 66 sentence pairs and were given three options from which they could choose one of the three responses provided ('Sentence A is better than B,' 'Sentence B is better than A' and 'Sentence A and B are equally acceptable'). Each task was coded for accuracy. The results of both tasks showed learners displaying Arabic-like behavior with regard to their judgments of English, which Hermas took to be evidence that representations in the L3 initial grammar were transferred predominantly from the L1. This is in turn was interpreted to mean that the L1 had a special status in terms of transfer selection. Hermas concluded that these data constituted evidence against a proposal giving the L2 a privileged status (see the L2 Status Factor hypothesis below), since French, the L2 of the bilingual participants, was not transferred. Similarly, the results were also interpreted as evidence against a proposal arguing for holistic – that is, at the language-to-language level overall, not property-by-property – structural similarity as the most deterministic factor (as argued by the TPM, see below), because French and English are holistically structurally closer than are Arabic and English.

Up to this point, the data seem to favor the privileged status of the L1 in the L3 initial interlanguage of these participants. However, as pointed out further by Hermas (2010: 354) himself, "46.11% accuracy [. . .] reveals that L2 French is itself influenced by Arabic," which suggests that the L2 French of (at least some, and perhaps many or all to some extent) the L3 learners had not overcome L1 transfer during L2 acquisition in the first place. Thus, determining whether the apparent transfer in L3 English originated directly from the L1 or via the L2 is complicated, since it may be the case that we are actually seeing transfer from a (L2) French interlanguage grammar that is itself similar to Arabic in the relevant domain because the original L1→L2 transfer had not yet been overcome. Foreshadowing discussions in the next chapter slightly, this very possibility underscores the importance of testing the L3 property of inquiry in at least the L2 (ideally in all three languages, but, if time is truly against the researcher, it is fairer to assume competence in the L1, at least for this type of learner) and, when doing so, of applying inclusion criteria for the study whereby selected participants can show unambiguous L1/L2 distinctions for the specific domain of L3 inquiry. After all, to show potential L1 transfer because one's selected learners have essentially only one representation (or indeed an L2 representation that is still influenced by the L1) does little to address the important query at hand. In fact, it can inadvertently lead to the opposite of the researcher's actual goal; that is, obscure the dynamic nature of multilingual transfer further.

The data that Hermas (2010) offered are interesting, notwithstanding the above. Since the author was aware of which participants did and did not have L1 influence in their L2 French, the way to determine whether transfer came directly from Arabic or from Arabic through French would be to examine the accuracy scores in L3 English of only those participants whose French was targetlike. If their L3 English still seemed to be influenced by Arabic, this would have constituted more compelling evidence that, for these learners, transfer came directly from the L1.

4.2.2 The L2 Status Factor

The L2 Status Factor is a hypothesis (L2SF; Bardel & Falk, 2007, 2012; Bardel & Sánchez, 2017; Falk & Bardel, 2011; Falk et al., 2015) contending that the nonnative language (the L2) has a privileged status as the source of transfer in L3/Ln acquisition. In cognitive terms, this argumentation is based on the declarative/procedural distinction posited by Paradis (2009). The Declarative/Procedural Model proposes that the grammars of native and nonnative languages are typically subserved by different memory systems. Whereas L1 grammar(s) are stored in procedural memory, all lexicons (L1 and beyond), as well as grammar proper acquired after puberty, are stored in declarative memory. Bardel and Falk (2012) drew on this distinction to claim that linguistic transfer was thus more likely to occur between the grammar of the

L3 and those of other nonnative languages than it was between the L1 and the L3. The L2SF, as originally conceptualized in Bardel and Falk (2007), has high predictive validity, making it a strong hypothesis in terms of testability. Because it advocates a privileged role for the L2, evidence of L1 transfer – particularly if this is replicated consistently – in cases not predicted to be exceptions by updates to the model, compromises the explanatory adequacy of this strong proposal or, at least, the generalizability thereof.

Following the sharp increase in work on L3/Ln morphosyntactic acquisition over the last decade, and the ensuing proliferation of new datasets, the L2SF has been revised and updated. Recent formulations of the model (Bardel & Sánchez, 2017; Falk et al., 2015) have turned to the task of accommodating L3 contexts, which were not the original focus of the model yet do not necessarily fall outside of its remit. The most important of these situations are those in which the association of L1 and L2 grammatical knowledge with procedural and declarative memory, respectively, may not be straightforward due to the timing and/or the context of acquisition, both of the L3/Ln and of previously acquired languages. These include, most notably, simultaneous bilinguals acquiring their first nonnative language (yet still their third grammar, which means that the selection problem also applies here), as well as L3 learners with considerable metalinguistic knowledge of their L1. According to Falk et al. (2015), the latter context would imply that these learners have some amount of L1-specific declarative knowledge, which may weaken or even effectively neutralize L2 status, since this is based on native and nonnative languages' reliance on different memory systems. Bardel and Sánchez (2017) argued that, once both grammars have equal potential for influence, the selection of the transfer source is constrained heavily by aspects of cognitive function (such as attention control and working memory), which are subject to considerable individual difference. Since these cognitive mechanisms are assumed to be involved in the comparison of incoming L3 input to previously acquired linguistic knowledge, the selection of a nontargetlike representation for transfer is attributed to shortcomings in this respect, rather than to a mismatch between the default source grammar and the target L3.

Although the above modifications might well be on the right track, as the authors themselves rightly point out, individual differences in executive functions and working memory abound. Accordingly, to the extent that there is a bona fide relationship between these and transfer selection in the relevant cases, it is difficult to model, and thus potentially diminishes the predictive validity of the original proposal to a certain extent. While it is the case that executive functions and working memory can be measured independently and correlational analyses

Declarative/Procedural Model =
L1 grammars are in Procedural Memory
L2 grammars & Beyond are in Declarative Me

can then be performed to test the assertion, it is not the case that we have independent reliable measures to determine when two grammars do, in fact, have truly equal potential of influence (to the extent this could be operationalized uncontroversially), whereby cognitive functions should come into play to determine transfer selection. With regard to the claim that L1 metalinguistic knowledge should have an effect on transfer per se, as opposed to CLE, in our opinion, this does not seem to accord with the generally accepted idea in generative linguistics that explicit and implicit knowledge do not have an interface at the level of competence, although they can proverbially dialog in performance. Suggesting metalinguistic knowledge should matter, then, either means that the authors of the L2SF believe there is an interface between explicit knowledge and underlying grammatical constitution – and they would not be alone in this – or that they do not abide by the functional difference between transfer (representation) and CLE. As reviewed in Section 1.4 in Chapter 1, this distinction is important as it pertains to the granularity of that which is described and explained, as well as to a question of precision in terms of modeling.

Falk and Bardel (2011) examined the acquisition of object placement in L3 German by speakers of English and French. In this study, they implemented the mirror-image methodology, whereby the order of acquisition of previously acquired languages is crossed, yielding an L1 English–L2 French (n=22) and an L1 French–L2 English group (n=22) in this case, both of which had German as their L3. By investigating the acceptability of object pronouns in preverbal and postverbal positions, the source of transfer can be identified unambiguously because English and French behave differently in this regard. Whereas English essentially requires object pronouns to be placed postverbally, French requires them preverbally, while German allows both preverbal and postverbal object pronouns depending on the context. Due to the fact the object pronouns are allowed in different structural positions in English and French, the behavior of the two groups should be different according to the predictions that the L2SF makes. The L1 English–L2 French group should prefer preverbal objects in L3 German, and the L1 French–L2 English should prefer postverbal objects. The authors employed a GJT consisting of 60 target sentences with object pronouns in different positions. In the event that a second object was present in the sentence, such an object was always a full DP instead of a pronoun. In addition, the authors controlled for the vocabulary to ensure that all the participants knew the lexical items in the test to avoid possible noise effects from the lack of lexical knowledge.

The GJT was coded for accuracy, and the results were examined and compared for both groups (L2 English versus L3 French). The results showed that the group with English as the L2 preferred postverbal object pronouns, whereas the group with French as the L2 preferred preverbal object pronouns. Falk and Bardel (2011) interpreted these findings to suggest that the L2 had a privileged status irrespective of language combination (and holistic structural similarity).

Fessi (2013) embodies a more recent example of a study in which the L2 is claimed to have a privileged status in adult L3 acquisition. Fessi examined the acquisition of the past tense in L3 Spanish by native speakers of Tunisian Arabic who were L2 speakers of French. The author collected data from 30 university students and examined their written production and knowledge of the aspectual distinction between the preterite and the imperfect past tense. Fessi began with the hypothesis that, if the L2 (French for these learners) is transferred, the effect on the L3 will be facilitative. On the other hand, if Tunisian Arabic (the L1) was the main source of transfer, then we should see instances of nonfacilitation in the L3 (from Tunisian Arabic). After examining the written production of these learners closely, Fessi claimed that the L2 played a larger role in the acquisition of the preterite/imperfect distinction in L3 Spanish. However, the author also acknowledged that the L2 was confounded with the more structurally similar language, making it impossible to determine whether the trigger for transfer selection was L2 status or the typological relatedness between French and Spanish.

4.2.2.1 An Exemplar Study: Bardel and Falk (2007)

The L2SF was first proposed by Bardel and Falk in their 2007 study; thus, it seems fitting to highlight this study as the exemplar for the model; see Box 4.2 for details.

Bardel and Falk (2007) examined the acquisition of either Dutch or Swedish by nine speakers with many different languages as their L1s and L2s. They examined the placement of negation, specifically as it relates to the verb-second (V2) phenomenon. V2 word order requires the finite verb of a clause to be placed in second position. This means that, in the canonical case and barring special consideration, there is only one permissible constituent that can precede the verb. In many cases this is the subject, but it need not be. Since the verb must come in second position in V2 languages, this means that, when a constituent other than the subject is in the initial position, surface SVO word order is impossible. Germanic languages are notorious examples of V2 languages – except for English, which has limited historical V2 remnants such as in questions and

Box 4.2 Exemplary study for the L2 Status Factor (Bardel and Falk, 2007)

Bardel and Falk (2007)	
Citation: Bardel C. and Falk Y. (2007) The role of the second language in third language acquisition: The case of Germanic syntax. *Second Language Research* 23(4): 459–484.	
L3/Ln	Swedish or Dutch
Previously acquired languages	Albanian, Dutch, English, German, Italian, Swedish
Linguistic domain examined	V2 phenomenon and placement of negation
Participants	Group 1 (n=5): L3/Ln learners of Swedish Group 2 (n=4): L3/Ln learners of Dutch
Task	45-minute oral interview

Procedure
  a) Session A: Videotaping and audio recording of ten lessons of Swedish
  b) Session B: Recording of four "one-to-one" lessons of the third language
      The production of the five participants targeted in this data collection was
      transcribed in CHAT format (MacWhinney, 2000).

Results

Table 4.2 *Negation placement, data collection A and B (adapted from Bardel and Falk, 2007: 475 and 478)*

	Data collection A		Data collection B	
	L2= V2	L1 = V2	L2= V2	L1 = V2
Preverbal				
+them	3	9	0	12
−them	0	2	0	0
Total +/− them	3	11	0	12
Postverbal				
+them	6	1	36	5
−them	6	2	35	7
Total +/− them	12	3	71	11

obligatory word order with negative constructions (e.g., Westergaard, 2007). Some V2 languages are "better behaved" than are others, meaning that some have V2 ubiquitously – in matrix and subordinate clauses, as in Icelandic – whereas others only have it in main clauses, as in German, where embedded clauses are verb-final.

As a consequence of Swedish being a V2 language, negation is placed after the main finite verb in surface word order. This is due to the fact that negation remains above the VP in its base position, and the verb has moved to the C'-position to satisfy the requirements of the V2 rule, as in (4) and (5) below:

(4)　　　Swedish　　　　　(5)　　　English

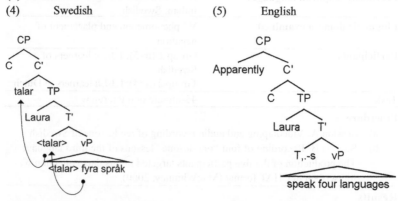

Sentence (4) is equivalent to the English sentence in (5). As seen in (4), Swedish verbs move to C' to satisfy the V2-requirement. In English, the verb in canonical sentences does not move to C', as in (5).

This is true for Dutch and German because they also need to satisfy the V2 requirement. As mentioned above, unlike German, Dutch and Swedish, English is not a V2 language; thus, sentential negation (the marker *not*) never occurs following the main finite verb, thereby making a sentence such as '*Laura speaks not Swedish' ungrammatical. Note that, although English does require V2 with negative adverbial constructions (for example 'Never had Lily believed she would win the lottery' versus '*Never Lily had believed that she would win the lottery'), this is different as it does not involve sentential negation. Unlike V2 languages, Albanian, Italian and Hungarian pattern like English with regard to the placement of negation.

There were two different data collection procedures. The first consisted of videotaping and audio recording ten lessons of Swedish. The production of the

Table 4.3 *The learners and their knowledge of V2 languages, data collection A (adapted from Bardel and Falk, 2007: 471)*

Learner	Sex	L1	L2	Target language
EN1	F	Dutch + V2	English	Swedish + V2
EN2	F	Dutch + V2	English	Swedish + V2
EN3	F	Dutch + V2	English	Swedish + V2
D/G1	F	English	German/Dutch + V2	Swedish + V2
D/G2	F	Hungarian	Dutch + V2	Swedish + V2

Table 4.4 *The learners and their knowledge of V2 languages, data collection B (adapted from Bardel and Falk, 2007: 462)*

Learner	Sex	L1	L2	Target language
EN4	F	Swedish + V2	English	Dutch + V2
EN5	F	Swedish + V2	English	Dutch + V2
D/G3	F	Italian	German/Dutch + V2	Swedish + V2
D/G4	F	Albanian	German + V2	Dutch + V2

five participants targeted in this data collection was transcribed in CHAT format (MacWhinney, 2000) to conduct the analysis of it. Table 4.3 contains the information about the five participants who took part in these classes.

The second data collection procedure consisted of recording one-to-one lessons. A total of four participants took part in this data collection procedure; their details are listed in Table 4.4.

The authors ensured that each participant had one V2 language and one non-V2 language as either their L1 or their L2. Two examples are participant *EN1* from the first data set, an L3 learner of Swedish (+V2) with L1 Dutch (+V2) and L2 English (non-V2), and participant *D/G4*, from the second data set, an L3 learner of Dutch (+V2) with L1 Albanian (non-V2) and L2 German (+V2). Bardel and Falk elicited the oral production of negative sentences because, as we have seen above, the placement of negation is strongly affected by the V2 property. They examined the oral data on an individual and group basis, and their findings showed that learners who had a V2 language as their L2 had a stronger advantage in acquiring either Dutch or Swedish (both V2) than did the learners who had a V2 language as their L1. These findings led to the proposal of the L2 Status Factor hypothesis for morphosyntax.

4.2.3   The Cumulative Enhancement Model

It should be acknowledged that the Cumulative Enhancement Model (CEM; Flynn et al., 2004) marks a shift in formal linguistic approaches to L3/L*n* acquisition that is not to be understated, particularly with regard to understanding the role of previous linguistic influence. A subfield of generative approaches to L3/L*n* acquisition of morphosyntax was already primed to emerge in the late 1990s and early 2000s, stemming principally from work that led to a doctoral dissertation. While of equal importance to the fostering of the modern L3/L*n* subfield of generative approaches to language acquisition, studies predating the CEM (e.g., Klein, 1995; Leung, 1998, 2001, 2002; Lozano, 2003) only began to ponder the question of whether or not L2 and L3 acquisition were one and the same and whether they must, therefore, be treated separately. Prior to 2004, however, studies examining L3/L*n* morphosyntax used models designed within and specifically for GenSLA. The work was largely comparative in nature between L2 and L3. From this basis, it became clear that the L2 and the L3 were sufficiently different environments (and that GenSLA theories could not be applied without modification), which led to the creation of the first truly bespoke model of L3/L*n* morphosyntactic development; the CEM was born.

The CEM has been highly influential in shaping the field since 2004. Even though they are competing positions, the L2SF and the TPM – the next L3/L*n* specific models to appear – are clearly inspired by the CEM. Many of the original insights of the CEM are echoed in all competing models of today, including the newest ones: the Linguistic Proximity Model (LPM, see Section 4.2.4; Westergaard, Mitrofanova, Mykhaylyk, & Rodina, 2017) and the Scalpel Model (see Section 4.3.5; Slabakova, 2017). The first most obvious insight, highlighted in the name of the CEM itself, is its claim that additional language learning has a cumulative effect, which means that previous linguistic experience in the form of grammatical knowledge matters, thus distinguishing between L2 and L3 acquisition. Before the CEM highlighted this, and indeed for too long after (perhaps even still) researchers did (do) not always consider potential differences between L2 and L3/L*n* learners.

Prior to the mid-2000s, so-called L2 groups in many – perhaps most – studies consisted of actual L2 learners and individuals with any number of previous bilingual competencies. That this might matter was simply not considered consciously, and no concrete evidence was supplied to suggest it does. L2 was effectively used as a synonymous, umbrella term for nonnative language. Thus, showing that grammatical development in L3 acquisition can be affected by not just the L1 resulted in two things: (a) the earnest starting point of the generative L3/L*n* subfield we have today, while (b) simultaneously highlighting an important oversight in how GenSLA research – and likely SLA studies in general – had been done previously. Although for some questions in GenSLA – for example, determining or questioning UG-accessibility itself – having mixed L2/L3 groups can matter less, there is no question that not discriminating between L2 and L3/L*n* in so many studies is likely one of the factors that contributed to the high incidence of variability and individual differences in L2 studies. This would then mean that some of the L2 variation is extraneous noise that could be reduced by heeding the implied warnings of L3 research.

The second insight, perhaps less obvious, that resonates in all other contemporary models is the argument that how previous linguistic knowledge alters the course of subsequent language acquisition is not random but is in fact highly restricted. In a sense, one could say that each existing model builds on both these important insights, as all embrace both, the first without reservation or further stipulation, while disagreeing with each other regarding the details of the second. In fact, it is this latter disagreement – and precisely what competing models claim the constraints for previous linguistic influence are – that differentiates them.

It is fair to say that, of all the three main models over the last decade – the CEM, the L2SF and the TPM – the CEM has changed the least. Although there have been some subsequent papers providing data and/or discussion that is claimed to support it further (e.g., Berkes & Flynn, 2012a), there has, to our knowledge, been no attempt to modify or clarify its original claims. Furthermore, there is nothing in the published record to suggest that the authors might feel some other researchers have misunderstood or inadvertently misapplied intended claims or predictions of the CEM. Conversely, as we have seen in Section 4.2.2 for the L2SF and will see in Section 4.3 for the TPM, the other models have been updated or articulated further on more than one occasion as more data that support and/or challenge them form critical masses over time. No theory should feel obliged to do so. To the extent that there is no need for refinement or clarification, any related discussion would be extraneous. Thus, we are working under the assumption that, since there is nothing to suggest otherwise, our interpretation that the CEM argues the L1, L2 or both can affect L3/L*n* acquisition, yet only when it is facilitative – to avoid redundancy – is correct. In other words, as described in virtually all the papers citing the CEM, it predicts transfer from any source as long as such transfer avoids nonfacilitation.

Nonetheless, we would like to acknowledge the possibility that, in the CEM authors' mind, *transfer* – at least as conceived of by the other models and in the ways that the papers citing the CEM have attributed to it – is not what we described in Section 1.4 in Chapter 1. This becomes particularly likely in consideration of Flynn's (1983, 1987) previous argumentation in GenSLA, where her early work in L2 acquisition is seminal. Flynn (1983, 1987) and Epstein et al. (1996) argued extensively for what is referred to in the literature as the *no transfer* at the initial state, yet *full access* to the UG position (see White, 2003b). In this light, it is interesting to note that, in the 2004 paper, the word *transfer* is used only once, and only refers to other (L2) models. As it concerns the CEM, the actual language used refers to enhancement without really specifying what that means: "Where appropriate, other languages known can *enhance* subsequent language acquisition. This claim contrasts with models that either implicitly or explicitly characterise subsequent language learning fundamentally in terms of a deficit model (e.g. negative *transfer*, and interference)" (Flynn et al. 2004: 5; emphasis our own). In follow-up work by Berkes and Flynn (2012), the term *transfer* is used much more frequently but does not refer unambiguously to the CEM itself. For example, on page 144, the term *transfer* is used several times with reference to the L2SF and the TPM – this being the section in which all three models and their contexts are discussed – but not with direct reference to the CEM. Alternatively, related to the CEM, it is stated "that language learning is cumulative, and it excludes redundancy in linguistic representation. One of the logical corollaries of such a hypothesis is that the accumulated linguistic knowledge necessarily enhances subsequent language learning" (Berkes & Flynn, 2012: 144). However, the above quote comes after the one below, embedded in the section that introduces the L3 models as just explained: "*Transfer* from the L1 to the L2 has been widely debated in second language research. L3 research picks up the thread and seeks to investigate the manner in which the specific languages known to the learner affect subsequent language learning" (Berkes & Flynn, 2012: 144; emphasis our own). Thus, it seems fair that the authors at least acknowledge that the CEM sits at the heart of the transfer source debate in L3/Ln and, when coupled with the fact that no one has ever been corrected by attributing the term *transfer* to the CEM, we feel justified in using the term in relation to the CEM.

It is also worth noting that the CEM does not only make predictions about the initial stages of L3 acquisition, mainly because it seems to predict transfer to occur when there is the need for it (incrementally on a property-by-property basis).[2] Thus, an L3 learner is not predicted to transfer a representation for, say, the syntax of negative quantifiers until she is exposed to relevant data in the L3 input. This specific exposure might take place after a considerable time of L3 contact overall, even if some exemplars of quantifiers (or any property) have been in the L3 input previously, they might not have been relevant (intaken) until later stages of L3 development.[3]

4.2.3.1 An Exemplar Study: Flynn, Foley and Vinnitskaya (2004)

As the CEM originally appeared in Flynn, Foley, and Vinnitskaya (2004), it seems particularly fitting to use it as the exemplar study (see Box 4.3).

Box 4.3 Exemplary study for the Cumulative Enhancement Model (Flynn et al., 2004)

Flynn, Foley, and Vinnitskaya (2004)	
Citation: Flynn S., Foley C. and Vinnitskaya I (2004) The cumulative enhancement model for language acquisition: Comparing adults' and children's patterns of development in first, second and third language acquisition. *International Journal of Multilingualism* 1(1): 3–16.	
L3/L*n*	English
Previously acquired languages	L1 Kazakh and L2 Russian
Linguistic domain examined	Restrictive relative clauses
Participants	Group 1 (n=33): L3 adult learners of English (divided across three different levels of proficiency) Group 2 (n=31): L3 child learners of English (divided into three groups)
Task	Task 1: Elicited imitation task
Procedure Elicited imitation task of three types of relative clauses in different positions (subject versus object head position; gap subject position versus gap object positions). In total, it yielded a total of 12 possible combinations. *Lexically headed, specified:* The lawyer who criticized the worker called the policeman. *Lexically headed, unspecified*: The person who criticized the engineer greeted the man. *Free relatives*: Whoever entered the office introduced the professor.	

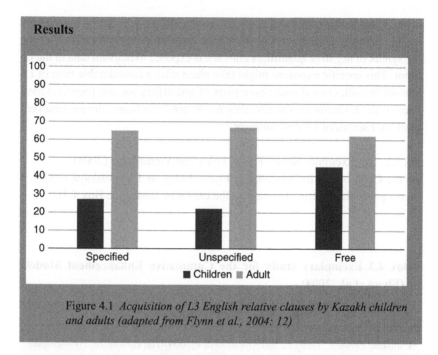

Figure 4.1 *Acquisition of L3 English relative clauses by Kazakh children and adults (adapted from Flynn et al., 2004: 12)*

The production of relative clauses by L1 Kazakh–L2 Russian learners of L3 English was the grammatical domain of focus. As there was no mirror-image control group, the main crux of the argument was in relation to a comparison between these L3 learners and L1 Japanese and L1 Spanish learners of L2 English, the former being L1 speakers of a head-final and the latter of a head-initial language. Both Russian and English behave similarly in that they are head-initial languages, whereas Kazakh is head-final. Compare the right-versus left-branching structure in (6) and (7), and the required movement implicit in the left-branching agglutinative language.

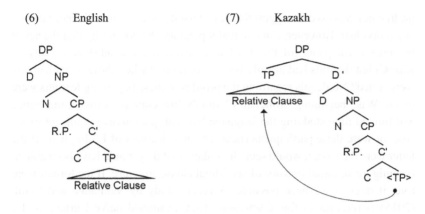

(6) English

(7) Kazakh

The Kazakh sentence in (7) is the equivalent of the English sentence in (6). In head-final languages, such as Kazakh, the relative clause moves to [Spec, DP] (see Özçelik 2016 for some issues and possible solutions).

Flynn et al.'s (2004) results showed that both groups (irrespective of age and proficiency) had targetlike production of restrictive relative clauses in English. Thus, the authors took these findings to be evidence that transfer selection in adult additive multilingualism took place if maximal facilitation could obtain as a result. Had it been the case that the L1 of the participants (Kazakh) had been transferred, nonfacilitation would have ensued.

Of course, hindsight provides the semblance of clarity. Therefore, to be fair, one can only judge any claims made by a study within its then-current context. The L2SF and the TPM did not exist in 2004, but it might be useful to see what their predictions would be to identify if maximal facilitation is the only or best explanation for why Russian was transferred instead of Kazakh. Since Russian was the L2 as well as the language offering facilitation, one cannot preclude that there is a default L2-effect; that is, that the data here could equally support the L2SF. It might be the case that the predictions of the TPM are also one and the same, if the parser would be inclined to take Russian to be more typologically proximal than Kazakh;[4] perhaps the fact that both Russian and English are head-initial languages might indicate this. Thus, it might be the case that the data cannot disentangle facilitation from L2 status from typological proximity.

A final question is whether or not what is noted is transfer (or however they conceived of facilitation from previous linguistic representation) at all. Recall that there was a range of L3 proficiency levels across the 33 subjects in the study's design. The fact that Russian was seen to be influential despite L3 proficiency was used to suggest that Kazakh did not have any influence at all on any individual. However, can one really preclude the possibility that the seven beginner participants (of the 33) had transferred the head-directionality of Kazakh but that this had already been reconfigured when these seven learners were tested? No details regarding the profiles of these beginning learners were given. Was "beginning proficiency" simply low communicative competence and limited time studying the language but with potentially significant exposure, or were these participants (near) ab initio learners of L3 English? If the latter were the case, it would seem less likely that they would have been able to reconfigure an initial transfer of head-final clause structure. If the former were true, it might have been possible. A recent study by VanPatten and Smith (2015) is relevant in this discussion. They examined naïve learners of L2 Japanese and showed how quickly head-directionality can be acquired by adult nonnative learners. Participants were provided with an input treatment in which they were flooded with Japanese SOV sentences and were subsequently tested on these sentences plus other head-final constructions (polar questions and embedded clauses). The results for the reaction times showed that some of these learners generalized head-final syntax across the board (for example, in embedded clauses to which they were never exposed) after being exposed to SOV main clause sentences in one grammatical treatment, suggesting that macro parameters such as head-directionality might be reconfigured after very limited exposure.

Follow-up work by Berkes and Flynn (2012a) examined the structural knowledge of relative clauses in L3 English by L1 Hungarian–L2 German speakers. German is a head-initial language, as are English and Hungarian; however, it is underlyingly SOV, as seen in its obligatory verb-final word order in embedded clauses. Thus, looking at word order within relative clauses and within this linguistic triad allowed the investigation of a property that behaves differently in the three languages under investigation. To test the prediction that transfer was only facilitative, the authors examined 42 L1 German–L2 English and 36 L1 Hungarian–L2 German–L3 English learners. The experimental task consisted of an elicited imitation task targeting three types of relative clauses (lexically headed and specified, lexically headed and unspecified, and free relative clauses).

The results were transcribed and coded for accuracy. Minor errors such as pronunciation errors or lexical errors were disregarded. Berkes and Flynn counted relative clauses produced in a targetlike manner as an accurate response. Their results showed significant differences for the L1 German–L2 English group regarding the production of free relatives and lexically headed

PM — Linguistic Proximity Model

relative clauses. They attributed these findings to influence from German. When they examined the production of relative clauses by the L3 group, performances were distinct (the significant difference disappeared). The authors took their results to be evidence that there was facilitation in L3 acquisition over what would have been nonfacilitation from L2 German to L3 English. They claimed that this was direct evidence against a proposal suggesting that the last learned language (or the L2 in this case) would have privileged status over the L1 (Hungarian for their learners). Their results could also be taken to show evidence against a proposal suggesting that the structurally closer language overall would be transferred. Thus, there seems to be evidence against the predictions of both the L2SF and the TPM, as German should have been transferred in the L3 group in both cases (albeit for different reasons), although Hungarian offered some facilitation here. However, since the TPM is concerned with describing the initial representation, one wonders whether learners who scored an average of 19.8 out of 50 – the cohort labeled low proficiency – were indeed close to ab initio L3 learners. If, in fact, this experiment indicated their initial representation (initial-stages transfer), these data would indeed constitute counterevidence to both the L2SF and the TPM.

4.2.4   The Linguistic Proximity Model

The Linguistic Proximity Model (LPM; Westergaard et al., 2017) shares some of its tenets with the CEM and the TPM. The LPM also claims that transfer selection is not restricted to either the L1 or L2. Nevertheless, as for the CEM and in disaccord with the TPM, there is no stipulation that transfer would have a single source (L1 or L2) for all properties at the initial stages, or elsewhere in development. It also shares the CEM's view regarding the completeness of transfer; transfer is not wholesale as in the TPM (see Section 4.3.1 for discussion) but is rather domain-by-domain as needed over the course of development. In common with the TPM is the view that structural proximity, not maximal facilitation per se as argued by the CEM, is deterministic for which language – the L1, the L2 or both – is chosen to transfer or otherwise influence the L3 process. However, unlike the TPM, the LPM allows for the possibility of both languages – apparently when relevant given comparative structural similarities – to show influence at the same time, following somewhat naturally from its a priori rejection of full representational transfer in the initial stages. In summary, the LPM argues that transfer is conditioned strongly (not necessarily restrictively) in L3/Ln acquisition, that influences happen on a property-by-property basis when necessary or relevant along the developmental L3 continuum, and that misanalysis can give rise to nonfacilitation.

It is prudent to highlight that the authors of the LPM likely have a different view of transfer from that which we explained in detail in Section 1.4 in Chapter 1: the model does not seem to make a distinction between *transfer* and *CLE*, at least not in practice. The LPM does not argue that the terminological distinction for which we advocated, whereby transfer relates to representational copying in a developing L3 interlanguage and CLE relate to bleeding over from the L1 or L2 grammars into L3 performance, is wrong per se (in this sense, the LPM is neutral in the available writing). As we understand it, the LPM is principally interested in capturing and describing L3 behavior across development that can be attributed to the dynamic nature of previous linguistic knowledge/experience/influence, whether or not this reflects transfer or CLE. However, something important is lost when the distinction between transfer and CLE is glossed over, particularly within the paradigm in which these models exist. Since the mid-1960s (Chomsky, 1965), generative approaches to language acquisition have operated under the assumption of a potential difference between competence and performance, and have sought actively, where possible, to ensure they are tapping into the former, not the latter. "We thus make a fundamental distinction between *competence* (the speaker-hearer's knowledge of his language) and *performance* (the actual use of language in concrete situations). Only under the idealization set forth in the preceding paragraph is performance a direct reflection of competence. In actual fact, it obviously could not directly reflect competence" (Chomsky, 1965: 4). The "idealization set forth in the preceding paragraph" above refers to that which is entailed as part and parcel of performance; that is, the increased complexity of variables that influence it, of "which the underlying competence of the speaker-hearer is only one" (Chomsky, 1965: 4). There should be no doubt that performance is important to describe and explain. The question is whether or not we seek to focus on one or the other – generative approaches have long focused on *competence*. If the LPM intends to maintain this classical distinction yet shift its focus to *performance* from a formal linguistic perspective, this should be welcomed. However, the LPM needs to clarify its position on this matter as opposed to others ascribing, as we are inclined to do, such value to it. This is important because it affects its status in relation to the other models, in particular the TPM, against which the LPM has sought to position itself.

If the LPM's focus is primarily on describing linguistic performance, then its neutral stance concerning the difference between transfer and CLE is justified, even if the terminological distinction we have applied is correct. This would mean that the LPM could in principle accept the general generative tenet that there is also a distinction between competence and performance; however, in a somewhat novel departure for the generative norm, it chooses to focus on the latter. It would also necessarily mean that its focus is simply different from that of the TPM. If they are targeting different things primarily, such that the LPM focuses on performance across development and the TPM on competence of initial-stages representations, then they are not truly comparable. Evidence in favor of one, in juxtaposition, will not always be relevant to invalidate the other. For example, if one shows evidence of influence unpredicted by the TPM but there is good reason to believe that this could be a performance effect (not tapping competence per se), it would simply not be relevant for TPM evaluation, yet it would remain highly relevant for the level in which the LPM is potentially most interested. The beauty of models such as the LPM is precisely their focus on L3 development at all stages, where performance variables are guaranteed to be dynamic. Understanding what constrains such variables to the best of our ability is also a step in the right direction toward the future of generative approaches to L3/L*n* acquisition.

Before we can move toward this future in which models such as the LPM lead the way to uncovering the dynamic nature of L3 development itself, the LPM (and similar models; see Section 4.2.5 for the Scalpel Model, where this applies equally) will need to undergo refinements to reveal its predictive validity. As discussed in Section 4.1 above, the goal of all theories, and thus their intrinsic value, is not solely to achieve descriptive coverage – what can be attributed to their claims when observed in data – but indeed to develop explanatory adequacy – what they can predict before data are collected and what thus ultimately justifies claims of attribution (see also Section 1.6 in Chapter 1). One advantage of all other models described so far – an L1 default effect, the L2SF and the CEM – as well as the TPM, is that they make robust predictions a priori. Accordingly, they are truly testable against one another. The predictions of the LPM, however, are elusive, particularly with regard to when nonfacilitation is expected. It is not sufficient to accept that nonfacilitation is possible, as this is essentially an acknowledgment of what the vast majority of L3/L*n* morphosyntactic transfer studies over the past decade or so have already shown (see Chapter 5 for a full discussion). "Non-facilitative influence occurs when learners misanalyze L3 input (and/or have not had sufficient L3 input), and mistakenly assume that a property is shared between the L3 and either or both of the previously acquired languages" (Westergaard et al., 2017: 671). Recall that the LPM claims that transfer/CLE is property-by-property and influenced by structural proximity throughout development. Under such a proverbially patient view, what mechanisms give rise to misanalysis? In fact, what one needs to know are the principles through which misanalysis can be predicted before it is observed in the data.

Until and unless the LPM provides a mechanism through which it can predict behavior beforehand and thus be meaningfully falsified, it cannot be vetted fairly in its own right or against the other models. This is a crucial step for researchers to be able to design studies testing the LPM moving forward. Compatibility of data is not itself evidence in favor of a particular position, nor is it the standard science tends to apply for theoretical evaluation. Given the general statement above, virtually all data sets showing nonfacilitation could be (made) compatible in principle, precisely because, as yet, nothing has been offered to determine what constrains misanalysis itself. Evidence from L3 data in the literature shows that misanalysis is not inevitable; thus, there must surely be something that future iterations of the LPM will argue constrains and thus predicts when it should and should not obtain.

Doing so is also necessary for another important step that relates to applying the LPM retroactively to the studies that predate it. In order for any new theory to be deemed viable, it needs to explain its present data and make predictions for future studies, as well as be able to cover and explain that which is already available in the literature. Articulating such predictions, therefore, will make the LPM not just testable going forward but also backward, to the extent that it can predict and explain existing data sets in the field.

To be fair, what we know of the LPM is only one year old at the time of writing this book; thus, the model has not had as many opportunities to make refinements in light of critiques, emerging data and the like as have the other models. The LPM was proposed in light of the data presented in Westergaard et al. (2017; see Mykhaylyk, Mitrofanova, Rodina, & Westergaard, 2015, for an earlier treatment of the same data). As the LPM is very fresh in the field, it cannot possibly have a confluence of studies designed specifically with it in mind or even including it juxtaposed against other studies. We now turn to Westergaard et al.'s data as the exemplar study for the LPM.

4.2.4.1 An Exemplar Study: Westergaard et al. (2017)

Westergaard et al. (2017) used a GJT with two word-order conditions (verb-second [V2] in Norwegian and subject-auxiliary inversion in English) to determine the source of transfer/CLE in a group of Norwegian–Russian bilinguals learning English as their L3 (see Box 4.4).

Russian and English pattern similarly in the sense that they are not V2 languages, whereas Norwegian is (see the tree diagrams for V2 movement in Section 4.3.2). With regard to the other property examined, both English and Norwegian require subject-auxiliary inversion in interrogatives, whereas Russian does not – compare (8–10).

Box 4.4 Exemplary study for the Linguistic Proximity Model (Westergaard et al., 2017)

Westergaard, Mitrofanova, Mykhaylyk, & Rodina (2017)

Citation: Westergaard M, Mitrofanova N, Mykhaylyk R, & Rodina, Y. (2017) Crosslinguistic influence in the acquisition of a third language: The Linguistic Proximity Model. *International Journal of Bilingualism 21*(6): 666–682.

L3/Ln	English
Previously acquired languages	L1 Norwegian, L1 Russian
Linguistic domain examined	Verb-second and subject-auxiliary inversion
Participants	Group 1 (n=22): 2L1 (Norwegian–Russian)
	Group 2 (n=46): L1 Norwegian
	Group 3 (n=31): L1 Russian
Task	Grammaticality judgment task

Examples

Condition A (Adv-V: a, *V-Adv: b)   Condition B (Aux-S: a, *S-Aux: b)

   a) Susan often eats sweets.   a) What will the little girl read?
   b) *Susan eats often sweets.   b) *What the little girl will read?

Results

Table 4.5 *Percentage of correct responses in all the conditions (adapted from Westergaard et al., 2017: 10).*

	Condition A		Condition B	
	Adv-V	*V-Adv	Aux-S	*S-Aux
L1 Nor	55	65	81	80
2L1 Nor–Rus	65	84	82	79
L1 Rus	83	85	67	78

(8)   Norwegian   (9)   Russian   (10)   English

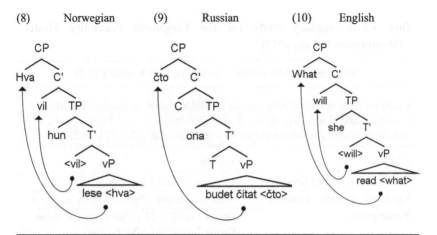

> The Norwegian (8) and Russian (9) sentences are the equivalent of the English sentence in (10). As seen in (8) and (10), there is subject-auxiliary inversion in Norwegian and English as a result of the auxiliary moving to C. This is not the case in Russian, as seen in (9).

The use of these three languages and the properties chosen for such a study allow Westergaard et al. (2017) to discriminate between possible nonfacilitation and facilitation from either Norwegian or Russian into L3 English. The collected data were from three groups of learners of English: One group of 2L1 Norwegian–Russian learners of L3 English and two groups of L2 learners of English (L1 Norwegian and L1 Russian). It is worth highlighting that the L3 learners in this study were not the typical ones reviewed in other studies thus far (adult sequential bilinguals acquiring an L3) but rather early childhood bilinguals (2L1 speakers) acquiring another language in adolescence.[5] Westergaard et al. included two conditions targeting declarative sentences with and without verb movement, and sentences with subject-auxiliary inversion with 12 items in each condition (half grammatical, half ungrammatical), as well as fillers in a one-to-one ratio.

The findings for the declarative condition showed that the group of bilinguals rejected significantly more sentences reflecting V2 in English than did the group of monolingual Norwegian learners of L2 English. The fact that the group of bilinguals performed better in this condition is taken to be evidence for an effect of Russian. Alternatively, all learners were equally accurate in the subject-auxiliary inversion condition, contrary to what was expected, namely that the bilinguals would be superior. Nevertheless, the juxtaposition of these two trends can be taken as evidence that both languages can play a role in the acquisition of L3 English. The fact that influence from both languages on L3 English can be seen is argued to be evidence in favor of a model of L3 acquisition that envisions transfer to occur on a property-by-property basis based on structural similarity at the specific property level. In fact, there seems to be an effect that is conferred by bilingualism (in Norwegian and Russian).

In accord with the discussion above, one might ask at what level the differences exposed sit, particularly since these bilinguals had been exposed to the L3 English for a significant time (that is, none were at what could be called the initial stages, in which the initial representations for the L3 inter-language could be tapped). Do they reflect transfer in the sense we have advocated herein, or are they performance variables that highlight the so-called bilingual efficiency effect in multilingualism, as advocated by others such as Cenoz (2003)?

4.2.5 The Scalpel Model

To be exhaustive, we now review the Scalpel Model (Slabakova, 2017) – the second of the two very recent proposals – for L3/Ln acquisition, although the structure of how we do so, in contrast to the coverage of other models thus far, is necessarily distinct. This is because, unlike the other models we reviewed, no specific study in which the author proposes the Scalpel Model to explain original data has been conducted, nor does the model otherwise derive natu-rally from a single or set of specific L3 studies done by the author that would lead to it being proposed. Instead, Slabakova (2017) proposed the model on a more epistemological level, offering insights into how L3/Ln development might be hypothesized to work by bringing together variables – some of which had not been factored into existing models previously – that are argued to be deterministic for language acquisition in general. She highlighted how, on balance, such variables could have distinct weights and set unique paths in multilingual acquisition. She appealed to data from various studies to justify the set of hypotheses offered, which we will highlight in what follows. Thus, no exemplar study will be reviewed, unlike in previous sections, simply because there is not yet one to consider.

The novel claim of the Scalpel Model is that there are several factors that affect L3/Ln transfer and which couple together to justify the proposal that it should occur property-by-property. The name of the model originates from the author likening the process to the precision of a surgeon's scalpel:

> This view of L3A[quisition] argues that the activated grammatical possibi-lities of the L1-plus-L2 combined grammar act with a scalpel-like precision, rather than as a blunt object, to extract the enhancing, or facilitative, options

of L1 or L2 parameter values. However, the scalpel can be blunted or shunted or slanted by additional factors pertaining to the relevant properties, such as processing complexity, misleading input, and construction frequency in the target L3.   (Slabakova, 2017: 655)

The general idea is that a bilingual mind acquiring yet an additional language is well prepared to execute the L3/L*n* task quite precisely. Using either the L1 or L2 when more useful would indeed allow for more precision, but the evidence base we have in L3/L*n* transfer studies shows that a lack of razorlike precision is not at all infrequent. As can be seen in the above quote, Slabakova is not blind to this fact. When the proverbial scalpel makes an inopportune incision, it should be for any or a combination of the factors she lists, such as processing complexity, frequency considerations and more. As we will review in Chapter 5, the quantity of studies that show evidence of transfer/CLE from previous linguistic knowledge that is not simply nonfacilitative but which occurs even when the other available grammar would have been more precise (facilitative) is extremely substantial (more than a simple majority of data in the literature). As we discussed in Section 4.2.4 for the LPM, the Scalpel Model currently suffers from the same issues of predictive validity, in our view, in virtually the same ways. Thus, we refer the reader to the previous section for details instead of repeating them here.

To clarify, as is the case of the LPM, the Scalpel Model is a welcome addition to the field, not the least because it also intends to focus on the entirety of the L3 acquisition process and the dynamic nature thereof. Equally, it is a very new model that has not yet had the opportunity to be properly vetted empirically, nor has it had the luxury of being revised over time. Future iterations would be welcome that clarify how we can predict *when* the scalpel is blunted in finer detail, providing a rubric to understand how processing complexities, misleading input and construction frequency can be modeled predictively for the specific domains of grammar tested in individual studies. Nevertheless, the insights it provides by drawing our attention to the role these (and likely other variables) play are indeed sig-nificant, and embody a step in the right direction for the field as a whole. We are confident that they will feature prominently in explaining outcomes and paths in L3 acquisition.

As mentioned above, like the CEM and the LPM, the Scalpel Model makes the case that transfer/CLE can, in principle, come from either the L1 or the L2, but that it is not wholesale from one system, obtaining on a property-by-property basis at any time during development. As Slabakova states,

Why would wholesale transfer be more economical in creating new morpho-syntactic representations? It stands to reason that at the initial stages, the Language Acquisition Device (LAD)/parser is adding new linguistic objects: words, grammatical features in old functional categories, maybe even some constructions. The influence of one grammatical system means blocking off or inhibiting the other grammatical systems already acquired, which is costly in terms of processing resources. Why would the LAD/parser expend resources on blocking off some crosslinguistic influence that may turn out to be profitable later on? In fact, from the point of view of what we know about language neural functional organization, interconnection, and interference between L1 and L2 in the brain, it may be more economical, as Amaral and Roeper (2014) suggest, to proliferate and then differentiate sub-grammars. In sum, it may be *more difficult* to block off some linguistic information than to take it on board and check if it works.   (Slabakova, 2017: 658)

We address the very same question that Slabakova asks in Section 4.3.1 below, albeit taking a very different position. As always, there are multiple interpretations of the same evidence and arguments. Suffice to say, for now, that we clearly have a different reading of what can be gleaned from the relevant psycholinguistic, neurolinguistic, and neuro-cognition research.[6] We will appeal to this literature to argue that whole-sale transfer is, in fact, cognitively more economical in the first instance of multilingual acquisition precisely because the mind lacks specific experience to know that "blocking off some crosslinguistic influence ... may turn out to be profitable later on" (Slabakova, 2017: 658). In fact, as researchers, we know what will and will not be facilitative because we are working backward – applying our knowledge as linguists and having the advantage of observations from empirical outcomes – to explain what is observed. That is, we know this precisely because we have access to evidence that suggests it. How could a mind still lacking proper experience of multilingualism, and thus without such evidence, know what the outcomes might be a priori?

Another nontrivial issue, which we address in detail in Section 4.3.1 and which is discussed in González Alonso and Rothman (2017a), involves the above claim that wholesale transfer would entail the blocking off of the other system thereafter. Just as full or partial transfer in L2 acquisition does not entail no access to other mental linguistic sources, namely UG, full transfer in L3/Ln would not entail inaccessibility to both mental linguistic resources in the mind: the other specific grammar and UG. According to the Full Transfer/Full Access (FT/FA) model, the L2 initial state is comprised of the representations of the L1's final-state grammar (complete transfer); however, there is argued to be unabridged access to the other internal grammar, UG. Thus, that complete transfer coincides with a cessation of access to other mental grammatical resources does not follow from the original concept of full transfer. This tradition, then, is fully embraced in L3/L*n* models that advocate the transfer of a full system, at least in the case of the TPM (again, see Section 4.3.1 below). Full transfer is merely a statement about the initial L3 interlanguage grammars and the sources from which they come; the process of L3 acquisition itself, as in L2 acquisition, is bound to be dynamic and to draw on all available internal and external resources. In our view, nothing to the contrary has been claimed in models advocating this position in any instance of bilingual and multilingual acquisition.

Moreover, the claim that "the influence of one grammatical system means blocking off or inhibiting the other grammatical systems" (Slabakova, 2017: 658) does not reflect our understanding of the relevant psycholinguistic literature accurately. As we reviewed in Chapter 3 and will discuss in various parts of Section 4.3 below, one of the most well-established facts shown in the psycholinguistic research on activation and inhibition is that both/all languages are activated simultaneously literally all the time, even when there is no functional/ utilitarian reason for this (e.g., Dijkstra, 2005; Kroll, 2008; Kroll, Bobb, & Wodniecka, 2006; Thierry & Wu, 2007). Therefore, wholesale transfer or not, blocking off activation of another language would be impossible. Thus, Slabakova's claim that wholesale transfer would or could block the other system is, in our view, in contradiction with the aforementioned literature. Conversely, what transfer from a single source might do is to reduce the activation of the other language to a point at which resource allocation can be more efficient, a point to which we return and on which we will expand in Section 4.3.1 below.

It is not immediately clear in Slabakova's (2017) writing whether that which she suggests regarding wholesale transfer, for the reasons she advocates and which we have addressed immediately above, is intended to refer to wholesale transfer in general or just to the case of L3/L*n* acquisition. It seems likely that she would only be referring to L3/L*n* acquisition in light of the historical context. Slabakova has been a prolific figure in GenSLA for over two decades. Some of her most seminal work has argued for support of the FT/FA model by Schwartz and Sprouse (1996) since the time of her doctoral dissertation (see Slabakova, 2001, for a monograph, updated version). Via personal communication with her, we can confirm that her intention does indeed seem, as we understand it, to apply only to L3/L*n* acquisition: "it makes a lot of sense to me that Full transfer will happen at the initial stage of L2 acquisition. Understandably so, since there is no other source" (Slabakova, personal communication, April 24, 2018). We further understand that she also questions what is meant or could be meant by full transfer in the first place; that is, the extent to which it has been debated properly in GenSLA whether or not the label is meant to refer to the potential for full transfer as opposed to actual full transfer in the sense of transposing a copy of the (entire) L1 system to the initial state of L2 acquisition, the former being what Westergaard (2017) has proposed. This, of course, embodies an empirical question for which much, yet perhaps not exactly the right, smoking-gun type of evidence exists. Our reading of the source, Schwartz and Sprouse (1996), confirmed recently with one of the original authors (Sprouse, personal communication, March 3, 2018), is that the authors are clear about what full transfer means, namely a full copy of L1 grammatical representations. This does not preclude Westergaard's (2017) proposal from being a better alternative a priori. At stake, however, is not the potential for more contemporary alternatives being on a better track, but rather fidelity to the construct of full transfer as existing in the published literature.

> According to the FT/FA model, the entirety of the L1 grammar (excluding the phonetic matrices of lexical/morphological items) is the L2 initial state (hence the term 'Full Transfer'). This means that the starting point of L2 acquisition is quite distinct from that of L1 acquisition: in particular, it contends that all the principles and parameter values as instantiated in the L1 grammar immediately carry over as the initial state of a new grammatical system on first exposure to input from the target language (TL). This initial state of the L2 system will have to change in light of TL input that cannot be generated by this grammar; that is, failure to assign a representation to input data will force some sort of restructuring of the system ('grammar'), this restructuring drawing from options of UG (and hence the term 'Full Access'). In some cases, this restructuring may occur quite rapidly; in others, much more time may be needed. As this process of restructuring continues, each intermediate system is a distinct Interlanguage (grammar).   (Schwartz & Sprouse, 1996: 41)

In line with the above, our understanding of the argument in the Slabakova (2017) quote is that it should apply to both L2 and L3 regardless, since it is also the case that in L2 acquisition "at the initial stages, the Language Acquisition Device (LAD)/parser is adding new linguistic objects: words, grammatical features in old functional categories, maybe even some constructions" (Slabakova, 2017: 658). If it is her intention to claim that this only applies to past L2 acquisition, further articulation of why this should be – or general clarification on this matter – would be extremely welcome in future iterations of writing on the Scalpel Model.

It is perhaps worth mentioning a final aside here. In our understanding, the Scalpel Model (as well as the LPM) does not take issue with the notion of restructuring as outlined in Schwartz and Sprouse's quote, but essentially with whether or not there is copying of the entire L1 grammar instead of continuous access to the L1 for potential transfer during L2/*Ln* development. However, the very notion of grammatical restructuring itself depends on representations being copied in the first place, which can then be restructured or modified following parsing failures from relevant L2 input. If we were to assume that what Schwartz and Sprouse's full transfer means is that one retains the potential to transfer individual properties of the L1 grammar, the need for restructuring in the proportions seen in the literature should be significantly less. After all, having full transfer potential as opposed to full transfer should mean having an economic raison d'être; less nonfacilitative transfer would then obtain than it apparently does as gleaned from the publication record. In Section 4.3.1, we will offer an argument precisely for why full transfer should be the default case in at least L2 and L3 acquisition equally, also offering some reasons why this could change for the L4 and beyond.[7]

Beyond theoretical reasons why wholesale transfer might be disfavored, Slabakova appeals to support in the literature that she claims shows this. She rightfully points out that, in order to show wholesale transfer, one ideally needs to test for multiple properties in the same learners. When doing so, if various domains of grammar reflect distinct transfer sources, one would have evidence of nonwholesale transfer in favor of a property-by-property approach. In principle, such a claim is clearly on the right track, provided it is tested in an appropriate set of learners, when transfer can be differentiated reliably from target language acquisition. This can only be done meaningfully under two scenarios, one of which is preferred to the other: (i) at the very beginning stages of L3/*Ln*, and/or (ii) when distinct sources (L1 for one and the L2 for the other) are shown for at least two different properties, and both show nonfacilitation. Alternatively, if one argues for two sources via evidence of greater facilitation in the L3 at stages past the initial ones, it is impossible to know whether facilitation derives from previous linguistic knowledge or simply reflects acquisition of the domain in the target grammar at an earlier stage than expected. Showing multiple sources of nonfacilitation would make for a stronger case, since such is less likely to be a byproduct of L3 development itself.

Slabakova (2017) cited evidence for the above primarily from a study by Bruhn de Garavito and Perpiñán (2014) with English–French bilinguals, who were tested after three weeks of an L3 Spanish class. Thus, it is clear that these learners were at the initial stages of learning the L3. Bruhn de Garavito and Perpiñán tested a selection of properties, meeting one of the possible scenarios above for testing the notion of wholesale transfer, namely coordination of subject pronouns, focus constructions, adverb placement, clefts and object clitics. For most of these properties, French differs from both the L2 (English) and the target L3 (Spanish). The participants completed a bimodal (written and aural) AJT, as well as a production task. In the AJT, French transfer was attested across all properties. However, in the elicited production task, the data offer some level of mixed results for a particular property, fragmented subject answers, as in the question: *Who arrived late?* Answer: *Him*. In such questions, a default accusative/ oblique subject is typically offered in English and French, whereas a nominative subject is required in Spanish. Slabakova appeals to these mixed results as her primary reference for L3 transfer originating from various sources.

Let us look at the original text to see what Bruhn de Garavito and Perpiñán (2014) stated (the emphasis is our own):

> we observed that for the second person responses, learners overwhelmingly prefer *tú*, the target response, which could come from Spanish itself or from the French pronoun *tu*, in which case it would be an instance of L1 transfer. Another interpretation for this pronoun would be to analyze this *tú* as the provided possessive, but this explanation seems more remote. In any case, it seems that these L3 learners have adopted correctly the strong pronouns of Spanish, at least for the 2nd person singular. With respect to the first person, the learners mostly produced *mí*, which is the oblique Spanish pronoun. This is an ungrammatical response in Spanish, but its pronunciation is very similar to that of 'me' in English, the default accusative form that would rightly appear in this [sic] fragment responses. **If this *mí* is coming from 'me'** in English, then we would have an instance of transfer from the L2. There are, however, **other possible interpretations** for this response, one of them being the Spanish possessive *mi*, and another one being the direct calque from **the oblique French form *moi***, also appropriate in this context.   (Bruhn de Garavito & Perpiñán, 2014: 10)

As can be seen, the authors themselves did not actually claim to have found transfer from multiple sources with any level of certainty, since they highlighted that French could also be the source, or that an appropriation of the target language Spanish possessive pronoun *mi* could be the source. Furthermore, the fact that the apparently ambiguous evidence comes only from production (not from the AJT) already calls such a strong claim into question, given that production can reflect much more than grammatical competence, particularly after three weeks. As discussed in Section 4.2.1, production of this sort (performance) might tap better into CLE, in the sense in which we make the distinction in this book. While this logic holds in general, there are other explanations that should be ruled out for this particular data set before one can claim it shows evidence in the way suggested by Slabakova (2017). These options were already underscored by Bruhn de Garavito and Perpiñán (2014), as highlighted in bold above. What is observed could equally originate from the French oblique 'moi,' not simply the English oblique 'me' to which Slabakova appeals. Thus, it is not clear what the empirical evidence complicating wholesale transfer actually is. Alternatively, as we will discuss in detail in Section 4.3.1.2, there is quite robust evidence suggesting the potential for wholesale transfer when one takes properties across comparable studies into account. In nine studies by 13 individual researchers in various cohorts, testing 11 different domains of morphosyntax of L3 BP as the target L3 by highly proficient English–Spanish bilinguals, Spanish has been shown to be the transfer source, without exception and irrespective of which language is the L1 or the L2.

4.3   The Typological Primacy Model

In this section, we present the Typological Primacy Model (TPM; Rothman, 2010, 2011, 2013, 2015), offering the most updated and comprehensive review of the model to date. We capitalize on the luxury of space that only a book can provide to explain the TPM's origins on several levels, to justify the working assumptions it makes (how and why they are applied), to clarify any misconceptions ascribed to it in the published literature and to offer some new insights and modifications based on continued work from several research groups over the past few years. As the focus of the TPM is particularly on describing, predicting and explaining the initial stages in L3 grammar – the first true L3 interlanguage system – it is worth repeating what we said at the end of Section 1.1 in Chapter 1. As it is the case in generative L2 theory, the significance of describing and understanding the composition of the first developing L3 grammars is not to be understated. Accurately describing the initial L3/L*n* interlanguage grammars effectively delimits the success of developmental and ultimate attainment theories (González Alonso & Rothman, 2017a); it would be spurious to attempt to chart development or to understand its dynamics if one does not know precisely the starting point upon which it is built. As in the case of L2 acquisition, the path of development and its dynamics, inclusive of comparative differences from other groups of learners of the same target language, can only be revealed and interpreted meaningfully when considering what the potentially different starting point of grammatical departure is in each case. DuPlessis, Solin, Travis and White (1987) effectively argued – a point later strengthened by Schwartz's (1992) inclusion of the child L2 and adult L2 comparison with the same languages into the debate – in reply to Clahsen and Muysken (1986), that differences in trajectory between L1 and L2 acquisition cannot always be used to argue against UG continuity without considering potential transfer effects. The point duPlessis et al. raised is that L1 transfer could, and predictively does, change the developmental course for L2 learners, precisely because the grammatical point of departure is different. Thus, determining if transfer happens initially is tantamount to predicting what the L2 developmental path should be: If L1 transfer obtains, X is predicted; if not, Y is predicted (Y equaling the same path as L1 acquisition for the target language). The same holds for L3/L*n* development; developmental and even ultimate attainment prediction is subject to knowing as many facts about the initial interlanguage representations as possible. In fact, as the strength of any building is inherently related to the strength of its foundation, so too are developmental theories relative to their accuracy in describing the initial points of departure of that which they seek to explain.

4.3.1 The Framework: Why Wholesale Transfer?

The TPM maintains not only that access to, and thus transfer from, both the L1 and the L2 is a distinct possibility (in fact, the very initial L3/L*n* state comprises by its claims a period in which both L1 and L2 are accessible) but also that the choice of the L1 or the L2 is highly constrained and is thus ubiquitously predictable in the initial stages of L3 development. Unlike the default models of transfer (L1 primacy and L2SF), the TPM – like the CEM, the LPM and the Scalpel Model – predicts that the L1 or the L2 can be the sources of L3 transfer. In this latter grouping of nondefault transfer models, it stands alone by stipulating that one or the other language, but crucially not both, is selected as the initial source of transfer in all domains of L3 morphosyntactic representation. Some emphasis is warranted for the words *initial* and *representation* in the previous sentence. As González Alonso and Rothman (2017a) discussed, while the TPM claims a single, complete source (L1 or L2) for initial stages transfer, this does not preclude surface-level influence from the other language early on and throughout, or indeed secondary transfer (representational) at later stages from the language not originally selected. For example, if initial transfer is nonfacilitative and L3 restructuring is thus required, it might be the case that, when the parser detects sufficient L3 input to determine this, the property from the other language is transferred in its place (instead of genuine learning from scratch). In much the same way that the L1 is considered a filter to UG in L2 acquisition by full transfer accounts, the typologically selected grammar, and potentially the other in later stages of L3/L*n* acquisition, can be viewed as analogous UG-filter (s) in multilingualism. Therefore, secondary transfer would be property-by-property in this sense, and would occur only as a byproduct of L3 development itself. In other words, the TPM is compatible with arguments from the LPM/ Scalpel Model in many aspects, except for one crucial, nontrivial point: the claimed completeness of transfer from a single source as the initial L3 inter-language grammar. Nevertheless, González Alonso and Rothman warned that disentangling subsequent transfer from L3 acquisition itself can prove compli-cated at later stages.

It is also prudent to highlight the TPM's stance concerning the difference between transfer and CLE – relating to the word *representation* we wished to highlight in the above sentence – which is a distinction that we have already discussed in detail in Section 1.4 in Chapter 1 and in several previous sections in this chapter. The TPM is clear in this regard; transfer sits at the level of grammatical representations, whereas CLE embody influence that is not repre-sentational in nature. Thus, one should expect transfer to be more systematic and CLE to be variable, particularly with regard to being more susceptible to processing considerations (seeming influence from X language being increas-ingly more likely as factor of increased burdening of processing resources). The TPM's stipulation of wholesale transfer is, essentially, an extension of the full transfer hypothesis from the GenSLA literature (e.g., Schwartz & Sprouse, 1996; White, 2003b). Simply extending a proposal from the L2 literature is hardly sufficient to justify the TPM's claims, particularly since we have advocated for a nuanced, independent treatment of L3, unless justified by empirical findings. Rothman (2013, 2015) and González Alonso and Rothman, (2017a) offered two main arguments to justify the TPM's stipulation of complete transfer of one or the other available systems on theoretical and empirical grounds, of which we now offer a more detailed discussion.

4.3.1.1 Theoretical Rationale

On the theoretical side, the TPM maintains that full transfer makes sense as the null hypothesis for an inexperienced multilingual mind. In fact, as the mind of an L3 learner will have had experience acquiring two previous languages, it is already an expert at being bilingual. Particularly in the case of L3 learners who are late sequential bilinguals, experience of having acquired an L2 will have conditioned their minds to understand that language learning need not occur from scratch but that using their previous linguistic (L1) knowledge to boot-strap L2 learning reduces what would be (some) unnecessary, redundant acquisition instead.

The TPM also argues that wholesale transfer is reasonable from a cognitive economy perspective; crucially, from the proverbial vantage point of an experience-driven adaptive mind. At the start of L3 acquisition, the learner's mind will be experiencing true multilingualism for the first time. That is, it will not yet have had the *right* experiences to suggest that wholesale transfer can induce nonfacilitation specifically for multilingualism, and the grammar will thus require reconfiguration for some properties. To the extent that there was full L1 transfer in L2 acquisition, the mind will have had some experience with nonfacilitation. Crucially, however, the L3 acquisition process is the very first time at which the mind will have been able to make an informed decision ("informed" being what the TPM and all other nondefault models of L3/L*n* transfer endeavor to articulate), as opposed to a default-induced one – in L2 acquisition, it is the L1 or nothing at all. Therefore, in the experience of the naïve multilingual mind, there is nothing to ward off full transfer, since it is possible that the choice between two candidates might yield significantly greater value than would forced L1-default transfer in L2 acquisition. It is important to highlight that, as with all other psychological processes, everything described here is assumed to be subconscious, a point to which we will return in detail below. Thus, it need not appear overly intuitive – least of all to those of us who spend time belaboring all these minute details, unlike typical human beings – but must simply meet the burden of being more economical from an adaptive mind's perspective instead. Because we know that the mind/brain remains highly plastic, adjustable to its experiences throughout the lifespan (see Fuchs & Flügge, 2014, for review) or at least much later than previously argued (e.g., Lenneberg, 1967), L3 experiences of nonfacilitation might very well mean that full transfer will be disregarded as a viable option when the mind is an experienced multilingual one, meaning L4 acquisition and beyond.

Finally, González Alonso and Rothman (2017a) argued that it is defensible to regard full transfer as more economical a priori because transfer in one swoop means that each property does not have to be considered juxtaposed against two highly activated grammars throughout development. As discussed in Chapter 3 and schematized in Figure 4.2, the use of an additional language entails that at least two active sets of representations compete for selection at several levels of language processing and production (see, e.g., Bialystok et al., 2012; Hervais-Adelman, Moser-Mercer, & Golestani, 2011; Kroll, Dussias, Bogulski, & Valdés Kroff, 2012). Resolution of this competition is required for successful communication, and this process of selection places increased demands on both the linguistic and executive control systems.

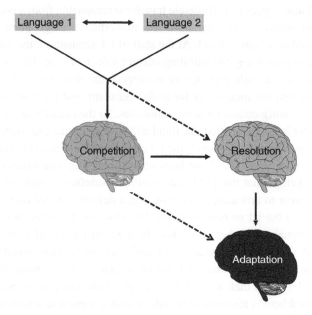

Figure 4.2 *Competition/resolution leads to neuroanatomical and cognitive function adaptive outcomes*

As schematized in Figure 4.2, the brain is argued to adapt both functionally and structurally to handle these demands optimally (Abutalebi & Green, 2016), but this comes as a – potentially beneficial – consequence of simultaneous activation itself. Although such research shows all grammars in bi-/ multilingual minds to be activated simultaneously, the same research indicates that there are differences in relative activation whereby grammars that are not needed contextually are suppressed to a low level of activation. If L3 transfer were to occur on a property-by-property basis, maintaining activation of the L1 and L2 at a sufficiently high level for comparison over the extended period of acquisition would be too costly for a cognitive system that is hardwired to conserve and maximize resources. This should be true unless (or until) specific multilingual experience justifies the resource allocation, as may be the case for the second and beyond multilingual experiences of L4/L*n* acquisition. This, of course, is an empirical question that can only be answered in the future via carefully designed studies comparing L3 and L*n* acquisition.

4.3.1.2 Empirical Rationale

With regard to the empirical basis for the TPM's argument, there are two main sources. The first is related to the sheer number of L1 transfer studies in L2 acquisition – in and well beyond generative circles – that consistently find pervasive transfer effects. If it is the case that full transfer happens in L2 acquisition as an initial point of departure, why would transfer not continue to be wholesale in L3 acquisition? Recall, as we pointed out in Section 4.1 above, that there is no formalized model of transfer in GenSLA suggesting property-by-property transfer. The partial transfer approaches, such as full transfer, are also initial-state proposals. As discussed, they are only partial with regard to what parts of the L1 grammar are transferred systematically (for example, lexical as opposed to functional categories) at the initial state but not at the grammatical-domain-by-grammatical-domain level across development. Even if transfer is argued to be partial in this sense, it still entails ubiquitous yet restricted transfer from a single source, the L1. Thus, it is incumbent on L3/L*n* approaches that wish to argue against wholesale transfer to do one of three things. First, they would need to explain how and/or why the hundreds of studies that claim to support full transfer in the L2 literature are in fact mistaken, and thus why it is defensible to claim that full transfer never happens, even in L2 acquisition. Alternatively, if they do not wish to claim this, they would need to justify precisely why and following what mechanisms L2 and L3 acquisition would be different in this regard; that is, why would full transfer be abandoned in multilingualism? In addition, since no previous formal L2 theory has advocated specifically for property-by-property representational transfer throughout development, such theories should motivate why and what mechanisms justify the difference for L3 acquisition in comparison to L2 acquisition. In other words, this line of argument should focus on *how* previous constraints in terms of predicting nonfacilitative transfer systematically do not apply equally in L3 acquisition.

More important, however, are the data available from L3 acquisition studies themselves. As we will see in a detailed analysis in the next chapter, a significant proportion of available studies show that typological/structural similarity is a deterministic predictor for the selection of the L3 transfer source (a view shared by the LPM and the Scalpel Model). Contrary to what some might realize, however, this has been shown across an impressive array of language triad combinations, which include pairings of languages in which the genetic relationship is irrelevant (details of which we review in Section 4.3.4.2.2). Of even greater relevance and significance is the fact that, when one brings together comparable studies in which the L1, the L2 and the L3 are the same and considers the sheer number of properties tested collectively, the idea of wholesale L3 transfer seems increasingly likely. Take, for example, the case of English and Spanish as the L1 and L2 with BP as the target L3. Nine studies by 13 individual researchers in various cohorts between 2009 and 2018 alone have tested 11 different domains of morphosyntax. Spanish – the typologically closer language to BP overall, yet crucially not with regard to the domains tested – has literally always been shown to be the transfer source, irrespective of whether this language was the L1 or the L2. Therefore, we are certain that at least 11 morphosyntactic properties of Spanish transfer to BP, from which it seems fair to claim that transfer is likely to be complete across the entire morphosyntactic system. After all, it is not feasible to test all domains of morphosyntax. As in in all other fields of scientific inquiry, when a critical mass of data is supporting a generalization, it is reasonable to make such a claim on this basis.

4.3.2   Why the TPM Rejects the Role of Consciousness in Determining Typological Similarity

As alluded to in several places, the TPM – to be unequivocally clear from the outset – does not claim any level of conscious perception in determining relative typological or structural proximity; in fact, it rejects it. As detailed by Rothman (2013, 2015), by typology, the TPM is referring decisively to linguistic structure-based similarity or proximity, nothing more nor less. Notwithstanding, claims by others to the contrary continue to be an all too common misappropriation of the authors' claims. This is likely to stem from the misalignment of Kellerman's (1983) framing of *psychotypology*, which refers to a speaker's conscious evaluations of typological relationships, on one hand, and what Rothman (2011) meant by using the same term, on the other. As explained in Rothman (2013, 2015), Rothman (2011) believed himself to be referring to the parser's – that is, completely subconscious – perception of typological/structural similarity, and thus potentially injected inadvertent confusion. Psychotypology seemed to be a particularly appropriate term, since psychological processes tend to be subconscious, and the parser is a psychological construct. Regardless of the provenance of confusion, let us be definitively clear here once again: the parser, and only the parser, determines which grammar is chosen for transfer via typological comparative consideration. When it happens to be the case that an individual can articulate which grammar is typologically more similar to the L3 correctly, namely the L1 or the L2, this is an epiphenomenal coincidence. A question that arises from the claims above is related to how the parser determines relative structural similarity, which we will address explicitly in Section 4.3.3.[8]

It is worth mentioning that the above discussion does not mean that it is not fruitful to seek to understand what the relationship between perception and outcome might be in this regard, particularly when the languages involved in the triad reasonably warrant it. Nevertheless, any claim suggesting that the TPM takes typology to be determined consciously, that a learner's perception could alter what it argues the parser and cognitive economy are hardwired to do, or expecting that there should be a correlation between perception and outcome, reflects a fundamental misunderstanding of the TPM (see Rothman 2015; González Alonso & Rothman, 2017a). Santos (2013) tested the relationship between perceived typology – *psychotypology* in Kellerman's terms – and outcome explicitly and showed a nice correlation between them for the languages on which she was working: English, Spanish and Portuguese. Having shown this to be a successful endeavor highlights the worthiness of asking such a question, as long as one understands that it runs in parallel to the claims of the TPM and that which it seeks to capture. In fact, the TPM makes no predictions for this question, although an extension of Kellerman's (1983) psychotypology construct certainly does.

An important consequence of there being no consciousness involved is related to the predictive space and validity of the model. The TPM does not make predictions only for genetically related languages. In fact, irrespective of the typological/structural similarity between languages of a historically related nature (such as Baltic, Germanic, Romance, Slavic and Turkic languages, for example), the parser does not know linguistic descriptions in the sense that we linguists create, study and discuss them. What makes languages with a genetic relationship typologically similar is the overwhelming number of similarities they share at various levels of linguistic structures (and they, in turn, are cues). However, universally speaking, languages exist within the confines of a finite number of relevant structures. Thus, Rothman (2013, 2015) updated the TPM to highlight exactly what the linguistic parser uses to determine underlying typological and structural proximity implicitly, and thus to make an informed decision as early as the abundance of cues or lack thereof will permit, depending on the language triads, to promote transfer of the L1 or the L2 system, to which we now turn.

4.3.3   How Does the Parser Determine Typological Proximity?

An implicational hierarchy of cues that induce the selection of the transfer source was first introduced in Rothman (2013; see also Rothman, 2015;

Rothman, Alemán Bañón, & González Alonso, 2015). The parser is argued to first examine similarity at the lexical level and, when sufficient, transfer would be induced by this level alone. In most cases, this would result in transfer for what seem to be obvious choices. For example, this would obtain for genetically related languages, which, in turn, become good candidates for situations in which lay individuals can guess correctly which system transfers and give the impression that consciousness matters. However, in the real world of bilinguals acquiring a third or more language, the relationships of the grammars are not such that this is always possible (see Section 4.3.4.2.2). Would there be no predictions in the absence of what is obvious? Of course, the answer is no.

In the event there is insufficient lexical crossover for the parser to establish similarity, the next level of cues (less language-specific as the lexical level is) comes into play, which is proposed to be phonetics/phonology/phonotactics, followed by morphological form and encoded features (again, if phonology does not suffice) and, finally, syntactic structure, in that order. What determines *sufficient* is highly related to the specific languages in the tripartite grouping, thus allowing room for any and all potential combinations, as well as accounting for differences in the timing of when L3 transfer might take place within the initial stages (if the lexicon is sufficient, it will be quicker than when subsequent domains are involved). The general idea is schematized in Figure 4.3.

The order of the hierarchy is not random. Beyond the first level of lexis, upon which we comment below, it reflects acquisition in a natural sense, starting from the smallest discernible units of representation and how children break into language (e.g., Clark, 2003; Crain & Lilo-Martin, 1999; Guasti, 2002, 2017; O'Grady, 2005; Snyder, 2007). It also makes it possible for the parser to render an informed decision independent of language-relatedness factors. This is important for the application of the TPM because, to have universal application – that is, beyond genetically related language pairings – it must be based on a set of articulated cues that is equally obvious to a computational parser regardless of the combination of languages. After all, as alluded to above, what happens in the case of an L1 Kuwaiti Arabic–L2 Norwegian speaker being confronted with L3 Hindi? Or what if a Catalan–Spanish bilingual learns L3 English – a more likely scenario? Which of the two previous systems is closer to the L3 target? The implicational hierarchy will reveal this at some level, no matter what the pairing is.

This implicational hierarchical approach inherently provides an opportunity for cross-disciplinary work between formal theorists and acquisitionists, precisely because, in the event that the typological motivation for selection cannot come from the lexicon, knowledge of the particular languages' phonological,

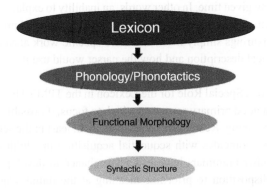

Figure 4.3 *The Typological Primacy Model's cue hierarchy. Note that the relative size of the font and the ovals are meant to evoke the relative weight/ order of applicability that each cue level has overall in the implicational hierarchy*

morphological and syntactic systems will become paramount. It is important to justify theoretically why the next available level of the implicational hierarchy should – or frankly should not – serve as the sufficient comparative domain for the parser to make a typologically informed (subconscious) decision. Examples with real language pairings of how this can be determined in principled ways beyond the lexicon, that is, on the basis of comparative phonological systems or, if still tied at that level, morphological type (for example, agglutinative versus synthetic) and so on, are presented in Section 4.3.3.3 below. Nevertheless, the general logic is worth reiterating. Selection is done subconsciously by a parser that is assumed to be linguistically preprogrammed but able to handle context sensitivity – something that is true of any instance of language acquisition, including monolingual child L1, see Rothman and Chomsky (2018) – which is adorned with language-specific experience from two previously acquired systems in the case of multilingualism. Cognitive economy essentially mandates that the previous experience, now in the form of two grammatical systems, be used. Since there is more than one, this results, subconsciously, in statistical comparisons by the same parser. Whether or not we have yet described – or have the knowledge to do so ourselves without help from our theorist colleagues – the linguistic features that comprise both systems sufficiently or accurately enough to consistently see/predict/determine how this process unfolds for any given tripartite pairing is irrelevant. The general construct operates regardless of a current ability to understand all of its component parts at any given time. In other words, an inability to explain exactly which language-specific units are being used to determine typological proximity selection in specific pairings simply means we have specific work ahead at the crossroads of theoretical description and how the parser would use it.

4.3.3.1   Why Is There a Special Role for the Lexicon in the TPM's Hierarchy?

Lexis is likely to be a good primary source on which to focus, if possible, when initially parsing for meaning. Recall that L3 acquisition, at least in the sense we are dealing with here, coincides with sequential acquisition in adulthood (or certainly after two other grammars have had a fair chance to develop fully). Thus, a natural predisposition to prioritize meaning at the initial stages (an involuntary "sink or swim" reaction), at least until sufficient exposure to justify the formation of an L3 interlanguage grammatical system proper (via transfer from L1/L2) has taken place, might be at play.

Some discussion of formal linguistic approaches to psycholinguistics and processing is relevant in this discussion. According to Clahsen and Felser's (2006b, 2018) influential Shallow Structure Hypothesis (SSH), nonnative speakers are destined to have so-called shallow processing throughout development. The idea is predicated on shortages in computational resources and an argued lack of automatization in L2 processing – at least partly due to a fundamental difference between children's and adults' abilities to build or manipulate abstract linguistic representations in real time. Cunnings (2017) painted a different picture, claiming alternatively that, with increasing proficiency (particularly at the highest levels), nonnative speakers can and do construct similarly specified grammatical (syntactic) parses to those of monolinguals. Recognizing that obvious differences between L1 and L2 processing need to be explained (see also, e.g., Grüter, Rohde, & Schafer, 2017; Kaan, 2014), Cunning's (2017) approach appealed to considerations of working memory and other cognitive resource allocations argued to lead L1 versus L2 speakers to weight cues that guide memory retrieval differently. As a result, the latter group is more prone to interference during memory retrieval.

Irrespective of which of the above positions is on the right (or better) track, few would argue – the reason for appealing to both is precisely because neither position, different as they are, would disagree – that some level of shallow processing likely defines the beginning proficiency levels of nonnative processing during which parsing for meaning is crucial for proverbial survival. Lexical similarities – when useful – potentially offer a crutch to sustain this. Our point is not simply to sustain the claim that comparative lexis is vital at the beginning stages, but that it could also lead the parser to make an evaluation of overall typological proximity before, strictly speaking, grammatical information is used to do the same. After all, if the lexicon of one language is vastly more helpful in allowing initial parsing for meaning, then it is not particularly farfetched to assume implicitly that the overall grammar is more similar and thus will be more helpful going forward, hence promoting transfer source selection.

4.3.3.2 Beyond the Lexicon: The Other Levels of the TPM's Hierarchy

As we know, lexical similarities will simply not be relevant to all language triads either because (a) all three languages are equally different from each other in this regard, or (b) there is a true tie, such as when all three languages originate from the same language family or the L1 and L2 are equally similar or distinct in lexis from the target L3 (see Section 4.3.4.2.2 for further discussion and actual examples). It is here that grammatical cues must come into play. Phonology and phonotactics make use of the smallest manageable units of linguistic analysis. Phones and phonemes are clearly played with in a proverbial sense very early on in child language acquisition (well before syntax proper) and are good candidates to make comparative choices: Is coronal a contrastive feature? Does the language have complex codas or permit only singletons? Is the language stress-timed or syllable-timed? The hierarchy continues to build up to form larger units, in which similarities that are otherwise clandestine to the nonlinguist can be uncovered: Is the language agglutinative, analytic or synthetic in its morphology? Does the language have dedicated morphology to express the same things (grammatical aspect, person, number, gender and so on)? What is the underlying word order? How informative (thus important) is syntactic structure to meaning (as in, for example, structural versus morphological case)? As we hope can be appreciated from this relatively small list, much can be relevant at various levels, and can be useful to the parser in order to determine the (typologically speaking) best guess between an L1 and L2 for transfer, regardless of what the actual L1, L2 and L3 are (see Rothman, 2013, 2015, for a much more in-depth explanation of the finer workings of each level, inclusive of examples with hypothesized language pairings).

4.3.3.3 Summarizing the TPM's Hierarchy via Some Practical Examples

Let us consider, for example, a situation in which an English–Italian bilingual (L1 English, L2 Italian or vice versa) has just moved to Copenhagen, and is now being exposed to Danish. The learner's parser will have to examine the input received from Danish and, according to the above hierarchy, will first focus on the lexicon as a linguistic cue. Since English and Danish are related languages – although both are from the Germanic family, they are not at all mutually intelligible – there is a considerable crossover with regard to vocabulary. This does not mean that the parser has any indication that these two languages are related genetically. However, sufficient crossover at the level of the lexicon is likely to make the parser determine that English is the most typologically proximate language to Danish from the two available choices, namely Italian and English. This should mean that the lexicon is sufficient – properties at other levels of the hierarchy might be supportive but will not be needed – and that the parser will chose to transfer English quite quickly.

Let us now consider another learner, a Turkish–German bilingual who has just moved to Tokyo and has started to learn Japanese. The parser's job will be considerably more cumbersome and will require comparison at more levels of the hierarchy before relative similarity can be established. First, the parser will start to examine the possible lexical crossover and, after a short while, will realize that the lexicon is not particularly helpful. It will then move on to the next levels of the hierarchy until properties at some level indicate which language should be promoted. If on the right track, the TPM, combined with a careful comparative consideration of the two grammars (phonologically, morphologically and syntactically), will reveal predictions regarding exactly what in the hierarchy – at what level – the balance should tip in favor of one or the other language being predicted for transfer. This also means that the TPM provides a means to determine relative timing for how long it will take for transfer selection to occur; transfer is predicted to happen in less time for the first case than in it is in the latter scenario, as the latter requires more input before the parser can reach an informed conclusion.

This also highlights the specific linguistic nature of the TPM and its interdependence with descriptions of grammar in formal linguistic theory. To apply the hierarchy, one needs to evaluate the L3 at various linguistic levels to argue for what, exactly, the parser uses to make its decision. We now present a real example from the literature to drive this point home. Puig-Mayenco and Marsden (2018) examined the acquisition of the syntactic distribution of the polarity item *anything* in L3 English by Catalan–Spanish bilinguals. Showing evidence of Catalan influence in the L3, they argued to provide support for the TPM. Given that Spanish and Catalan are so closely related/typologically similar overall (but crucially not for the translation equivalent of this polarity item), on what basis did the authors assess that Catalan was the typologically more similar language to English? This quandary is in accordance with scenario (b) discussed in Section 4.3.3.2 immediately above. Catalan and Spanish are from the same language family (Romance), both differ from English (which is Germanic) and both cross over equally significantly with English at the lexical level. Following the TPM's cue hierarchy, Puig-Mayenco and Marsden argue that the next level would render Catalan the clear winner; for example, Catalan is closer prosodically to English than is Spanish, the former being stress-timed and the latter syllable-timed.

4.3.4 Empirical Support

The TPM was formally proposed by Rothman (2010), which is to say this was the first publication in which the model was named. However, the precursor logic to the model was discussed previously in Rothman and Cabrelli Amaro (2010) in light of data comparing the L2 and L3 acquisition of French and Italian as target languages. Although it is true that the results of Rothman and Cabrelli Amaro confound typological proximity and L2 status, as will be detailed below, because the study represents the genesis of this model, it seems fitting to begin describing the empirical basis of the TPM with this as our detailed exemplar. An added bonus of this choice will then be our ability to highlight how and why the TPM aligns itself with a particular design methodology – the mirror-image method – that enables a differentiation, in terms of predictions, of the growing list of L3/Ln models.

Bear in mind that, at the time of this study (data collection took place in 2006), there were only two formal models: the L2SF and the CEM. Originally, Rothman and Cabrelli Amaro (2010) set out to test the following simultaneously: (a) the potential differences between L2 and L3 grammatical acquisition, and (b) the comparison of two formal models against each other (while at the same time offering a method that could also show L1-default primacy, if applicable). With regard to query (a), their four-group design was truly fit for purpose. Two of the four groups were L2 learners, and two were L3 learners (matched for target language proficiency and input exposure, as they were all beginning learners from the same first semester university class with no other previous exposure to the target L3). The L1 (English) remained constant across all learners. The L2 of the L3 groups was also held constant, and was Spanish. The target languages tested in the study were always French and Italian, the L2 for the L2 groups and the L3 for the L3 groups. Thus, the authors were able to compare the L2 French to the L3 French group, and the L2 Italian to the L3 Italian group whereby differences, if any, between them would ideally be attributable to the previous linguistic experience that the L3 groups had. If this occurred, it would show that L2 experience with Spanish altered or affected the developmental path of Italian and French acquisition by English natives, which would be good evidence to suggest that L2 and L3 acquisition were not simply one and the same.

With regard to query (b), the design is adequate in its proper context. As the goal of (b) was essentially to test whether or not nonfacilitative transfer could obtain contrary to the predictions of the CEM, and if Spanish, the L2, was transferred into L3 French given the domain of grammar tested, the design was well-positioned to comment on the two models existing at the time. Given the goals and the logic of the original design, French was the most important language because it was the key one for both queries (a) and (b). The L2 versus L3 comparison would provide particularly good evidence for (a). If there were no differences, we would have had evidence of an L1 default effect and thus no support to claim that, with regard to initial-stages transfer, the L2 and the L3 are distinct. If differences obtained and could be likened to Spanish, we would have had good evidence that L2 and L3 acquisition can be different with regard to transfer, which inevitably affects the trajectories of developmental sequencing for these groups: learning French for a native English speaker would not always be the same formal task for all learners depending on what intervenes.

The addition of Italian was, as first conceived, essentially a way to strengthen any conclusion one could make for (b). Since the working hypothesis was that nonfacilitative transfer would be shown in the case of L3 French, Rothman and Cabrelli Amaro wanted to be able to show that nonfacilitative transfer itself was in fact not random but was linguistically constrained instead. Because Italian and Spanish are the same for the domain tested, the hypothesis was that one could show facilitative effects for L2 transfer in this case. Thus, Spanish L2 transfer would simultaneously show both a facilitative and a nonfacilitative effect, providing quite strong evidence against some predictions of the CEM, and strongly supporting the L2SF if the hypotheses were to be confirmed.

What was not considered until the data confirmed the predictions so squarely was that there could be another factor at play, obscured from meaningful disentangling given this design. Typological – underlying structural – proximity between Spanish and the two other Romance languages could explain exactly the same outcomes. In other words, perhaps it was simply happenstance that Spanish was the L2, and what was actually determining its transfer was not its L2 status, but rather its typological proximity to both French and Italian. Although possible, the design of the study could not have permitted a proper differentiation of the typological effect from that of L2 status. Nevertheless, Rothman and Cabrelli Amaro came to feel that this was not just a possible but also indeed a likely explanation. They pondered on this at length in the discussion and conclusion sections of their 2010 paper but rightfully conceded that such a proposal needed more robust data and a method that could tease apart an L2 factor from typological influence. In many ways, then, the TPM was born during this project, despite not being called such formally until follow-up work.

4.3.4.1 An Exemplar Study: Rothman and Cabrelli Amaro (2010)

As shown in Box 4.5, the key difference between the groups in Rothman and Cabrelli Amaro (2010), groups 2–3 and 4–5, was whether these native, L1 English speakers were already successful L2 Spanish speakers or not at the time of starting to learn French or Italian. The domain of grammar studied included various properties related to the syntax of pronominal subject arguments, specifically properties related to null-subject licensing.

Exploring the syntax of null subjects in these linguistic combinations is interesting for several reasons, the most important of which is that, according to the predictions of the TPM, Spanish proves to be the nonfacilitative option for the L3 learners of French, yet the facilitative one for Italian. Both English and French are nonnull subject languages (Jones, 1996; Radford, 2012). What this means is that, for both languages, overt subjects (phonologically spelled out/pronounced) are obligatory in both main and embedded clauses.[9] Spanish and Italian, conversely, are classical null-subject languages (e.g., Alexiadou & Anagnostopoulou, 1998; Camacho, 2014; Jaeggli & Safir, 1989; Rizzi, 1982), and the subject of either main or embedded clauses can be – and usually is – unpronounced; a null element (a *pro*) that carries the same *phi*-features as expressed in the rich verbal morphology occupies the canonical subject position. Although both overt and null subjects are technically possible in all syntactic positions – except for expletives which are obligatorily null – this does not mean that the choice of one or another is unconstrained. In fact, null subjects are the default option whereby its overt counterpart typically requires some discourse motivation to be selected (such as a change in topic or contrastive focus), a point to which we return below. The difference in syntactic structure between null and overt subject sentences – how the subject requirement of all finite predicates, the Extended Projection Principle (EPP; Chomsky, 1981, 1982), is fulfilled differently – can be seen in the trees in (11) and (12).

Box 4.5 Exemplary study for the Typological Primacy Model (Rothman & Cabrelli Amaro, 2010)

Rothman and Cabrelli Amaro (2010)	
Citation: Rothman J. and Cabrelli Amaro J. (2010) What Variables Condition Syntactic Transfer? A Look at the L3 Initial State. *Second Language Research 26*: 189–218.	
L3/L*n*	Italian or French
Previously acquired languages	English and Spanish
Linguistic domain examined	Null subject
Participants	Group 1: Native speakers of English Group 2: L2 learners of French (English NSs) Group 3: L2 learners of Italian (English NSs) Group 4: L3 learners of French (L1En–L2Sp) Group 5: L3 learners of Italian (L1En–L2Sp)
Task	Task 1: Grammaticality judgment/correction task Task 2: Context/sentence-matching Overt Pronoun Constraint (OPC) task

Example GJT
 	
a) *Je pense que pleut.
b) *I think is raining.
c) Io credo che piova.
	Example Coreference interpretation OPC task
	¿Chi non sa che Ø può dormire tardi questi giorni?
	Who do you suppose does not know he can sleep later these days?
	   I. the same as Chi;
	   II. someone else

Results

Table 4.6 *Rejection (out of 10) in the GJT in each condition by each group (adapted from Rothman & Cabrelli Amaro, 2010: 204)*

	Null expletive	Overt expletive	Null referential	Overt referential
Eng NS	9.42	0.00	0.00	9.08
L2 French	8.00	0.20	0.20	8.09
L2 Italian	1.00	7.11	7.11	1.22
L3 French	6.18	2.00	2.00	2.91
L3 Italian	0.50	8.60	8.60	0.60

(11)   English   (12)   Spanish

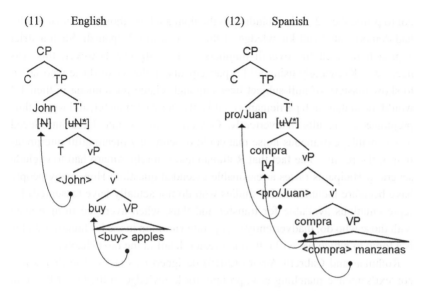

The Spanish sentence in (12) is the equivalent to the English sentence in (11). Although there are competing approaches, we adopt Adger's (2003) analysis here to depict the structural differences at hand. In (11), finite T bears an EPP feature [uN*], which attracts the closest lexical item with an N feature resulting in raising to [Spec, TP]. In (12), the EPP feature is checked by triggering v-raising in an agreement relationship between the rich verbal morphology bearing *phi*-features and the *pro* subject in the [Spec, TP] position. If an overt subject is spelled out in a language such as Spanish, it will be in Spec of some functional projection of the left periphery (CP, for ease of exposition), as depicted by Juan (see Adger, 2003: 216).

Choosing L1 English–L2 Spanish bilinguals meets the first criterion for L3 testing, as it is a population that, in principle, has two distinct representations available for transfer into the L3. *In principle* is meant to carry an effect. Simply because someone has been exposed to an L2 and has achieved relatively high proficiency in a global sense does not necessarily mean that he or she has (yet) acquired the domain of grammar in the L2 at the time of L3 (initial-stages) testing. As discussed in other chapters and earlier in this one (see Section 4.2.1.1), the consequences of not being certain whether the L2 representation has been acquired, and is thus available for transfer, are too severe to leave this unchecked. The study by Rothman and Cabrelli Amaro (2010) was one of the first to point this out and to sidestep the potential confound by testing the L3 learners for the same domain in L2 Spanish as an inclusion criterion for the study. That is, they tested the L2 after the L3 in order not to prime the L2, only including in the final analysis those participants who had demonstrated full knowledge of the domain in L2 Spanish. Such a strict approach reduced the overall numbers of L3 subjects; however, this was necessary. Knowingly using all L3 participants, inclusive of those who failed to show mastery of null-subject licensing and related phenomena in their L2 would mean that such participants could only show L1 transfer, and would thus prejudice the results inadvertently. Obviously, this would have introduced unacceptable, extraneous noise that could obscure any meaningful interpretation of the results. The fact that Rothman and Cabrelli Amaro had to exclude several participants raises a reasonable extended question: How many people have been/are included in L3 studies who do not actually have (assumed) L2 representations available for transfer and thus, when averaged in aggregate with those who do, inadvertently exaggerate variation in the L3 literature? This is a topic to which we will return in greater detail in the next chapter.

Rothman and Cabrelli Amaro (2010) designed two tasks. The first was a context/sentence-matching task, probing for knowledge of the Overt Pronoun Constraint (OPC; Montalbetti, 1984, 1986), and the second was a GJT with corrections examining various canonical properties of the Null Subject Parameter. Before going any further into the actual design of these tasks, it is worth explaining what the OPC is and the logic behind using it. The OPC is essentially a footnote of sorts to Principle B of the Binding Theory (Chomsky, 1981), which is an elaborate way of saying it is a restriction on how coreference interpretations can obtain between matrix (main) clause referential subjects and embedded clause ones.

The OPC captures the following truism of null-subject grammars: An overt pronoun in an embedded clause cannot be bound by a quantified expression or wh-phrases (that is, variable expression) from a main clause whenever the alternation overt/null pronoun is available (Montalbetti, 1984, 1986). In other words, bound variable interpretations are precluded in null-subject grammars. This universal principle is only visible in null-subject languages precisely because the null versus overt alternation only occurs therein. The logic for using the OPC is twofold: (a) it is a reliable index of null-subject grammars as it pertains to all or most null-subject languages (but see Gürel, 2003), and (b) its presence in L2 Spanish would indicate underlying, qualitative similarity to natives in L2 representation for null-subjectness precisely because it is a related property that cannot be transferred from English and, unlike the properties tested in the GJT, it is never taught and is undetermined in available L2 input. In fact, the OPC is an excellent candidate for a poverty of the stimulus (POS; see Section 2.1.1 for a detailed explanation of POS) effect (see, e.g., Lozano, 2003; Pérez-Leroux & Glass, 1999; Rothman, 2009a). Thus, Rothman and Cabrelli Amaro (2010) adopted the position that the OPC was an ideal property to test as an index of underlying representation in the L2, which would, if transferred, also index the underlying representation of null-subject licensing in the L3.

Consider the following sentences in Spanish and English in (13) and (14), in which the subscripts indicate the possibility of coreference: [i]=coreference with a matrix subject as indicated, and [j]=coreference with a disjoint referent from the discourse.

(13) a. Este   chico$_i$ cree   que *pro$_{i/j}$* es el más inteligente
        This   boy   believe$_{3rd\text{-}sing}$ that pro$_{i/j}$ is the more intelligent
        de todos.
        of all

     b. Este   chico$_i$ cree   que *él$_{i/j}$* es el más inteligente
        This   boy   believe$_{3rd\text{-}sing}$ that he is the more intelligent
        de todos.
        of all

     c. Cada   chico$_i$ cree   que *pro$_{i/j}$* es el más inteligente
        Each   boy   believe$_{3rd\text{-}sing}$ that pro is the more intelligent
        de todos.
        of all

     d. Cada   chico$_i$ cree   que *él*$_{i/j}$ es el más inteligente
        Each   boy   believe$_{3rd\text{-}sing}$ that pro is the more intelligent
        de todos.
        of all
        'This boy/each boy believes he is the smartest of all.'

(14)   a. This boy$_i$ believes he$_{i/j}$ is the smartest of all.
        b. *This boy$_i$ believes *pro$_{i/j}$* is the smartest of all.
        c. Each boy$_i$ believes he$_{i/j}$ is the smartest of all.
        d. *Each boy$_i$ believes pro$_{i/j}$ is the smartest of all.

An immediate difference to be noted between (13) and (14) above is the fact that Spanish has two versions for each of the grammatical (a, c) English sentences (b, d are ungrammatical), obviously because only Spanish has a null/overt alternation possibility for the embedded subject pronoun. Another difference is that, in Spanish, there is a restriction on coreference interpretations for overt embedded subject pronouns with a specific type of main clause subject only, essentially variable expressions (quantified determiner phrases [QDPs] or wh-words). Technically, both sentences in (14) are ambiguous, as the main clause and disjoint reference are available equally, showing that the type of main clause subject (variable expression or not) is treated the same. In fact, native speakers of English will likely default to main clause coreference (The boy$_i$ believes that he$_i$ [himself] is the smartest of all) without further context. However, the discourse could easily be such that disjoint reference (The boy$_i$ [Johnny$_i$] believes that he$_j$ [Roger$_j$] is the smartest of all) is coerced or even required.

The ambiguity just described in English does not hold entirely true for Spanish. For (13 a, b), what was just described for English holds. Technically, in (13 a, b), coreference between the embedded pronoun, be it overt or null, is possible with the matrix subject, as well as someone else from the discourse. However, it is useful to explain, as we did for English, what the preferences are for Spanish pronouns. As captured neatly in Carminati's (2002) Position of Antecedent Hypothesis (PAH), Romance null-subject languages such as Italian and Spanish display robust anaphoric interpretive biases whereby null embedded subjects are most naturally interpreted with main clause coreference, and overt embedded pronouns with discourse disjoint reference. These are tendencies; however, the point is that main clause coreference is possible with both embedded pronoun types. The situation changes dramatically in (13d) but not in (13c). In other words, only the embedded null pronoun, as per the OPC, can be coreferential with a variable (QDP) subject, whereas the overt counterpart cannot. This is not a question of preference as described by the PAH but is a question of grammaticality, as indicated by the (*) notation.

The OPC task examined knowledge of the sentence types described above in L2/L3 Italian and L2/L3 French. Recall that, as a criterion for inclusion, L3 learners would have had to have shown knowledge of the OPC-specific restrictions in L2 Spanish that were tested separately. The OPC applies in exactly the same way to Italian but does not apply to French. To indicate knowledge of the OPC in Italian, the learners would have needed to demonstrate several distinctions across the four sentence types in (13). They would have needed to show a distinction between (13b) and (13d), indicating they knew that overt embedded subjects cannot take matrix clause coreferences freely; in other words, that the type of matrix clause subject matters. They would also have needed to show knowledge of the contrast in (13c) and (13d), indicating they knew that the type of embedded subject, null or overt, mattered when applying coreference potential to QDP main clause subjects. Together, these two distinctions would indicate that they have not come up with a rule that simply says across the board 'overt subjects cannot co-refer to main clause subjects,' but rather know the highly specific and underdetermined restriction of when such a rule applies. In French, because their examples are like (14) and not (13), evidence of the

OPC applying would be found if sentences like (14b), main clause coreference, are not accepted.

Cabrelli Amaro and Rothman's (2010) results showed that both L2 groups (Italian and French) behaved similarly, which is not surprising since they were beginners. Both groups had transferred the only available option, English, in their L1. This means that they already had target interpretations for French and disobeyed the OPC in interpreting sentences such as (13d) in Italian. When examining both groups of L3 learners, they behaved similarly to each other, albeit very differently from the L2 groups. Spanish, the L2, was the language transferred when acquiring both Italian and French, in that the behavioral scenario described at the end of the preceding paragraph obtained.

The results of the other experiment, a traditional GJT with correction, had four main conditions shown in (15)–(18) below, in which the order French, English, and Italian always applied.

(15)   Null expletive subjects

      a. *Je pense que___ pleut.
      b. *I think___ is raining.
      c. Io credo che piova.

(16)   Overt expletive subject

      a. Nous pensons qu'il fait chaud.
      b. We think that it is hot.
      c. *Noi crediamo que lo faccia caldo.

(17)   Null referential subject

      a. *La madame dit que __ sommes très intelligents.
      b. *The lady says that __ are very intelligent.
      c. La signora dice che __ siamo molto intelligenti.

(18)   Overt referential subject

      a. Je sais que je t'aime.
      b. I know that I love you.
      c. #Io so che io ti amo.
         #=Pragmatically odd

The results aligned nicely with the OPC task, as the L2 learners always showed English transfer, rejecting null subjects in Italian, whereas the L3 learners showed effects of Spanish transfer, accepting things in Italian that must have come from Spanish (unlike their L2 counterparts) and introducing rejections in French that could not come from English, as in the case of overt expletives.

4.3.4.2   Other Empirical Work

In this section, we will review other studies. As it seemed fitting to highlight Rothman and Cabrelli Amaro's (2010) study as the exemplary study for the TPM because it was the seed of the idea, we would be remiss to not review in some detail the first paper in which the model's name and general tenets were introduced; thus, we will also provide some details about Rothman (2010). In addition, we will concisely walk the reader through a subset of further supportive evidence from studies since 2010.

4.3.4.2.1 Rothman (2010)

The findings of Cabrelli Amaro and Rothman (2007; Rothman & Cabrelli Amaro 2010) led Rothman (2010) – although published in the same year, the data were collected 18 months later – to implement a new design that would be able to disentangle L1 or L2 privileged status from typological selection determinacy: the mirror-image design. It was based on this ability to differentiate the aforementioned that Rothman found data that supported the idea of a primacy effect of linguistic structure in L3/L*n* transfer selection, from which the TPM was officially born.

Rothman (2010) tested two mirror-image groups of L3 learners of BP: a group of native speakers of Spanish who were highly proficient L2 speakers of English, and the opposite, a group of native speakers of English who were highly proficient in L2 Spanish. Two so-called interrelated properties were targeted: (i) word order differences in declarative and interrogatives with transitives and two types of intransitives (unergative and unaccusative), and (ii) attachment preferences (high or low) for relative clauses that patterned differently in Spanish and BP, and which are much closer in English and BP. English is an SVO language with strict canonical word order in declaratives, yet has interesting alterations in questions (VS) due to do-insertion. Spanish word order is much less strict. Underlyingly, it is an SVO language but, in declaratives, various other word orders are possible for discourse considerations with transitive and unergative verbs, and VS (not SV) is the default word order for unaccusatives. Questions, in most dialects of Spanish, require subject-verb inversion of the main verb (in other words, inversion is not a result of Aux-insertion as it is in English) for all verbal types. BP is quite different; like the other two languages, it is underlyingly SVO. It rarely deviates from SVO word order; in fact, except for unaccusatives in questions only, VS(O) order is more or less patently ungrammatical. Both English and BP are low attachment preference languages, whereas Spanish prefers high attachment for relative clause interpretations. Thus, in a sentence such as 'María quería hablar con la hija de la pescadera que se cortó el pelo' (Mary wants to talk to the daughter of the fishmonger who had a haircut), it is more likely that the daughter had her hair cut and not the female fishmonger, whereas the opposite would be the pattern in English and BP.

Rothman (2010) designed two tasks, the first being a GJT that tapped into word order restrictions with six target conditions with different patterning combinations among the three languages, as described above and summarized in Table 4.7.

The second task consisted of an attachment preference task in which the participants were presented with two types of relative clauses, some being ambiguous and some unambiguous, in which grammatical gender morphology in adjectival agreement was used to force either a low or high attachment interpretation. The relative clauses in which one or another interpretation was left uncoerced would predict different ambiguity resolution if Spanish or English (overt gender in possessive adjectives were used for English to do this) were to be transferred. If they interpreted the ambiguous relative clauses with a low attachment preference, this would indicate English transfer. Conversely, a high attachment preference would indicate Spanish transfer.

Table 4.7 *Distribution of SV order and VS order in BP, English and Spanish (adapted from Rothman, 2010: 261)*

		Trans. decl.	Unerg. decl.	Unacc. decl.	Trans. inter.	Unerg. interrog.	Unacc. interrog.
SV order	BP	Ok	Ok	Ok	Ok	Ok	Ok
	English	Ok	Ok	Ok	*	*	*
	Spanish	Ok	Ok	#/Ok	*	*	*
VS order	BP	*	*	#/Ok	*	*	#/Ok
	English	*	*	*	Ok	Ok	Ok
	Spanish	#/Ok	#/Ok	Ok	Ok	Ok	Ok

All the L3 learners of BP, irrespective of whether they were L1 or L2 Spanish speakers, displayed relative clause attachment preferences and word order grammaticality judgments in line with the way in which native speakers of Spanish do. The results showed two important things: (i) that typological proximity seemed to override other potential factors determining transfer selection, such as L2 status, and that (ii) nonfacilitation in L3 acquisition occurs, which was not anticipated by the CEM (Section 4.2.3).

4.3.4.2.2 A Brief Look at Further Support

As highlighted above in Section 4.3.1.2, the language pairing reviewed for Rothman (2010) – BP as the target L3 and English/Spanish as alternating L1s and L2s – has indeed provided much support for the TPM (e.g., Cabrelli Amaro, 2013b; Cabrelli Amaro, 2015; Cabrelli Amaro, Amaro, & Rothman, 2015; Giancaspro, Halloran, & Iverson, 2015; Ionin, Grolla, Santos, & Montrul, 2015; Montrul, Dias, & Santos, 2011; Rothman, 2010, 2011; Santos, 2013). Other Romance languages have also contributed to this support, including French, Italian and Spanish as L3 targets when another Romance language is the L1 or L2 (e.g., Borg, 2013; Bruhn de Garavito & Perpiñán, 2014; Cabrelli Amaro et al., 2018; Rothman & Cabrelli Amaro, 2010). Across these Romance-language studies alone, many domains of morphosyntactic (and its interfaces) transfer have been examined, including tense, aspect, and mood, several properties related to subject and object arguments, bare nominals (genericity and existential interpretations), verbal argument structure, sentential word order, adjectival syntax and meaning, among others. In all of these cases, even when the other language available – most often English – could have provided more facilitative transfer, the previously acquired Romance language was the source of transfer.

A reasonable question to ask, one that we have discussed in this chapter directly and alluded to indirectly is this: How far does the typological effect extend? Does it apply beyond the Romance family? Does it only truly capture an otherwise obvious effect of genetically related transfer when only one of two could win? In Section 4.3.3.3, we reviewed a study by Puig-Mayenco and Marsden (2018) in some detail, which offers evidence to suggest that the parser's use of underlying typological and structural cues does indeed go well beyond the level of language family. Although this study also involved two Romance languages and one Germanic language, unlike the above studies, English was the target L3. This means that the L1 and L2 were the genetically related, highly similar (across the board) languages. Therefore, choosing between one Romance language and another for transfer could not be done on the basis of genetic relationship to the target L3. The authors argued convincingly – see details in Section 4.3.3.3 – that typological factors and how the parser weighted them as articulated by the TPM makes the right predictions for what was observed in their data.

Let us also consider the opposite, yet similar scenario, in which two Germanic languages were the L1 and the L2, and the target was an L3 Romance language. Stadt, Hulk, and Sleeman (2016) examined V(erb)-to-T(ense) movement in L3 French by L1 Dutch–L2 English participants via a GJT. English, unlike French, does not display such movement. Dutch, as a consequence of being a V2 language, displays French-like surface word order in relevant contexts (such as adverbial placement). The results of the GJT showed that the learners transferred English to French, which provides evidence of both L2 transfer and an overall typological effect simultaneously. If it is not obvious why English would be chosen by the TPM, the reader is referred to Section 4.3.3 above. Although both the L1 and L2 in this case were Germanic languages, recall that the TPM argues for a primary lexical similarity effect used by the parser as a first pass. As a result of the Norman occupation of the British Isles from 1066, many words from (old) French were borrowed into (middle) English, from which a very high percentage of modern English vocabulary derives (e.g., Algeo, 2010), perhaps upwards of 25% (Bielenia-Grajewska, 2009). This is in sharp contrast to other Germanic languages such as Dutch, German and Flemish, and the Scandinavian ones, which have no such history. There is no question that of the two English stands out as (by far) the lexically more similar language.

Due to the fact that there was no mirror-image group, we cannot adjudicate meaningfully between the L2 Status Factor and the TPM, a similar scenario to Rothman and Cabrelli Amaro (2010). In fact, this confound was later acknowledged by the authors. In a follow-up attempting to tease apart a default L2-factor from an overall typological one, Stadt, Hulk and Sleeman (2018) added an additional group, keeping the L1 and L2 constant from the previous study – an exact mirror image not being practical, they did the next best thing and changed the target L3 to German (that is, L1 Dutch–L2 English to L3 German). In so doing, they did not see an L2 English effect in L3 German as they did in the 2016 study, which we take as an influence from L1 Dutch. Juxtaposing this against the L2 English effects on L3 French from Stadt, Hulk, and Sleeman (2016), it seems more likely that typological considerations were at play in both cases. The second study minimally shows that there is not a default L2 effect. If there had been, English should have shown its influence once again in this pairing. Therefore, we can see how the TPM can be applied irrespective of specific language pairings and that it is explanatory for data sets when linguistic cues are applied in accordance with the TPM's hierarchical rubric, whether or not intuition alone (that is, when the genetic relationship is obvious) leads to the same choice.

The work of Stadt et al. (2018) also stands out as an exemplary study in another way that is worthy of discussion in this section. To our knowledge, it is the only study in which all three languages were from the same (Germanic) family. As a standalone study, then, it is a good test case for the TPM and further highlights its explanatory power, as it demonstrates that the TPM's cue hierarchy provides a level of granularity from which ecologically valid predictions can meaningfully be made. Whether these predictions bear out and whether the TPM's current articulation of the cue hierarchy is correct is parenthetical to the epistemological point; the mere fact that it can make predictions among three closely related languages in the same language family a priori underscores its ability to be falsified and tested. It happens to be the case that its predictions also bear out, as detailed in the above paragraph. Again, based on the TPM's cue hierarchy, the parser should choose Dutch, the L1. The reasons for this were partially revealed above; recall from the explanation of why English is TPM-predicted in Stadt et al. (2016) that the English lexicon is less Germanic overall than are its sisters and cousins. Dutch and German, lexically speaking, are much closer despite the fact that all three languages share significant crossover, perhaps because German and Dutch share a level of mutual intelligibility – particularly in the written form – that English does not have with either. The lexical proximity is likely to be reinforced by other domains, such as phonology (for example, the final obstruent devoicing of Dutch and German, which is absent in English; Piroth, 2003) and syntax (such as the obligatory main clause V2 in Dutch and German and SOV [verb-final] constituent order in embedded clauses; Koster, 1975; Vikner, 1995).

Because the TPM hypothesizes a parser that is blind to genetic relationships as we know them (linguists and nonlinguists alike) yet does use the underlying linguistic properties that abound in such cases, there is still another real-world context that we have not yet reviewed: the case when none of the languages have any overt family relationship at all. A few studies have provided evidence in favor of the TPM, such as that of García Mayo and Slabakova (2015), who examined object drop in L3 English with the mirror-image groups alternating between Basque and Spanish as the L1 and L2. Basque is described as a three-way pro-drop language (e.g., Ortiz de Urbina, 1989), in which subjects, accusative and dative objects – overtly marked as ergative, absolutive and dative – can be left phonologically empty (in other words, they can be dropped). Both specific and generic Basque objects can be dropped freely (Duguine, 2008; Landa, 2009). Although Spanish also allows some instances of object drop, its distribution is restricted in comparison to Basque. Only [−definite, −specific] objects can be left phonologically empty (e.g., Bruhn de Garavito & Guijarro-Fuentes, 2002; Campos, 1986; Clements, 1994, 2006; Rothman & Iverson, 2013). English does not allow for generic and specific objects to be dropped.[10] Basque is a linguistic isolate with no living relatives and, except for borrowings from Spanish and English, has a unique vocabulary at the lexical level that is not similar to either Spanish or English. English, on the other hand, shares significant lexical crossover with Spanish via the Norman infiltration discussed previously (Latin being the common source of vocabulary in old French and Spanish). This alone is sufficient for Spanish to be selected by the TPM criteria for transfer; however, many other domains of grammar are likely to reinforce this choice − for example, Basque is an agglutinative language with an active-inactive case marking system and has an underlying SOV word order, which further highlights the greater similarity between Spanish and English.

The TPM's prediction should be that, if Basque is transferred, sensitivity to ungrammatical dropped objects in English should not differ in line with semantic constraints, such as definiteness and specificity. If Spanish is transferred, a distinction should be noted because Spanish, unlike Basque, restricts object drop to [−definite, −specific] contexts. As it turned out, Spanish seemed to exercise influence; that is, there was a dip in sensitivity for dropped objects in English, but only for objects that were [−definite, −specific]. This was true whether Spanish was the L1 or the L2 (likely entailing whether Spanish was the dominant language or not, given the context of Basque–Spanish bilingualism). This was also true even though Basque Spanish − the native Spanish dialect spoken in the Basque Country − has been described as potentially allowing more object drop than do other Spanish dialects; although more objects can be dropped in Basque Spanish, it is not obligatory (Larrañaga & Guijarro-Fuentes, 2012).

It should also be noted that the participants in this study were not beginner L3 learners. We have stressed how the TPM makes its clearest predictions for transfer in the initial stages, insofar as its main interest is tapping into initial representations. However, we have also highlighted how initial-stages transfer makes developmental predictions − if nonfacilitative transfer occurs early, it will eventually have to be unlearned during the course of L3 acquisition itself. Thus, evidence such as this from later stages might best be used to argue for a typological effect more generally and can be highlighted as compatible with the TPM; after all, we cannot be entirely certain of when Spanish transfer took place without a time machine! That being acknowledged, one could make the case that what García Mayo and Slabakova (2015) showed is indeed remnant transfer from the initial stages, since this domain should be particularly difficult to unlearn. If this is true, the Spanish effect could be predicted to linger in otherwise high levels of English proficiency.

On what basis might we claim it should be a particularly stubborn property to reconfigure? In this case, there will be no negative evidence from English input to induce a parsing failure; that is, to promote grammatical restructuring. Spanish allows for overt objects – which English requires – in [−definite, −specific] contexts as well, it just happens to prefer dropped objects here. Therefore, the input from English is not ungrammatical for the underlying transferred Spanish representation, it is just not the preferred configuration. In turn, the initially transferred syntax can parse the equivalent English sentences. There would need to be a secondary source, an indirect cue in English input, to induce a relevant parsing failure for restructuring, and this scenario could either never happen or could prolong the eventual convergence on the complete English representation even in advanced stages of proficiency.

Finally, we wish to highlight the range of language pairings that have been argued to show support for a primacy effect of comparative typology in L3/L*n* transfer selection. Doing so shows that the range of languages goes well beyond what might be otherwise known. For example, Özçelik (2013) tested L1 Uzbek, L2 Russian and L3 Turkish; Mollaie, Jabbari and Javad Rezaie (2016) tested L1 Persian, L2 French and L3 English; Na Ranong and Leung (2009) tested L1 Thai, L2 English and L3 Chinese; and Kulundary and Gabriele (2012) examined L1 Tuvan, L2 Russian and L3 English. As was the case with García Mayo and Slabakova (2015), all have examined very interesting combinations that include languages from a wide array of families.

4.3.5 *Conclusions about the TPM*

It is also important to acknowledge previous work that contributed to the thinking that underlies the TPM's emergence as a formalized model, such as Foote's (2009) study of transfer in the domain of grammatical aspect, in which typology was also considered to be a primary factor in the Romance-to-Romance transfer found in her study. As you will recall from Chapter 3, work in L3/L*n* lexical acquisition had also claimed a primacy effect for typology in transfer effects in the multilingual lexicon, such as the work of Singleton and O'Laire (2006). As we have reviewed, there has been no shortage of work in morphosyntax since 2010 indicating the key role of comparative typology for transfer effects. It is not clear that all of the data showing such an effect are supportive of all the claims and stipulations of the TPM. What is clear, however, is that typological/structural similarity is deterministic. Newer models, such as the LPM and the Scalpel Model, also take typological/structural similarity as a main variable, albeit in ways that manifest differently, a point to which we will return in Chapter 6.

4.4 Taking Stock: Moving Toward an Overview of What the Available Data Can Tell Us

Our goal in this chapter was to provide a comprehensive overview of the current theoretical proposals within generative approaches to L3/L*n* morphosyntax and, in so doing, to offer the most detailed articulation of our approach, the TPM, to date. The luxury of space that this forum affords made it ideal for both purposes, and we hope that the reader is well equipped to get the most out of Chapter 5 – a detailed, comparative analysis of the data this nascent field has produced thus far – with an understanding of the field's theoretical landscape. Most importantly, this includes the basics of the main variables that potentially constrain transfer source selection in L3/L*n* acquisition; for example, structural similarity, maximal facilitation, order of acquisition and so on. After all, models are multifaceted constructs based on the assumption that some variables are more deterministic than others in conditioning some natural phenomenon and, as such, can be reduced to the strongest possible version of themselves, one in which predicted outcomes are entirely bound to a single main variable (or group of variables with equal weight in the model). Therefore, knowing what factors characterize a model most prominently is essential to understanding and evaluating it properly. This relates to our discussion of the *strongest falsificator* in Section 1.6 in Chapter 1: Our objective when discussing L3/L*n* theoretical proposals in the way in which we did in the above was to provide the reader with the necessary tools to be able to test the models. For this reason, our discussion focused on the current state of the explanatory power of each theory (at least in our view), the argumentation underlying its claims and the systematicity of its predictive validity. If we have succeeded in this task, an interested reader will now be aware of what type of evidence, when accumulated to a critical mass, is in a position to falsify each model. When this was not immediately clear from the published record, we have discussed potential shortcomings and suggested directions for refinement toward a maximally articulated, minimally ambiguous version of the model.

Of equal importance, in our view, is the set of methodological considerations that have surfaced at various points throughout the chapter, and which relate to potential confounds in the interpretation of available data sets in light of the different models. While some of them are relatively small factors that were raised in our critical discussion of selected studies, others have been addressed extensively in epistemological articles (see Bardel & Falk, 2012; Rothman, 2015, for order of acquisition; González Alonso & Rothman, 2017a, for L3 developmental stage at testing). In fact, a cohort of fine-grained, highly articulated models is of little use to the advancement of a field if methodological factors introduce extraneous noise that essentially and inadvertently confound predictions of otherwise competing theories. A considerable part of our efforts should, therefore, be directed to ensuring that our methods provide a clear window, not a foggy pane, into the insights of different theoretical proposals – ideally, to as many different theories as possible simultaneously. Much of our progress in this sense, as is typical in science, will inevitably be a byproduct of hindsight with regard to unwitting missteps we will have taken in designing our studies that could only be appreciated via a rearview mirror. However, we hope that having identified some reliable ways of avoiding recurrent confounds will be helpful as the field grows. Lest this be misunderstood as a criticism applied to everyone but ourselves, be assured that our concern and advice is also meant to be self-facing. Recall the detailed explanation of how the TPM actually came to be; namely, unwittingly given the confounding of L2 status with potential underlying typological determinacy in Rothman and Cabrelli Amaro (2010). Our point is actually meant to be a simple one. In order to fulfill the general goal of empirical research, we need to be able to eliminate as many logical possibilities as possible – even and especially our own – to draw closer to answering the questions we pose accurately. The only way to eliminate possibilities fairly – that is, all models we have discussed herein – is via an accurate understanding of what the theory proposes and with a method that speaks to its predictions and falsification effectively. Precisely because each theory is truly a logical position, the cost is too high to discard any prematurely (or indeed to effectively eliminate a subclaim within a theory) on the basis of misconception.

Just as Chapter 4 was concerned with the theories, Chapter 5 will address the data directly. While reviewing a vast majority of the available studies of transfer in L3/L*n* morphosyntax systematically is certainly no small task, even in a comparatively young field such as ours, it is still viable given the relative size of the sample. Beyond feasibility, the moment is ripe for such a collective assessment of the data. Almost 20 years into its history, the field has gathered a critical mass of data that is now sufficiently powerful to be combined as a macro dataset. With the benefit of insights gleaned from the aggregate of available data, we can take a step back and consider the overall explanatory power of the variables proposed as being deterministic for transfer source selection, beyond the descriptive accuracy they have for individual data sets.

Notes

1. Although a functional distinction between transfer and CLE – even if other labels are used to make the same distinction – is not unique to generative linguistics (see Herdina & Jessner, 2002; Paradis, 2004), what is taken to constitute the linguistic representations themselves on which transfer operates, as meant herein, is very much a generative notion.

2. The notion of incremental transfer has precedence in earlier literature and complimentary paradigms. For example, Zobl (1980) argued for the selectivity of transfer along two axes: a formal axis and a developmental axis. The notion of incremental transfer refers to the developmental axis. According to Zobl (1980: 49) "learners must attain a certain level of development with respect to an L2 structure before transfer is activated" (see Schwartz, 1999, for details and a critique). This position is echoed until this day in processability theory, which claims that transfer occurs incrementally when, and only when, a domain of grammar is processible by a then-current developing interlanguage (Pienemann, 2005).

3. By "intaken" we are referring to the distinction between input versus intake, as discussed in great detail in Gass (1997). In this sense, input refers to all linguistic material available to the learner, whereas intake refers to the subset of input that is being processed by the learner. In other words, intake is the proportion of input that is being fed into the mechanisms for grammatical (re)configuration. It is possible, in fact likely, that not all of the available input, particularly at the beginning stages, is being intaken in this sense. This theoretical construct is particularly important for theories advocating property-by-property transfer. Differential timing in the development of a particular property should correlate to when sufficient input is intaken, not necessarily to when it was first available.

4. The TPM's proposal for how comparative typological or structural assessment is done by the parser is explained in Section 4.3.3. To really determine whether the TPM also predicts Russian over Kazakh – since both are equally lexically distinct – one would need to assess the relative phonology, morphology and morphosyntax of the three languages comparatively at a much deeper level. As it is a moot point for our purposes here, we will not do this, not least because formal descriptions of Kazakh are not nearly as abundant as are descriptions for the other two languages. Our use of head-directionality as a proxy permits the same epistemological point.

5. Rothman (2015) posed the question and discussed whether or not the TPM should be restricted to adult sequential bilinguals who venture the acquisition of yet another language in adulthood, or whether its predictions should apply equally across all types of bilinguals acquiring a chronological L3 (the third language by

mere counting). He discussed potential reasons for differences that age and other variables that differentiate sets of bilingual types might confer. He was ultimately inconclusive as to whether or not it should matter, albeit hinting toward it not mattering. However, Rothman rightfully concluded that answers to such a query beyond conjecture are ultimately an empirical question and, as of 2015, there were insufficient data. Bardel and Sánchez (2017) also discussed potential differences related to various sets of bilinguals who are traditional adult L2 learners acquiring an L3 (see Section 4.2.2). It is important to bear this in mind when understanding the results in Westergaard et al. (2017) and that evidence of the type they provide – from younger, simultaneous bilinguals acquiring an L3 – helps to rectify the dearth in the available data to which one had access even just a few years prior in order to address questions related to potential age and bilingual type differences properly. In Chapter 6, we will return to this question explicitly.

6. Although agreement by others that we have interpreted the implications of the relevant psycho-/neurolinguistics and neurocognition literature appropriately does not mean we are correct – logically, it only means that others agree. Nonetheless, it is interesting to point out that, in querying, to ensure our reading was at least a tenable one, some of the main figures in the relevant field, such as Ellen Bialystok, Judith Kroll, David Green and Viorica Marian, found our understanding to be on track, as were the implications thereof. It is relevant to understand what the main motivators of these positions think in this case, as we are also consumers of their research. For example, in a personal communication with Bialystok of June 4, 2018, she wrote: "My view is that there is absolutely no blockage – just as L1 and L2 are jointly active for bilinguals, L3 joins the party if there is a third language. The idea of inhibition or suppression seems to me (now) to be demonstrably false [that only one system is activated at a time]. Since it has been empirically ruled out for L1/L2 bilinguals, it would be incoherent for suppression/inhibition/*blockage* to suddenly show up for trilinguals." In a personal communication with Marian (June 3, 2018) she responded to the same query as follows: "I would predict that the transfer of representations from a previously acquired system would indeed NOT block off access to the other system(s) available to a bilingual acquiring yet another additional language."

7. Slabakova, in personal communication (April 24, 2018) suggested "that a complete and actual transfer of the L1 grammar into the L2 would mean transfer of quite a lot of lexical items" in consideration of how minimalism (Chomsky, 1995) envisages the bundling of features on functional morphology – the basis of grammatical structure – being encoded in the lexicon (on lexical heads). We do not agree that this is an issue, particularly in light of Sprouse (2006), in which an updated version of the FT/FA model compatible with minimalism is presented. Central to this version of the model is the transfer of L1 lexical items, necessarily encompassing their morphosyntactic and semantic features (but minus labels); acquisition would thus consist of relabelling the lexical items and, sometimes, rebundling the features. Both operations would be triggered by input in the L2, which induces parsing failures.

8. Linguistic typology as a system of classification is based on shared formal (grammatical) features across languages independently of genetic relationship. What this

means, in essence, is that linguistic typology is complementary, but crucially not equivalent, to linguistic genealogy – that is, the classification of languages into families according to their documented or presumed common origin. For example, both Japanese and Tamil are head-final languages (phrase heads are typically preceded by their complements) and are therefore typologically similar with regard to head-directionality; however, it seems unlikely that they are even remotely related. That being said, genetically related languages tend to have moderately high degrees of overlap in typological terms when their grammars are compared as a whole. Thus, by typology, the TPM refers to underlying structural similarity (see González Alonso & Rothman, 2017; Rothman, 2011, 2015, for discussion). Throughout the book, we use the term 'typology' in strictly linguistic terms, 'typological proximity/similarity' as measured over the entire grammar, and 'typological transfer' to be the one predicted by the specific learner-internal mechanisms proposed in the TPM; that is, by anecdotal perceptions of overall similarities.

9. We do not ignore the fact that English allows for extremely restricted instances of so-called dropped subjects; however, these are not instances of bona fide null-subject licensing. For example, English allows for a phenomenon often referred to as diary drop, a restricted instance of topic-drop, whereby overt subjects can be omitted in colloquial registers – historically, a manner in which personal diaries/journals were written, hence the name – if and only if in first, unstressed position, and only in contexts in which the subject can otherwise be readily understood from previous discourse (e.g., Haegeman, 2007; Haegeman & Ihsane, 1999; Haegeman & Ihsane, 2001). For example, as an informal answer to the question 'What did you do yesterday?' it would acceptable to reply, 'Went to the movies with some friends.' However, *'Yesterday, went to the movies with some friends' would be a definitively ungrammatical response, precisely because the subject is not in the first position and is thus not a topic that can be dropped. English has no other markings of a null-subject language: Expletives are obligatorily overt, it has very weak agreement morphology, there is no possibility of unpronounced embedded subjects, it does not abide by the Overt Pronoun Constraint, it has nominative→oblique case in existential copula constructions such as *A: Who is it? B: It's me/ *I am/am I* and so on.

10. Although it is generally true that English does not permit phonetically unrealized objects with transitive verbs in spoken language, it does permit them in a highly limited register related to recipes and similar types of writing such as 'beat [Ø] until stiff then put [Ø] in oven and bake [Ø] for 45 minutes' (Culy, 1996: 91). Depending on one's position with regard to the universality of an object position projection in VP, irrespective of the lexical choice of V, as argued in Cummings and Roberge's (2003) transitivity requirement, all implicit objects in English – in which typically transitive verbs have an unergative use, such as 'Push [Ø] harder!', 'Do you sing [Ø]?', 'She will steal [Ø] without remorse' – could be considered instances of null objects. We put this issue aside since the claims regarding English here are not our own but rather analyses of English assumed by García Mayo and Slabakova (2015) in their study.

5   A Review of Published Work

5.0   General Introduction

As we saw in great detail in Chapter 4, interest in the L3/Ln acquisition of morphosyntax is thriving. It is not surprising that a substantial amount of research in this emerging field has focused on transfer and/or cross-language effects (CLE) in L3/Ln learning. Examining how previous linguistic experience affects subsequent learning has been a staple topic in nonnative language acquisition for as long as people have been examining L2 acquisition seriously. This curiosity likely springs from both theoretical interests and personal reflection. Even as young lay people – before we were linguists studying this – we recall having some conscious, if not intuitive, feelings that our native languages both propelled and restricted our learning of the additional languages we were studying. Of course, research over many decades – many hundreds, if not thousands of well-designed studies – has shown how far beyond intuitive anecdote the effects that previous linguistic knowledge has on additional language learning go. Thus, it seems natural that interest would potentially be even greater in additive multilingualism (L3/Ln) than it is in additive bilingualism (L2), if only because of the greater potential complexity involved. With increased sources from which to choose, determining what variables, if any, condition how previous linguistic knowledge affects the L3/Ln process makes the challenge of investigating this more exciting than it is in L2 acquisition in some ways. After all, the L3 context affords a new opportunity for those who study nonnative acquisition. The question is no longer "How does the L1 affect subsequent language acquisition?", but "How does transfer unfold when the mind has choices at its disposal?"

The above discussion embodies a very important question. Understanding how previous linguistic knowledge influences additive multilingualism must, in our view, take center stage in our nascent field if we are to have the fairest chance of determining how L3/Ln development works and of being able to predict outcomes. Transfer/CLE is a principal, deterministic variable that factors into developmental sequencing.[1] First spoiler alert: The data covered in the systematic review in this chapter make the previous statement unequivocally clear. Transfer/CLE necessarily alters the formal learning task – the grammatical learning task shifts in response to transfer/CLE – and the developmental path changes accordingly. Transfer/CLE alters the learning task from the very point of influence going forward, meaning that the timing thereof matters. For the purposes of ultimately describing and explaining L3 development overall, it is useful to see whether transfer/CLE is present at any point in the L3/L*n* developmental continuum. The question becomes "How might the timing of examining this differentially affect what can be gleaned from it?"

Although the Typological Primacy Model (TPM) is principally focused on the initial-stages interlanguage representations, whereas other models seem to be more interested in the entirety of the L3 developmental process, their foci are much more similar than such a stark difference might lead one to believe. All of the models, and all of the authors of the papers that factor into the systematic review in this chapter, recognize that L2 and L3 acquisition present themselves differently across the developmental continuum. It is acknowledged by all models that the way in which L3 unfolds is not random and that transfer/CLE plays a significant role in such nonrandomness. All models invariably contain two underlying assumptions: (i) that one or more variables can reveal the nonrandom nature of when and/or why transfer/CLE takes place, and (ii) that these variables are weighted such that, all things being equal, one variable takes precedence over the others.

The way that L3 unfolds is not random and transfer or CLE plays a big role in the non-randomness

Recall that, as discussed in Chapter 4, the TPM is not uninterested in, nor does it deny the potential of, later stage influence at various levels of L3/L*n* development. Its focus on the initial stages of interlanguage is galvanized by its concerns with our ability to know reliably when in the developmental process transfer actually occurred if tested beyond the initial stages. Just because *something* is detectable at the L3 intermediate proficiency level, for example, this does not pinpoint, even indirectly, when this *something* first obtained via transfer. We simply know that, at the intermediate L3 proficiency level – that is, the time of testing – it was present. This point is important since the formal learning task is altered at the time of influence itself. Modeling developmental trajectories is thus dependent on pinpointing timing in addition to source. Of course, evidence of absence is not necessarily absence of evidence. Therefore, in the event that the predicted transfer source at the initial stages is not shown at the intermediate level and beyond, this cannot be used to argue against the prediction, precisely because (nonfacilitative) transfer could have been worked out by that point. Furthermore, it is not always clear that one can differentiate transfer from L3 development itself when learners have had sufficient experience with the target grammar. When apparent influence seems unlikely to stem from the target grammar – that is, it is nonfacilitative – we can assume more safely that it originates from previous linguistic experience. Nonetheless, we still are confronted with the same potential issues of timing and its determinism for modeling the formal L3 learning task.

All models are concerned with L3 development and ultimate attainment. It just so happens that the TPM presents more conservatively, given its preoccupation with our ability to tease apart, a posteriori and reliably, potential noise from the signal when we examine learners beyond a particular point in L3 development. However, the preoccupation is simply one of accuracy in labeling. That is, the TPM claims nothing about the necessity for and the utility of the data collected past the initial stages themselves. All L3 data collected using sound methodology are important for the biggest question in our field, which is understanding the complexities of L3 acquisition and use from start to finish with ecological validity. Just as is the case in L2 acquisition studies, however, not all data are as useful for each research subquestion. The query to which we will return toward the end of this chapter, then, is whether or not all data are positioned equally to address the question of transfer source and timing. With these caveats in mind, we will consider all the data at our disposal, from an impressive number of studies, irrespective of the proficiency level of the L3 learners when the data were collected.

In line with scientific reasoning in general, we concede that, in all likelihood, none of the models that currently exist is correct in absolute terms as yet, including the TPM. Chapter 4 outlined the epistemology behind the models, the scope thereof and what is at stake in theoretical terms. Because we take as a given that none is perfect and that insights from various models will ultimately be needed to explain the entirety of the existent data from the literature, it is useful, if not essential, to have an in-depth look at as much of the data as possible in a single place. This is what we endeavor to do by means of a systematic review of the existing literature in Chapter 5.

As discussed in Section 1.6 in Chapter 1 and throughout Chapter 4, all models have the same burden: Ideally, they must be able to describe and explain the preponderance of data that is relevant to their hypothesized remit (that is, all data that the model claims to cover). We will consider how each model fairs in light of the data as a whole, particularly as it relates to Jacobs's (2000) notion of the *strongest falsificator* – see Section 1.6 in Chapter 1. Second spoiler alert: No model covers all the data. However, we will see that there are clear trends suggesting that some insights are on the right track. We will consider what methodological factors correlate with particular outcomes, and provide a critical discussion of what this means. Given that the data cover a range of L3 proficiencies, we will also be able to gain some insights into the true dynamic nature of L3 development.

5.1 Why a Systematic Review?

To understand what the combined data from the literature say in their own right and in relation to the models discussed in Chapter 4, we offer an updated systematic review. This is based on the systematic review in Puig-Mayenco, González Alonso and Rothman (2018), albeit departing from it in several ways. To begin, having been done over a year later, it includes 21 more experiments (across 17 further publications), increasing the total number of experiments considered from 71 to 92. These 17 new publications brought with them 24 new scholars whose work was not factored into the previous systematic review. The fact that there are so many more studies that could be included, and so many new researchers producing work in this subfield, demonstrates the trending expansion of interest. Of course, the generalizability of correlations revealed by systematic reviews benefits exponentially from the ever-larger sets of data considered. To our knowledge, the cohort of studies we consider from the literature is an exhaustive one; below, we will explain the criteria for retrieval and inclusion. The presentation of the systematic review herein also departs in significant ways from Puig-Mayenco et al., not least because of the space a book permits as opposed to that available in an academic article. The tone here is unique, as the intended audience is different. Our goals across the two overlap only partially. The present chapter takes full advantage of space to unpack all that could and should be said stemming from this macro-analysis at various levels. It is thus written simultaneously for the novice reader and for the researcher who is already fully invested in this subfield.

As terminology can be confusing, we wish to clarify from the beginning that this chapter does not offer a meta-analysis in the traditional sense, for reasons that pertain both to the nature of the studies themselves and to our specific motivations. Meta-analyses provide calculations based on individual studies' effect sizes – or some other measure of strength – to synthesize quantitative information from related studies. The ensuing result summarizes an entire body of research with regard to the effects of a particular treatment on a specific population that is targeted by all the studies included (e.g., Boulton & Cobb, 2017; Norris & Ortega, 2000; Plonsky & Oswald, 2012). By combining several studies in one large data set, meta-analyses seek to alleviate the *sampling problem* – namely, that one normally has access to only a small subset of the population of interest and should therefore be cautious when generalizing outwards from the narrow scope of a single study's results. The majority of the studies reviewed here do not meet the requirements to conduct a meta-analysis of the type just described, as effect sizes are crucial for performing a proper meta-analysis. Unfortunately, effect sizes are not reported in many of the relevant studies, nor can they be estimated directly or indirectly from the information reported in the studies in line with how this could be done as per Boulton and Cobb, (2017) and Plonsky and Oswald (2012, 2014), among others. Had we performed a proper meta-analysis, more than 50% of the included studies would not have been usable. This would have prejudiced the emerging picture unfairly, since literally all the available studies claiming to show evidence for some of the variables for which we coded (see Section 5.4) would have necessarily been cast aside.

There is considerable value in attempting to capture a panoramic view of the relevant available data, even if this cannot be done as a meta-analysis per se. Instead, we offer a formal systematic review of the field. Systematic reviews follow a clear, predefined structure to find, assess and analyze studies that have all attempted to answer a similar question in the absence of effect sizes available in the composite studies (Plonsky & Kim, 2016; Roessingh, 2004). Our main goal is to explore, describe, and provide a critical analysis of methodological practices currently followed in studies on morphosyntactic transfer in L3/L*n* acquisition in an effort to shed better light on what the collective whole of the data reveal. If successful in this endeavor, we should prepare the ground for more robust consensuses. A systematic review could show that some disparities in argumentation and seemingly mutual exclusivity of positions are predicated more on methodological issues than on anything else. It could also reveal, in a principled way, if the plurality of the available data warrants the discarding of any positions argued previously. Thus, we aim to uncover, to the extent that they exist, potential associations between methodological choices or practices and otherwise robust effects related to macro variables that differentiate the models. If we are on the right track, we will be able to offer insights into consolidating consistency in experimental design for purposes of reliability, replicability and maximum comparability across studies.

5.2   Study Retrieval and Inclusion Criteria

Three types of studies were included in the review:

   (a)   studies published in peer-reviewed publications (journal articles, book chapters and conference proceedings),

   (b)   defended doctoral dissertations with a special emphasis on transfer in L3/L*n* acquisition, and

   (c)   very recent research presented at conferences in early 2018 after peer-reviewed abstract submission.

Category (c) is limited for obvious reasons – as two of the 92 experiments are unpublished work and do not appear in the databases, we would need access to the data. For categories (a) and (b), the search was conducted via Google Scholar, ProQuest and Language and Linguistic Behavior Abstracts (LLBA). Relevant studies were located using keywords such as the terms *third language* or *multilingualism* + *morphosyntax*, as well as the specific models' names – *Cumulative Enhancement Model (CEM), L2 Status Factor (L2SF), TPM, Linguistic Proximity Model (LPM)* and *Scalpel Model*. Articles citing each model's main publications were also inspected. Table 5.1 contains citations for the main articles in which the models were first presented and/or follow-up articles that add significant stipulations, modifications and/or clarifications to the original idea. The table shows that the three original models are cited frequently in the literature – as are the new models, considering the time that has lapsed between when each was published and April 25, 2018, the date on which we completed the final search for inclusion.

After each citation was examined manually, a second filter was applied: We included only those publications that (a) presented original L3 datasets – in other words, we excluded epistemological commentaries, review articles and papers in which the models were cited but the empirical study did not pertain to L3 – and (b), met one or more of the following criteria:

   (i)   they focused on transfer in L3/L*n* morphosyntax;

   (ii)   they focused specifically on testing the models of L3/L*n* acquisition discussed herein; and/or

   (iii)   they focused on modeling L3/L*n* morphosyntax.

In total, 63 independent research projects were included in the analysis. When a research project contained more than one experiment, each experiment was coded as an individual study. In the final analysis, a total of 92 different

Table 5.1 *Number of citations in Google Scholar (date of retrieval April 25, 2018)*

Article	N of citations	Total
Cumulative Enhancement Model		
Flynn, Foley, & Vinnitskaya (2004)	281	
Flynn, Vinnitskaya, & Foley (2008)	8	318
Berkes & Flynn (2012a)	29	
L1 Position		
Lozano (2003)	64	
Hermas (2010)	26	114
Hermas (2014)	21	
The L2 Status Factor		
Bardel & Falk (2007)	301	
Falk & Bardel (2011)	137	465
Falk, Lindqvist, & Bardel (2015)	27	
The Typological Primacy Model		
Rothman (2010)	85	
Rothman (2011)	183	345
Rothman (2015)	77	
The Linguistic Proximity Model		
Mykhaylyk et al. (2015)	6	25
Westergaard et al. (2017)	19	
The Scalpel Model		
Slabakova (2017)	17	17

experiments/studies were examined. Hereafter, we refer to these as "studies" for the sake of simplicity. Each study and details pertaining to it can be found in Appendix A at the end of the book. Appendix A provides the publication details (author and year), the language combination(s) tested in the study (L1, L2 and L3) and the domain of morphosyntax examined.

5.3   Demographics of Included Studies

The 92 different studies in the dataset were published/defended by 66 different researchers – in various cohorts – between 2003 and 2018. While there are a few publications before 2003 that could be considered, for example some conference proceeding papers from Ingrid Leung's then-developing dissertation (Leung, 1998), these data sets were inevitably included in later journal publications. In an effort not to duplicate data sets, we opted for the journal article in such cases. As alluded to in Section 5.2 above, there has been a sharp

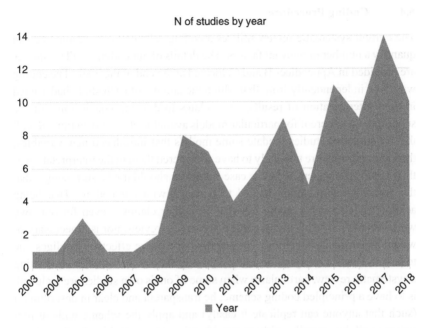

Figure 5.1 *Distribution of datasets from 2003 to 2018*

increase in research on L3/L*n* morphosyntax from a formal linguistic per-spective, particularly over the past few years. This can be seen clearly in Figure 5.1.

In terms of targeted populations, the datasets contain data from language triads with 25 different languages as either the L1, the L2 or the L3: Albanian, Arabic, Azeri, Basque, Brazilian Portuguese, Catalan, Dutch, English, Farsi (Persian), Flemish, French, German, Hungarian, Japanese, Italian, Latin, Mandarin (Chinese), Mazandarani, Norwegian, Old Church Slavonic, Russian, Spanish, Swedish, Turkish and Tuvan. Research included in the systematic review comes from all corners of the globe, most notably from data collected in Europe and North America, but also from Africa (Fessi, 2013; Hermas, 2010, 2015), Middle East and Central Asia (Fallah & Jabbari, 2018; Kulundary & Gabriele, 2012; Mollaie et al., 2016), (South-)East Asia (Kong, 2015; Na Ranong & Leung, 2009), and South America (Parma, 2017) in recent years. A total of 2,234 people were tested across the 92 studies. This number is absolute without double counting; that is, it is the total number of subjects tested across the 63 research projects.

5.4   Coding Procedure

The current systematic review utilizes a coding scheme to operationalize and quantify a number of relevant factors. The details of our coding of all 92 studies are provided in Appendices B and C, located at the end of the book. The coding was done independently from that which the authors of each study had argued in their interpretation of results, as it relates to drawing conclusions for the support or lack thereof for particular models available at any given time. Recall that a number of studies predate some models that introduced new variables; thus, the authors were not likely to have considered them in the interpretation of their results. It happens to be the case – and this should not be surprising – that the author's interpretation tended to coincide with our coding. That being acknowledged, simply going by what an author claims – even for our own work – is not the right way to guide a systematic review, nor is it necessary or would be particularly helpful. The standard procedure effectively obliges one to be blind to data interpretation. The only way to be unbiased when conducting a systematic review, particularly when some of one's own studies are included, is to have a principled coding scheme, be transparent and clear in describing it (such that anyone can replicate it easily) and apply the scheme without prejudice to all data equally, without consideration of any positing by the authors themselves. The data are indexical; the interpretation of data is not necessarily so. The beauty of such an analysis is that the coded numbers render statistics that can then be (re)interpreted with greater power.

We coded each study consistently, following the same two-step process. We coded for two sets of variables: (i) macro and (ii) methodological variables. These will be explained in much greater detail below. Suffice to say for now that macro variables correspond to transfer source/type, and methodological ones correspond to choices in empirical design that could, in principle, condition how we interpret the subset of studies ascribed to a particular macro variable. We must bear in mind that any given data set could simultaneously provide evidence for multiple variables for which we coded. To cite one example, L2 status and typological proximity are not inherently incompatible; thus, a given data set could receive a positive valuation for both. After all, the potential for support or lack thereof is not binary: There are five macro variables that map onto six positions to consider with partially overlapping claims. In this sense, a neutral coding scheme can probe for potential compatibilities with more than one model at the same time.

The first step was to code each experiment in binary terms for five macro variables meant to capture the source (and type) of transfer:

(a) *L1 transfer,*
(b) *L2 transfer,*
(c) *Typological transfer* (in line with the TPM's cue hierarchy, described in Section 4.3.3),
(d) *Hybrid transfer* (simultaneous or alternative transfer from both languages), and
(e) *Nonfacilitative transfer.*

Appendix B provides the details of the values we assigned to each of the variables per study. We will provide further details of each macro variable in Section 5.4.1 below. Table 5.2 provides a summary of these macro variables and the coding value associated with each level. In principle, it is possible for any given data set – unlikely as it might be to the extreme – to receive a check for a plurality of factors at the same time. We will revisit the possibility of overlap immediately below, using a tangible example from our set of 92 studies reviewed. By coding in this way, no single macro variable – or the models to which they apply differently – is prejudiced.

The data set from each study was then further coded for five relevant methodological factors. The purpose of this was to run statistical tests later to see where correlations exist between the use of a specific methodology and source/ type (the macro variables) of transfer/CLE. Understanding the extent to which methodological practices correlate significantly with specific subsets of the data related to different sources (and types) of transfer can help us to move toward our goal of consolidating consistency in experimental design. Of course, correlations between methodological choice and outcomes can be positive or (inadvertently) negative. We will discuss, argue for and defend our interpretation of what the potential correlations in this regard reveal, with which we do not expect everyone to agree. That being said, what should be incontrovertible is that the coding

Table 5.2 *Binary value assignment to macro variables and factors in the study*

Macro variables	Levels
L1 transfer	Yes=($\checkmark$); No=(X)
L2 transfer	Yes=($\checkmark$); No=(X)
Typological transfer	Yes=($\checkmark$); No=(X)
Hybrid transfer	Yes=($\checkmark$); No=(X)
Nonfacilitative transfer	Yes=($\checkmark$); No=(X)

scheme we are adopting allows us to reveal correlations without prejudice up and until the point at which one begins to interpret the implications. In other words, we submit that whatever one's interpretations of the correlations are, revealing them is a fruitful expedition a priori.

The five methodological variables for which we coded are

(a) *Proficiency* of the participants in the L3,

(b) *Testing beyond the L3* (that is, whether participants were tested only in the L3 or also in one or more of the previously acquired languages),

(c) *Production or comprehension* (whether the study examined production or comprehension data),

(d) *Mirror-image groups,* whether mirror-image participant groups were examined (for example, L1 Spanish–L2 English–L3 Catalan versus L1 English–L2 Spanish–L3 Catalan), and

(d) *Genetic relationship* (whether either or both previous languages were genetically related to the L3; for example, L1 Spanish–L2 English–L3 Catalan, where Spanish and Catalan are genetically related, versus L1 Japanese–L2 English–L3 Arabic, where none of the languages are related).

Appendix C provides the details of the values we assigned for each of the variables per study. These variables are explained in greater detail in Section 5.4.2. As with the macro variables, these methodological factors were coded as binary variables. As noted above, in principle, each study could check off several (or all) of these variables at a time. Table 5.3 contains a summary of the factors and a description of variable levels.

5.4.1   Macro variables

The five macro variables listed in Table 5.2 were coded to reflect whether a given study's results were potentially compatible with the constructs of

Table 5.3 *Methodological factors included in the study*

Methodological factors	Levels
Proficiency in the L3	Beginner; Post-beginner
Testing beyond the L3	L3 only; L3/L2 and/or L1
Production or comprehension	Production; Comprehension
Mirror-image groups	Yes; No
Genetic relationship	Related; Not related

exclusive *L1* or *L2 transfer, typological transfer, hybrid transfer* or *nonfacilitative transfer.* In various combinations or lack of combinations of positive values, these five variables enable one to claim support for and/or compatibility of a given data set with the six available models reviewed in Chapter 4. Four of the five variables relate to the source of transfer/CLE, whereas one – *nonfacilitative transfer* – relates to the type. The reason for coding for this single type variable relates to our ability to interpret the results juxtaposed against the models. The *nonfacilitative transfer* variable will prove crucial in differentiating the CEM's predictions from those of the others. As we will see, and as we address immediately below, the models' predictions are mainly straightforward, but, given that there are six, there is considerable overlap in some of the models' predictions in principle. To understand the dynamic nature of how these models relate to one another more fully, we now turn to a discussion of how each conforms to the macro variables we coded, making a distinction between what is truly supportive as opposed to compatible evidence, and what the strongest falsificator (Jacobs, 2000; see Section 1.6 in Chapter 1) is per model.

Positive valuations for *L1* or *L2 transfer* would provide clear, supportive evidence for the L1 default position or the L2SF, respectively, if and only if *typological transfer* were not valued positively at the same time. *L1* or *L2 transfer* are not mutually exclusive with *typological transfer* per se; thus, when positive valuations co-occur, this means the data are merely compatible with (not strongly supportive of) either the L1 default position or the L2SF. Data sets valued positively for *L1* or *L2 transfer* without *typological transfer* would mean that the design could rule out *typological transfer* – for example, a mirror-image design – and thus constitutes the best evidence of bona fide support for the default models. For these, the simultaneous valuation of the *nonfacilitative transfer* variable does not matter, since neither precludes absolute L1 or L2 transfer from being nonfacilitative. *Hybrid transfer* is ruled out in principle because of how this variable was coded (see Section 5.4.1.1). As a result, positive valuations for *hybrid transfer* or *typological transfer,* when not co-occurring with *L1 or L2 transfer* positive values – for example, when a mirror-image design shows no default status at play – are the strongest falsificator(s) for these two default transfer positions in Jacobs's (2000) terms.

The TPM would be supported if *typological transfer* were valued positively, either exclusively or with a positive value for *nonfacilitative transfer.* The TPM, as discussed above, is compatible when either *L1* or *L2 transfer* is valued positively and co-occurs with a positive valuation for *typological transfer* (irrespective of what the valuation for *nonfacilitative transfer* is). Given the

TPM's claims, a positive valuation for *hybrid transfer* is the most problematic when tested at the initial stages of L3/Ln, since this is not predicted to obtain a priori. *Hybrid transfer* at the initial stages is, therefore, the TPM's strongest falsificator.

The CEM makes strong claims related to *nonfacilitative transfer*; therefore, positive valuation for the *nonfacilitative transfer* variable is the CEM's strongest falsificator. The CEM is otherwise compatible with positive valuations of all other variables, except perhaps for certain instantiations of what we include under the label *hybrid transfer*, as explained in Section 5.4.1.3. When a positive valuation for *hybrid transfer* relates to some amalgamated L1/L2 influence on the same linguistic property (that is, a hybrid representation), then this might be ruled out by the CEM as a function of its claims regarding nonfacilitation. An L1/L2 amalgamated influence is highly likely to result in some level of nonfacilitation for the L3 learning task – it will need to be reconfigured – and should therefore be precluded by the model. However, when a positive valuation for *hybrid transfer* reflects application to the data from an experiment that tested two properties and found L1 transfer for one and L2 transfer for the other, this could be compatible with the CEM if both are facilitative choices, precisely because it could show how facilitation itself is selectively deterministic.

It is difficult to determine what the strongest falsificator would be for the LPM and the Scalpel Model. As discussed in Sections 4.2.4 and 4.2.5 in Chapter 4, what the precise predictions of these models are is not yet clear, which makes it impossible to determine their strongest falsificator. A good candidate for the strongest falsificator might arise by showing that transfer, which is assumed by both models to occur at the property-by-property level, is exceedingly imprecise given the entirety of the data. If there is any advantage to property-by-property transfer, it must surely rest in the greater precision that would be entailed for selecting the right grammar at the most opportune time of L3 development – in line with the CEM's original claim. This being said, both the LPM and Scalpel Model clearly acknowledge that nonfacilitation occurs. As discussed in Section 4.2.4, neither model has yet offered a rubric whereby one can capture predictively when nonfacilitation is expected. Thus, the authors will rightly claim that these models do not preclude nonfacilitation per se. However, should it not follow that nonfacilitation should be relatively infrequent and/or predictable in a way that can retroactively offer a good fit for the majority of available data? If we are on the right track, a confluence of evidence showing nonfacilitation should be problematic for these approaches, at least until they offer a fine-grained mechanism with predictions that hold across the available data.

CEM = Cumulative Enhancement Model

Both models question in the strongest terms the claim that transfer is wholesale. Therefore, evidence suggesting that transfer is wholesale would provide strong evidence against a central claim of these models. However, for practical reasons, we will not factor this into our coding scheme directly. It is nearly impossible to prove a negative (that is, that transfer is *not* wholesale) as opposed to hypothesizing that it is when justified on a confluence of evidence suggesting it could be; that is, by generalizing from the existing evidence base. What would constitute sufficient evidence to assuage the doubts of those who reject it? It is a logical question to ask, since no one would consider it reasonable to have to test every domain of grammar to corroborate wholesale transfer indexically at the beginning L3 stages. As discussed in Section 4.3.1.2 in Chapter 4, when one examines the studies across the 92 that keep the L1, L2 and L3s constant and test the true initial stages, it is defensible to propose wholesale transfer on the merits of super-aggregate data, a point to which we will return when describing in more detail the methodological variables for which we coded in Section 5.4.2.

Positive valuations for *L1* or *L2 transfer* that could be sustained on the basis of the plurality of available data would chip away at the strength of some of the LPM's and Scalpel Model's claims. After all, property-by-property transfer makes it unlikely that the source will always be from the same language. In principle, both models are otherwise compatible with positive valuations of the other variables, but evidence of *hybrid transfer* would serve to provide some supportive evidence for a subset of the claims made by these models.

5.4.1.1 L1 and L2 (as Default) Transfer

As the heading of this section suggests, the default *L1 transfer* and *L2 transfer* variables are the easiest to assess and the most straightforward to explain. In the case that an available data set provides evidence exclusively for L1 or L2 transfer, one or the other was coded positively. In principle, these two variables are mutually exclusive, precisely because a positive value for one precludes the other – if we see *exclusive* L1 transfer, then L2 transfer cannot obtain by definition. Conversely, we would have an instance of *hybrid transfer*, for which we explain the coding parameters in Section 5.4.1.3 below. In theory, there is one logical scenario in which both could be valued positively, but this would be tantamount to a fatal methodological design, at least in the sense of being able to provide any meaningful evidence for the transfer source question at hand. When an L1 and an L2 have the same underlying grammatical configuration for a given property, evidence of transfer in an L3 would be completely ambiguous but, technically speaking, would be compatible with exclusive L1 and L2 transfer simultaneously. Given this inherent confound, it is not surprising that such a scenario applied to very few of the 92 studies we examined.

It is possible that other confounding factors can conspire to make *L1 transfer* and *L2 transfer* appear absolute – because, in a given data set, they are – yet not serve as sufficiently strong data from which to make or justify generalizations regarding the default status of one or the other. This occurs when data sets are compatible with either value but cannot rule out other options such as *typological transfer*. In fact, *L1 transfer* and *L2 transfer*, as defaults, are sufficient to disprove each other. Since both can be compatible with other variables, however, studies need to endeavor to have designs that permit ruling out other confounded explanatory variables before generalizations can be made. We return to this in Section 5.4.1.5, in which we look at some published studies to which the above issue pertains.

5.4.1.2   Typological Transfer

Typological transfer is assessed in our coding scheme in strict accordance with the TPM's cue hierarchy, as discussed in Section 4.3.3 in Chapter 4. Therefore, *typology* refers to overall structural similarity. This was done to ensure that the coded variable could be used later – as was the case for all the other coded variables – to assess the coverage each model has – supportive, compatible and non-supportive alike – across the super-aggregate of 92 studies. As the TPM makes highly specific claims, it seems reasonable, if not necessary, to use its hierarchy to determine the valuation for *typological transfer*; otherwise, how the TPM itself could be evaluated would not be clear. Thus, *typological transfer* refers to the source of transfer in consideration of the L3 compared to the L1 and L2 at the overall level of the languages (grammar-to-grammar), not necessarily regarding the specific property tested in the study.

In addition to this making it possible to evaluate TPM coverage later, it is also the case that the "type" macro variable *nonfacilitative transfer* value indicates whether or not there has been the best selection at the property level by linguistic proximity (structural similarity property-by-property). Such information is therefore not lost in the way we have coded for *typological transfer* herein. For example, if a study is valued positively for *nonfacilitative transfer*, this would mean that the language selected was not the one of the two offering the closer structure at the property level. In a way, the variable *typological transfer*, along with the others, seeks to explain why *nonfacilitative transfer* is valued positively so often.

5.4.1.3   Hybrid Transfer

Hybrid transfer refers to those cases in which influence from both languages could be observed for the same group, in any of three possible situations:

(a)   combined influence on the same linguistic property (a true hybrid value),

(b)   influence on different properties; that is, in a single experiment with two conditions, one is seemingly influenced by language X(L1), and the other by language Y(L2), and

(c)   those situations in which it was not possible to exclude a hybrid value (tease apart the L1 from the L2) because both the L1 and L2 were functionally the same.

As (b) and (c) are more straightforward by simply knowing the facts of the L1 and L2 alone, let us look at a potential scenario that we would label (a). For example, in an interpretation task, it could be the case that participants assigned an interpretation aligning with their L1 to a condition in the L3 40% of the time and 60% to the interpretation aligning with the L2. Essentially, this macro variable operationalizes two different, but related, theoretical positions, namely that transfer occurs selectively on a property-by-property basis (e.g., Flynn et al, 2004; Slabakova, 2017), and that it may consist of a combined influence from both languages, even within a single linguistic property (Westergaard et al, 2017). As mentioned above, however, it is not clear that (a) would follow from the CEM, although the other cases would. The LPM and the Scalpel Model seem to advocate that (a)–(c) are possible. This is not a view that could be ascribed to the TPM or to a strong version of L1 default transfer and the L2SF.

5.4.1.4   Nonfacilitative Transfer

The *nonfacilitative transfer* variable is extremely straightforward. It relates to whether or not the transferred property facilitates the learning of the L3; in other words, whether – particularly in consideration of the sources at hand – that which was transferred for a given domain was the best option. In the event that transfer/CLE requires restructuring during the course of L3 development, this can be said to be nonfacilitative because it will induce redundancy in grammatical acquisition. Recall from Section 4.2.3 in Chapter 4 that the CEM is very clear in this regard: Previous linguistic experience will either facilitate the learning task or it will not become involved at all. The CEM stands alone as having such a stipulation; thus, the coding of this variable in the positive relates most directly to evidence challenging this specific stipulation of the CEM.

5.4.1.5   Possible Confounds

As discussed in the introduction to this subsection, not all of these variables are mutually exclusive. Let us consider some real-world scenarios from the published literature to show how this plays out. To do so, we will refer to a couple of the exemplar studies detailed in Chapter 4: Rothman and Cabrelli Amaro (2010) in Section 4.3.4.1, and Flynn et al. (2004) in Section 4.2.3.1. As presented in Chapter 4 in greater detail, due to confounds in their designs, these studies provided simultaneous evidence for several of the factors for which we coded separately. Recall that, in Rothman and Cabrelli Amaro (2010) – L1 English–L2 Spanish–L3 French versus L1 English–L2 Spanish–L3 Italian – the results suggested that transfer occurred from the L2 into the L3 for both groups (that is, L2 Spanish into both L3 Italian and L3 French). Since Spanish, a Romance language like French and Italian, was the L2 for both groups of L3 learners, the *L2 transfer* and *typological transfer* variables are confounded in this case, and thus both receive a positive valuation. Since Spanish transfer is nonfacilitative in the case of L3 French for the domain under investigation (null subjects), the *nonfacilitative transfer* variable also received a positive value assignment. In the case of Flynn et al. (2004), *L2 transfer* and *typological transfer* were also confounded. Recall that the data came from L1 Kazakh, L2 Russian and L3 English. Given the proximity of Russian to English (as compared to Kazakh), as argued in Section 4.2.3.1 in Chapter 4, both of these macro variables received a positive value assignment in the coding matrix.

The overlap in variable valuation is not isolated to a mere few examples, as we have just seen. It is, in fact, much more ubiquitous than we might hope. Overlap is inevitable to a certain extent given the complexities of real-world considerations; for example, the availability of participants. Spoiler alert number three: Figure 5.2 not only shows this clearly but also reveals the actual numbers from our analysis of the 92 studies, depicting the four macro variables related to transfer source.

The circles in Figure 5.2 are drawn to scale. The numbers not in the white boxes add up to 92, the total number of studies evaluated. The numbers in the overlapping parts of a larger circle always add up to the numbers in the white boxes and, as a whole (that is, counting all of the numbers in overlapping and nonoverlapping regions), add up to the total of 92 studies. For example, the numbers in the three relevant pieces of the circle related to *typological transfer* 28+25+6 equal 59, which is indeed the total number of studies showing *typological transfer* overall. In each part of the circle, the number of studies and the compatible theories are listed. Thus, as can already be appreciated,

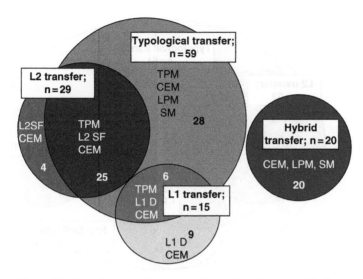

Figure 5.2 *Venn diagram showing overlap in the valuation of the four macro variables related to transfer source, as well as the compatibilities of the six models of L3 morphosyntactic transfer*

looking only at these four macro variables related to source is not sufficient to evaluate the models properly in a comparative sense. Even when there is no overlap, as for *hybrid transfer*, more than one model is compatible, at least in principle.

Let us consider how much more we can explain or if there is anything that can be gleaned by adding the fifth macro variable, the one related to type, which is done in Figure 5.3 below.

The large oval encompasses all 82 of the 92 studies that showed *nonfacilitative transfer*. The reduced numbers in the white boxes reflect the 10 studies removed to accommodate a visual depiction of the fifth variable along with the four source ones. We would like to draw your attention to some advantages of adding this fifth variable that might escape the human eye. Recall that the CEM is not compatible with a positive valuation for *nonfacilitative transfer*. Accordingly, the CEM has been removed as a compatible theory in all of the portions of the circle in which it appeared in Figure 5.2. Thus, *nonfacilitative transfer* as a macro variable has considerable coverage and advantage in evaluating models, details of which we return to later in this chapter. Suffice it to say that, for our present purposes, the additional variable helps; we can see that 82 of the 92 studies provide evidence for the CEM's strongest falsificator.

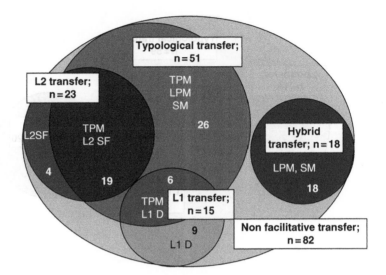

Figure 5.3 *Venn diagram for the four transfer source macro variables as related to the type variable (nonfacilitation)*

As can be seen in Figure 5.3, however, potential ambiguity across the other models is not reduced significantly.

In light of the above, coding for methodological variables is an attempt at better understanding the overlaps still seen in Figures 5.2 and 5.3. Referring to the confound in Rothman and Cabrelli Amaro (2010), namely that L2 status and typological proximity cannot be separated, it is worth pondering what, methodologically, could be applied to disentangle these factors. It seems likely that a mirror-image approach would have done just that. In Rothman's (2010) study of word order restrictions and relative clause attachment preferences, for example, the mirror-image groups were L1 Spanish–L2 English–L3 BP and L1 English–L2 Spanish–L3 BP learners. The L1 and L2 transfer macro variables were not coded positively, even though one group did indeed show L1 and the other L2 transfer. The controlled nature of the mirror-image design shows that L1 or L2 transfer is not an absolute default and, in this case, selection seems compatible with overall typological and/or structural proximity. In the above cases in which confounds applied, the default status of L1 or L2 transfer was compatible with the results, but could very well have been a byproduct of not having another group to control potential issues of design. With the revealing nature of the mirror-image design, we feel confident in assigning a positive value only to typological transfer for cases such as Rothman (2010) because there is no ambiguity in the matter: Given the mirror-image design and the results, default transfer is ruled out. The same approach is applied consistently across the board; for example, as it pertains to Falk and Bardel's (2011) study, which also had mirror-image groups: L1 English–L2 French–L3 German and L1 French–L2 English–L3 German. In this study, evidence of L2 transfer is valued uniquely because there is no ambiguity; evidence that the L2 always transfers is claimed, thus confirming an L2 default status in these data precisely because there was the potential to show otherwise.

5.4.2 Methodological Factors

In addition to the transfer source and type (macro) variables, we coded for five methodological ones. These have no direct link to or any reason to align with any of the models per se. Each represents a choice in methodological application that, in principle, any study can choose freely. These variables might reveal tendencies related to how data cluster toward support for and/or compatibility with various models. For example, if it is the case that using or not using a mirror-image design correlates positively and/or negatively with particular outcomes, we can ponder what this means in terms of gaining a better understanding of how to assess data in general and for comparative evaluation across the models. When brought together, a discussion of the correlations that occur can also place us in a position to comment on best methodological practice for the field in the future.

5.4.2.1 Proficiency in the L3

This variable concerns whether participants were tested at the initial stages of L3/L*n* acquisition or later in development. Recall that not all theories presented are equally intended to model transfer throughout L3/L*n* development. The TPM, in particular, contends that the grammar of one of the learner's previous languages is transferred in its entirety shortly after first exposure. For this reason, evaluations of the TPM using data from learners well beyond initial L3/L*n* stages are largely irrelevant for this purpose. Furthermore, learners make fewer errors as their proficiency increases, which means that, as we move away from the initial stages, it is less likely to find errors, including those that can be attributed to transfer from previously acquired languages. In other words, the concentration of instances of our object of study (linguistic transfer) is inversely proportional to proficiency level, which makes the initial stages a more suitable testing ground. After all, failure to see an influence at intermediate or advanced levels reveals nothing about whether or not it occurred at a lower level proficiency and has since been overcome.

Since the other models make predictions that hold equally at any stage of L3/ Ln development, data from novice learners are valid for the purpose of vetting these theories. It seems reasonable, then, to assume that the stage at which participants were tested may have an impact on the way a dataset can appear to support one model instead of others. Given that the scope of the TPM, the most restrictive model in this sense, is most relevant to the initial stages, we used two levels in our coding of this factor: *beginners* and not beginners (in other words, *post-beginner* learners), which capture the necessary distinction for our purposes.[2]

5.4.2.2   Testing beyond the L3

Determining the source of transfer in L3/Ln acquisition is not always straight-forward. In a property-by-property sense, it is not possible to test all language combinations for the purpose of this question. That is, the tripartite language pairing in juxtaposition to the grammatical property being tested and in consideration of the research question being asked, matters a great deal. In order for the combination to be an appropriate one – in the sense of being able to address the question of transfer source – one must first ensure that the L1 and L2 themselves have different values for the property tested in the mind of each participant. Failure to meet this criterion immediately nullifies the applicability of any result, specifically for the question at hand: How could one determine from which of two entities something derives if the two entities are identical with regard to the relevant property?

Once it is established that the grammars themselves have two different values for the target property in principle, we have a suitable combination with which to begin; all things being equal, relative influence from one grammar or the other can be teased apart empirically. However, the mere fact that the languages in an L1/L2 combination have, in principle – that is, at least for native monolinguals of the two languages – distinct representations for a given property, does not mean that an individual L2 learner herself has (already) acquired two distinct representations. Decades of work in second language acquisition documenting differences in ultimate attainment and lingering effects of L1 transfer, even at so-called near-native levels of L2 acquisition, show that such an assumption would be inappropriate, if not naïve (e.g., Abrahamsson & Hyltenstam, 2009; Bley-Vroman, 1989, 2009; Bylund, Abrahamsson, & Hyltenstam, 2012; Clahsen & Felser, 2006a; DeKeyser, 2000; Granena & Long, 2013; Hawkins & Casillas, 2008; Hawkins & Chan, 1997; Johnson & Newport, 1989; Long, 2005; Meisel, 2011; Sorace, 2011; Tsimpli & Dimitrakopoulou, 2007).

Of course, if an individual's L2 representation does not differ from that of her L1 for a particular property then, as an individual, she or he could not possibly transfer that which has not yet been acquired. Not having distinct representations means that the individual is not a suitable candidate for L3 transfer testing because, having only a single representation – or, rather, identical representations in two different languages – to transfer in the first place, the overarching criterion of being able to identify the transfer source is not met. In such a case, transferring the value for the L1 or for the L2 – they being one and the same in this scenario – would never permit, from the very outset, a teasing apart of the contributory factors affecting the principal variable of focus (that is, transfer source). Thus, choosing to include such subjects in a final analysis or never being entirely certain – not testing them in their L1 and L2 to verify that they do indeed have distinct representations for the property tested – would be a futile exercise, if not inadvertently misleading (González Alonso & Rothman, 2017a).

The ideal way to overcome the potential issues derived from not choosing appropriate language combinations, and/or appropriate subjects in terms of L2 attainment for the domain of grammar, is relatively simple. In the first place, one must simply choose a property that has distinct representations in the grammars that constitute the contributing L1 and L2s in the triad. If testing a specific grammatical property is, for independent reasons, more important to the researcher than is the combination of languages, then selecting the right combination of languages becomes crucial. Secondly, testing each participant's competence for the specific grammar domain of interest in the L1 and L2 (or at least the L2) in order to identify the actual state of linguistic representations available for L3 transfer is also crucial. We classified studies into two types: those in which participants were tested in the L3 alone (*L3 only*) with an apparent assumption that the property tested was acquired in the L2 and thus available for transfer and those in which, at a minimum, the L2 was tested, if not both the L1 and L2, in which case it could be stated with certainty that two distinct representations were available.

5.4.2.3 Production or Comprehension

Research in related areas of language development, such as L2 acquisition and heritage language bilingualism, has discussed mismatches in the outcomes of studies as a function of the type of methodology used, particularly along two axes: on-line (that is, real-time) versus off-line measures, and comprehension versus production tasks (e.g., Bialystok, 1979, 1982; Bowles, 2011; Dussias, 2003, 2004; R. Ellis, 2005; Godfroid et al., 2015; Jegerski, Keating, &

VanPatten, 2016; Villegas, 2014, among others). Given this record in parallel subfields, it is reasonable to consider that the type of task employed might also be an important factor in L3/L*n* acquisition research, and that we might find some patterns of correlation between studies' methodologies and the general direction of their results. Owing to the dearth of relevant studies that have employed truly on-line measures (for example, eye-tracking and event-related potentials) in adult L3 acquisition, there is insufficient data to explore potential effects within the on-line/off-line methodological continuum. There is, however, considerable variability in the field regarding whether studies analyze production or comprehension data. Therefore, we coded each study according to whether it employed a *production* or *comprehension* methodology.

5.4.2.4   Use of Mirror-Image Groups

As we have seen many times over the course of this book, the L2SF and L1 default proposals assign a prominent role to the L2(s) and the L1(s), respectively, whereas the CEM, the TPM, the LPM and the Scalpel Model predict the source of transfer on the basis of factors that hold irrespective of the order of acquisition of the L1/L2. As seen in great detail in Section 5.4.1.5 above, this division contributes to the overlapping predictions by various theories.

Since the most powerful dataset is one that is able to consider as many theories as possible within the same experimental design, some authors (e.g., Falk & Bardel, 2010; Rothman, 2010; Rothman & Cabrelli Amaro, 2010) have encouraged the use of mirror-image participant groups, among which the L3 is shared and the L1 and L2 are the same languages, but in the reverse order of acquisition. In reality, finding such groups is not always practical. However, when possible, they can help to differentiate the predictions of various models, in particular whether or not an L1 or an L2 truly has a privileged status. This methodological factor has a straightforward binary coding: *use* or *no use of mirror-image* groups.

5.4.2.5   Genetic Relationship

Linguistic typology, most often understood in a genealogical or genetic sense – that is, as relating to languages with a (more or less distant) common origin – has featured prominently in theories of L3/L*n* acquisition, both in lexis and in morphosyntax, as we have seen in Chapters 3 and 4. For some of these theories, typology is merely a proxy of learner-external features that often correlate with the learner-internal (that is, linguistic and cognitive) variables that actually matter. Simply put, genetic relatedness and/or a long history of close contact between two languages are factors that guarantee some degree of overlap between them, most evidently in vocabulary, but also sometimes in syntax, morphology, phonology, information structure and so on – although the latter group of features is more likely to overlap in languages of the same family than it is as a result of contact. For this reason, and if models such as the TPM and the LPM are on the right track in suggesting that L1/L2 to L3 structural similarity is the most deterministic variable for transfer source selection, genetic relatedness could be a (broad-brushstroke) pointer to the language that is most likely to constrain L3/L*n* acquisition, at least initially. However, the assessment of similarity between the L3 and prior linguistic knowledge is an internal process, in which a linguistic parser that knows nothing of the expert analyses behind linguistic typologies, as we scholars understand them, is guided by variables present in the input that only ever correlate partially with those taxonomies. Nevertheless, research on language combinations with and without the presence of genetic relatedness is essential to calibrate the predictive validity of our models, which should hold beyond the (linguistic) contexts in which they were first proposed.

For this variable, we coded studies depending on whether a genetic relationship between the L3 and the L1 or the L2 existed. A negative valuation for this variable was assigned to studies in which neither the L1 nor the L2 was (at least straightforwardly) related to the L3 – an extreme example would be L1 Korean–L2 English–L3 Turkish.

5.5 Results: Correlations of Methodological Variables within Each Macro-Variable Category

In order to navigate the results of this systematic review more easily, we will first break them down by the macro variables discussed in the previous section. Within each section based on the macro variables, we provide an overview of how the methodological variables distribute across the subset of the total studies in which the outcome can be ascribed to the macro variable in question. Note that the tables summarizing by methodological factor distributions in each subsection necessarily reflect only the subset of studies pertinent to each macro variable; thus, percentages should be read with both these subset totals and the grand superset total of all 92 studies in mind. We will walk the reader through the proper interpretation of these tables and will explain all the numbers therein in Section 5.5.1, in which the first table of this type is presented.

We provide a series of graphs visually depicting similar information to that in the tables, yet broken down in a more user-friendly manner by each

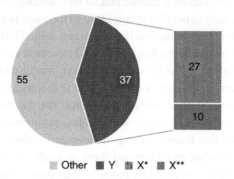

Figure 5.4 *Hypothetical graph explaining how to read the graphs in this section*

methodological variable in a further effort to assist the reader to digest the description of such a large amount of information. Let us look at a hypothetical graph in order to explain how to read the actual ones correctly.

In Figure 5.4, we can see how methodological variable X (coded for X* versus X**) was distributed across the subset of studies (37 of 92) valued positively for the macro variable Y. The sum of the light gray and the dark, dotted gray areas of the pie chart is always equal to 92, the superset of studies input into the systematic review. The dotted section represents the subset of studies valued positively for a given macro variable; in this case, 37 are valued positively for macro variable Y. The stacked bar extending from the dotted slice of the pie shows the distribution of the relevant Y subset for a given methodological variable. In summary, from the present chart, we can see that 37 studies reflected a positive valuation for Y, of which 27 were valued positively for methodological variable X* and the remaining 10 for X**.

In consideration of a battery of Fisher's exact tests – recall that each methodological variable is coded in a binary fashion – we report whether any significant associations are observed between methodological variables and the specific outcome captured by the macro variable for each subsection. The choice of this statistical test instead of the more common Pearson chi-square was motivated by the fact that some of the cells did not meet the minimum raw count requirements of a chi-square test. Since we are limited by availability in the published literature itself, Fisher's exact test was the more appropriate method to explore the associations in 2x2 contingency tables when some of the cells had lower numbers (e.g., Wong, 2011).

We present the statistical analyses in a matter-of-fact manner on the first pass; that is, without interpretation. Once all the data have been presented in a neutral way, we return to the significant correlations revealed to interpret them and to comment on implications that we believe they have for the field going forward.

5.5.1   L1 Transfer

The first macro variable we consider is that of *L1 transfer*. Recall that this refers to the subset of data sets reflecting transfer that seems to come exclusively from the L1. We take special care to walk the reader through Table 5.4, as we did for the graph above, since similar charts are presented in the remaining macro-variable subsections that should be read in the same manner.

Of the 92 studies considered, 15 (16.3% of the total) showed transfer coming exclusively from the L1. Table 5.4 includes raw counts and percentages relative to the same distributions of each methodological variable across the entire sample of 92 studies. A look at the first rows provides a tangible example of this. *Proficiency in the L3,* binarily coded as *beginner* or *post-beginner,* has a distribution of five (studies) and 10 (studies), respectively, across the relevant subset of 15 studies (first two cells in the column "n(umber) in L1T"). For the more visually inclined reader, the same information just described is provided in Figure 5.5.

Table 5.4 *Distribution of studies by methodological factor within the L1 transfer subset (n=15), and p values for Fisher's exact tests on the associations between distribution and outcome. Values in bold indicate a significant result (p<0.05).*

Variable	Level	n in L1T (%)	n in Other (%)	Sig. (*p*)
Proficiency in the L3	Beginner (n=42)	5 (11.9%)	37 (88.1%)	0.39
	Post-beginner (n=50)	10 (20%)	40 (80%)	
Testing beyond the L3	L3 only (n=73)	13 (17.8%)	60 (82.2%)	0.72
	L3 (+L2/L1) (n=19)	2 (10.5%)	17 (89.5%)	
Production or comprehension	Comprehension (n=57)	12 (21.1%)	35 (78.9%)	**0.04**
	Production (n=35)	3 (8.6%)	32 (91.4%)	
Mirror-image	No use (n=62)	13 (21%)	49 (79%)	0.13
	Use (n=30)	2 (6.7%)	28 (93.3%)	
Genetic relationship	Related (n=42)	4 (9.5%)	38 (90.5%)	0.15
	Not related (n=50)	11 (22%)	39 (78%)	

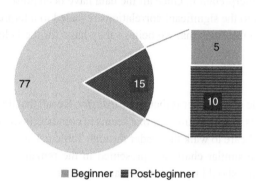

■ Beginner ■ Post-beginner

Figure 5.5 *Pie chart of proficiency in the L3 (methodological variable) distribution over the L1 transfer (macro-variable) studies*

Continuing with the methodological variable *proficiency in the L3*, the following column ("n in Other") in Table 5.4 reports the number of studies in which *beginners* or *post-beginners* were used, respectively, within the remainder of the 92 studies in which the L1 was not identified as the sole source of transfer. Of these remaining 77 (or the light gray part of pie chart in Figure 5.5), 37 examined beginners, and 40 examined post-beginners. In both columns, percentages are relative to the subset of studies for each of the binary choices associated with each variable (and thus the relevant subset of the 92). Accordingly, 11.9% relates to five studies showing L1 transfer exclusively with beginners in the 42 studies overall that used beginners, and 20% to the 10 studies showing L1 transfer in post-beginners in the 50 studies in which post-beginner learners were examined (note that 42+50 equals the superset of 92). Note then, as this will be the case for all such relevant comparisons going forward, that the percentages always equal 100%, and the number of studies equal 92 when relevant to the superset; for example, for *proficiency in L3* in Table 5.4., 5+10+37+40=92 – and to the overall number of the relevant subset – for example, for *L1 transfer* (n=15) in light of *proficiency* (5+10=15) – when pertaining to that cohort. Perhaps more simply, the superset is the quadrant of four cells presented (highlighted in gray) – the subset of focus plus the remainder of the superset – and the relevant subset is the doublet of vertical cells in the column specifically highlighting the relevant subset (always the third column), outlined by a bold frame in Table 5.4.

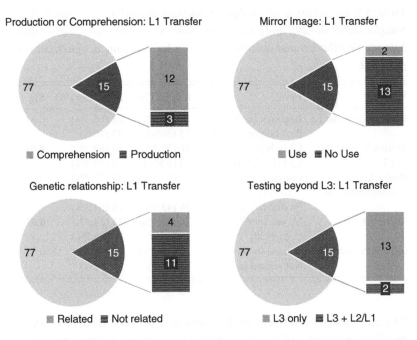

Figure 5.6 *Pie chart for the methodological variable distribution across the L1 transfer (macro-variable) studies*

In Figure 5.6, there is a series of pie charts depicting how the other four methodological factors were distributed across the 15 *L1 transfer* studies. As can be seen, only two of the 15 tested participants' knowledge of the property of inquiry beyond the L3, 12 of the 15 used comprehension methods, 11 of the 15 tested language triads that did not contain a genetic pairing and only three of the 15 used a mirror-image method.

Fisher's exact tests revealed a single significant association; the use of comprehension data (12 versus 3) in these studies' experimental designs correlated positively ($p=0.04$).

5.5.2   L2 Transfer

Recall that the macro-variable *L2 transfer* referred to datasets from studies that show transfer/CLE exclusively from the L2. A subset of 29 from the superset of 92 studies (31.5%) was valued positively.

From the numbers in Table 5.5, and more visually in Figure 5.7, we can appreciate how the methodological variables distributed across the relevant

Table 5.5 *Distribution of studies by methodological factor within the L2 transfer subset (n=29), and p values for Fisher's exact tests on the associations between distribution and outcome. Values in bold indicate a significant result* (p<*0.05*).

Variable	Level	n in L2 (%)	n in Other (%)	Sig. (p)
Proficiency in the L3	Beginner (n=42)	14 (33.3%)	28 (66.7%)	0.82
	Post-beginner (n=50)	15 (30%)	35 (70%)	
Testing beyond the L3	L3 only (n=73)	26 (35.6%)	47 (64.4%)	**0.04**
	L3 (+L2/L1) (n=19)	3 (15.8%)	16 (84.2%)	
Production or comprehension	Comprehension (n=57)	13 (22.8%)	44 (77.2%)	0.06
	Production (n=35)	16 (45.7%)	19 (54.3%)	
Mirror-image	No use (n=62)	28 (45.5%)	34 (54.8%)	**0.01**
	Use (n=30)	1 (3.3%)	29 (96.7%)	
Genetic relationship	Related (n=42)	15 (35.7%)	27 (64.3%)	0.51
	Not related (n=50)	14 (28%)	36 (72%)	

29 studies valued positively for L2 transfer. There is a relatively balanced distribution for three of the methodological variables: *proficiency in the L3, production or comprehension* and *genetic relationship*. Of these, 14 of the 29 are valued positively for beginners, and the remaining 15 of the 29 for post-beginners. Furthermore, 13 of the 29 were valued positively for comprehension, and the remaining 16 of 29 for production. Another 14 of the 29 were valued as not being related, and the remaining 15 of 29 as being related. For the two other methodological variables, the distributions are highly skewed: For *testing beyond the L3*, only three of the 29 studies were valued positively for L3+L2/L1, while for *mirror-image* only one study was valued positively for use. This means that only three studies tested for knowledge of the L3 target domain in the L2. In this case, one could say that the ends justify the means. Since L2 transfer was found, it must be the case that the property in the L2 was acquired. The numbers also reveal that only one study used a mirror-image design, without which data interpretation is somewhat ambiguous in relation to the models, particularly with regard to compatibility with, as opposed to strong supportive evidence for, the L2SF. We return to this point in Section 5.6 below.

As shown in Table 5.5 above, there was a positive correlation between *L2 transfer* and specific valuations for two methodological factors. The first related to *testing beyond the L3*, when only the L3 was tested (that is, without testing for

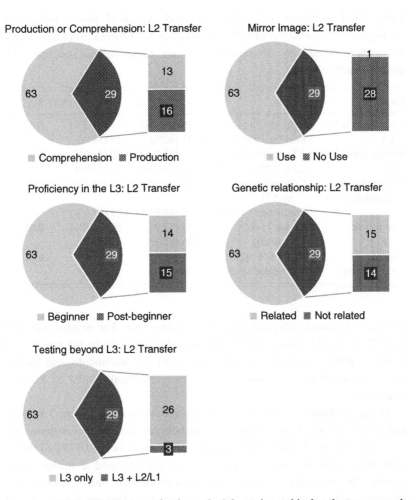

Figure 5.7 *Pie charts for the methodological variable distribution across the L2 transfer (macro-variable) studies*

knowledge of the domain in the L2 or L1/L2; 26, or 35.6%, versus 3, or 15.8%; p=0.04). The second association was the correlation of *L2 transfer* when a mirror-image design was not employed (28, or 45.5% versus 1, or 3.3%; p=0.01).

5.5.3 Typological Transfer
Recall that the macro variable *typological transfer* uses the TPM rubric to determine a positive or negative valuation and that this variable, as all

Table 5.6 *Distribution of studies by methodological factor within the typological transfer subset (n=59), and p values for Fisher's exact tests on the associations between distribution and outcome. Values in bold indicate a significant result (p<0.05).*

Variable	Level	n in TT (%)	n in Other (%)	Sig. (*p*)
Proficiency in the L3	Beginner (n=42)	28 (66.7%)	14 (33.3%)	0.67
	Post-beginner (n=50)	31 (62%)	19 (38%)	
Testing beyond the L3	L3 only (n=73)	43 (58.9%)	30 (41.1%)	0.06
	L3 (+L2/L1) (n=19)	16 (84.2%)	3 (15.8%)	
Production or comprehension	Comprehension (n=57)	37 (64.9%)	20 (35.1%)	0.91
	Production (n=35)	22 (62.9%)	13 (37.1%)	
Mirror-image	No use (n=62)	33 (53.2%)	29 (46.8%)	**0.01**
	Use (n=30)	26 (86.7%)	4 (13.3%)	
Genetic relationship	Related (n=42)	34 (81%)	8 (19%)	**0.01**
	Not related (n=50)	25 (50%)	25 (50%)	

others, is assessed independently of the other four. The results indicated that 59 of the 92 studies (64.1%) were valued positively for *typological transfer*. Table 5.6 shows the distribution of the methodological factors across these 59 studies, and the respective statistical results of Fisher's exact tests.

As can perhaps be more easily appreciated visually in Figure 5.8, there was a more or less balanced distribution between the binary valuations for two of the five methodological variables: *proficiency in the L3* (28 of the 59 used beginners) and *mirror-image* (26 of the 59 used a mirror-image group). The other three variables were more skewed. *Testing beyond the L3* revealed that only 16 of the 59 studies tested the learners beyond the L3 (meaning that they also tested the L2 or L1/L2). However, it is worth highlighting that these 16 studies comprise 84.2% of all the studies in the 92 superset that tested beyond the L3 (19/92). *Production or comprehension* showed that 37 of the 59 studies used comprehension methodologies. *Genetic relationship* revealed that 34 of the 59 studies used *related* language pairings. It is worth highlighting that 25 studies did not use related languages, yet still showed *typological transfer*, precisely because this adds some independent credence to the TPM's cue hierarchy (not necessarily to the model itself but to the effectiveness of the cue hierarchy for capturing relative typological transfer).

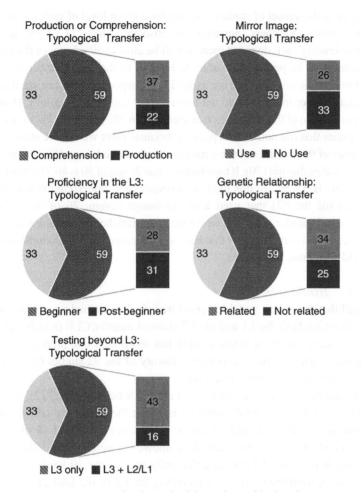

Figure 5.8 *Pie chart for the methodological variable distribution across the typological transfer (macro-variable) studies*

Statistical analyses revealed that, for studies showing typological transfer, there were two significant methodological variable correlations. The first was via the use of a *mirror-image* methodology. Contrary to the L1 and L2 transfer macro variables in which *mirror-image* also correlated, the significant association tion here was found in the opposite direction. This is a good moment to have a deeper examination of the numbers and percentages from the tables, since we will focus on some that are potentially confusing. Recall that percentages are relative to the subset of studies relevant for a given level of each methodological variable. Numbers, however are absolute. Thus, 33 of 59, which is approximately half, does not mean it will be around 50% because the number, to determine its percentage value, is relative to the total number of studies within a given sublevel. We are using 33 on purpose, as you can see there is a similar number that use or do not use a mirror-image methodology. However, the percentage of the 26 studies that used it is 86.7% versus 53.2% for the other 33 studies that did not. This is possible because there were more studies in the superset of 92 that did not use a mirror-image methodology (62), compared to those studies that did (30). It then follows that 26 out of 30 is 86.7%, whereas 33 out of 62 is 53.2%. In this light, it is revealing to underscore that, of the 30 studies (of the 92) that used a mirror-image design, 26 of them showed typological transfer, a point to which we will return below. *Genetic relationship* revealed – not surprisingly – that having a language family relationship within a triad correlated positively.

5.5.4   Hybrid Transfer

Recall that the macro variable *hybrid transfer* was valued positively for data sets in which both the L1 and the L2 showed transfer/CLE (a truly hybrid or amalgamated effect, or when a study has more than one property and both languages affect distinct properties). Twenty of the 92 studies (21.7%) were valued positively for *hybrid transfer*.

As can be appreciated visually in Figure 5.9 below (page 222), there was a more or less balanced distribution between the binary valuations for one of the five methodological variables: *proficiency in the L3* (8 of 20 used beginners). The other four variables showed a more skewed distribution. *Testing beyond the L3* revealed that only two of the 20 studies tested the learners beyond the L3 (that is, including the L2 or the L1/L2). *Production or comprehension* showed that 11 of the 20 used production methodologies, while *mirror-image* showed that 18 of the 20 did not employ such a design, and *genetic relationship* revealed that 16 of the 20 studies used unrelated language pairings.

As can be seen in Table 5.7, the statistical analysis revealed that there were two significant methodological variable associations (*production or comprehension* and *mirror-image*). Considering whether a particular study showing hybrid transfer (n=20) employed a production versus a comprehension type of method seems to matter, as *production* seems to correlate (p=0.01). Moreover, not using a mirror-image methodology also correlates within this cohort (p=0.03).

Table 5.7 *Distribution of studies by methodological factor within the hybrid transfer subset (n=20), and p values for Fisher's exact tests on the associations between distribution and outcome. Values in bold indicate a significant result (p<0.05).*

Variable	Level	n in HT (%)	n in Other (%)	Sig. (*p*)
Proficiency in the L3	Beginner (n=42)	8 (19.1%)	34 (80.9%)	0.32
	Post-beginner (n=50)	12 (24%)	38 (76%)	
Testing beyond the L3	L3 only (n=73)	18 (24.7%)	55 (75.31%)	0.21
	L3 (+L2/L1) (n=19)	2 (10.5%)	17 (89.5%)	
Production or comprehension	Comprehension (n=57)	9 (15.8%)	48 (84.2%)	**0.04**
	Production (n=35)	11 (31.4%)	24 (68.6%)	
Mirror-image	No use (n=62)	18 (29%)	44 (71%)	**0.02**
	Use (n=30)	2 (6.7%)	26 (93.3%)	
Genetic relationship	Related (n=42)	4 (9.5%)	38 (90.5%)	0.06
	Not related (n=50)	16 (32%)	34 (68%)	

5.5.5   Nonfacilitative Transfer

Recall that the last macro variable, namely the occurrence of *nonfacilitative transfer*, refers to the apparent transfer/CLE from a previously acquired language that does not facilitate grammar building toward the target L3. In other words, transfer occurs from a previously acquired language X when transfer from a previously acquired language Y would have been a better choice considering the L3 learning task at hand.

As seen in Table 5.8 below (page 223) and more visually in the graphs in Figure 5.10 below (page 224), there is a more or less balanced distribution between the binary valuations for two of the five methodological variables: *proficiency in the L3* (41 beginners versus 41 post-beginner) and *genetic relationship* (37 related versus 45 not related). The other three methodological variables present a skewed distribution, albeit along a continuum: *testing beyond the L3* (64 tested the L3 only versus 18 that tested L3+L2/L1), *production or comprehension* (51 comprehension versus 31 production) and *mirror-image* (27 use versus 55 no use).

A stark difference from the other methodological variables can be appreciated at a glance in Figure 5.10; the proportion of light gray to dotted dark gray is very different. The overwhelming amount of dotted dark gray reveals that the vast majority of the 92 studies were valued positively for *nonfacilitative transfer* (82 of the 92 studies, or 89.1%). It is worth mentioning that, within the 10 studies in which *nonfacilitative transfer* was not valued positively, four

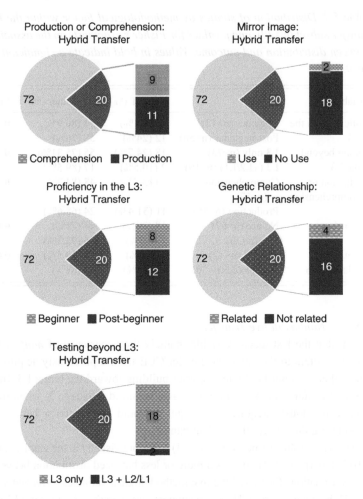

Figure 5.9 *Pie chart for the methodological variable distribution across the hybrid transfer (macro-variable) studies*

of these could not (on their merits) probe for the possibility of nonfacilitative transfer from either language. That is, the linguistic property or properties tested could only provide facilitative transfer (from any previously acquired language) or nothing at all. Accordingly, it is impossible to determine whether nonfacilitative transfer could occur for the same learners and the same languages when testing different properties. For this reason, these four studies were listed as "not applicable," and were excluded from the analysis. The

Table 5.8 *Distribution of studies by methodological factor within the nonfacil-itative transfer subset (n=82), and p values for Fisher exact tests on the associations between distribution and outcome.*

Variable	Level	n in NT (%)	n in Other (%)	Sig. (p)
Proficiency in the L3	Beginner (n=42)	41 (97.6%)	1 (2.4%)	0.12
	Post-beginner (n=46)	41 (89.1%)	5 (10.9%)	
Testing beyond the L3	L3 only (n=69)	64 (92.7%)	5 (7.2%)	1
	L3 (+L2/L1) (n=19)	18 (94.7%)	1 (5.2%)	
Production or comprehension	Comprehension (n=54)	51 (94.4%)	3 (5.5%)	0.43
	Production (n=34)	31 (91.1%)	3 (8.2%)	
Mirror-image	No use (n=58)	55 (94.8%)	3 (5.7%)	0.24
	Use (n=30)	27 (90%)	3 (10%)	
Genetic relationship	Related (n=41)	37 (90.2%)	4 (9.8%)	1
	Not related (n=47)	45 (95.7%)	2 (4.3%)	

statistics reported in Table 5.8 show that no significant associations were found; that is, irrespective of all potential methodological choices, nonfacilitative transfer was found equally robustly.

5.6 Interpreting the Data: Contextualizing and Understanding What Correlations Mean for Subsets and the Superset of Studies

Having presented all of the data in a fairly neutral, matter-of-fact manner, we now turn to an interpretation of the results. We are guided by the two original questions we introduced at the beginning of this chapter:

(i) What can the super-aggregate data tell us about the role of previous linguistic knowledge in sequential multilingualism?

(ii) How do different methodological practices correlate with the results in (i)?

The first question is, of course, relevant to cognitive science more generally; that is, beyond our immediate concerns in L3/L*n* acquisition. As we discussed at length in several subsections of Chapters 1 and 4, the constructs of economy and efficiency are fundamental to our understanding of learning and cognitive/neurological function. Multilingualism is unique in allowing us to appreciate more clearly how previous experience bootstraps the acquisition of additional

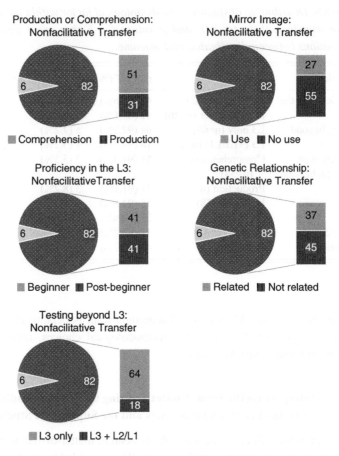

Figure 5.10 *Pie chart for the methodological variable distribution across the nonfacilitative (macro-variable) studies*

knowledge – at least within the same domain – for reasons of economy and/or maximal efficiency. After all, the mechanisms of cognitive economy are only fully at play – or appreciable – when prior knowledge consists of at least partially competing options. What is then essentially confounded in L2 acquisition – because the choice is limited to whether or not to make use of previous experience – becomes a full-fledged scenario from L3 acquisition onwards, as the first branch of that decision tree ('make use of previous experience') is itself split into two or more options. Considering the role of prior linguistic knowledge in sequential multilingualism thus has the potential to inform theories of cognitive economy in ways that other learning scenarios of language acquisition are, by their very nature, incapable of exploring.

What is particularly important about the second question (ii) above, which can also be projected to have implications beyond our field, is the insight it provides into the relative weight of methodology in accounting for results – particularly the inconsistencies across studies – we observed. That our theories determine our questions, and these in turn determine our methods – because different inquiries are best informed by data of different types – is hardly controversial. However, it is important to be aware of when differences in focus truly justify differences in outcomes. When they do not, examining the correlations between methodology and results is particularly useful because it allows us to remove extraneous noise introduced by our measurements from the equation. Doing this foregrounds the contribution of the original variables and has (at least) two beneficial consequences: It increases comparability across studies, and it often helps to reconcile findings that seem to be in contradiction of each other.

The data in the previous section were presented from the perspective of the macro variables as the lead; conversely, the following discussion is guided by each of the methodological variables; that is, we isolate the data category captured by each methodological variable, drawing on all five macro variables. For example, when we discuss *proficiency in the L3*, we combine all the relevant subsets of data from *L1 transfer, L2 transfer, typological transfer, hybrid transfer,* and *nonfacilitative transfer.* Doing so flips the presentation of data from Section 5.5 on its head in an attempt to interpret what everything means, albeit at the level of subsets, and particularly the superset of 92 studies. When significant correlations among methodological variables and one or more macro variables have been reported above, we offer interpretation(s) within the subset(s) of studies in which this applies, as well as what this means for the interpretation of the superset of studies. Only through a simultaneous consideration of these two levels of granularity in the data will we be able to extract lessons applicable to both theory and practice in L3/L*n* acquisition studies.

While we have been explicit about the importance of considering associations within their actual scope – that is, in the different subsets of studies in which the data are compatible with each macro variable – it is important that we underscore this point once more before proceeding with our discussion. In other words, there is significant potential for a causation fallacy herein. Correlations do not (necessarily) imply causation; that is, the simultaneous occurrence of two phenomena does not necessarily mean that one causes the other. Nonetheless, it might be tempting to assume that only because (a lack of) mirror-image groups is significantly associated with the *L2 transfer* macro variable, this means one is more likely to obtain an *L2 transfer*-compatible outcome if no mirror-image groups are employed in a given study. The error in such an assumption is most apparent in those cases in which one methodological factor is associated significantly with two different macro variables. Returning to our example, *mirror-image methodology* is also significantly associated, and in fact in the same direction (its lack of use), with the macro variable of *hybrid transfer*. Of course, it is unlikely that the same (lack of) methodological practice causes two mutually exclusive outcomes; thus, cases such as this one make it easier to see that these correlations must be interpreted as nested within the outcome factor: They simply provide a more fine-grained picture of studies that are compatible with a certain macro variable, and therefore have the potential to improve our understanding of that subset.

The first result that is worth discussing is the absence of significant associations among any of the macro variables and the participants' *L3 proficiency*. This is not surprising from merely glancing at Tables 5.4 through 5.8 above. In fact, the distribution of studies in each of the subsets is surprisingly balanced for this methodological factor in particular, with the exception of *L1 transfer*, where twice as many studies (10 versus 5) examined participants who were at post-beginner levels of proficiency. This evenness, of course, translates to the superset, in which both levels of the factor describe almost half of the studies each.

This absence of significant associations for the *L3 proficiency* variable, however, does not contribute much information beyond the fact that roughly equal numbers of beginners and nonbeginners have been tested across the superset of studies reviewed here and that we cannot, on the basis of these results, explain the particular outcomes of any one subset as potentially related to L3 proficiency. If you recall our discussion of this factor in Section 5.4.2.1 above, as well as throughout Section 4.3 on the TPM in Chapter 4, the potential confounds introduced by testing participants far beyond initial exposure are subtle but far from trivial. Because acquisition proper is consolidated as a function of proficiency, it is generally impossible to determine what path led to the acquisition of a given property without access to the developmental sequence. It follows from this that observations of learners well past the initial stages are problematic for determining the original interlanguage transfer source in cases of targetlike L3 knowledge because we are unable to reverse-engineer the process that led to these representations. Was it transfer, or was it a consequence of L3 learning/acquisition? Have there been any changes from an initially transferred representation that was different from that which we can observe now? Without some sense or snapshot of time – for example, from longitudinal or at least cross-sectional data – we simply cannot distinguish between the results of these very different developmental paths. Nonetheless, determining which of them is true of the property we are examining is essential to adjudicate between competing theories. Because it is impossible to estimate how often and to what extent the confounds related to this methodological factor may be misleading – with regard to the source of transfer – we will not discuss this beyond the methodological word of caution expressed here. We will, however, return to this factor in Section 5.7 below, in which we will show just how subtle yet profoundly impactful these potential effects might prove to be.

In Section 5.4.2.2 above, we have introduced potential confounds that arise from leaving the grammatical domain(s) of interest untested in the previously acquired languages of our participants, which we operationalized here as the methodological variable *testing beyond the L3*. Recall that, when the L1 and the L2 do not have distinct representations for the L3/Ln property under investigation, this effectively nullifies any potential to determine transfer source: No matter what is transferred, one cannot distinguish among sources. This is as true of grammatical properties that take the same shape in both languages – where the confound would reflect shortcomings in experimental design – as it is of cases in which the L3 learner possesses nontargetlike L2 knowledge that falls short of showing a difference from the L1.

Uncertainty regarding exactly what constitutes the L3 learner's prior linguistic knowledge is undesirable in any case: We know from monolingual/ dialectal variation, attrition, regressive transfer and multi-competence studies that even L1 knowledge is potentially vulnerable and thus cannot be taken for granted. However, this uncertainty is particularly problematic with regard to the L2 knowledge one is justified to assume. If we consider the insights from decades of research in SLA (see, e.g., Ortega, 2011; Slabakova, 2016; VanPatten & Williams, 2015, for reviews), it seems obvious that we cannot simply take it as given that L3 learners have acquired target or native-like knowledge of the relevant domains in the L2 by the time of testing, which means that the L1 and the L2 do not necessarily constitute distinct sources of transfer for these learners, irrespective of what is true of theoretical descriptions of the L1 and L2 as native grammars. This is compounded by the fact that nontargetlike knowledge in the L2 is often not just off-target; it also aligns with the L1. This combination of variability in L2 competence and L1 effects in L2 acquisition compromises our ability to attribute transfer unambiguously to the

L1 or the L2 source, unless we can ascertain directly that the grammatical property under investigation does indeed have the expected shape in the L2 of the same participants.

When we examine the associations between the methodological factor *testing beyond the L3* and studies' outcomes, we can see that these are significant for the two order-of-acquisition macro variables: *L1 transfer* and *L2 transfer*. This reveals that the vast majority of the studies that are compatible with these macro variables (13 of 15 for *L1 transfer* and 26 of 29 for *L2 transfer*) have not tested any languages besides the L3 with regard to the specific linguistic domain under investigation. While the proportion is far from balanced in other subsets – carried over to the superset, where this applied to 73 of the 92 studies – it is particularly uneven in the case of these two macro variables. For the reasons we have just explained, this is notably more problematic for an *L1 transfer* account, as it is more likely for the confound at hand to conceal L1-like L2 knowledge than it is for the opposite to be the case. In fact, this is the one scenario in which it might matter less that the L2 has not been tested. Why might this be? Assuming that the L1 and L2 have, in principle (that is, as native grammars), distinct representations of the particular grammatical domain tested, studies showing L2 transfer could only have shown this if the grammatical property had indeed been acquired in the L2 (see Iverson, 2009a, 2010, for a similar argument).[3] That being acknowledged, we hope it would be uncontroversial to claim that, as a field, we should be moving toward common standards that avoid a priori issues. It could be the case that many more studies among the 63 claiming to not show transfer would have done so if they had controlled for this variable. Thus, as we move toward greater conformity of minimal criteria for testing multilingual transfer/CLE, it seems best practice to ensure that we know the status of the L1 and of the L2 in terms of what each individual included in our studies can show.

Our analysis revealed significant associations between the type of methodology used – comprehension or production tasks – and two macro variables, namely, *L1 transfer* and *hybrid transfer*. These are associated with different values of the factor. Within the *L1 transfer* subset of 15 studies, a significant majority of them (12 versus 3) employed comprehension methodologies. Conversely, 11 of the 20 studies compatible with *hybrid transfer* were based on production data (e.g., Angelovska & Hahn, 2017; Fallah, Jabbari, & Fazilatfar, 2016). This discrepancy between production and comprehension data is not new; in fact, it has also been reported in other instances of acquisition, such as child L1 (e.g., Hendriks, 2014), child L2 (e.g., Unsworth, 2007), and adult L2 acquisition (e.g., Gershkoff-Stowe & Hahn, 2013). Given these precedents, it should not be entirely unexpected that this divide appears in L3 acquisition as well. A question that remains, however, is why production methodologies would feature so prominently in studies that are compatible with *hybrid transfer*. Let us attempt an explanation.

Comprehension involves decoding (linguistic) information contained in the input that we hear, read or see, by juxtaposing this input against a system of language-specific representations – in other words, a grammar and a lexicon. The reverse is essentially true of production; however, there are arguably more factors at play between the system of representation and the spoken, written or signed outcome of language production. These further, more complex requirements (such as speech/sign motor planning, self-monitoring of the outgoing signal and so on) are likely to introduce some degree of extraneous noise to the observed effects, thus blurring our window into the mental linguistic representations that lie at the core of both receptive and productive language use. This argument has notably been made before by Grüter (2005/2006) with regard to testing L2 initial state models. For these reasons, it is possible that the mixed outcomes in terms of transfer source that are characteristic of *hybrid transfer* are, at least in part, a consequence of this distortion, rather than a reflection of true hybridity in the underlying representations of the emerging L3 system.

As you may recall from our description of the *mirror-image groups* variable in Section 5.4.2.4 above, the mirror-image methodology (e.g., Falk & Bardel, 2010; Rothman, 2010) was specifically conceived and endorsed by authors of competing models to disentangle the potential effects of order of acquisition (that is, a purported L1 or L2 status factor) from those of other likely explanatory variables (such as maximal facilitation and typological similarity), which could be left confounded if only one L3 group were to be examined. This argument is now compellingly quantified in the present analysis, which has shown that the presence or absence of the mirror-image methodology is unevenly distributed in three of five subsets in our data. This can be seen in the significant associations among this methodological variable and three of the macro variables, namely, *L2 transfer, hybrid transfer* and *typological transfer*. However, as these associations do not always go in the same direction, we will examine them separately.

In the case of *typological transfer*, the association seems to reflect, in principle, the fact that the methodology was not employed in the majority of the studies in which the data were valued positively for this type of transfer. In itself – that is, as it relates only to this subset of studies – this is highly relevant to our interpretation of these data, since the mirror-image design guarantees that typological transfer is explanatory above and beyond any potential effects of order of acquisition – as well as of other variables, such as maximal facilitation, which are similarly controlled for in this methodology (see Rothman, 2010). However, as pointed out in Section 5.5.3 above, it is extremely important here to consider the distribution of this methodological variable across the entire superset of 92 studies. Overall, the mirror-image group design was not employed by the majority of studies in the superset data: While 30 (32.7%) made use of it, 62 (67.3%) did not. From this subset of 30 studies that, for the reasons we have discussed, are better positioned to disentangle the potential effects of L1/L2 status and typological similarity, a vast majority (26, or 87.9%) were valuated positively for *typological transfer* (e.g., Giancaspro, Halloran, & Iverson, 2015; Rothman, 2010). It is in consideration of this distribution across the superset that we can more confidently relate the insights of the mirror-image design to the outcome captured by the *typological transfer* variable. While all of the four source-related macro variables receive some support from studies that have not employed mirror-image groups, the results point less ambiguously in the direction of *typological transfer* when these variables are compared in a testing ground designed specifically to dissociate their potential effects.

The associations among the mirror-image factor and the other two macro variables – *L2* and *hybrid transfer* – are negative, indicating that most of the studies providing compatible or supportive evidence for these variables did not use mirror-image participant groups (e.g., Foote, 2009; Hermas, 2010; Na Ranong & Leung, 2009). Similarly to that which occurred with *L2 transfer* and *testing beyond the L3* above, these results are not particularly problematic for a *hybrid transfer* account, since the confound this methodology is designed to address is automatically ruled out if transfer from both languages is found within the same group. However, and for the same reasons we have just highlighted in previous paragraphs, the fact that a significant majority of studies compatible with the *L2 transfer* macro variable did not employ mirror-image groups undermines the supportive validity of their data somewhat because alternative explanations cannot be ruled out as confidently as might otherwise have been the case if the method had been employed. This should not be interpreted as a statement of counterevidence: This association, in and of itself, does nothing to prove an L2 default position wrong. However, it does highlight the fact that the (unambiguous) evidence base in favor of an *L2 transfer* strong hypothesis is less robust than one might glean from taking individual study interpretations at face value, as foreshadowed in the Venn diagrams provided in Figures 5.2 and 5.3.

The association with *L2 transfer*, then, suggests that studies compatible with this macro variable do not necessarily show this outcome unequivocally. Given this circumstance, it is reasonable to ask what other explanations are actually compatible with the data in these studies. Twenty-five of the 29 studies showing *L2 transfer* also had a positive valuation for *typological transfer*. Put in percentages, unambiguous data pointing to default L2 transfer are reduced to 4.3% of the total (4 of 92 studies). Similarly, six of the 15 studies that ascribed to *L1 transfer* can also be accounted for by *typological transfer*, leaving only 6.5% of the total (6 of 92) as potentially unambiguous evidence in favor of *L1 transfer*. Even within this relatively low number, it is possible that other variables are able to provide alternative accounts of the data, since several methodological factors have higher counts in their negative valuations within this subset. First, only two of the 15 *L1 transfer* studies compared mirror-image groups. Similarly, only two of the remaining 13 studies tested the same domain of grammar in the L2 to ensure that each previous language had a distinct representation and that *L1 transfer* could be teased apart meaningfully from *L2 transfer*. This leaves a mere 2.17% (2 of 92) of the total studies as unambiguous support for a default *L1 transfer* position.

Such numbers leave little room for strong versions of L1 and L2 default theories. As the body of evidence suggesting that both L1 and L2 transfer are in principle possible grows, it is progressively more difficult to justify a model in which order of acquisition dominates other variables. Note that this does not mean that order of acquisition – or, rather, the complex combination of cognitive and learner-external factors for which it is a proxy – is not a potentially relevant variable. As we saw in Section 3.3 in Chapter 3, more than 30 years ago Ringbom (1987) had already considered that an interaction between native status and typological similarity was the most powerful predictor of transfer source selection, at least at the lexical level. That being said, if a model were to have order of acquisition as the ultimate explanatory variable based on the data that are currently available, it would have to incorporate an articulated account of when this is not predicted to be the case – that is, precisely when the model predicts transfer from the non-default language(s) to occur. As explained in Section 4.2.2 in Chapter 4, the latest work associated with the L2 Status Factor hypothesis takes this requirement most seriously (Bardel & Sánchez, 2017; Falk et al., 2015), invoking the role of L1-specific metalinguistic knowledge (MLK). The main argument is that L1 transfer has two (compatible) triggers: The first is the presence of high degrees of L1 MLK. The second is individual differences in working memory, which may lead to unexpected L1 transfer on some occasions when other conditions should lead us to expect transfer from the L2. While these are notable improvements to the theory in terms of articulation, the methodological designs in the vast majority of studies thus far – all the 92 reviewed here, including those conducted by these authors in previous years – are not suitable to evaluate these claims because none of them controlled for MLK and working memory simultaneously.

Perhaps unsurprisingly, the only macro variable to show a significant association with the *genetic relationship* factor is *typological transfer*. In numbers, this reflects the fact that 34 of the 59 studies compatible with this macro variable examined linguistic triads with some internal degree of relatedness. In fact, these represent up to 80.9% of the subtotal of 42 studies with a genetically related language combination. While some readers might then be tempted to conclude that typological transfer is to be expected in these cases only (cum hoc, ergo propter hoc), a closer examination of the distribution of studies within that cell suffices to render this unlikely: Up to 25 other studies in which unrelated language triads were employed are also compatible with *typological transfer* as predicted by the TPM's hierarchy.

In fact, in considering the aggregate results of this systematic review, it is ultimately inevitable to address the most straightforward of all: relative coverage of the entire superset. In this sense, *typological transfer*, as determined by a strict application of the TPM's hierarchy, is compatible with 64.1% of the data (59 of the 92 studies in total). Recall again the Venn diagrams in Section 5.4.1.5 above; therein, one can see that the data covered by *typological transfer* have significantly more than twice the coverage of the second macro variable with the highest degree of compatibility, *L2 transfer*. The subset of studies associated with *typological transfer* is heterogeneous in its methodological profile, with the exception of *genetic relationship*, which adopts a prominent role in the subset. However, as we have discussed several times, this does not mean that *typological transfer* only occurs in studies with genetically related language combinations, as shown by the other 25 studies valued positively for this macro variable. In connecting the dots between our macro variables and the models we discussed at length in Chapter 4, we should clarify that the wide coverage of *typological transfer* across the superset data does not mean support for *all* stipulations of the TPM. As it stands, the current systematic review – by the very nature of the variables it has addressed – can only confirm that the TPM's hierarchy is supported substantially by the available data, as it formed the basis of the most explanatory source macro variable in the analysis. While no single variable can be expected to account for all the data (as our results show clearly), it seems fair to conclude from this review that the degree of overall similarity between the L3 and previously acquired languages, however (in)conspicuous, is a crucial predictor of transfer source selection in L3/L*n* acquisition. For this reason, it seems inevitable for theories attempting to model any stage of L3/L*n* acquisition – or, indeed, its developmental sequence – to include overall structural similarity as a strong variable.

For similar reasons of coverage, it is important to address the data regarding *nonfacilitative transfer*. This macro variable was meant to capture the type (not the source) of transfer, precisely because the claims of one major model, the CEM, rest on assumptions related to transfer type and outcome (with regard to target L3 acquisition). As we have explained in several places within Chapters 4 and 5, a fundamental claim of the CEM is that previously acquired languages will only intercede in L3/L*n* acquisition if the result of such involvement is facilitative toward the acquisition of the target L3 property. When there is no potential for facilitation, Flynn et al. (2004: 14) assumed that prior linguistic knowledge "[was] neutral." A claim of this type generates a very straightforward strongest falsificator for this model: If nonfacilitative transfer is shown to obtain with some consistency in L3/L*n* acquisition, the CEM is falsified. The coverage (compatibility) of the *nonfacilitative transfer* macro variable in this review's data set is unequivocal: Up to 82 (89.1%) of the total 92 studies showed some instance of nonfacilitative transfer/CLE.

Lest one have the impression that transfer/CLE is almost always nonfacilitative in the real world, we should provide a context to indicate why it is found so ubiquitously in the laboratory world of L3/L*n* acquisition studies. One might argue that this overwhelming presence of nonfacilitative transfer reflects an epistemological bias of sorts, whereby researchers probe for nonfacilitative transfer in their L3 groups instead of focusing on potential facilitative effects of prior knowledge. Two things must be clarified in response to such an argument. The first is that, in some sense, this is true: More often than not, L3/L*n* studies focus on transfer instances that result in nontargetlike behavior. However, this practice is a result of two very well-motivated concerns: (i) a study must seek to collect data that are relevant to as many theories as possible simultaneously, and nonfacilitative transfer is the most straightforward way of incorporating the CEM precisely because of this model's stipulation/prediction that nonfacilitation is impossible, and (ii) by definition, nonfacilitative transfer is always –that is, at any point in the developmental sequence – distinguishable from true acquisition, which essentially means that it is easier to identify unambiguously. In the real world, however, transfer/CLE contributes much more positively than might be suggested here for reasons of methodological convenience. The second part of the response to the bias argument is actually more straightforward: Maximal facilitation claims are restrictive, strong hypotheses.

Accordingly, they have little if any tolerance to counterevidence, which suffices to falsify them – in some meaningful quantity, of course, but 82 studies would be an undeniably meaningful amount irrespective of the total sample size. For this reason, whether or not the current distribution of studies along this macro variable is a result of some sort of inclusion or focus bias is irrelevant: It is sufficient that this evidence occurs with the consistency that it does.

Given these facts, one may ponder whether there is value in continuing to consider the CEM in its original – and, to date, most recent – formulation in our design and interpretation of L3/L*n* morphosyntax studies moving forward. After all, one of the most uncontroversial lessons from this systematic review is that any theory of morphosyntactic transfer in L3/L*n* acquisition that aspires to account for (at least some of) the data the field has collected thus far must at the very least have a place – and, ideally, clear predictions – for nonfacilitative transfer from prior linguistic knowledge. Some of the theories we discussed in Chapter 4, such as the LPM and the Scalpel Model, are the most recent proposals that agree with the general principles and motivation of the CEM – that is, nonredundancy in sequential language acquisition and cumulative enhancement – yet contemplate the possibility of nonfacilitative influence from previously acquired languages.

Since the currently available data combine to highlight the pervasiveness of nonfacilitative transfer/CLE, the most important challenge for these new theories in their transition to becoming explanatorily adequate models is inevitably related to modeling these occurrences. This is not an easy task, given the kinds of assumptions on which cumulative enhancement-type of theories rely. In models such as the CEM, the LPM and the Scalpel Model, the involvement of prior knowledge is not merely taken to serve the specific purpose of easing the learning task – this is in fact shared by the TPM and, to some extent, even by other models such as the L2SF, albeit more indirectly. It is also assumed that this prior knowledge is handled by mechanisms that are particularly precise and well suited for the job of using it for the benefit of target (L3/L*n*) language acquisition. Thus, one might reasonably expect nonfacilitation to be predicted by the theory and to obtain relatively rarely at that. In defining these mechanisms as precise, one is claiming implicitly that failure is highly restricted, if not exceptional, and is therefore governed by a specific typology of factors that trump the normal functioning of those mechanisms geared toward maximal facilitation (see, e.g., Slabakova, 2017). The task, then, becomes not only to identify and operationalize those factors but, crucially, to assign them a specific (that is, quantified) weight in the model in order for predictions to be derived from various outcomes of their interaction. On the other hand, one could argue, from such positions, that nonfacilitation is not only exceptional but is also random. However, this would be at odds with most of what we have observed in L3/Ln studies thus far. For example, much of the data for which the *typological transfer* macro variable is able to account in this review consists of instances of nonfacilitative transfer – and we hope to have shown convincingly in our discussion above that there appears to be nothing unsystematic about it. In short, if nonfacilitative transfer occurs with some degree of systematicity, then it is predictable; if it is predictable, our models must be able to deal with it and anticipate its occurrence, however sporadic.

5.7 Implications of Methodological Choice: A Snapshot from the Existing Literature

An obvious benefit of systematic reviews is the power of numbers. Trends emerge or do not in a way that is difficult to bias inadvertently, at least numerically. In fact, one always runs the risk of implicit bias when interpreting any results, even ones that come from systematic reviews. That being acknowledged, the numbers are the numbers, nonetheless. Although there are likely to be disagreements concerning how certain trends in the data should be understood, pervasive evidence such as the *nonfacilitative transfer* results we have just discussed is difficult to counter. Disagreeing, as some will do, that such robust evidence should be sufficient to falsify definitively the claims of the CEM (its strongest falsificator is met), nothing will change the fact that 89.18% of these 92 studies showed the relevant evidence they did. When a trend is as ubiquitous as *nonfacilitative transfer* was in the data, it is likely easier to understand what the explicit and even implicit implications are. However, not all potential issues can be extrapolated from the numbers in a systematic review. That is, not all trends worthy of reflection and discussion can be highlighted based on such an approach. Consequences of the nature of the studies themselves come together with sacrifices at the level of analytical granularity required to be able to compare as much data as possible. To be sure, there are relevant lessons at the crossroads of theoretical proposals and methodological applications that could not be modeled in this (or any) systematic review; these are questions and issues worthy of serious consideration that the analysis could not address given the nature of the overall superset of data.

We now turn to a specific example of potential methodological issues in which confounding effects can be highlighted. We have already alluded to several throughout the book; for example, the importance of knowing what is available for transfer – that is, testing L2 knowledge at a minimum, and ideally

L1 knowledge too – and disentangling default status (L1 versus L2) from typological or hybrid transfer. We now turn to very recent data from our own work that highlight yet another aspect to hammer home the general point we are making, which is related to teasing apart transfer from L3 developmental effects.

As discussed in Section 5.4.2.1, understanding the role of L3 proficiency at the time of testing is an important issue. One might believe that the concern is only really relevant for testing the TPM – after all, this seems to be the only account that is primarily focused on the initial stages. As explained in great detail in Section 4.3 in Chapter 4, it is not accurate to assume that the TPM only considers or offers predictions that are limited strictly to the initial stages: The model merely argues that the initial stages are the ideal point to test or determine transfer (distinguishing it from other types of crosslinguistic influence). The TPM's predictions beyond the initial L3 interlanguage pertain to how the learning task should play out over development, in line with full transfer of whatever system the TPM predicts, the target L3 input and access to UG – in many ways, an extension of the Full Transfer/Full Access model of L2 acquisition to L3/L*n* (Schwartz & Sprouse, 1996). Understanding if proficiency at the time of testing can inadvertently muddy the waters of determining the transfer source of the initial interlanguage grammar should be a concern of equal importance for all models. Since each model is supposed to predict and explain patterns of transfer/CLE, it should naturally follow that all are concerned with being able to differentiate one from the other at the level of representation. Similarly, to the extent that knowing the constitution of the L3 initial-stages grammar is a crucial part of modeling developmental sequencing and ultimate attainment, reliably distinguishing between transfer and byproducts of L3 learning themselves is important for all theories. We have suggested that testing beyond the initial stages, while interesting in its own right and absolutely necessary in order to talk about L3 acquisition overall, can be risky for the purposes of isolating the transfer source itself. However, we have not had the opportunity until now to review data that speak specifically to this risk better than our words could ever convey. We now turn to an extremely recent data set that does just that.

Puig-Mayenco and Rothman (in press) examined data from 60 L3 learners of English who were Catalan (Cat) and Spanish (Sp) bilinguals, divided into two different groups according to order of acquisition. Group A: L1Cat–L2Sp (N=35, mean age 50.4, *SD*=9.3) and Group B: L1Sp–L2Cat (N=25; mean age=48.6; *SD*=9.1). All the participants were tested at the end of a two-month language course designed and advertised specifically for people who had never taken English previously – in principle true ab initio learners. By targeting such learners and establishing the context themselves, the authors sought to control the exact amount and type of L3 input the learners received from the very initial stages of the L3 acquisition process. Few prior studies had attempted similar control over input, ensuring a true ab initio state (Grey, Sanz, Morgan-Short, & Ullman, 2018; Sanz et al., 2015). Those that did approached the task in a very different way. They used an artificial or mini-grammar method (a Latin mini-grammar in Sanz et al. and Brocanto2 in Grey et al.), exposing the learner to a strictly limited set of lexical items and, at most, a few domains of morphosyntax in a learning paradigm. They then tested for which, if any, of the previous linguistic systems had the most influence on the L3 after only a few hours of exposure (at best) and with very limited time allowed for consolidation. Insightful as such an approach is (see Rothman, Alemán Bañón, & González Alonso, 2015), it exchanges the ecological validity of a typical L3 learning experience for increased control of important variables. The methodology in Puig-Mayenco and Rothman (in press) is meant to be a plausible compromise between ecological validity and the relative control over input the other studies have introduced. Provided that the learners are truly ab initio, the methods are comparable in their attempts to tap early stages of interlanguage grammar. Because participants might confuse very low (perceived) proficiency in English with ab initio status at the time of self-selection for the course – or simply do not care but want to take the course anyway – we used data from a detailed questionnaire to ascertain who had previous exposure to the L3 (English), instructed or otherwise, as well as to gain insight into specific details of their linguistic backgrounds.

Puig-Mayenco and Rothman (in press) focused on interpretations of negative quantifiers (NQs) and negative polarity items (NPIs) in two different contexts: (a) in preverbal position with the presence of the sentential negative marker, and (b) in (nonveridical) conditional contexts. The sentences examined contained either the NQ *nobody/nothing* or the NPI *anyone/anything* in the subject position of a transitive verb in context (a), as in (1)–(2), and in the object position of transitive verbs in context (b), as in (3)–(4) – whereas (1) and (2) reflect ungrammaticality with the intended interpretation, (3) and (4) are grammatical, albeit with different interpretations (of necessity).

(1) #Nobody does not write a letter. (Acceptable only with a double negation reading).
(2) *Anybody does not write a letter.
(3) Laura will call us if John eats nothing.
(4) Laura will call us if John eats anything.

The choice of these constructions and these lexical items is interesting for two main reasons: (i) *nobody/nothing* and *anyone/anything* are interpreted differently in these contexts in English, and (ii) Spanish and Catalan only have one lexical item to express both meanings – but, crucially, Catalan and Spanish (can) have different interpretations in these contexts.

With regard to the English interpretations, sentence (1) above gives rise to a double negation (DN) interpretation only – effectively canceling semantic negation otherwise, it is ungrammatical. Sentence (2) is simply ungrammatical. In sentence (3), *nothing* must have a negative reading – Laura will call if and only if John does not eat anything – and *anything* in sentence (4) can only have an existential reading – if there exists anything at all that John eats, then and only then will Laura call. The single lexical items used in these contexts in Spanish and Catalan present differently. When the negative concord item (NCI) occurs in the preverbal position with sentential negation (SN), the Spanish version of the sentence also gives rise to a DN reading, as in (5): 'There is nobody that does not write a letter'; that is, 'Everyone writes a letter,' whereas the Catalan version gives rise to a single-negation interpretation, as in (6): 'Nobody writes a letter.'

(5)   #Nadie   no   escribe   una carta.   *Spanish*
       Nobody   not   write   a   letter
       'Nobody   does not write a letter.' (DN reading)

(6)   Ningú   no   escriu   una carta   *Catalan*
       Nobody   not   write   a   letter
       'Nobody writes a letter.' (SN reading)

In a conditional context, Spanish *nada* 'nothing' in sentences such as (7), despite being ungrammatical, is interpreted as having a negative reading ('Laura will call me if Pedro says nothing,' where calling is contingent upon him saying nothing), as the English NQs would be. Alternatively, Catalan *res* 'nothing' in this same context has the same interpretation as an English NPIs; that is, it takes an existential reading as in (8): 'Laura will call me if Pere says anything at all.'

(7)   *Laura   me llamará   si   Pedro   dice   nada.   *Spanish*
       Laura   will.call.me if   Pedro   says   nothing
       'Laura will call me if Peter says nothing.'

(8)   La Laura   em trucarà   si   en Pere   diu   res.   *Catalan*
       Laura   will.call.me if   Pere   says   anything
       'Laura will call me if Peter says anything.'

The fact that Catalan and Spanish behave differently in this context allowed the authors to probe for transfer source in a sentence-picture matching interpretation task, which was devised taking the subtle differences in interpretation into account. Participants were presented with two pictures depicting the two possible interpretations of an English sentence. Only one interpretation should be expected, depending on the transfer source (Catalan or Spanish). There were two conditions in each context, labeled (a) and (b) in the list below:

  1a. negative quantifier+sentential negation (*do/does not*)
  1b. negative polarity item+sentential negation
  2a. conditional+negative quantifier
  2b. conditional+negative polarity item

There were four items in each condition. Figures 5.11 and 5.12 exemplify two experimental items of the second context in both conditions (2a and 2b).

Mary will call us if Peter says anything.

Existential reading   Negative reading

Figure 5.11 *Example of the experimental item in the CON+NPI condition*

Mary will call us if Peter says nothing.

Existential reading   Negative reading

Figure 5.12 *Example of the experimental item in the CON+NQ condition*

For presentation purposes, the expected interpretation depending on the language is indicated in the appropriate frame (English above, Catalan and Spanish below).

A look at the questionnaires revealed that not all of the 60 participants had understood the difference between ab initio – 'no exposure at all' was explained as a criterion for enrolment – and beginner proficiency. In fact, the latter was tested by means of a standardized test (Oxford Quick Placement Test), and all of the participants scored within the beginner proficiency range. However, beginner proficiency can coincide with years of exposure at the individual level, and proficiency measures are global, whereas the authors were interested in – and thus tested – knowledge of a particular domain of grammar. Puig-Mayenco and Rothman (in press) nevertheless made the decision to run all participants in the statistical model, adding prior exposure to English (measured in months) as a variable. In other words, they consciously decided to capitalize on the reality of the learners' backgrounds to provide a test case for the argument at hand: Although often confounded, beginner proficiency and ab initio exposure are not equivalent, and collapsing them so can inadvertently obscure results. Indeed, the results were not equally straightforward in all conditions for the sample as a whole (N=60): Participants assigned categorical Catalan interpretations to negative quantifiers and NPIs in three of the four conditions but gave mixed interpretations of the remaining condition (Con +NQ), as can be appreciated visually in Figure 5.13.

All things being equal, the results would show some level of that for which we coded in the systematic review as *hybrid transfer*: Three properties seemed to be transferred from Catalan, while the fourth aligned with Spanish. However, all things were *not* equal with regard to previous exposure to the L3. How could we know if exposure mattered, thereby making proficiency an inadequate proxy for initial stages in (part of) this data set? In order to address this question and the results displayed in Figure 5.12, Puig-Mayenco and Rothman (in press) conducted two generalized linear mixed-effects logistic regression analyses, one targeting the first context (NQ/NPI+SN), and one targeting the second context (conditional structures). Would previous L3 exposure or other factors explain the variation in transfer source, or would the models reveal no interactions, suggesting that we were seeing bona fide hybrid transfer? The models included several independent variables: experimental condition, order of acquisition (that is, whether Catalan was the participants' L1 or L2), proficiency score in English and, crucially, months of exposure to the L3. The model revealed a single significant interaction: that between condition and previous exposure, the effect of which was located in the conditional

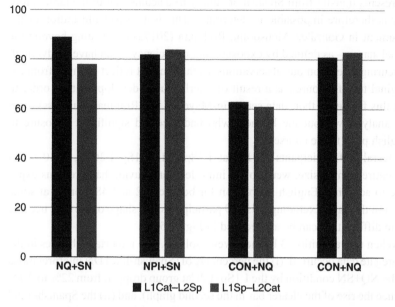

Figure 5.13 *Percentages of Catalan-like interpretation by condition and by group (adapted from Puig-Mayenco & Rothman, in press)*

sentences – where the apparent hybridity in transfer source had been detected – showing that the more (L3) English exposure participants had received prior to the course, the more negative were their interpretations of NQs in conditional contexts.

Had the authors ignored or failed to uncover this interaction, the data would have been consistent with models predicting property-by-property transfer from either language. Specifically, these results would lend support to the LPM or the Scalpel Model – as opposed to the CEM – since transfer in the fourth condition would be nonfacilitative. The significance of exposure in the model, however, brings two covert facts to light: (i) not all participants were in fact ab initio L3 English learners, as confirmed by the questionnaire data, and (ii) those who were not performed differently from the rest of the group in one of the conditions. Now, a first look at the readings of these participants in the CON+NQ condition may lead us to think that, since this interpretation aligns with Spanish, the participants were showing a source of transfer other than Catalan. However, this is also – and crucially – a targetlike interpretation; that is, what would be expected in L3 English. Whether these participants' behavior represents transfer from Spanish or simply true acquisition of the target property is therefore impossible to determine. This is a perfect illustration of the argument in González Alonso and Rothman (2017a) that testing beyond the initial stages – as defined by exposure, not proficiency – can have inadvertent, obscuring effects on our observations, as these might reflect changes from the original transfer source as a result of interlanguage development. In order to test this further in their data set, Puig-Mayenco and Rothman (in press) reran the analysis without the learners who had received significant exposure to English prior to the course.

Overall, 19 participants (12 L1Cat–L2Sp and 7 L1Sp–L2Cat), or 30.2% of the entire sample size, were not ab initio learners, having had previous exposure to academic English instruction for between 12 and 48 months at some point in the past. Excluding these 19 participants, the shape of the data became quite different, as can be appreciated in Figure 5.14.

When true ab initio L3 learners were isolated, two important changes in the aggregate data occurred: (i) the percentage of (Spanish-like) DN interpretations in the NQ+SN condition by the L1Sp–L2Cat group dropped from 22% to 9.7% (hence the rise of the clearer bar in the second graph), and (ii) the Spanish- (and English-)like reading of NQs in the CON+NQ condition dropped from 40% to approximately 10% for both groups, aligning these responses with those of NPIs. As a result, the evidence for hybrid transfer across the entire sample of 60 participants, which relied on the fact that one category received Spanish-like interpretations (unlike the other three), disappeared: Both groups, now comprised exclusively of true beginners, gave existential readings for NQs and NPIs in a conditional sentence frame, which suggested that their interpretations were influenced by Catalan only, irrespective of whether this language was their L1 or L2.

The subtle effects of exposure discussed here constitute a cautionary tale against precipitous evaluations of some models' claims. As we saw, taking beginning proficiency as a proxy for exposure in this study would have led to the conclusion that various models entirely, or specific subclaims of models, were unsupported by the data, that transfer was clearly not complete, and more. To our knowledge, this is the first data set of its kind for which, as a byproduct of the larger study design, the authors were able to look at the data retroactively in order to disentangle the confound and evaluate the tenability of these claims. Although these data do not prove that models that would be rejected without a more nuanced approach (such as the TPM) are in fact confirmed, they underscore the importance of using the correct type of data to make certain claims, particularly when considering rejecting a model in its entirety. Note that the

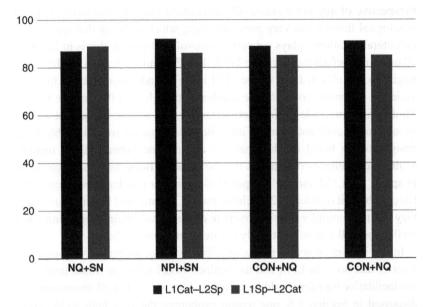

Figure 5.14 *Percentages of Catalan-like interpretation by condition and by group, after removing participants with high exposure to English (adapted from Puig-Mayenco & Rothman, in press)*

point we are making here is exclusively about data appropriateness for specific questions; it is by no means a commentary on the relevance of postinitial-stages data sets for the study of L3/L*n* acquisition as a whole.

Returning to the exposure-proficiency confound, if the participants with previous L3 exposure presented so differently from those who had truly never been exposed to it, one might question what this means for the vast majority of data in L3 studies that conflate beginning proficiency with true L3 initial stages, or take the position that one can make claims for transfer at any point in the L3 developmental continuum. How can we be absolutely certain that one has discarded other explanations for what seems to be transfer, unless this is done under controlled input exposure?

5.8 Taking Stock

What we have seen in this systematic review is enlightening. To summarize, we see that no single model is supported uncomplicatedly by the entirety of the super-aggregate data. We have seen that nonfacilitative transfer is ubiquitous, irrespective of any other potentially interacting variable. We have seen that typological transfer has very good coverage, which is to say that typological (structural) similarity plays a deterministic role. Of course, this is in line with all of the nondefault models – the TPM, the LPM and the Scalpel Model. What might tip the odds in favor of the TPM is the consideration of these first two variables in conjunction with one another. Although the LPM and the Scalpel Model do not preclude nonfacilitative transfer, they also do not predict when it should and should not obtain. Future iterations that do so will enable us to design studies based on this that can differentiate between these models: Mutual compatibility of data can thus be reduced. Being later to the game, so to speak, the LPM and the Scalpel Model are in a privileged position. They have the benefit of at least 92 available studies, summarized herein, from which they can meaningfully test the coverage of their future claims regarding when facilitation will and will not apply before even releasing them.

In the interim, it seems that a specific advantage of property-by-property transfer that both the LPM and the Scalpel Model advocate would imply that nonfacilitative transfer would be minimal. Alas, it is not at all uncommon. As discussed in Section 5.6, one reason explaining the very high incidence of nonfacilitative transfer is related to the choice of properties tested and the specific goal of seeing whether nonfacilitation is possible contra the CEM. That being said, the fact that nonfacilitation is documented across dozens of different grammatical domains and across so many language combinations might lead one to question the utility and functionality of property-by-property transfer. Should it not translate to a much lower incidence of nonfacilitation? If not, how is it particularly useful and economical?

We have also seen and discussed that methodology matters which, of course, should come as no surprise. We need to triangulate various types of methodologies, as well as variables considered in our analyses, to tease apart covarying factors affecting our ability to make definitive conclusions. As discussed in Section 1.6, the goal of any science is to propose and discard models, theories and hypotheses as quickly as possible. One of the only truisms of science over the years is that any given claim is eventually proven imprecise or just plain wrong although it seemed extremely logical at the time of its first proposition. The expression "hindsight is 20/20" or that looking backward creates, conveniently, the clearest picture is actually correct. To even talk of hindsight in the first place, a path that brings one to it must have been paved. It is still early days in the formal linguistic study of L3/Ln morphosyntax; however, a critical mass of work has been done, whereby we can look back fairly and meaningfully and even look forward – something we will do in the next chapter. Suffice to say that there is sufficient evidence to suggest that there is no default L1 transfer, nor a predisposition to bias toward this. In fact, there are data that sʰᵤ.. L1 and L2 transfer, and some that are difficult to motivate via an interaction with another variable, such as typological proximity. However, in light of the literature as a whole, one has to concede that these are minorities in the overall available data. The proliferation of data showing nonfacilitation leaves little hope for the strong version of the CEM, although its place in the history of this subfield will remain undeniable. Therefore, in our opinion, the future of L3/Ln studies would be wise to continue to consider a subset of available models, testing them more rigorously and fairly while still encouraging them to progress in terms of the coverage and the details of their predictions.

Notes

1. Having argued for the difference between transfer and CLE in Chapter 1, it is useful to point out that, in this chapter, we will refer to 'transfer/CLE' as if they are interchangeable, either when the distinction we explained in Section 1.4 does not matter in a ubiquitous sense and/or to capture the fact that some models do not ascribe to the distinction. While we have used this nomenclature occasionally and when relevant in parts of Chapters 3 and 4, doing so is particularly fit for purpose in the context of this chapter, precisely because we will present a systematic review of the field. After all, researchers who do ascribe to the distinction are still interested in both and, as we have argued, data collected after the initial stages are often, in our view, ambiguous regarding whether they reflect remnants of initial-stage transfer, potentially nonrepresentational CLE or simply transitional properties of L3 interlanguage development itself. As a good portion of the data that will be used in the systematic review originated from postinitial-stages learners, using the label 'transfer/CLE' seems appropriate in the contexts in which we use it. When the distinction matters in this chapter, we will use the terms separately.
2. One could argue that the range of levels within what we have included under post-beginner is in fact immense. Indeed, some studies have investigated intermediate learners (e.g., Santos, 2013), and others have focused on highly advanced, even near-native learners (e.g., García Mayo & Slabakova, 2015; Slabakova & García Mayo, 2015). However, and besides the reasons we have just suggested, we have limited the levels of this variable to two for ease of comparability: Measures of proficiency vary greatly across studies (ranging from self-assessment to standardized tests), and thus it would have been difficult – if even possible – to develop an independent taxonomy in which the studies could be assigned to different levels with confidence.
3. There is always the possibility that having acquired an L2 has effects on L1 representations, which is exponentially more likely in certain contexts of bilingualism. For example, in the case that one finds oneself in L2 immersion with limited access to and use of one's L1, the potential for L1 attrition increases (Iverson & Miller, 2017; Schmid, 2011); thus, one should not take for granted that the L1 of any

individual can simply be assumed. Recently, Schmid and Köpke (2017) have suggested that all bilinguals, regardless of type or context, reflect some level of L1 attrition simply by virtue of being bilingual. To the extent this is on the right track, it makes it even less defensible to assume L1 knowledge to be that which is described in the literature without actually testing it.

6 Moving On and Going Forward in L3/Ln Acquisition

6.0   General Introduction

The goal of this final chapter will be to tie up loose ends while reflecting on where the field is currently and where we believe it will – or, in our view, should – be going in the near future. At the same time, this chapter serves as a locus to discuss some recent, exciting research that did not fit squarely into previous sections of the book in any obvious way, yet begins to address forward-thinking questions. In fact, some of this new research already frames what we see as the future expansion of formal linguistic approaches to L3/Ln acquisition, particularly work that examines

(a) understudied instances of morphosyntactic transfer sourcing in child additive multilingualism (Hopp, 2018) and in early bilinguals acquiring an L3/Ln in adulthood (e.g., Iverson, 2009b, 2010; Puig-Mayenco & Marsden, 2018; Westergaard et al., 2017),

(b) the consequences of L3 development for previously acquired morphosyntactic systems or potential regressive transfer (Cabrelli Amaro, 2017a; Cabrelli Amaro et al., 2015; Cheung et al., 2011; Matthews et al., 2014),

(c) questions asking whether it is equally difficult to overcome L1 as opposed to L2 transfer during the course of L3 acquisition (Cabrelli Amaro, Iverson, et al., 2018),

(d) work that brings together multiple domains of grammar, such as syntax and phonology, to see if transfer is complete across modules (Cabrelli Amaro, Pichan, et al., 2018; Llama, 2017), and

(e) work that breaks new ground methodologically, such as studies that apply neurolinguistic methods – electroencephalography (EEG) or event-related potential (ERP) – to the questions we have discussed throughout the book (Grey et al., 2017; González Alonso et al., 2019; Rothman et al., 2015).

6.1   Is Transfer the Same in L3 Acquisition for All Bilingual Types?

Throughout the book, our discussions have mainly idealized a situation in which an L3 would be the same for all, taking the sequential bilingual (adult L2 learner) who then seeks to acquire an additional language in adulthood as the point of reference. As you will recall from Section 1.3 in Chapter 1, L3/L*n* learners can come in various shapes and sizes. Numerically and chronologically, a third language is quite simple to determine, as simple as counting 1, 2 and 3 (see Hammarberg, 2010, 2018, for a more nuanced discussion). However, this does not mean that all L3s are the same as relates to the application of the models we have discussed, much less the patterns of transfer that we might be able to expect. Might the age of the learner at the time of onset of L3/L*n* acquisition matter? Might the type of bilingual – age at the time of onset of bilingualism – matter for adult L3/L*n* acquisition? Put more simply, are all bilinguals the same when it comes to previous linguistic effects on sequential multilingualism?

The above question has been considered by Rothman (2013, 2015) in relation to the Typological Primacy Model (TPM), and by Bardel and Sánchez (2017), as well as by Falk et al. (2015) in relation to the L2 Status Factor (L2SF). We have discussed and alluded to this important question directly and indirectly throughout the book, particularly in various parts of Chapter 4, albeit from a different perspective from which we are about to discuss it here. As explained in Chapter 4, Falk et al. (2015) suggested that, for individuals with metalinguistic knowledge in the L1, the L2SF's effects could be preempted, and Bardel and Sánchez (2017) claimed that, when one had metalinguistic knowledge in both languages or none in either (as could be the case of naturalistic child bilinguals, simultaneous or child L2), individual differences in working memory and other cognitive functions could be more deterministic than would be a default L2 effect. Such footnotes to the application of the L2SF are quite welcome, since they extend the model and/or insights it captures beyond the sequential multilingualism of adult L2 learners. In summary, these discussions acknowledge that different types of bilingualism might display different patterns in transfer/CLE as a result of differences in their bilingual experiences.

Rothman (2013, 2015) pondered this general question directly. At the time of writing these articles (2012 and 2013, respectively), there were limited data available that could be teased out from the masses to address such a query directly. Playing devil's advocate, Rothman (2015) presented arguments both for and against types of bilingualism being a factor that could trump the effects advocated by the TPM and other models. On one hand, he highlighted how age factors, patterns of use that often differ among bilingual types, access to input and other factors might conspire to result in different patterns, while simultaneously suggesting reasons that such factors might not matter. Ultimately, this is an empirical question, one that is still very difficult to answer given the vast imbalance of studies with relevantly comparable populations. From the few studies (compared to the overwhelming majority) that have examined cases of L3, can we generalize acquisition for bilinguals who are not adult L2 learners? We strongly believe that understanding the potential differences among various types of bilinguals is something that will come (or should come) increasingly into focus in the near future. Not only does it embody an important theoretical question that has multifarious potential implications but, if our cognitive-based research is ever to have proper links to practical applications in teaching, we will need to know if models pertain to all instances of L3 acquisition or only to subsets thereof (González Alonso & Rothman, 2017b). In the real world, many types of bilinguals learn, numerically speaking, a third or further additional language. Thus, if cognitive research can help to create fit-for-purpose teaching of bilingual learners of an additional language, it is crucial to know how bilinguals differ in their patterns and therefore their needs, or if it is justified to have singular, catchall approaches.

With the above in mind, it is then worth revisiting this important question in 2019 to see if data now exist that give better answers than were possible in Rothman (2013, 2015). A quick glance at the participant profiles in relevant studies reveals that the vast majority of the research still examines the sequential L3 acquisition of successful adult L2 acquirers (see Appendix A from the systematic review conducted in Chapter 5, where such information for all the studies considered is available). However, studies in which early bilinguals – that is, not only adult L2 learners – are examined when acquiring yet another language do exist (e.g., Iverson, 2009b, 2010; Slabakova & García Mayo, 2015; Westergaard et al., 2017). Although these studies are relatively few, they do not seem to suggest overwhelmingly that the models reviewed in Chapter 4 do not apply or are ruled out from applying to other sets of bilinguals. It should be noted, however, that even those studies that examine nonadult L2 and other types of bilinguals tend to investigate *adult* L3 acquisition. Therefore, there is a genuine dearth of data looking at L3/L*n* acquisition in childhood, at least from a formal linguistic, experimental perspective that considers the models reviewed in Chapter 4. As the field expands in the years to come, we strongly encourage more studies that examine child L3/L*n* acquisition. As we know from the emergence of research on child L2 acquisition that started in the 1990s (see Chondrogianni, 2018; Haznedar, 2013), adult and child L2 acquisition only overlap partially and thus require independent hypothesizing and modeling. By analogy, we are confident that adult and child L3/L*n* will also only overlap partially. That being said, the same models might be applicable to both cases with regard to transfer. It would not be terribly surprising if empirical studies were to show this consistently, precisely because much of the partial overlap between child and adult L2 relates to similar patterns of L1 transfer effects. A very recent study stands out in this discussion, that by Hopp (2018), not least because it is the first study to test these theories in children and is a well-conceived and orchestrated study. Hopp (2018) marks, we hope, a shift in the field whereby studies examining child L3/L*n* acquisition will soon become common practice. For as many adult L2 learners and other types of bilinguals there are who attempt mastery of additional languages in adulthood, there is a significant population of children around the world acquiring sequential L3/L*n*. This includes all sequential language learning of heritage language bilingual children (such as Turkish heritage bilinguals in Germany in Hopp's 2018 study), immigrant child L2 learners exposed to yet another language in childhood and balanced, simultaneous child bilinguals in bilingual environments learning a first foreign language in childhood. Given the ubiquity of English as a lingua franca being taught at ever-earlier ages around the world, the incidence of child L3/L*n* acquisition is likely to be highly significant in terms of raw numbers.

6.1.1   Hopp (2018)

As mentioned, Hopp's (2018) study is one of the very first to attempt to test the L3 models of adult successive multilingualism in young child L3 acquisition. The study examines the L3 English grammar of Turkish–German bilinguals growing up in Germany (that is, heritage speakers of Turkish). Grammatical phenomena permitting a teasing apart of German and Turkish as the source of transfer are employed, such as word order, because it presents differently in the three languages under investigation. English, the target language, is the more restrictive one among the three, in that it is an SVO language in both main and embedded clauses. German is a V2 language in main clauses and SOV in embedded clauses. Turkish, as with German embedded clauses, is an SOV language; however, this is true for both main and embedded clauses. As a result of verb raising to second position in German, this language displays verb-adverb constructions (for example, *Max spielt oft Klavier;* 'Max **often** plays the piano'), absent in English or Turkish, at least in the context on which Hopp was focusing. In addition to differences pertaining to word order, the study also explores null subjects and the absence of definite articles. Only Turkish allows for null subjects and the absence of definite determiners, which provides yet another difference between the three languages.

The experimental group consisted of 31 Turkish–German heritage bilingual children whose L1 was Turkish and L2 was German – the latter being their dominant language at the time of testing. In order to not confound effects of multilingualism and transfer, Hopp included a group of 31 L2 learners of English whose L1 was German, thus allowing him to compare the Turkish–German bilinguals to the German learners of English. The first task was a sentence-repetition task, targeting four different constructions (corresponding to the linguistic differences across these three languages). The second task in the study was an oral production task to examine grammatical productivity, which used a picture story developed in the MAIN project (Multilingual Assessment Instrument for Narratives; Gagarina et al., 2012). In this task, six different pictures form a narrative with common characters and actions.

The results showed that, irrespective of the task, no significant differences emerged between the two groups. Recall that the crucial differentiation between the groups was that the L3 group had acquired Turkish and German, and the L2 group had only acquired German at the onset of L3 English. Hopp (2018) explained these findings by arguing that the L3 learners of English had transferred German, irrespective of previously acquired knowledge. He suggested that these findings could be accounted for by the TPM, which would predict transfer from German.

Hopp (2018) also acknowledged that, without the implementation of the mirror-image methodology (as discussed at length in Chapter 5), it is impossible to disentangle the predictions of the L2SF and the TPM. However, doing so does not seem feasible in this case: As Hopp points out, it would be very difficult – if possible at all – to find a homogenous group of L1 German–L2 Turkish bilinguals. Moreover, the fact that he tested several unrelated domains of grammar showing that German was always transferred, offers strong evidence in favor of full transfer, in that there was no indication that some of the several properties tested showed effects of hybrid transfer. On the whole, it seems that the available models can be tested in child L3/L*n* acquisition, and thus provide at least an initial pathway to begin the field's expansion in this direction.

6.2 Consequences for the L1 and L2: Does the L3 Affect Them in the Same Way?

Until this point of the book, we have not considered what the consequences of transfer in L3/L*n* might be for the mental representations in any degree of detail, nor the performance and/or processing of previous linguistic systems over the course of and indeed after L3 acquisition is complete. Not having done so sits at the crossroads of two facts: (a) the dearth of relevant evidence in this emerging field from which generalizations in this regard can be made responsibly, and (b) the self-selection of our focus, which has been of progressive transfer as opposed to regressive transfer. Nevertheless, interest in describing and explaining regressive transfer – the effect that the new target, in this case the L3/L*n*, has on the previously acquired systems – has recently taken center stage. Can and to what extent does an L3 have an effect on either the L1 or the L2 of the multilingual learner? Which variables, if any, determine when regressive transfer occurs, and to what extent? Will we need bespoke, independent models for this, or will variables such as structural distance between the languages, L1 or L2 default status, facilitation, working memory and other cognitive functions suffice to make predictions regarding regressive transfer for group trends and/or individual differences?

Although many generative scholars have taken the position that there is an absolute steady state to acquisition – a point along the learning continuum at which development stops and a grammar is proverbially set in stone – we do not. The facts of bilingualism across the many forms it can take (from naturalistic, simultaneous child acquisition to adult sequential L2 acquisition) do not match well with the construct of an absolute steady state, at least one that would somehow be impervious to significant changes over the lifespan. Whereas some generative scholars assume and advocate for a weaker notion of a steady state, whereby only narrow syntax is virtually impervious to change once established (e.g., Sorace, 2011; Tsimpli & Sorace, 2006), we actually ascribe to a view whereby all domains of grammar can potentially change over the lifespan, depending on conditions for maintenance (Iverson, 2012; Iverson & Miller, 2017). While syntax proper might be more resistant to change than, say, the interface with discourse/pragmatics, nothing is truly invulnerable depending on lifespan contexts. We know from decades of work that L1 attrition occurs (see Schmid & Köpke, 2017, and peer commentaries to this keynote article in *Linguistic Approaches to Bilingualism* for discussion and review), particularly after prolonged exposure to the L2 and decreased access to the L1 or the opportunity to use the L1 (Iverson & Miller, 2017). We also know that, when

L1 attrition occurs, much of the changes to the L1 can be attributed directly to the other, now competing, L2 system. Finally, we know that even the processing strategies of an L1 can be supplanted by those used in the L2, again after prolonged experience with the L2 (Dussias & Sagarra, 2007). If L1 modification is a consequence of L2 acquisition, especially in particular contexts, then a logical question arises: What happens in the context of L3 acquisition after prolonged L3 exposure over time?

The above question has been investigated by a small cohort of researchers in recent years. Hui (2010), Matthews et al. (2014) and Tsang (2016) examined the influence of acquiring either German or French as the L3 on the L2 English of L1 Cantonese speakers, each study examining different domains of grammar in the same combination independently. Taken together, the results of these studies suggest that an L3 can indeed have an effect on previously acquired languages: The L3 groups of these studies patterned differently in the L2 from other groups that had the same L1 and L2 combination and the same overall L2 proficiency, yet lacked an L3. Llinàs-Grau and Puig-Mayenco (2016) showed a similar trend, whereby L4 German was argued to affect L3 English. This study compared the rate of *that*-deletion in embedded clauses by advanced L3 learners of English with and without German as an L4. Significant differences between both groups were interpreted as facilitative influence from German into English, which is argued to be an instance of regressive transfer from the L4 to the L3. It should be said, however, that these studies assumed that any possible effect would be found uniquely from the L3/L4 to the L2/L3, depending on the case. In other words, they did not consider or test whether or not an L3/L*n* could have a regressive transfer effect on an individual's native language.

Cabrelli Amaro, Amaro and Rothman's (2015) study distinguishes itself from the aforementioned cohort precisely because this study examined the potential effect an L3 could have on both the L2 and the L1. Assuming that typological proximity might favor regressive transfer, if it were to happen at all, they used the mirror-image approach to see if such instances of backward influence would have an equal effect when the typologically more similar language to the L3 was an L1 or an L2. In other words, they set out to test whether the same language, as an L1 or L2, would be equally susceptible to change. Two groups of Spanish–English bilinguals acquiring L3 BP were tested: (a) L1 Spanish–L2 English, and (b) L1 English–L2 Spanish. The domain of inquiry was subject-to-subject raising across a dative experiencer, as in 'John seems to me to be intelligent.' While English and BP allow for such raising, Spanish does not allow it due to differences in the feature configuration of embedded T' across the languages. At advanced stages of L3 proficiency, the results showed clear influence from the L3 to the L2 (BP→Spanish), but not BP to Spanish influence across the board. In other words, Spanish was only affected for the L2 Spanish, not the L1 Spanish group. This is particularly interesting in light of the fact that these learners had also been tested at the initial stages, at which point both groups showed knowledge of the ungrammaticality of subject-to-subject raising in their L1 or L2 Spanish and influence from their Spanish when tested in L3 BP. Obviously, something changes for L2 Spanish throughout development that seems to have been resisted when Spanish was an L1. The findings of this study, along with evidence in Cabrelli Amaro (2017b) for phonology, led Cabrelli Amaro to formulate the Differential Stability Hypothesis (DSH; Cabrelli Amaro, 2017a). Reminiscent of some arguments offered in the Phonological Permeability Hypothesis (Cabrelli Amaro & Rothman, 2010; see Section 3.4 in Chapter 3 for details), the main tenet of the DSH is that an L2 system is less stable than is an L1 system, and is thus more likely to be influenced by a third language. However, as rightly pointed out by Cabrelli Amaro and Iverson (2018), available studies on the topic have used cross-sectional data, which have been useful to formulate hypotheses for regressive transfer in multilingualism, but longitudinal designs are needed to move forward and to corroborate the findings thus far.

As this topic in L3 acquisition develops, as is the case in L3 progressive transfer studies, we will want to answer a few related questions. The data available thus far suffer from unavoidable confounds by virtue of there not yet being a critical mass of relevant studies. For example, what if the observed trend is more reflective of a role of typological similarity effects? The data set from Cabrelli Amaro et al. (2015) might add some independent evidence for there being more than a typological effect, as the data indicate this only occurs when the typologically similar language is an L2. Do we see an L2SF in reverse? That is, is there a privileged role for an L2 being affected? If so, why? There are many other questions related to uncovering the dynamic processes of transfer in reverse that future research will address.

6.3 Is It Easier to Overcome L1 versus L2 Transfer during L3 Development?

As discussed throughout the book, L3 development as an explicit focus has not received much attention in the formal linguistic L3 literature. While there is no lack of studies that have investigated more advanced L3 proficiencies than ab initio and low-proficiency L3 beginners (see the numbers discussed in Chapter

5), there is a dearth of studies that have considered development itself, even when the L3 learners examined have had significant exposure to the L3. Most of these studies also examined transfer/CLE of other languages, based on the hypothesis that either transfer source can be reliably identified at later stages or because they assumed that transfer occurs over the course of L3 development itself (e.g., García Mayo & Slabakova, 2015; Hermas, 2015; Lozano, 2003; Puig-Mayenco & Marsden, 2018; Slabakova & García Mayo, 2015). Whereas we have advocated herein that the best path forward for determining multilingual transfer sources is at the initial stages in isolation of more advanced developmental stages, it is not the case that examining L3 development in and of itself should suffer as a consequence. It is true that L3 development is not completely independent from L3 transfer studies: After all, what is transferred and when will inevitably affect the learning trajectories that developmental studies seek to describe and explain.

Cabrelli Amaro, Iverson, Giancaspro and Halloran (2018), by contrast, investigated the effects of having initially transferred an L1 versus the effects of having transferred an L2 on the actual developmental path of the L3. In other words, they asked whether overcoming nonfacilitative transfer was equally challenging depending on whether the said transfer comes from an L1 or an L2. To this end, they tested the knowledge of differential object marking (DOM) in L3 BP by Spanish–English bilinguals, covarying the order of acquisition with a mirror-image methodology. Their focused experimental groups had an advanced knowledge of Portuguese, and they compared them to two groups of Spanish–English bilinguals who were beginners of L3 BP in Giancaspro, Halloran and Iverson (2015). In that study, Giancaspro et al. (2015) found that both experimental groups transferred Spanish as opposed to English, irrespective of order of acquisition; in other words, they transferred DOM to BP, where it does not actually form part of the grammar – as is equally true of English. If we see similar patterns of behavior, that is if both groups have eradicated DOM from their BP grammar or have similar degrees of lingering effects from Spanish transfer, then this would be consistent with concluding that there is no difference in overcoming L3 transfer effects when they come from an L1 or an L2. If neither scenario obtains, it would indicate a difference in overcoming nonfacilitative transfer depending on the type of grammar from which it is copied; that is, a native or a nonnative one. Cabrelli Amaro et al. (2018) found that only those learners who had Spanish as their L2 seemed to be able to overcome nonfacilitative DOM transfer to their BP. The L1 Spanish–L2 English advanced learners of BP, on the other hand, behaved like the beginner learners of BP from Giancaspro et al.'s (2015) study. Why should this be the case? Why would overcoming nonfacilitative transfer from an L2 be easier than doing so from an L1? Is this simply the opposite of that which was noticed in Section 6.2? If so, might what we observe in both cases provide converging evidence for a type of L2SF effect in reverse order, or at least support for some of the suggestions related to how the L2 and L3 are structured more similarly and, therefore, have a greater degree of or opportunity to influence one another (e.g., Bardel & Falk, 2012)?

The L3 learner begins with an initial hypothesis, which will either be the L1 or L2 representation, but the developing interlanguage L3 grammars will need to sustain it as correct by proverbially testing it against the input received in the L3. As the learner receives more input that can prove initial hypotheses false (cause parsing failures) or sustained (by not having parsing failures), reanalysis will be conducted, leading to convergence on the L3 target to match the input. However, the process for this might be different precisely because the cumulative experience that a specific learner will have had with the L1 or the L2 will differ considerably. Following from the general assumption that one has more cumulative experience with one's L1 than with an L2 – at least this was true of the learners tested in the present study – Cabrelli Amaro et al. (2018) took the position that such experience matters. In addition to transferred representations, relative entrenchment of those representations also transfers. In other words, L2 transfer is more easily overcome because there is weaker entrenchment of the property from which to retreat. Whatever the ultimate explanation is and the extent to which we replicate what few studies thus far have shown, understanding the regressive consequences for previously acquired languages with both descriptive and explanatory adequacies must be a significant piece of the proverbial puzzle that is L3/Ln acquisition.

6.4   A Note on Cross-Module Converging Evidence

To our knowledge, there are very few studies that present evidence from the same learners across modules of the grammar. If there really is full transfer, as the TPM suggests, we might expect to find converging evidence of this from studies that examine domains of morphosyntax, as well as phonology. We have discussed details of these few studies throughout the book; for example, Llama's (2017) dissertation, which examined processing strategies for relative clause (low versus high) attachment preferences as a proxy for syntax, while also testing phonology proper in the same learners. The evidence to date is not only scarce but is also somewhat messy by its very nature. While Llama (2017) is to be commended for the attempt – it is one of the very first – the abundant noise in her data, as she acknowledges, precludes a definitive answer regarding whether or not one can expect to find cross-module converging data based on these results. In the first place, there are issues with taking relative clause attachment preference as a proxy for syntax, not to mention the unexpected variation she found in this regard, even in so-called control populations. What emerges from the argumentation in Llama (2017) is the call for the value and necessity of studies of this type in the first place. We could not agree more.

Although possible in principle, it seems unlikely that L3 morphosyntactic and phonology systems – and by phonological system, we are referring to just that, not including articulatory phonetics as other constraints, as even physiological ones can obscure the teasing apart of the signal from the noise in this respect – would have completely different variables at play for determining what is selected for L3/*Ln* transfer. It seems then fair to attempt to adopt current models and to test the extent to which phonology and morphosyntax play out given the predictions of each theory. Of course, this means testing at the right time during the acquisition process, as well as in the right domains in light of the language pairings, ideally with consideration of all the methodological issues discussed in Chapter 5. Converging evidence from more than one grammatical system would provide quite strong evidence, regardless of the nature of the resulting data, for several key questions that currently dominate the field, as well as unique ones that can only be addressed via such an approach. Is previous linguistic influence the same for morphosyntax and phonology? Does one module take longer to converge on in L3 acquisition relative to the other? If so, why?

Such bespoke questions offer unique opportunities for cross-fertilization between those fields that work on the L3/*Ln* acquisition of morphosyntax and phonology, areas that to date have developed in relative isolation of one another. As we have seen when phonologists and syntacticians collaborate in L2 acquisition, models with greater explanatory power emerge, such as the case of the Prosodic Transfer Hypothesis (Goad & White, 2006). In addition to seeing if specifically designed studies can yield converging cross-module evidence, research that considers the relative contribution of both phonology and morphosyntax to the patterns of L3/*Ln* transfer and developmental learning, wherever they emerge – for example, in morphological omission and/or commission errors – will be in the best position to explain the complicated patterns in the data. We look forward to an expanding field of formal linguistic approaches to L3/*Ln* acquisition in which such collaborations are increasingly common.

6.5   Complementary Evidence from Neurolinguistic Methodologies

For decades, generative scholars have worked with on-line methodologies such as reaction times in reading and listening, as well as with visual-world and eye-tracking during reading, combining formal linguistic insights, description and predictions into questions that can best be described as processing-based (e.g., Clahsen, Balkhair, Schutter, & Cunnings, 2013; Cunnings, 2017; Cunnings, Patterson, & Felser, 2015; Dekydtspotter, McGuire, & Mossman, 2013; Jacob & Felser, 2016; Jegerski, 2012, 2014, 2015; Juffs, 2005; Juffs & Harrington, 2011; Lago, Stutter García, & Felser, 2018). Neurolinguistic methods that are also related to language processing (EEG and ERP) and neuroanatomical adaptations (magnetic resonance imaging; MRI) have seen a lesser but still significant uptake in formal linguistic L2 studies, particularly in recent years (e.g., Alemán Bañón, Fiorentino, & Gabriele, 2014; Alemán Bañón, Miller, & Rothman, 2017; Jessen & Felser, 2018; Pliatsikas, Johnstone, & Marinis, 2014, 2017; see Roberts, González Alonso, Pliatsikas, & Rothman, 2018, for a review). Such methods have been crucial on several fronts. An obvious benefit of this research has been the integration of the granularity of formal linguistic descriptions and related predictive power for acquisition and processing behavior with increasing ecological validity related to the role of domain-general cognitive and environment variables.

To date, there has not yet been the same injection of truly processing-focused psycholinguistic and neurolinguistic research in the study of formal linguistic approaches to L3/Ln morphosyntactic acquisition as there has been in L2 acquisition studies. Perhaps this is due to the comparative size of L2 studies and L3/Ln studies overall, the relative age of the subfields, the more limited set of questions that have been pondered in L3/Ln studies and/or the greater difficulty in finding L3/Ln subjects relative to L2 ones. Whatever the case may be, we are positive that the future of L3/Ln morphosyntactic studies, from a formal linguistic perspective, will benefit from a similar injection of processing and neurological methods, as well as considerations or the combination of psycholinguistic questions and theories. As we saw in Chapter 3, the study of the L3/Ln multilingual lexicon is well ahead of morphosyntax in this regard.

A very interesting recent study related to L3 morphosyntax is that by Grey et al. (2017). This study stands out for several reasons, partly because of the combination of its methods – behavioral and neural correlates via ERPs – its focus on grammatical learning in morphosyntactic domains and its main question, which focuses on quantifying the much-claimed advantage that bilinguals purportedly have over monolinguals in subsequent grammatical acquisition. As discussed throughout the book, it is often difficult to find sufficient numbers of subjects (to be confident that one can generalize responsibly to an extent) at precisely the right point in L3 development to test what we need fairly. As a result, the authors shrewdly sidestep some of these issues by using an artificial grammar paradigm, the acquisition of Brocanto2 (see also Morgan-Short, Sanz, & Ullman, 2010). As suggested by Rothman et al. (2015) – details related to the ecological validity of comparisons between artificial grammar learning and natural language learning aside (see Ettlinger, Morgan-Short, Faretta-Stutenberg, & Wong, 2016; Robinson, 2010) – using artificial grammars might prove to be a good solution for the aforementioned real-world obstacles because one is able to control the amount, type and context of input all learners receive in the L3/L*n*. Grey et al. (2017) tested early Mandarin–English bilinguals compared to English monolinguals in the acquisition of Brocanto2. Although this is not the typical case in the formal L3/L*n* approaches to the morphosyntax of adult L2 to L3, we can learn much from it nevertheless.

Following grammar instruction in and/or exposure to Brocanto2, the monolingual and bilingual subjects practiced comprehension and production. They then judged grammaticality at low and high levels of proficiency while ERPs were recorded. Although the monolinguals and bilinguals did not differ in performance on behavioral measures with Brocanto2, the ERP patterns were distinct. At high proficiency levels, both groups showed a P600, a common neurological component in ERPs associated with syntactic repair – among other things – and found consistently in native-speaker processing of morphosyntactic violations. A reasonable interpretation of these results would be that previous exposure to more than one language is not required for success in ultimate attainment in subsequent languages. However, the groups differed in significant ways when tested with lower Brocanto2 proficiency; only the bilinguals showed a P600, indicating that previous exposure to more than one language could affect the speed of successful L3 acquisition, providing independent evidence for the so-called bilingual advantage in additional language acquisition (e.g., Cenoz, 2003; Sanz, 2000).

Where this advantage/difference comes from is not clear. In line with the theories we have examined, particularly because the difference seems to be at the beginning, when levels of proficiency are low, one wonders how the models on which we have focused would apply and what predictions they might make. Since Brocanto2 is a true artificial grammar – not a miniature version of a natural grammar – it seems quite difficult to argue how the features across these languages line up with regard to typological proximity and the like with any degree of precision. Nevertheless, what research of this type emphasizes is that the application of neurolinguistic methodologies and the use of artificial grammars can indeed inform relevant questions within L3/Ln theorizing. To our knowledge, there are no completed studies using EEG/ERP or MRI – neurological measures – that test the models of L3/Ln on which we have focused, despite compelling reasons to do so. Rothman et al. (2015) offered an ERP methodology designed specifically to test the L3/Ln morphosyntactic models directly. They also combine EEG with artificial grammars of a specific type, namely mini-grammars based on Spanish and English lexis, respectively. Each of these mini-grammars contains 12 bare nouns (stripped of language-specific morphology) and 12 adjectives that take novel agreement morphemes for number and gender. The morphemes are the same across the two grammars, which respect the phonotactics of both Spanish and English, yet differ significantly in form regarding how number (English and Spanish) and gender (Spanish only) are expressed in the source languages. The mini-grammars also provide unique articles, also inflected for gender and number. The procedure is a standard one – in terms of training and testing – for novel artificial grammar-learning paradigms; see, for example, Grey et al. (2017). After novice learners are exposed to these languages and perform to criterion on behavioral measures for accuracy (at or above 80%) – that is, they seem to "get" the patterns of grammaticality after being exposed to all the sentences (at least 480 exemplars, since the training repeats a new set of 480 exemplars for individuals who do not meet the accuracy criterion in the first training phase – the EEG experiment begins. In this phase, ERPs are recorded within a standard violation paradigm; in other words, participants are first exposed to ungrammatical sentences in the experimental phase. The idea is to use the ERP components specifically in the sentences containing agreement violations to provide detailed information of what the learners are doing; that is, what (linguistic or otherwise) mechanisms underlie their behavior. Is it (phonological) pattern matching, which should elicit an N400 component, given that it would represent a failed expectation of some sort, or is it syntactic repair, which should elicit a P600? By having four groups (two sets of mirror-image groups per mini-grammar) the predictions, as detailed in Table 6.1 below, should yield differences across the pairing depending on whether the TPM, the CEM or the L2SF is supported (the models available at the time of writing).

As it turned out, developing such a methodology, particularly using an ERP technique – partly due to the sheer number of novel exemplars needed for this approach – has required some modifications, including increasing the number of lexical items in the language and, most recently, modifications to be able to address the LPM and the Scalpel Model. The full study has thus taken some

Table 6.1 *Predictions of electrophysiological components by model of L3/Ln morphosyntactic transfer in Rothman et al.'s (2015) methodology*

	CEM		L2SF		TPM	
	Number	Gender	Number	Gender	Number	Gender
L1 Spanish–L2 English–L3 Mini-English	P600	P600	P600/N400	N400/No effects	P600/N400	No effects
L1 English–L2 Spanish–L3 Mini-English	P600	P600	P600/N400	P600/ N400	P600/N400	No effects

time to develop and is, at the time of writing this book, still in the process of implementation. As a result, we do not have sufficient data to warrant reporting the results here. That being said, one thing is clear. Adopting a neurolinguistic methodology that can uncover the qualitative nature of what L3/Ln learners are doing at the very initial stages of (synthesized) L3 learning, despite its time-consuming nature, is both possible and potentially highly informative. By relying on involuntary brainwave components used standardly as an indicator of the processing of distinct domains of grammar; for example, syntactic repair versus semantic processing or phonological matching, to adjudicate among the L3/Ln models is, we believe, a step in the right direction. Complementing the behavioral work done in the field thus far with psycholinguistic methodologies that, in principle, could add converging evidence for particular claims or challenge them could help us to prune the models we have in a responsible manner and may possibly even suggest that some have reached a critical mass of negative evidence and can thus be put aside.

6.6   Taking Stock: A Few Closing Points

Our brief discussion of the topics covered in this final chapter is meant to be a pointer toward the most notable directions in which the field is already expanding however gradually it might be doing so in some cases. That we welcome and encourage research in these new or understudied areas should not, however, be taken as a suggestion to shift focus away from progressive transfer or the initial stages of L3/Ln acquisition. Instead, we hope that new perspectives contribute further pieces of the puzzle, highlighting where and how variables we have already considered as a field (such as L2 status and typological proximity) might apply differently in different modalities and contexts of transfer/CLE. That being said, we nevertheless hope to have made an impact with this book, providing evidence and arguments to reconsider and, to the extent possible, reconcile our current positions.

If there is anything that should be uncontroversial from the results of our systematic review in Chapter 5, it is that no current theory is capable of dealing with the entirety of the data the field has collected thus far although, on balance, some fare better than do others. These proposals, whether or not they have been articulated explicitly in models, have highlighted the role of an impressive number of variables, all of which are likely to be relevant to some extent. The formidable task ahead then, if we want to move on and forward (instead of sideways, as we suggested in Section 1.6 in Chapter 1), is to derive testable predictions that we can verify empirically from as many models as possible simultaneously. This requires commitment from both the theorist and the experimenter: As theorists, we must strive to provide predictions that are as unambiguous and as concrete as possible; in other words, we must commit to the strongest possible version of our models at any given stage. As experimenters, we must strive to elaborate on designs that are as powerful as they can be, given predictions from the available theories; in other words, we must commit to casting the widest possible net over the field's theoretical gamut. At this point in the development of formal linguistic approaches to L3/Ln acquisition, with five available models and numerous other independently proposed deterministic variables, we will benefit the most from data that can speak to several – all, to the extent possible – models at once, however difficult such data are to come by and however long they take to collect. In the meantime, systematic reviews such as the one we have offered in this book will help us look beyond individual data sets and (more) fractional designs, and at the bigger picture.

As is true of all instances of language development, well-collected data from any and all stages of L3/Ln acquisition are equally important, even if not equally relevant for all questions. Thus, we look forward to future work that addresses initial and developmental stages, as well as ultimate attainment, regressive transfer and other crucial issues that we have discussed throughout the book. We hope to have made a case, both to the novice reader and to our colleagues in the field, for the epistemological necessity of converging on a better understanding of the initial stages. Progress, we submit, starts with building the strongest possible foundations and bridges for the proverbial edifice we have yet to see fully erected. We look forward to the near future, in which we will have better answers to all the questions considered in this book, as well as to questions of which the field has not yet even conceived.

Appendix A

List of studies in the systematic review: An item number (#) has been assigned to each individual experiment/study within a given publication. The table lists all languages involved in each study, as well as the type of bilinguals the participant groups were at the onset of L3 acquisition (adult L2ers or early bilinguals, including simultaneous bilinguals). An asterisk signals the target L3 for each study.

#	Item (Publication: Experiment)	Languages	Learners
1	Angelovska (2017): A	*English, German, Russian	Adult L2ers
2	Angelovska (2017): B	*English, German, Russian	Adult L2ers
3	Antonova-Ünlü & Sağın-Şimşek (2015)	*Turkish, Russian, English	Adult L2ers
4	Bardel & Falk (2007)	*Swedish, Dutch, English, German, Hungarian	Adult L2ers
5	Bayona (2009)	*Spanish, English, French	Adult L2ers
6	Ben Abbes (2016): A	*French, English, Turkish, Spanish	Adult L2ers
7	Ben Abbes (2016): B	*French, English, Turkish, Spanish	Adult L2ers
8	Ben Abbes (2016): C	*French, English, Turkish, Spanish	Adult L2ers
9	Berends et al. (2017)	*Dutch, English, French	Adult L2ers
10	Berkes & Flynn (2012b)	*English, German, Hungarian	Adult L2ers
11	Bohnacker (2006)	*Swedish, German, Hungarian	Adult L2ers
12	Borg (2013): A	*Spanish, French, English	Adult L2ers
13	Borg (2013): B	*Spanish, French, English	Adult L2ers
14	Bruhn de Garavito & Perpiñán (2014): A	*Spanish, French, English	Adult L2ers
15	Bruhn de Garavito & Perpiñán (2014): B	*Spanish, French, English	Adult L2ers

#	Item (Publication: Experiment)	Languages	Learners
16	Cabrelli Amaro (2013b)	*BP, English, Spanish	Adult L2ers
17	Cabrelli Amaro, Amaro, & Rothman (2015): A	*BP, English, Spanish	Adult L2ers
18	Cabrelli Amaro, Amaro, & Rothman (2015): B	*BP, English, Spanish	Adult L2ers
19	Chin (2009)	*Spanish, Chinese, English	Adult L2ers
20	Clements & Domínguez (2018): A	*Chinese, English, Spanish	Adult L2ers
21	Clements & Domínguez (2018): B	*Chinese, English, Spanish	Adult L2ers
22	Falk (2017)	*German, Spanish, Italian, French, Swedish	Adult L2ers
23	Falk & Bardel (2011)	*German, French, English	Adult L2ers
24	Falk, Lindqvist, & Bardel (2015)	*German, Swedish, Dutch, English, Greek, Hungarian, Russian, Arabic, Catalan, French, Italian, Mandarin, Portuguese, Spanish, Latin, Old Church Slavonic, Swedish Sign Language	Adult L2ers
25	Fallah & Jabbari (2018): A	*English, Mazandarani, Persian	Early bil.
26	Fallah & Jabbari (2018): B	*English, Mazandarani, Persian	Early bil.
27	Fallah, Jabbari, & Fazilatfar (2016): A	*English, Mazandarani, Persian	Early bil.
28	Fallah, Jabbari, & Fazilatfar (2016): B	*English, Mazandarani, Persian	Early bil.
29	Fallah, Jabbari, & Fazilatfar (2016): C	*English, Mazandarani, Persian	Early bil.
30	Fessi (2013): A	*Spanish, Arabic, French	Adult L2ers
31	Fessi (2013): B	*Spanish, Arabic, French	Adult L2ers
32	Fessi (2013): C	*Spanish, Arabic, French	Adult L2ers
33	Flynn, Foley, & Vinnitskaya (2004)	*English, Kazakh, Russian	Early bil.
34	Foote (2009)	*Spanish, French, Italian	Adult L2ers
35	García Mayo & Slabakova (2015)	*English, Basque, Spanish	Early bil.
36	Ghezlou, Koosha, & Lotfi (2018)	*English, Azeri, Persian	Early bil.
37	Giancaspro, Halloran, & Iverson (2015)	*BP, English, Spanish	Adult L2ers

#	Item (Publication: Experiment)	Languages	Learners
38	Hermas (2010): A	*English, French, Arabic	Adult L2ers
39	Hermas (2010): B	*English, French, Arabic	Adult L2ers
40	Hermas (2015): A	*English, French, Arabic	Adult L2ers
41	Hermas (2015): A	*English, French, Arabic	Adult L2ers
42	Hopp (2018): A	*English, German, Turkish	Early bil.
43	Hopp (2018): B	*English, German, Turkish	Early bil.
44	Imaz Aguirre & García Mayo (2017): A	*English, Basque, Spanish	Early bil.
45	Imaz Aguirre & García Mayo (2017): B	*English, Basque, Spanish	Early bil.
46	Ionin, Grolla, Santos, & Montrul (2015)	*BP, English, Spanish	Adult L2ers
47	Iverson (2009b): A	*BP, English, Spanish	Adult L2ers
48	Iverson (2009b): B	*BP, English, Spanish	Adult L2ers
49	Izzo, Cenni, & De Smet (2017)	*Italian, French, German, English, Dutch	Adult L2ers
50	Jaensch (2008)	*German, English, Japanese	Adult L2ers
51	Jaensch (2012): A	*German, English, Spanish, Japanese	Adult L2ers
52	Jaensch (2012): B	*German, English, Spanish, Japanese	Adult L2ers
53	Jaensch (2012): C	*German, English, Spanish, Japanese	Adult L2ers
54	Jin (2009)	*Norwegian, English, Chinese	Adult L2ers
55	Kong (2015)	*French, English, Chinese	Adult L2ers
56	Kulundary & Gabriele (2012): A	*English, Russian, Tuvan	Adult L2ers
57	Kulundary & Gabriele (2012): B	*English, Russian, Tuvan	Adult L2ers
58	Leung (2005a): A	*French, English, Vietnamese	Adult L2ers
59	Leung (2005a): B	*French, English, Vietnamese	Adult L2ers
60	Leung (2007a)	*French, English, Cantonese	Adult L2ers
61	Leung (2008)	*French, English, Cantonese	Adult L2ers
62	Lindqvist & Falk (2014)	*Swedish, English, French, Latin, Turkish, Greek	Adult L2ers
63	Lozano (2003)	*Spanish, English, Greek	Adult L2ers
64	Mollaie, Jabbari, & Rezaie (2016): A	*French, English, Persian	Adult L2ers
65	Mollaie, Jabbari, & Rezaie (2016): B	*French, English, Persian	Adult L2ers

#	Item (Publication: Experiment)	Languages	Learners
66	Montrul, Dias, & Santos (2011): A	*BP, English, Spanish	Adult L2ers
67	Montrul, Dias, & Santos (2011): B	*BP, English, Spanish	Adult L2ers
68	Na Ranong & Leung (2009)	*Thai, English, Chinese	Adult L2ers
69	Park (2016)	*Korean, English, Japanese, Tamil, Malay	Early bil.
70	Parma (2017): A	*BP, English, Spanish	Adult L2ers
71	Parma (2017): B	*BP, English, Spanish	Adult L2ers
72	Puig-Mayenco & Marsden (2018)	*English, Catalan, Spanish	Early bil.
73	Puig-Mayenco, Miller, & Rothman (2018)	*English, Catalan, Spanish	Early bil.
74	Puig-Mayenco & Rothman (in press)	*English, Catalan, Spanish	Early bil.
75	Rothman (2010): A	*BP, English, Spanish	Adult L2ers
76	Rothman (2010): B	*BP, English, Spanish	Adult L2ers
77	Rothman (2011): A	*BP, English, Spanish	Adult L2ers
78	Rothman (2011): B	*BP, English, Spanish	Adult L2ers
79	Rothman & Cabrelli Amaro (2010): A	*French/Italian, English, Spanish	Adult L2ers
80	Rothman & Cabrelli Amaro (2010): B	*French/Italian, English, Spanish	Adult L2ers
81	Sánchez & Bardel (2017)	*English, German, Catalan, Spanish	Adult L2ers
82	Santos (2013): A	*BP, English, Spanish	Adult L2ers
83	Santos (2013): B	*BP, English, Spanish	Adult L2ers
84	Santos (2013): C	*BP, English, Spanish	Adult L2ers
85	Sanz, Park, & Lado (2015)	*Latin, Spanish, Japanese, English	Adult L2ers
86	Siemund, Schröter, & Rahbari (2018)	*English, Russian, Vietnamese, Turkish, German	Early bil.
87	Slabakova & García Mayo (2015)	*English, Basque, Spanish	Early bil.
88	Stadt, Hulk, & Sleeman (2016)	*French, English, Dutch	Adult L2ers
89	Stadt, Hulk, & Sleeman (2018)	*French/German, English, Dutch	Adult L2ers
90	Tavakol & Jabbari (2014)	*German, Italian, English, Persian	Adult L2ers
91	Tsang (2009)	*Chinese, Tagalog, English	Adult L2ers
92	Westergaard et al. (2017)	*English, Norwegian, Russian	Early bil.

Appendix B

Individual scoring for macro variables, binary coded for statistical purposes. If a (✓) has been assigned, this means that the study/experiment's results are compatible with the macro variable; conversely, (X) indicates incompatibility. For *nonfacilitative transfer*, an N/A valuation indicates that the study's design offered no possibility to assess this variable. Item numbers (#) are the same as in Appendix A.

#	L1 transfer	L2 transfer	Typological transfer	Hybrid transfer	Nonfacilitative transfer
1	X	X	X	✓	✓
2	X	X	X	✓	✓
3	✓	X	✓	X	✓
4	X	✓	✓	X	✓
5	X	✓	✓	X	N/A
6	X	X	✓	X	✓
7	X	X	✓	X	✓
8	X	X	✓	X	✓
9	X	✓	✓	X	✓
10	X	X	X	✓	X
11	X	✓	✓	X	✓
12	X	X	✓	X	X
13	X	X	✓	X	X
14	X	X	X	✓	✓
15	X	X	✓	X	✓
16	X	X	✓	X	✓
17	X	X	✓	X	✓
18	X	X	✓	X	✓
19	X	✓	✓	X	✓
20	✓	X	X	X	✓
21	X	X	X	✓	✓
22	X	✓	X	X	✓

#	L1 transfer	L2 transfer	Typological transfer	Hybrid transfer	Nonfacilitative transfer
23	X	✓	X	X	✓
24	X	X	X	✓	✓
25	X	X	X	✓	✓
26	X	X	X	✓	✓
27	X	X	X	✓	✓
28	X	X	X	✓	✓
29	X	X	X	✓	✓
30	X	✓	✓	X	N/A
31	X	✓	✓	X	N/A
32	X	✓	✓	X	N/A
33	X	✓	✓	X	X
34	✓	X	✓	X	✓
35	X	X	✓	X	✓
36	X	✓	✓	X	✓
37	X	X	✓	X	✓
38	✓	X	X	X	✓
39	✓	X	X	X	✓
40	✓	X	X	X	✓
41	✓	X	X	X	✓
42	X	✓	✓	X	✓
43	X	✓	✓	X	✓
44	X	X	X	✓	✓
45	X	X	X	✓	✓
46	X	X	✓	X	✓
47	X	X	✓	X	✓
48	X	X	✓	X	✓
49	X	✓	✓	X	✓
50	X	✓	✓	X	✓
51	X	✓	✓	X	✓
52	X	✓	✓	X	X
53	X	✓	✓	X	✓
54	✓	X	X	X	✓
55	X	X	X	✓	✓
56	X	X	X	✓	✓
57	X	X	X	✓	✓
58	X	✓	✓	X	✓
59	X	✓	✓	X	✓
60	X	✓	✓	X	✓
61	X	✓	✓	X	✓
62	X	✓	X	X	✓

#	L1 transfer	L2 transfer	Typological transfer	Hybrid transfer	Nonfacilitative transfer
63	✓	X	✓	X	✓
64	✓	X	X	X	✓
65	✓	X	X	X	✓
66	X	X	✓	X	✓
67	X	X	✓	X	✓
68	✓	X	✓	X	✓
69	✓	X	✓	X	✓
70	X	X	✓	X	✓
71	X	X	✓	X	✓
72	✓	X	✓	X	✓
73	X	X	✓	X	✓
74	X	X	✓	X	✓
75	X	X	✓	X	✓
76	X	X	✓	X	✓
77	X	X	✓	X	✓
78	X	X	✓	X	✓
79	X	✓	✓	X	✓
80	X	✓	✓	X	✓
81	X	✓	X	X	✓
82	X	X	X	✓	X
83	X	X	✓	X	✓
84	X	X	✓	X	✓
85	✓	X	X	X	✓
86	X	✓	✓	X	✓
87	X	X	✓	X	✓
88	X	X	✓	X	✓
89	X	✓	✓	X	✓
90	X	X	X	✓	✓
91	X	X	X	✓	✓
92	X	X	X	✓	✓

Appendix C

Individual scoring for methodological variables, binary coded for statistical purposes. Levels are labeled (1) or (2) for each variable, as follows: Proficiency in the L3 (1=Beginner, 2=Postbeginner); Testing beyond the L3 (1=L3 only, 2=L3+L2 and/or L1); Production or comprehension (1=Comprehension, 2=Production); Mirror-image groups (1=No use, 2=Use); and Genetic relationship (1=Related, 2=Not related). Item numbers (#) are the same as in Appendix A.

#	Testing beyond the L3	Proficiency in the L3	Production or comprehension	Mirror image	Genetic relationship
1	1	2	2	1	2
2	1	2	2	1	2
3	1	2	2	1	2
4	1	2	2	1	2
5	1	2	1	1	1
6	1	2	2	1	2
7	1	2	1	1	2
8	1	2	2	1	2
9	1	2	1	1	1
10	1	2	2	1	2
11	1	1	2	1	2
12	1	2	1	2	1
13	1	2	1	2	1
14	1	1	2	2	1
15	1	1	1	2	1
16	2	1	1	2	1
17	2	1	1	2	1
18	2	2	1	2	1
19	2	2	1	1	2
20	2	2	2	1	2
21	2	2	1	1	2

#	Testing beyond the L3	Proficiency in the L3	Production or comprehension	Mirror image	Genetic relationship
22	1	1	2	1	1
23	1	2	1	2	1
24	1	1	2	1	1
25	1	1	2	1	2
26	1	1	1	1	2
27	1	1	2	1	2
28	1	1	1	1	2
29	1	1	1	1	2
30	1	2	1	1	2
31	1	2	2	1	2
32	1	2	1	1	2
33	1	1	2	1	2
34	1	2	1	1	1
35	1	2	1	2	2
36	1	2	1	1	2
37	2	1	1	2	1
38	1	1	1	1	2
39	1	1	1	1	2
40	1	2	1	1	2
41	1	2	1	1	2
42	1	1	1	1	1
43	1	1	2	1	1
44	1	2	1	1	2
45	1	2	1	1	2
46	1	2	1	2	1
47	2	1	1	2	1
48	2	1	2	2	1
49	1	1	2	1	1
50	1	2	2	1	1
51	1	2	2	1	1
52	1	2	2	1	1
53	1	2	2	1	1
54	1	1	1	1	1
55	1	2	2	1	2
56	1	2	1	1	2
57	1	2	1	1	2
58	1	1	2	1	2
59	1	1	2	1	2
60	1	1	1	1	2
61	1	1	2	1	2

#	Testing beyond the L3	Proficiency in the L3	Production or comprehension	Mirror image	Genetic relationship
62	1	1	2	1	2
63	1	2	1	1	2
64	1	2	1	1	2
65	1	2	1	1	2
66	1	2	2	2	1
67	1	2	1	2	1
68	2	2	1	1	1
69	1	2	2	1	2
70	1	1	1	2	1
71	1	1	2	2	1
72	1	1	1	2	2
73	1	1	1	2	2
74	2	1	1	2	2
75	2	1	1	2	1
76	2	1	1	2	1
77	2	1	1	2	1
78	2	1	1	2	1
79	2	1	1	1	1
80	2	1	1	1	1
81	1	2	2	1	1
82	2	2	1	2	1
83	1	2	1	2	1
84	2	2	2	2	1
85	1	1	1	2	1
86	1	2	1	1	1
87	1	2	1	2	2
88	1	1	2	2	2
89	1	1	1	1	2
90	1	1	2	1	2
91	1	2	1	1	2
92	1	2	1	1	2

References

Abrahamsson, N., & Hyltenstam, K. (2009). Age of onset and nativelikeness in a second language: Listener perception versus linguistic scrutiny. *Language Learning, 59*(2), 249–306.

Abutalebi, J., & Green, D. W. (2007). Bilingual language production: The neurocognition of language representation and control. *Journal of Neurolinguistics, 20*(3), 242–275.

Abutalebi, J., & Green, D. W. (2016). Neuroimaging of language control in bilinguals: Neural adaptation and reserve. *Bilingualism: Language and Cognition, 19*, 689–698.

Achard, M., & Lee, S. (2016). Toward a model of multilingual usage. In L. Ortega, A. E. Tyler, H. I. Park, & M. Uno (Eds.), *The usage-based study of language learning and multilingualism* (pp. 255–274). Washington, DC: Georgetown University Press.

Adger, D. (2003). *Core syntax: A minimalist approach.* Oxford: Oxford University Press.

Albert, M. L., & Obler, L. K. (1978). *The bilingual brain.* New York: Academic Press.

Alemán Bañón, J., Fiorentino, R., & Gabriele, A. (2014). Morphosyntactic processing in advanced second language (L2) learners: An event-related potential investigation of the effects of L1-L2 similarity and structural distance. *Second Language Research, 30*(3), 275–306.

Alemán Bañón, J., Miller, D., & Rothman, J. (2017). Morphological variability in second language learners: An examination of electrophysiological and production data. *Journal of Experimental Psychology: Learning, Memory and Cognition, 43* (10), 1509–1536.

Alexiadou, A., & Anagnostopoulou, E. (1998). Parametrizing AGR: Word order, V-movement and EPP checking. *Natural Language and Linguistic Theory, 16*, 491–539.

Algeo, J. (2010). *The origins and development of the English language.* Boston, MA: Wadsworth Cengage Learning.

Alonso Alonso, R. (Ed.) (2016). *Crosslinguistic influence in second language acquisition.* Bristol: Multilingual Matters.

Alonso Alonso, R., Cadierno, T., & Jarvis, S. (2016). Crosslinguistic influence in the acquisition of spatial prepositions in English as a foreign language. In R. Alonso Alonso (Ed.), *Crosslinguistic influence in second language acquisition* (pp. 93–120). Bristol: Multilingual Matters.

Amaral, L., & Roeper, T. (2014). Multiple grammars and second language representation. *Second Language Research, 30*(1), 3–36.

Ambridge, B., & Lieven, E. (2011). *Child language acquisition: Contrasting theoretical approaches*. Cambridge: Cambridge University Press.

Angelovska, T. (2017). (When) do L3 English learners transfer from L2 German? Evidence from spoken and written data by L1 Russian speakers. In T. Angelovska & A. Hahn (Eds.), *L3 syntactic transfer: Models, new developments and implications*. Amsterdam: John Benjamins.

Angelovska, T., & Hahn, A. (Eds.) (2017). *L3 syntactic transfer: Models, new developments and implications*. Amsterdam: John Benjamins.

Ansaldo, A., Marcotte, K., Scherer, L., & Raboyeau, G. (2008). Language therapy and bilingual aphasia: Clinical implications of psycholinguistic and neuroimaging research. *Journal of Neurolinguistics, 6*(21), 539–557.

Antón, E., Duñabeitia, J. A., Estévez, A., Hernández, J. A., Castillo, A., Fuentes, L. J., Davidson, D. J., & Carreiras, M. (2014). Is there a bilingual advantage in the ANT task? Evidence from children. *Frontiers in Psychology, 5*, 398.

Antonova-Ünlü, E., & Sağın-Şimşek, Ç. (2015). The use of verbal morphology in Turkish as a third language: The case of Russian–English–Turkish trilinguals. *International Journal of Bilingualism, 19*(3), 347–362.

Aronin, L., & Singleton, D. (2012). *Multilingualism*. Amsterdam: John Benjamins.

Azevedo, M. (2005). *Portuguese: A linguistic introduction*. Cambridge: Cambridge University Press.

Baetens Beardsmore, H. (1993). An overview of European models of bilingual education. *Language, Culture and Curriculum, 6*(3), 197–208.

Baker, C. (2006). *Foundations of bilingualism and bilingual education*. Clevedon: Multilingual Matters.

Baker, C. (2007). Becoming bilingual through bilingual education. In P. Auer & L. Wei (Eds.), *Handbook of multilingualism and multilingual communication* (pp. 131–152). Berlin: Mouton de Gruyter.

Bardel, C., & Falk, Y. (2007). The role of the second language in third language acquisition: The case of Germanic syntax. *Second Language Research, 23*(4), 459–484.

Bardel, C., & Falk, Y. (2012). Behind the L2 Status Factor: A neurolinguistic framework for L3 research. In J. Cabrelli Amaro, S. Flynn, & J. Rothman (Eds.), *Third language acquisition in adulthood* (pp. 61–78). Amsterdam: John Benjamins.

Bardel, C., & Lindqvist, C. (2007). The role of proficiency and psychotypology in lexical cross-linguistic influence: A study of a multilingual learner of Italian L3. In M. Chini, P. Desideri, M. E. Favilla, & G. Pallotti (Eds.), *Atti del 6o Congresso Internazionale dell'Associazione Italiana di Linguistica Applicata* (pp. 123–145). Perugia: Guerra Edizioni.

Bardel, C., & Sánchez, L. (2017). The L2 Status Factor hypothesis revisited: The role of metalinguistic knowledge, working memory, attention and noticing in third language learning. In T. Angelovska & A. Hahn (Eds.), *L3 syntactic transfer: Models, new developments and implications* (pp. 85–102). Amsterdam, NL: John Benjamins.

Basnight-Brown, D. M., & Altarriba, J. (2007). Differences in semantic and translation priming across languages: The role of language direction and language dominance. *Memory & Cognition, 35*(5), 953–965.

Basque Government, D.o.E. (2017). *Estadísticas del sistema educativo – Matrícula 2017–2018*. Retrieved from http://www.euskadi.eus/informacion/prematricula-2017-2018/web01-a2hestat/es/

Basque Government, D.o.E., & Government of Navarre, D.o.E. (2017). *VI Encuesta Sociolingüística*. Retrieved from https://bideoak2.euskadi.eus/2017/07/05/zupiria_hablantes/VI_INK_SOZLG-EH_gaz.pdf

Bates, E., & MacWhinney, B. (1982). Functionalist approaches to grammar. In E. Warner & L. Gleitman (Eds.), *Language acquisition: The state of the art* (pp. 173–218). New York: Cambridge University Press.

Bates, E., & MacWhinney, B. (1987). Competition, variation, and language learning. In B. MacWhinney (Ed.), *Mechanisms of language acquisition* (pp. 157–193). Hillsdale: Erlbaum.

Bates, E., & MacWhinney, B. (1989). Functionalism and the competition model. In B. MacWhinney & E. Bates (Eds.), *The crosslinguistic study of sentence processing* (pp. 3–73). Cambridge: Cambridge University Press.

Bayley, R., Cameron, R., & Lucas, C. (Eds.) (2013). *The Oxford handbook of sociolinguistics*. Oxford: Oxford University Press.

Bayona, P. (2009). The acquisition of Spanish middle and impersonal passive constructions from SLA and TLA perspectives. In Y. I. Leung (Ed.), *Third language acquisition and Universal Grammar* (pp. 1–29). Bristol: Multilingual Matters.

Bayram, F., Pascual y Cabo, D., & Rothman, J. (2018). Cross-generational attrition contributions to heritage speaker competence. In B. Köpke & M. S. Schmid (Eds.), *The Oxford handbook of attrition*. Oxford: Oxford University Press.

Bayram, F., Rothman, J., Iverson, M., Kupisch, T., Miller, D., Puig-Mayenco, E., & Westergaard, M. (2017). Differences in use without deficiencies in competence: Passives in the Turkish and German of Turkish heritage speakers in Germany. *International Journal of Bilingual Education and Bilingualism*, 1–27. doi: 10.1080/13670050.2017.1324403.

Beck, M. (1998). L2 acquisition and obligatory head movement: English-speaking learners of German and the local impairment hypothesis. *Studies in Second Language Acquisition, 20*, 311–348.

Ben Abbes, K. (2016). *The acquisition of French morpho-syntactic properties: Cross-linguistic influence in the learning of L3 French by Turkish/Spanish speakers who learned English as an L2*. Unpublished PhD dissertation, University of Essex.

Benati, A., & Schwieter, J. (2017). Input processing and processing instruction: pedagogical and cognitive considerations for L3 acquisition. In T. Angelovska & A. Hahn (Eds.), *L3 syntactic transfer: Models, new developments and implications* (pp. 253–275). Amsterdam: John Benjamins.

Berends, S., Schaeffer, J., & Sleeman, P. (2017). Cross-linguistic influence in adult second language learners: Dutch quantitative pronoun constructions. In M. LaMendola & J. Scott (Eds.), *Proceedings of the 41st Annual Boston University*

Conference on Language Development (pp. 74–87). Boston, US: Cascadilla Proceedings Project.

Berkes, É., & Flynn, S. (2012a). Further evidence in support of the Cumulative-Enhancement Model. In J. Cabrelli Amaro, S. Flynn, & J. Rothman (Eds.), *Third language acquisition in adulthood* (pp. 143–164). Amsterdam: John Benjamins.

Berkes, É., & Flynn, S. (2012b). Multilingualism: New perspectives on syntactic development. In T. K. Bhatia & W. C. Ritchie (Eds.), *The handbook of bilingualism and multilingualism (2nd ed.,* pp. 137–167). Chichester: Wiley.

Berkes, É., & Flynn, S. (2016). Multi-competence and syntax. In V. Cook & L. Wei (Eds.), *The Cambridge handbook of linguistic multi-competence* (pp. 206–226). Cambridge: Cambridge University Press.

Berkes, É., & Flynn, S. (2017). Toward a new understanding of syntactic CLI: Evidence from L2 and L3 acquisition. In T. Angelovska & A. Hahn (Eds.), *L3 syntactic transfer: Models, new developments and implications* (pp. 35–61). Amsterdam: John Benjamins.

Bernaus, M., Masgoret, A.-M., Gardner, R. C., & Reyes, E. (2004). Motivation and attitudes towards learning languages in multicultural classrooms. *International Journal of Multilingualism, 1*(2), 75–89.

Bernstein, J. (1993). *Topics in the syntax of nominal structure across Romance.* Unpublished PhD dissertation, City University of New York.

Berthoud, A.-C., & Lüdi, G. (2011). Language policy and planning. In R. Wodak, B. Johnstone, & P. E. Kerswill (Eds.), *The SAGE handbook of sociolinguistics* (pp. 479–494). New York: SAGE Publications.

Berwick, R. C., & Chomsky, N. (2015). *Why only us: Language and evolution.* Cambridge, MA: MIT Press.

Berwick, R. C., & Chomsky, N. (2017). Why only us: Recent questions and answers. *Journal of Neurolinguistics, 43,* 166–177.

Berwick, R. C., Pietroski, P., Yankama, B., & Chomsky, N. (2011). Poverty of the stimulus revisited. *Cognitive Science, 35*(7), 1207–1242.

Bialystok, E. (1979). Explicit and implicit judgments of L2 grammaticality. *Language Learning, 29*(1), 81–103.

Bialystok, E. (1982). On the relationship between knowing and using linguistic forms. *Applied Linguistics, 3*(3), 181–206.

Bialystok, E. (1988). Levels of bilingualism and levels of linguistic awareness. *Developmental Psychology, 24*(4), 560–567.

Bialystok, E. (2001). *Bilingualism in development: Language, literacy, & cognition.* New York: Cambridge University Press.

Bialystok, E. (2009). Bilingualism: The good, the bad, and the indifferent. *Bilingualism: Language and Cognition, 12*(1), 3–11.

Bialystok, E. (2011). Reshaping the mind: The benefits of bilingualism. *Canadian Journal of Experimental Psychology, 65*(4), 229–235.

Bialystok, E. (2016). The signal and the noise: Finding the pattern in human behavior. *Linguistic Approaches to Bilingualism, 6*(5), 517–534.

Bialystok, E. (2018). Bilingualism and executive function: What's the connection? In D. Miller, F. Bayram, J. Rothman, & L. Serratrice (Eds.), *Bilingual cognition and language: The state of the science across its subfields* (pp. 283–305). Amsterdam: John Benjamins.

Bialystok, E., Craik, F. I. M., & Luk, G. (2008). Lexical access in bilinguals: Effects of vocabulary size and executive control. *Journal of Neurolinguistics, 21*(6), 522–538.

Bialystok, E., Craik, F. I. M., & Luk, G. (2012). Bilingualism: Consequences for mind and brain. *TRENDS in Cognitive Sciences, 16*(4), 240–250.

Bialystok, E., & Hakuta, K. (1994). *In other words: The psychology and science of second language acquisition.* New York, USA: Basic Books.

Bielenia-Grajewska, M. (2009). Linguistic borrowing in the English language of economics. *Lexis: Journal in English Lexicography, 3,* 107–135. Retrieved from http://journals.openedition.org/lexis/643

Birdsong, D. (1992). Second language acquisition and the critical period hypothesis. *Language, 68,* 706–755.

Birdsong, D., & Molis, M. (2001). On the evidence for maturational constraints in second language acquisition. *Journal of Memory and Language, 44*(2), 235–249.

Bley-Vroman, R. (1983). The comparative fallacy in interlanguage studies: The case of systematicity. *Language Learning, 33*(1), 1–17.

Bley-Vroman, R. (1989). What is the logical problem of foreign language learning? In S. Gass & J. Schachter (Eds.), *Linguistic perspectives on second language acquisition* (pp. 41–68). New York: Cambridge University Press.

Bley-Vroman, R. (2009). The evolving context of the Fundamental Difference Hypothesis. *Studies in Second Language Acquisition, 31*(2), 175–198.

Bobb, S. C., & Kroll, J. F. (2018). Words on the brain: The bilingual mental lexicon. In D. Miller, F. Bayram, J. Rothman, & L. Serratrice (Eds.), *Bilingual cognition and language: The state of the science across its subfields* (pp. 307–324). Amsterdam: John Benjamins.

Bock, K., & Miller, C. (1991). Broken agreement. *Cognitive Psychology, 23*(1), 45–93.

Bohnacker, U. (2006). When Swedes begin to learn German: From V2 to V2. *Second Language Research, 22*(4), 443–486.

Borg, K. (2013). The acquisition of future of probability in L3 Spanish. In T. Judy & D. Pascual y Cabo (Eds.), *Proceedings of the 12th Generative Approaches to Second Language Acquisition Conference* (pp. 11–21). Somerville, MA: Cascadilla Proceedings Project.

Bornstein, M. H. (1984). A descriptive taxonomy of psychological categories used by infants. In C. Sophian (Ed.), *Origins of cognitive skills* (pp. 313–338). Hillsdale: Erlbaum.

Bornstein, M. H., Arterberry, M. E., & Mash, C. (2010). Infant object categorization transcends diverse object-context relations. *Infant Behavior and Development, 33*(1), 7–15.

Boulton, A., & Cobb, T. (2017). Corpus use in language learning: A meta-analysis. *Language Learning, 67*(2), 345–393.

Bowles, M. (2011). Meaning implicit and explicit linguistic knowledge. *Studies in Second Language Acquisition, 33,* 247–271.

Brohy, C. (2001). Generic and/or specific advantages of bilingualism in a dynamic plurilingual situation: The case of French as official L3 in the School of Samedan

(Switzerland). *International Journal of Bilingual Education and Bilingualism, 4*(1), 38–49.

Brown, A. (1991). A review of the tip-of-the-tongue experience. *Psychological Bulletin, 109*(2), 204–223.

Bruhn de Garavito, J., & Guijarro-Fuentes, P. (2002). L2 acquisition of indefinite object drop. In *Generative Approaches to Language Acquisition (GALA 2001) Proceedings* (pp. 60–67). Lisbon, Portugal: Associação Portuguesa de Linguística.

Bruhn de Garavito, J., & Perpiñán, S. (2014). Subject pronouns and clitics in the Spanish interlanguage of French L1 speakers. In L. Teddiman (Ed.), *Proceedings of the 2014 Annual Conference of the Canadian Linguistic Association* (pp. 1–11). Montreal: Canadian Linguistic Association.

Bullock, B. E., & Toribio, A. J. (Eds.) (2009). *The Cambridge handbook of linguistic code-switching*. Cambridge: Cambridge University Press.

Bybee, J. (1985). *Morphology: A study of the relation between meaning and form.* Amsterdam: John Benjamins.

Bybee, J. (1995). Regular morphology and the lexicon. *Language and Cognitive Processes, 10,* 425–455.

Bybee, J. (2010). *Language, usage and cognition.* Cambridge: Cambridge University Press.

Bylund, E., Abrahamsson, N., & Hyltenstam, K. (2012). Does first language maintenance hamper nativelikeness in a second language? A study of ultimate attainment in early bilinguals. *Studies in Second Language Acquisition, 34*(2), 215–241.

Bylund, E., Hyltenstam, K., & Abrahamsson, N. (2013). Age of acquisition effects or effects of bilingualism in second language ultimate attainment. In G. Granena & M. Long (Eds.), *Sensitive periods, language aptitudes, and ultimate L2 attainment* (pp. 69–101). Amsterdam: John Benjamins.

Bylund, E., & Jarvis, S. (2011). L2 effects on L1 event conceptualization. *Bilingualism: Language and Cognition, 14*(1), 47–59.

Cabrelli Amaro, J. (2012). L3 Phonology: An understudied domain. In J. Cabrelli Amaro, S. Flynn, & J. Rothman (Eds.), *Third language acquisition in adulthood* (pp. 33–60). Amsterdam: John Benjamins.

Cabrelli Amaro, J. (2013a). Methodological issues in L3 phonological acquisition research. *Studies in Hispanic and Lusophone Linguistics, 6*(1), 101–117.

Cabrelli Amaro, J. (2013b). Raising across experiencers in L3 Portuguese: Further evidence for psychotypological transfer. In S. Stavrakaki, P. Konstantinopoulou, & M. Lalioti (Eds.), *Advances in language acquisition* (pp. 272–281). Newcastle upon Tyne: Cambridge Scholars Press.

Cabrelli Amaro, J. (2015). Does the source of transfer affect the rate of L3 morphosyntactic development? Paper presented at the *40th Boston University Conference on Language Development (BUCLD 40)*. Boston, MA.

Cabrelli Amaro, J. (2017a). L3 morphosyntactic effects on L1 versus L2 systems: The Differential Stability Hypothesis. In A. Hahn & T. Angelovska (Eds.), *L3 syntactic transfer: Models, new developments and implications* (pp. 173–193). Amsterdam: John Benjamins.

Cabrelli Amaro, J. (2017b). Testing the Phonological Permeability Hypothesis: L3 phonological effects on L1 versus L2 systems. *International Journal of Bilingualism, 21*(6), 698–717.

Cabrelli Amaro, J., Amaro, F., & Rothman, J. (2015). The relationship between L3 transfer and structural similarity across development. In H. Peukert (Ed.), *Transfer effects in multilingual language development* (pp. 2–23). Amsterdam: John Benjamins.

Cabrelli Amaro, J., Flynn, S., & Rothman, J. (2012). Third language (L3) acquisition in adulthood. In J. Cabrelli Amaro, S. Flynn, & J. Rothman (Eds.), *Third language acquisition in adulthood* (pp. 1–6). Amsterdam: John Benjamins.

Cabrelli Amaro, J., & Iverson, M. (2018). Third language acquisition. In K. L. Geeslin (Ed.), *Handbook of Spanish linguistics.* Cambridge: Cambridge University Press.

Cabrelli Amaro, J., Iverson, M., Giancaspro, D., & Halloran, B. (2018). Implications of L1 versus L2 transfer in L3 rate of morphosyntactic acquisition. In K. Molsing, C. Becker Lopes Perna, & A. M. Tramunt Ibaños (Eds.), *Linguistic approaches to Portuguese as an additional language.* Amsterdam: John Benjamins.

Cabrelli Amaro, J., Iverson, M., & Judy, T. (2009). Informing adult acquisition debates: N-drop at the initial state of L3 Brazilian Portuguese. In A. Pires & J. Rothman (Eds.), *Minimalist inquiries into child and adult language acquisition: Case studies across Portuguese* (pp. 177–196). Berlin: Mouton de Gruyter.

Cabrelli Amaro, J., Pichan, C., Rothman, J., & Serratrice, L. (2018). Initial transfer across domains in L3 Italian by Spanish Heritage Speakers. Paper presented at the *28th European Second Language Association Conference (EUROSLA 28).* Münster, Germany.

Cabrelli Amaro, J. & Rothman, J. (2007). The Psychotypological Syntactic Transfer Hypothesis of the L3 initial state: Evidence from comparing L3 French and L3 Italian. Talk presented at the *5th International Conference on Third Language Acquisition and Multilingualism.* Stirling, UK, September 2007.

Cabrelli Amaro, J., & Rothman, J. (2010). On L3 acquisition and phonological permeability: A new test case for debates on the mental representation of non-native phonological systems. *International Review of Applied Linguistics in Language Teaching (IRAL), 48*(2–3), 273–294.

Cabrelli Amaro, J., & Wrembel, M. (2016). Investigating the acquisition of phonology in a third language – a state of the science and an outlook for the future. *International Journal of Multilingualism, 13*(4), 395–409.

Calvo, A., & Bialystok, E. (2014). Independent effects of bilingualism and socioeconomic status on language ability and executive functioning. *Cognition, 130*(3), 278–288.

Camacho, J. (2014). *Null subjects.* Cambridge: Cambridge University Press.

Campbell, T., Dollaghan, C., Needleman, H., & Janosky, J. (1997). Reducing bias in language assessment: Processing-dependent measures. *Journal of Speech, Language, and Hearing Research, 40*(3), 519–525.

Campos, H. (1986). Indefinite object drop. *Linguistic Inquiry, 17*, 354–359.

Caramazza, A., & Brones, I. (1979). Lexical access in bilinguals. *Bulletin of the Psychonomic Society, 13*(4), 212–214.

Carminati, M. N. (2002). *The processing of Italian subject pronouns.* Unpublished PhD dissertation, University of Massachusetts.

Castro, T., Rothman, J., & Westergaard, M. (2017). On the directionality of cross-linguistic effects in bidialectal bilingualism. *Frontiers in Psychology, 8,* 1382. doi:10.3389/fpsyg.2017.01382.

Cattell, J. M. (1887). Experiments on the association of ideas. *Mind, 12,* 68–74.

Cenoz, J. (2001). The effect of linguistic distance, L2 status and age on cross-linguistic influence in third language acquisition. In J. Cenoz, B. Hufeisen, & U. Jessner (Eds.), *Cross-linguistic influence in third language acquisition: Psycholinguistic perspectives* (pp. 8–20). Clevedon: Multilingual Matters.

Cenoz, J. (2003). The additive effect of bilingualism on third language acquisition: A review. *International Journal of Bilingualism, 7*(1), 71–87.

Cenoz, J. (2009). *Towards multilingual education: Basque educational research from an international perspective.* Bristol: Multilingual Matters.

Cenoz, J. (2015). Content-based instruction and content and language integrated learning: the same or different? *Language, Culture and Curriculum, 28*(1), 8–24.

Cenoz, J., & Genesee, F. (Eds.) (1998). *Beyond bilingualism: Multilingualism and multilingual education.* Clevedon: Multilingual Matters.

Cenoz, J., & Gorter, D. (Eds.) (2015). *Multilingual education: Between language learning and translanguaging.* Cambridge: Cambridge University Press.

Cenoz, J., Hufeisen, B., & Jessner, U. (Eds.) (2001). *Cross-linguistic influence in third language acquisition: Psycholinguistic perspectives.* Clevedon: Multilingual Matters.

Cenoz, J., & Jessner, U. (Eds.) (2000). *English in Europe: The acquisition of a third language.* Clevedon: Multilingual Matters.

Cenoz, J., & Valencia, J. (1994). Additive trilingualism: Evidence from the Basque Country. *Applied Psycholinguistics, 15,* 195–207.

Chamot, A. (1973). Phonological problems in learning English as a third language. *International Review of Applied Linguistics in Language Teaching (IRAL), 11*(3), 243–250.

Cheung, S. C., Matthews, S., & Tsang, W. L. (2011). Transfer from L3 German to L2 English in the domain of tense/aspect. In J.-M. Dewaele & G. De Angelis (Eds.), *New trends in crosslinguistic influence and multilingualism research* (pp. 53–73). Bristol: Multilingual Matters.

Chin, D. H. (2009). Language transfer in the acquisition of the semantic contrast in L3 Spanish. In Y. I. Leung (Ed.), *Third language acquisition and Universal Grammar* (pp. 30–54). Bristol: Multilingual Matters.

Chomsky, N. (1957). *Syntactic structures.* Berlin: Walter de Gruyter.

Chomsky, N. (1965). *Aspects of the theory of syntax.* Cambridge, MA: MIT Press.

Chomsky, N. (1975). *Reflections on language.* New York: Random House.

Chomsky, N. (1981). *Lectures on government and binding.* Dordrecht: Foris.

Chomsky, N. (1982). *Some concepts and consequences of the theory of government and binding.* Cambridge, MA: MIT Press.

Chomsky, N. (1995). *The minimalist program.* Cambridge, MA: MIT Press.

Chomsky, N. (2001). *Beyond explanatory adequacy.* Cambridge, MA: MIT Press.

Chondrogianni, V. (2018). Child L2 acquisition. In D. Miller, F. Bayram, L. Serratrice, & J. Rothman (Eds.), *Bilingual cognition and language: The state of the science across its subfields* (pp. 103–126). Amsterdam, NL: John Benjamins.

Clahsen, H., Balkhair, L., Schutter, J.-S., & Cunnings, I. (2013). The time course of morphological processing in a second language. *Second Language Research, 29*(1), 7–31.

Clahsen, H., & Felser, C. (2006a). Grammatical processing in language learners. *Applied Psycholinguistics, 27*, 3–42.

Clahsen, H., & Felser, C. (2006b). How native-like is non-native language processing? *TRENDS in Cognitive Sciences, 10*, 564–570.

Clahsen, H., & Felser, C. (2018). Some notes on the Shallow Structure Hypothesis. *Studies in Second Language Acquisition, 40*(3), 693–706.

Clahsen, H., & Muysken, P. (1986). The availability of universal grammar to adult and child learners: A study of the acquisition of German word order. *Second Language Research, 2*(2), 93–119.

Clahsen, H., & Muysken, P. (1989). The UG paradox in L2 acquisition. *Second Language Research, 5*(1), 1–29.

Clark, E. (2003). *First language acquisition.* Cambridge: Cambridge University Press.

Clements, J. (1994). Notes on topicalization and object drop in Spanish. In M. Mazzola (Ed.), *Issues and theory in Romance linguistics: Selected papers from the XXIII symposium on Romance languages* (pp. 219–237). Washington DC: Georgetown University Press.

Clements, J. (2006). Null direct objects in Spanish. In J. Clements & J. Yoon (Eds.), *Functional approaches to Spanish syntax* (pp. 134–150). New York: Palgrave.

Clements, M., & Domínguez, L. (2018). Testing the predictions of the Scalpel Model in L3/Ln Acquisition: The acquisition of null and overt subjects in L3 Chinese. In J. Cho, M. Iverson, T. Judy, T. L. Leal, & E. Shimanskaya (Eds.), *Meaning and structure in second language acquisition: In honor of Roumyana Slabakova.* Amsterdam: John Benjamins.

Clyne, M. (1998). Multilingualism. In F. Coulmas (Ed.), *The handbook of sociolinguistics* (pp. 301–314). Oxford: Blackwell Publishing Ltd.

Collins, A. M., & Loftus, E. F. (1975). A spreading-activation theory of semantic processing. *Psychological Review, 82*(6), 407–428.

Cook, V. (1991). The poverty-of-the-stimulus argument and multicompetence. *Second Language Research, 7*(2), 103–117.

Cook, V. (1992). Evidence for multicompetence. *Language Learning, 42*(4), 557–591.

Cook, V. (Ed.) (2003a). *Effects of the second language on the first.* Clevedon: Multilingual Matters.

Cook, V. (2003b). Introduction: The changing L1 in the L2 user's mind. In V. Cook (Ed.), *Effects of the second language on the first* (pp. 1–18). Clevedon: Multilingual Matters.

Cook, V. (2016). Premises of multi-competence. In V. Cook & L. Wei (Eds.), *The Cambridge handbook of linguistic multi-competence* (pp. 1–25). Cambridge: Cambridge University Press.

Cook, V., & Wei, L. (Eds.) (2016). *The Cambridge handbook of linguistic multi-competence.* Cambridge: Cambridge University Press.

Cornips, L. (1998). Syntactic variation, parameters and their social distribution. *Language Variation and Change, 10*(1), 1–21.

Cornips, L. (2018). Bilingual child acquisition through the lens of sociolinguistic approaches. In D. Miller, F. Bayram, L. Serratrice, & J. Rothman (Eds.), *Bilingual cognition and language: The state of the science across its subfields* (pp. 15–36). Amsterdam: John Benjamins.

Costa, A. (2005). Lexical access in bilingual production. In J. F. Kroll & A. de Groot (Eds.), *Handbook of bilingualism: Psycholinguistic approaches* (pp. 308–325). New York: Oxford University Press.

Costa, A., & Caramazza, A. (1999). Is lexical selection in bilingual speech production language-specific? Further evidence from Spanish–English and English–Spanish bilinguals. *Bilingualism: Language and Cognition, 2*(3), 231–244.

Costa, A., Miozzo, M., & Caramazza, A. (1999). Lexical selection in bilinguals: Do words in the bilingual's two lexicons compete for selection? *Journal of Memory and Language, 41*(3), 365–397.

Coulmas, F. (Ed.) (1998). *The handbook of sociolinguistics.* New York: Wiley-Blackwell.

Crain, S., & Lilo-Martin, D. (1999). *An introduction to linguistic theory and language acquisition.* Malden, MA: Blackwell Publishing Ltd.

Croft, W. (2000). *Explaining language change: An evolutionary approach.* London: Longman.

Culy, C. (1996). Null objects in English recipes. *Language Variation and Change, 8*, 91–124.

Cummings, S., & Roberge, Y. (2003). Null objects in French and English. Paper presented at the *33rd Linguistics Symposium on Romance Languages.* Indiana University, Bloomington, IN.

Cummins, J. (2003). Bilingual education: Basic principles. In J. Dewaele, A. Housen, & L. Wei (Eds.), *Bilingualism: Beyond basic principles* (pp. 56–66). Clevedon: Multilingual Matters.

Cummins, J. (2010). Bilingual and immersion programs. In M. Long & C. Doughty (Eds.), *The handbook of language teaching* (pp. 161–181). Malden: Wiley-Blackwell.

Cunnings, I. (2017). Interference in native and non-native sentence processing. *Bilingualism: Language and Cognition, 20*(4), 712–721.

Cunnings, I., Patterson, C., & Felser, C. (2015). Structural constraints on pronoun binding and coreference: Evidence from eye movements during reading. *Frontiers in Psychology, 6*, 840. doi:10.3389/fpsyg.2015.00840.

Daoust, D. (1998). Language planning and language reform. In F. Coulmas (Ed.), *The handbook of sociolinguistics* (pp. 436–452). Oxford: Blackwell Publishing Ltd.

Darwin, C. (1859). *On the origin of the species.* London: Routledge.

Davis, C., Sánchez-Casas, R., García-Albea, J. E., Guasch, M., Molero, M., & Ferré, P. (2010). Masked translation priming: Varying language experience and word type with Spanish–English bilinguals. *Bilingualism: Language and Cognition, 13*(2), 137–155.

De Angelis, G. (2005). Multilingualism and non-native lexical transfer: An identification problem. *International Journal of Multilingualism, 2*(1), 1–25.

De Angelis, G. (2007). *Third or additional language acquisition.* Clevedon: Multilingual Matters.

De Angelis, G., & Dewaele, J.-M. (Eds.) (2011). *New trends in crosslinguistic influence and multilingualism research.* Bristol: Multilingual Matters.

De Angelis, G., Jessner, U., & Kresic, M. (Eds.) (2015). *Crosslinguistic influence and crosslinguistic interaction in multilingual language learning.* London: Bloomsbury Academic.

De Angelis, G., & Selinker, L. (2001). Interlanguage transfer and competing linguistic systems in the multilingual mind. In J. Cenoz, B. Hufeisen, & U. Jessner (Eds.), *Cross-linguistic influence in third language acquisition: Psycholinguistic perspectives* (pp. 42–58). Clevedon: Multilingual Matters.

De Bot, K. (2000). Sociolinguistics and language processing mechanisms. *Sociolinguistica, 14*(1), 74–78.

De Bot, K. (2004). The multilingual lexicon: Modelling selection and control. *International Journal of Multilingualism, 1*(1), 17–32.

De Bot, K. (2016). Multi-competence and dynamic/complex systems. In V. Cook & L. Wei (Eds.), *The Cambridge handbook of linguistic multi-competence* (pp. 125–141). Cambridge: Cambridge University Press.

De Bot, K., & Jaensch, C. (2015). What is special about L3 processing? *Bilingualism: Language and Cognition, 18*(2), 130–144.

De Bot, K., Lowie, W., Thorne, S. L., & Verspoor, M. (2013). Dynamic Systems Theory as a comprehensive theory of second language development. In M. P. García Mayo, M. J. Gutiérrez Mangado, & M. Martínez-Adrián (Eds.), *Contemporary approaches to second language acquisition* (pp. 199–220). Amsterdam: John Benjamins.

De Bot, K., Lowie, W., & Verspoor, M. (2007). A Dynamic Systems Theory approach to second language acquisition. *Bilingualism: Language and Cognition, 10*(2), 7–21.

De Groot, A. M. B. (1992). Bilingual lexical representation: A closer look at conceptual representations. In R. Frost & L. Katz (Eds.), *Orthography, phonology, morphology, and meaning* (pp. 389–412). Amsterdam: North-Holland.

De Groot, A. M. B. (2010). *Language and cognition in bilinguals and multilinguals: An introduction.* New York: Psychology Press.

De Groot, A. M. B., Delmaar, P., & Lupker, S. J. (2000). The processing of interlexical homographs in translation recognition and lexical decision: Support for non-selective access to bilingual memory. *The Quarterly Journal of Experimental Psychology, 53* (2), 397–428.

DeKeyser, R. (2000). The robustness of critical period effects in second language acquisition. *Studies in Second Language Acquisition, 22*(4), 499–533.

Dekydtspotter, L., McGuire, M., & Mossman, S. (2013). Movement and binding-driven efficiencies in L2 sentence processing: On the role of UG-constrained acquisition in L2 acquisition. In E. Voss, D. Shu-Ju, & L. Zhi (Eds.), *Selected Proceedings of the 2012 Second Language Research Forum* (pp. 104–117). Somerville: Cascadilla Press.

DeLuca, V., Miller, D., Pliatsikas, C., & Rothman, J. (2019). Brain adaptations and neurological indices of processing in adult second language acquisition: Challenges for the Critical Period Hypothesis. In J. W. Schwieter (Ed.), *The handbook of the neuroscience of bilingualism (pp. 170–196)*. Oxford: Wiley-Blackwell.

De Mejía, A.-M. (2002). *Power, prestige and bilingualism*. Clevedon: Multilingual Matters.

Deumert, A. (2011). Multilingualism. In R. Mesthrie (Ed.), *The Cambridge handbook of sociolinguistics* (pp. 261–282). Cambridge: Cambridge University Press.

Dewaele, J.-M. (1998). Lexical inventions: French interlanguage as L2 versus L3. *Applied Linguistics, 19*(4), 471–490.

Dewaele, J.-M. (2002). Psychological and sociodemographic correlates of communicative anxiety in L2 and L3 production. *International Journal of Bilingualism, 6*(1), 23–38.

Dewaele, J.-M. (2005). Sociodemographic, psychological and politicocultural correlates in Flemish students' attitudes towards French and English. *Journal of Multilingual and Multicultural Development, 26*(2), 118–137.

Dewaele, J.-M. (2007). The effect of multilingualism, sociobiographical, and situational factors on communicative anxiety and foreign language anxiety of mature language learners. *International Journal of Bilingualism, 11*(4), 391–409.

Dewaele, J.-M., Petrides, V. K., & Furnham, A. (2008). Effects of trait emotional intelligence and sociobiographical variables on communicative anxiety and foreign language anxiety among adult multilinguals: A review and empirical investigation. *Language Learning, 58*(4), 911–960.

Dijkstra, T. (2003). Lexical processing in bilinguals and multilinguals: The word selection problem. In J. Cenoz, B. Hufeisen, & U. Jessner (Eds.), *The multilingual lexicon* (pp. 11–26). Amsterdam: Kluwer Academic.

Dijkstra, T. (2005). Bilingual word recognition and lexical access. In J. F. Kroll & A. de Groot (Eds.), *Handbook of bilingualism: Psycholinguistic approaches* (pp. 179–201). New York: Oxford University Press.

Dijkstra, T., Grainger, J., & van Heuven, W. J. B. (1999). Recognition of cognates and interlingual homographs: The neglected role of phonology. *Journal of Memory and Language, 41*(4), 496–518.

Dijkstra, T., & van Heuven, W. J. B. (1998). The BIA-model and bilingual word recognition. In J. Grainger & A. M. Jacobs (Eds.), *Localist connectionist approaches to human cognition* (pp. 189–225). Hillsdale: Erlbaum.

Dijkstra, T., & van Heuven, W. J. B. (2002). The architecture of the bilingual word recognition system: From identification to decision. *Bilingualism: Language and Cognition, 5*(3), 175–197.

Dijkstra, T., van Jaarsveld, H., & ten Brinke, S. (1998). Interlingual homograph recognition: Effects of task demands and language intermixing. *Bilingualism: Language and Cognition, 1*(1), 51–66.

Dimitropoulou, M., Duñabeitia, J. A., & Carreiras, M. (2011). Masked translation priming effects with low proficient bilinguals. *Memory & Cognition, 39*(2), 260–275.

Dirac, P. A. M. (1930). Note on exchange phenomena in the Thomas atom. *Mathematical Proceedings of the Cambridge Philosophical Society, 26*(3), 376–385.

Dodsworth, R. (2011). Social class. In R. Wodak, B. Johnstone, & P. E. Kerswill (Eds.), *The SAGE handbook of sociolinguistics* (pp. 192–206). New York: SAGE Publications.

Dörnyei, Z. (1994). Motivation and motivating in the foreign language classroom. *The Modern Language Journal, 78*(3), 273–284.

Dörnyei, Z. (2001). *Teaching and researching motivation.* Harlow: Longman.

Dörnyei, Z., & Ushioda, E. (2011). *Teaching and researching motivation (2nd ed.).* Harlow: Pearson Education.

Doyle, A., Champagne, M., & Segalowitz, N. (1978). Some issues in the assessment of linguistic consequences of early bilingualism. In M. Paradis (Ed.), *Aspects of bilingualism* (pp. 13–21). Columbia: Hornbeam Press.

Duguine, M. (2008). Silent arguments without *pro*. In T. Biberauer (Ed.), *The limits of syntactic variation* (pp. 311–329). Amsterdam: John Benjamins.

Duñabeitia, J. A., Hernández, J. A., Antón, E., Macizo, P., Estévez, A., Fuentes, L. J., & Carreiras, M. (2014). The inhibitory advantage in bilingual children revisited: Myth or reality? *Experimental Psychology, 61*(3), 234–251.

Duñabeitia, J. A., Perea, M., & Carreiras, M. (2010). Masked translation priming effects with highly proficient simultaneous bilinguals. *Experimental Psychology, 57*(2), 98–107.

DuPlessis, J., Solin, D., Travis, L., & White, L. (1987). UG or not UG, that is the question: A reply to Clahsen and Muysken. *Second Language Research, 3*(1), 56–75.

Dussias, P. E. (2003). Syntactic ambiguity resolution in L2 learners: Some effects of bilinguality on L1 and L2 processing strategies. *Studies in Second Language Acquisition, 25*, 529–557.

Dussias, P. E. (2004). Parsing a first language like a second: The erosion of L1 parsing strategies in Spanish-English Bilinguals. *International Journal of Bilingualism, 8*(3), 355–371.

Dussias, P. E., & Sagarra, N. (2007). The effect of exposure on syntactic parsing in Spanish-English bilinguals. *Bilingualism: Language and Cognition, 10*(1), 101–116.

Duyck, W. (2005). Translation and associative priming with cross-lingual pseudo-homophones: Evidence for nonselective phonological activation in bilinguals. *Journal of Experimental Psychology: Learning, Memory, and Cognition, 31*(6), 1340–1359.

Duyck, W., van Assche, E., Drieghe, D., & Hartsuiker, R. J. (2007). Visual word recognition by bilinguals in a sentence context: Evidence for nonselective lexical access. *Journal of Experimental Psychology: Learning, Memory, and Cognition, 33* (4), 663–679.

Duyck, W., & Warlop, N. (2009). Translation priming between the native language and a second language. *Experimental Psychology, 56*(3), 173–179.

Ecke, P. (2004). Words on the tip of the tongue: A study of lexical retrieval failures in Spanish-English bilinguals. *Southwest Journal of Linguistics, 23*(2), 33–63.

Ecke, P. (2015). Parasitic vocabulary acquisition, cross-linguistic influence, and lexical retrieval in multilinguals. *Bilingualism: Language and Cognition, 18*(2), 145–162.

Ecke, P., & Hall, C. J. (2013). Tracking tip-of-the-tongue states in a multilingual speaker: Evidence of attrition or instability in lexical systems? *International Journal of Bilingualism, 17*(6), 734–751.

Ecke, P., & Hall, C. J. (2014). The Parasitic Model of L2 and L3 vocabulary acquisition: Evidence from naturalistic and experimental studies. *Fórum Linguístico, 11*(3), 360–372.

Edwards, J. (2007). Societal multilingualism: Reality, recognition and response. In P. Auer & L. Wei (Eds.), *Handbook of multilingualism and multilingual communication* (pp. 447–467). Berlin: Mouton de Gruyter.

Einstein, A. (1905). Does the inertia of a body depend upon its energy-content? *Annalen Der Physik, 323*(13), 639–641.

Ellis, N. C. (1993). Rules and instances in foreign language learning: Interactions of explicit and implicit knowledge. *European Journal of Cognitive Psychology, 5*, 289–318.

Ellis, N. C. (1998). Emergentism, connectionism and language learning. *Language Learning, 48*(4), 631–664.

Ellis, N. C. (2005). At the interface: Dynamic interactions of explicit and implicit language knowledge. *Studies in Second Language Acquisition, 27*(2), 305–352.

Ellis, N. C., & Wulff, S. (2015). Usage-based approaches in second language acquisition. In B. VanPatten & J. Williams (Eds.), *Theories in second language acquisition: An introduction* (pp. 75–93). London: Routledge.

Ellis, R. (2005). Measuring implicit and explicit knowledge of a second language: A psychometric study. *Studies in Second Language Acquisition, 27*(2), 141–172.

Ennaji, M. (2005). *Multilingualism, cultural identity, and education in Morocco.* New York: Springer.

Epstein, S., Flynn, S., & Martohardjono, G. (1996). Second language acquisition: Theoretical and experimental issues in contemporary research. *Behavioral and Brain Sciences, 19*, 677–714.

Escudero, P., Boersma, P., Rauber, A. S., & Bion, R. A. H. (2009). A cross-dialect acoustic description of vowels: Brazilian and European Portuguese. *The Journal of the Acoustical Society of America, 126*(3), 1379–1393.

Ettlinger, M., Morgan-Short, K., Faretta-Stutenberg, M., & Wong, P. (2016). The relationship between artificial and second language learning. *Cognitive Science, 40*, 822–847.

Eubank, L. (1994). On the transfer of parametric values in L2 development. *Language Acquisition, 3*, 183–208.

Evans, V. (2014). *The language myth: Why language is not an instinct.* Cambridge: Cambridge University Press.

Falk, Y. (2017). On pronouns that drop (out of German). In T. Angelovska & A. Hahn (Eds.), *L3 syntactic transfer: Models, new developments and implications* (pp. 127–142). Amsterdam: John Benjamins.

Falk, Y., & Bardel, C. (2010). The study of the role of the background languages in third language acquisition. The state of the art. *International Review of Applied Linguistics in Language Teaching (IRAL), 48*(2–3), 185–220.

Falk, Y., & Bardel, C. (2011). Object pronouns in German L3 syntax: Evidence for the L2 Status Factor. *Second Language Research, 27*(1), 59–82.

Falk, Y., & Lindqvist, C. (2018). L1 and L2 role assignment in L3 learning. Is there a pattern? *International Journal of Multilingualism.* doi:10.1080/14790718.2018.1444044.

Falk, Y., Lindqvist, C., & Bardel, C. (2015). The role of L1 explicit metalinguistic knowledge in L3 oral production at the initial state. *Bilingualism: Language and Cognition, 18*(2), 227–235.

Fallah, N., & Jabbari, A. A. (2018). L3 acquisition of English attributive adjectives: Dominant language of communication matters for syntactic cross-linguistic influence. *Linguistic Approaches to Bilingualism, 8*(2), 193–216.

Fallah, N., Jabbari, A. A., & Fazilatfar, A. (2016). Source(s) of syntactic CLI: The case of L3 acquisition of English possessives by Mazandarani–Persian bilinguals. *Second Language Research, 32*(7), 825–843.

Fassi Fehri, A. (1993). *Issues in the structure of Arabic clauses and words.* Dordrecht: Kluwer.

Fauconnier, G., & Turner, M. (2003). *The way we think.* New York: Basic Books.

Fedzechkina, M., Jaeger, T. F., & Newport, E. (2012). Language learners restructure their input to facilitate efficient communication. *Proceedings of the National Academy of Sciences, 109,* 17897–17902.

Fedzechkina, M., Jaeger, T. F., & Newport, E. (2013). Communicative biases shape structures of newly acquired languages. In M. Knauff, M. Pauen, N. Sebanz, & I. Wachsmuth (Eds.), *Proceedings of the 35th Annual Conference of the Cognitive Science Society* (pp. 430–435). Austin: Cognitive Science Society.

Fedzechkina, M., Newport, E., & Jaeger, T. F. (2016). Miniature artificial language learning as a complement to typological data. In L. Ortega, A. E. Tyler, H. I. Park, & M. Uno (Eds.), *The usage-based study of language learning and multilingualism* (pp. 211–232). Washington, DC: Georgetown University Press.

Felix, S. (1985). More evidence on competing cognitive systems. *Second Language Research, 1,* 47–72.

Ferguson, C. A. (1959). Diglossia. *Word, 15,* 325–340.

Fernández, E. M. (2003). *Bilingual sentence processing: Relative clause attachment in English and Spanish.* Amsterdam: John Benjamins.

Fessi, I. (2013). Cross-linguistic influence in tense-aspect Spanish L3 acquisition: A study of Arabic Tunisian learners of L3 Spanish. *Revista Nebrija de Lingüística Aplicada a La Enseñanza de Lenguas, 20.* Retrieved from https://www.nebrija.com/revista-linguistica/files/articulosPDF/articulo_56fb9ec59aecb.pdf

Feynman, R. (1965). *The character of physical law.* Cambridge, MA: MIT Press.

Finkbeiner, M., Forster, K., Nicol, J., & Nakamura, K. (2004). The role of polysemy in masked semantic and translation priming. *Journal of Memory and Language, 51*(1), 1–22.

Fishman, J. A. (1964). Language maintenance and language shift as a field of inquiry. *Linguistics, 2*(9), 32–70.

Fishman, J. A. (1967). Bilingualism with and without diglossia; diglossia with and without bilingualism. *Journal of Social Issues, 23*(2), 29–38.

Fishman, J. A. (1991). *Reversing language shift.* Clevedon: Multilingual Matters.

Fitch, W. T., & Hauser, M. D. (2004). Computational constraints on syntactic processing in a nonhuman primate. *Science, 303*(5656), 377–380.

Fitch, W. T., Hauser, M. D., & Chomsky, N. (2005). The evolution of the language faculty: Clarifications and implications. *Cognition, 97*(2), 179–210.

Flege, J. E. (1987). The production of "new" and "similar" phones in a foreign language: Evidence for the effect of equivalence classification. *Journal of Phonetics, 15*, 47–65.

Flege, J. E., & Port, R. F. (1981). Cross-language phonetic interference: Arabic to English. *Language and Speech, 24*(2), 125–146.

Flynn, S. (1983). Differences between first and second language acquisition. In D. Rogers & J. A. Sloboda (Eds.), *Acquisition of symbolic skills* (pp. 485–500). London: Plenum Press.

Flynn, S. (1987). Contrast and construction in a theory of second language acquisition. *Language Learning, 36*, 1–37.

Flynn, S. (2009). UG and L3 acquisition: New insights and more questions. In Y. I. Leung (Ed.), *Third language acquisition and Universal Grammar* (pp. 71–88). Clevedon: Multilingual Matters.

Flynn, S., Foley, C., & Vinnitskaya, I. (2004). The Cumulative-Enhancement model for language acquisition: Comparing adults' and children's patterns of development in first, second and third language acquisition. *International Journal of Multilingualism, 1*(1), 3–16.

Flynn, S., Vinnitskaya, I., & Foley, C. (2008). Complementizer phrase features in child L1 and adult L3 acquisition. In J. M. Liceras, H. Zobl, & H. Goodluck (Eds.), *The role of formal features in second language acquisition* (pp. 519–533). Mahwah: Erlbaum.

Foley, C., & Flynn, S. (2013). The role of the native language. In J. R. Herschensohn & M. Young-Scholten (Eds.), *The Cambridge handbook of second language acquisition* (pp. 97–113). Cambridge: Cambridge University Press.

Foote, R. (2009). Transfer in L3 acquisition: The role of typology. In Y-K. I. Leung (Ed.), *Third language acquisition and Universal Grammar* (pp. 89–114). Bristol: Multilingual Matters.

Forster, K. I., & Davis, C. J. (1984). Repetition priming and frequency attenuation in lexical access. *Journal of Experimental Psychology: Learning, Memory, and Cognition, 10*, 680–698.

Fouser, R. J. (1997). Pragmatic transfer in advanced language learners: Some preliminary findings. *CLCS Occasional Paper, 50*, 1–44.

Fouser, R. J. (2001). Too close for comfort? Sociolinguistic transfer from Japanese into Korean as an L3. In J. Cenoz, B. Hufeisen, & U. Jessner (Eds.), *Cross-linguistic influence in third language acquisition: Psycholinguistic perspectives* (pp. 149–169). Clevedon: Multilingual Matters.

Fuchs, E., & Flügge, G. (2014). Adult neuroplasticity: More than 40 years of research. *Neural Plasticity, 14*, 1–10.

Fung, K.-T. D., & Murphy, V. A. (2016). Cross linguistic influence in adult L2/L3 learners: The case of French on English morphosyntax. *GSTF Journal on Education (JED), 3*(2), 6–15.

Gagarina, N., Klop, D., Kunnari, S., Tantele, K., Välimaa, T., Balciuniene, I., Bohnacker, U., & Walters, J. (2012). MAIN: Multilingual Assessment Instrument for Narratives. *ZAS Papers in Linguistics, 56.*

Galves, C. (2001). *Ensaios sobre as gramáticas do português.* Lisbon: Unicamp.

García, O. (1998). Bilingual education. In F. Coulmas (Ed.), *The handbook of sociolinguistics* (pp. 405–420). Oxford: Blackwell Publishing.

García, O. (2008). Introducing bilingual education. In O. García (Ed.), *Bilingual education in the 21st century: A global perspective* (pp. 3–17). Chichester: Wiley-Blackwell.

García Lecumberri, M. L., & Gallardo del Puerto, F. (2003). English FL sounds in school learners of different ages. In M. P. García Mayo & M. L. García Lecumberri (Eds.), *Age and the acquisition of English as a foreign language* (pp. 115–135). Clevedon: Multilingual Matters.

García Mayo, M. P. (Ed.) (2015). Special Issue – L3 acquisition: A focus on cognitive approaches. *Bilingualism: Language and Cognition, 18*(2), 127–129.

García Mayo, M. P., & Rothman, J. (2012). L3 morphosyntax in the generative tradition: From the initial state and beyond. In J. Cabrelli Amaro, S. Flynn, & J. Rothman (Eds.), *Third language acquisition in adulthood* (pp. 9–32). Amsterdam: John Benjamins.

García Mayo, M. P., & Slabakova, R. (2015). Object drop in L3 acquisition. *International Journal of Bilingualism, 19*(5), 483–498.

Gardner, N., Puigdevall i Serralvo, M., & Williams, C. H. (2000). *Language revitalization in comparative context: Ireland, the Basque Country and Catalonia.* In C. H. Williams (Ed.), *Language revitalization: Policy and planning in Wales* (pp. 311–361). Cardiff: University of Wales Press.

Gass, S. (1997). *Input, interaction, and the second language learner.* Mahwah, NJ: Lawrence Erlbaum Associates.

Genesee, F. (1987). *Learning through two languages: Studies of immersion and bilingual education.* Rowley, MA: Newbury House.

Genesee, F. (2008). What do we know about bilingual education for majority-language students? In T. K. Bhatia & W. C. Ritchie (Eds.), *The handbook of bilingualism* (pp. 547–576). Oxford: Wiley-Blackwell.

Genesee, F., Lindholm-Leary, K., Saunders, W. M., & Christian, D. (Eds.) (2006). *Educating English language learners: A synthesis of research evidence.* New York: Cambridge University Press.

Gershkoff-Stowe, L. & Hahn, E. (2013). Word comprehension and production asymmetries in children and adults. *Journal of Experimental Psychology, 114,* 489–509.

Ghezlou, M., Koosha, M., & Lotfi, A. R. (2018). Acquisition of adjective placement by L3 learners of English: Evidence for the L2 Status Factor. *International Journal of Applied Linguistics and English Literature, 7*(2), 175.

Giancaspro, D., Halloran, B., & Iverson, M. (2015). Transfer at the initial stages of L3 Brazilian Portuguese: A look at three groups of English/Spanish bilinguals. *Bilingualism: Language and Cognition, 18*(2), 191–207.

Giles, H., Bourhis, R. Y., & Taylor, D. M. (1977). Towards a theory of language in ethnic group relations. In H. Giles (Ed.), *Language, ethnicity and intergroup relations* (pp. 207–348). New York: Academic Press.

Ginsborg, J. (2006). The effects of socio-economic status on children's language acquisition and use. In J. Clegg & J. Ginsborg (Eds.), *Language and social disadvantage: Theory into practice* (pp. 9–27). New York: Wiley.

Givón, T. (1979). *On understanding grammar*. New York: Academic Press.

Goad, H., & White, L. (2006). Ultimate attainment in interlanguage grammars: A prosodic approach. *Second Language Research, 22,* 243–268.

Godfroid, A., Loewen, S., Jung, S., Park, J.-H., Gass, S., & Ellis, R. (2015). Timed and untimed grammaticality judgments measure distinct types of knowledge. *Studies in Second Language Acquisition, 37*(2), 269–297.

Goldberg, A. E. (2003). Constructions: A new theoretical approach to language. *TRENDS in Cognitive Sciences, 7*(5), 219–224.

Goldberg, A. E. (2006). *Constructions at work: The nature of generalization in language*. Oxford: Oxford University Press.

Gollan, T. H., Bonanni, M., & Montoya, R. I. (2005). Proper names get stuck on bilingual and monolingual speakers' tip-of-the-tongue equally often. *Neuropsychology, 19,* 278–287.

Gollan, T. H., Montoya, R. I., Cera, C., & Sandoval, T. C. (2008). More use almost always means a smaller frequency effect: Aging, bilingualism, and the weaker links hypothesis. *Journal of Memory and Language, 58*(3), 787–814.

Gollan, T. H., Montoya, R. I., Fennema-Notestine, C., & Morris, S. K. (2005). Bilingualism affects picture naming but not picture classification. *Memory & Cognition, 33*(7), 1220–1234.

Gollan, T. H., Montoya, R. I., & Werner, G. A. (2002). Semantic and letter fluency in Spanish–English bilinguals. *Neuropsychology, 16,* 562–576.

Gollan, T. H., Slattery, T. J., Goldenberg, D., Van Assche, E., Duyck, W., & Rayner, K. (2011). Frequency drives lexical access in reading but not in speaking: The frequency-lag hypothesis. *Journal of Experimental Psychology: General, 140*(2), 186–209.

González Alonso, J. (2012). Assessing multilingual lexical incorporation hypotheses through a primed picture-naming task. *Linguistic Approaches to Bilingualism, 2*(1), 91–107.

González Alonso, J., Alemán Bañón, J., DeLuca, V., Miller, D., Pereira Soares, S., Puig-Mayenco, E., Slaats, S., & Rothman, J. (2019). ERPs and artificial mini-grammars in third language transfer/learning. Talk presented at the *32nd Annual CUNY Conference on Human Sentence Processing*. Boulder, CO: University of Colorado,.

González Alonso, J., & Rothman, J. (2017a). Coming of age in L3 initial stages transfer models: Deriving developmental predictions and looking towards the future. *International Journal of Bilingualism, 21*(6), 683–697.

González Alonso, J., & Rothman, J. (2017b). From theory to practice in multilingualism: What theoretical research implies for third language learning. In T. Angelovska & A. Hahn (Eds.), *L3 syntactic transfer: Models, new developments and implications* (pp. 277–298). Amsterdam: John Benjamins.

González Alonso, J., Rothman, J., Berndt, D., Castro, T., & Westergaard, M. (2017). Broad scope and narrow focus: On the contemporary linguistic and psycholinguistic study of third language acquisition. *International Journal of Bilingualism, 21*(6), 639–650.

Gorter, D., Zenotz, V., & Cenoz, J. (Eds.) (2014). *Minority languages and multilingual education*. Berlin: Springer.

Graena, G., & Long, M. (2013). Age of onset, length of residence, language aptitude, and ultimate L2 attainment in three linguistic domains. *Second Language Research, 29*(3), 31–43.

Grainger, J., & Dijkstra, T. (1992). On the representation and use of language information in bilinguals. In R. J. Harris (Ed.), *Cognitive processing in bilinguals* (pp. 207–220). Amsterdam: North-Holland.

Grainger, J., & Frenck-Mestre, C. (1998). Masked priming by translation equivalents in proficient bilinguals. *Language and Cognitive Processes, 13*(6), 601–623.

Granena, G., & Long, M. (Eds.) (2013). *Sensitive periods, language aptitude, and ultimate L2 attainment*. Amsterdam: John Benjamins.

Green, D. W. (1986). Control, activation, and resource: A framework and a model for the control of speech in bilinguals. *Brain and Language, 27*(2), 210–223.

Green, D. W. (1998). Mental control of the bilingual lexico-semantic system. *Bilingualism: Language and Cognition, 1*(2), 67–81.

Green, D. W., & Abutalebi, J. (2013). Language control in bilinguals: The adaptive control hypothesis. *Journal of Cognitive Psychology, 25*(5), 515–530.

Green, D. W., & Wei, L. (2014). A control process model of code-switching. *Language, Cognition and Neuroscience, 29*(4), 499–511.

Greenberg, J. H. (1963). Some universals of grammar with particular reference to the order of meaningful elements. In J. H. Greenberg (Ed.), *Universals of language* (pp. 73–113). London: MIT Press.

Grey, S., Sanz, C., Morgan-Short, K., & Ullman, M. (2018). Bilingual and monolingual adults learning an additional language: ERPs reveal differences in syntactic processing. *Bilingualism: Language and Cognition, 21*(5), 970–994.

Grosjean, F. (1982). *Life with two languages: An introduction to bilingualism*. Cambridge, MA: Harvard University Press.

Grosjean, F. (1989). Neurolinguists, beware! The bilingual is not two monolinguals in one person. *Brain and Language, 36*(1), 3–15.

Grosjean, F. (1998). Transfer and language mode. *Bilingualism: Language and Cognition, 1*(3), 175–176.

Grosjean, F. (2001). The bilingual's language modes. In J. Nicol (Ed.), *One mind, two languages: Bilingual language processing* (pp. 1–22). Oxford: Blackwell.

Grüter, T. (2005/2006). Another take on the L2 initial state: Evidence from comprehension in L2 German. *Language Acquisition, 13*(4), 287–317.

Grüter, T., & Rohde, H. (2013). L2 processing is affected by RAGE: Evidence from reference resolution. Paper presented at the *12th Generative Approaches to Second Language Acquisition Conference (GASLA)*. Gainesville, Florida: University of Florida.

Grüter, T., Rohde, H., & Schafer, A. (2017). Coreference and discourse coherence in L2: The role of grammatical aspect and referential form. *Linguistic Approaches to Bilingualism, 7*(2), 199–229.

Guasti, M. T. (2002). *Language acquisition: The growth of grammar.* Cambridge, MA: MIT Press.

Guasti, M. T. (2017). *Language acquisition: The growth of grammar* (2nd ed.). Cambridge, MA: MIT Press.

Gürel, A. (2003). Is the Overt Pronoun Constraint universal? Evidence from L2 Turkish. In J. M. Liceras, H. Zobl, & H. Goodluck (Eds.), *Proceedings of the 6th Generative Approaches to Language Acquisition Conference.* Somerville, MA: Cascadilla Proceedings Project.

Gut, U. (2010). Cross-linguistic influence in L3 phonological acquisition. *International Journal of Multilingualism, 7*(1), 19–38.

Haegeman, L. (2007). Subject omission in present-day written English: On the theoretical relevance of peripheral data. *Rivista Di Grammatica Generativa, 32,* 91–124.

Haegeman, L., & Ihsane, T. (1999). Subject ellipsis in embedded clauses in English. *English Language and Linguistics, 3*(1), 117–145.

Haegeman, L., & Ihsane, T. (2001). Adult null subjects in the non-pro-drop languages: two diary dialects. *Language Acquisition, 9*(4), 329–346.

Hahn, A., & Angelovska, T. (2017). Input-practice-output: A method for teaching L3 English after L2 German with a focus on syntactic transfer. In T. Angelovska & A. Hahn (Eds.), *L3 syntactic transfer: Models, new developments and implications* (pp. 299–320). Amsterdam: John Benjamins.

Håkansson, G., Pienemann, M., & Sayehli, S. (2002). Transfer and typological proximity in the context of second language processing. *Second Language Research, 18* (3), 250–273.

Hakuta, K., Bialystok, E., & Wiley, E. (2003). Critical evidence: A test of the Critical-Period Hypothesis for second-language acquisition. *Psychological Science, 14*(1), 31–38.

Hall, C. J. (1992). *Morphology and mind.* London: Routledge.

Hall, C. J. (2002). The automatic cognate form assumption: Evidence for the parasitic model of vocabulary development. *International Review of Applied Linguistics in Language Teaching (IRAL), 40*(2), 69–87.

Hall, C. J., & Ecke, P. (2003). Parasitism as a default mechanism in L3 vocabulary acquisition. In J. Cenoz, B. Hufeisen, & U. Jessner (Eds.), *The multilingual lexicon* (pp. 71–85). Kluwer.

Hall, C. J., Newbrand, D., Ecke, P., Sperr, U., Marchand, V., & Hayes, L. (2009). Learners' implicit assumptions about syntactic frames in new L3 words: The role of cognates, typological proximity, and L2 status. *Language Learning, 59*(1), 153–202.

Hammarberg, B. (2001). Roles of L1 and L2 in L3 production and acquisition. In J. Cenoz, B. Hufeisen, & U. Jessner (Eds.), *Cross-linguistic influence in third language acquisition: Psycholinguistic perspectives* (pp. 21–41). Clevedon: Multilingual Matters.

Hammarberg, B. (2006). Activation de L1 et L2 lors de la production orale en L3. Étude comparative de deux cas. *Acquisition et Interaction en Langue Étrangère (AILE), 24,* 45–74.

Hammarberg, B. (Ed.) (2009). *Processes in third language acquisition.* Edinburgh: Edinburgh University Press.

Hammarberg, B. (2010). The languages of the multilingual: Some conceptual and terminological issues. *International Review of Applied Linguistics in Language Teaching (IRAL)*, *48*(2–3), 91–104.

Hammarberg, B. (2018). L3, the tertiary language. In A. Bonnet & P. Siemund (Eds.), *Foreign language education in multilingual classrooms* (pp. 127–150). Amsterdam: John Benjamins.

Hammarberg, B., & Hammarberg, B. (1993). Articulatory re-setting in the acquisition of new languages. *Phonum*, *2*, 61–67.

Hammarberg, B., & Hammarberg, B. (2005). Re-setting the basis of articulation in the acquisition of new languages: A third-language case study. In B. Hufeisen & R. J. Fouser (Eds.), *Introductory readings in L3* (pp. 11–18). Tübingen: Stauffenburg Verlag.

Harnad, S. (1987). Psychophysical and cognitive aspects of categorical perception: A critical overview. In S. Harnad (Ed.), *Categorical perception: The groundwork of cognition* (pp. 1–27). New York: Cambridge University Press.

Hauser, M. D., Chomsky, N., & Fitch, W. T. (2002). The faculty of language: What is it, who has it, and how did it evolve? *Science*, *298*(5598), 1569–1579.

Hawkins, R., & Casillas, G. (2008). Explaining frequency of verb morphology in early L2 speech. *Lingua*, *118*, 595–612.

Hawkins, R., & Chan, C. Y. (1997). The partial availability of Universal Grammar in second language acquisition. *Second Language Research*, *13*(3), 187–226.

Hawkins, R., & Liszka, S. (2003). Locating the source of defective past tense marking in advanced L2 English speakers. In R. van Hout, H. Aafke, F. Kuiken, & R. Towel (Eds.), *The interface between syntax and lexicon in second language acquisition* (pp. 21–44). Amsterdam: John Benjamins.

Haznedar, B. (2013). Child second language acquisition from a generative perspective. *Linguistic Approaches to Bilingualism*, *3*(1), 26–47.

Haznedar, B., & Schwartz, B. (1997). Are there optional infinitives in child L2 acquisition? In E. Hughes & D. Greenhill (Eds.), *Proceedings of the 21st Annual Boston University Conference on Language Development* (pp. 257–268). Somerville, MA, MA: Cascadilla Press.

Hendriks, P. (2014). *Asymmetries between language production and comprehension*. New York: Springer.

Hendricks, A. E., & Adlof, S. M. (2017). Language assessment with children who speak nonmainstream dialects: examining the effects of scoring modifications in norm-referenced assessment. *Language, Speech, and Hearing Services in Schools*, *48*(3), 168–182.

Herdina, P., & Jessner, U. (2002). *A Dynamic Model of Multilingualism: Perspectives of change in psycholinguistics*. Bristol: Multilingual Matters.

Hermans, D., Bongaerts, T., de Bot, K., & Schreuder, R. (1998). Producing words in a foreign language: Can speakers prevent interference from their first language? *Bilingualism: Language and Cognition*, *1*(3), 213–229.

Hermas, A. (2010). Language acquisition as computational resetting: verb movement in L3 initial state. *International Journal of Multilingualism*, *7*(4), 343–362.

Hermas, A. (2014). Multilingual transfer: L1 morphosyntax in L3 English. *International Journal of Language Studies*, *8*(2), 1–24.

Hermas, A. (2015). The categorization of the relative complementizer phrase in third-language English: A feature re-assembly account. *International Journal of Bilingualism, 19*(5), 587–607.

Hernandez, A. E., Hofmann, J., & Kotz, S. A. (2007). Age of acquisition modulates neural activity for both regular and irregular syntactic functions. *NeuroImage, 36*(3), 912–923.

Herschensohn, J. (2000). *The second time around: Minimalism and L2 acquisition.* Amsterdam/Philadelphia: John Benjamins.

Hervais-Adelman, A., Moser-Mercer, B., & Golestani, N. (2011). Executive control of language in the bilingual brain: Integrating the evidence from neuroimaging to neuropsychology. *Frontiers in Psychology, 15*(2), 234.

Herwig, A. (2001). Plurilingual lexical organisation: Evidence from lexical processing in L1-L2-L3-L4 translation. In J. Cenoz, B. Hufeisen, & U. Jessner (Eds.), *Cross-linguistic influence in third language acquisition: Psycholinguistic perspectives* (pp. 90–114). Clevedon: Multilingual Matters.

Hochmann, J., Azadpour, M., & Mehler, J. (2008). Do humans really learn AnBn artificial grammars from exemplars? *Cognitive Science, 32*(6), 1021–1036.

Hopp, H. (2006). Syntactic features and reanalysis in near-native processing. *Second Language Research, 22*(3), 369–397.

Hopp, H. (2014). Working memory effects in the L2 processing of ambiguous relative clauses. *Language Acquisition, 21*(3), 250–278.

Hopp, H. (2018). Cross-linguistic influence in the child third language acquisition of grammar: Sentence comprehension and production among Turkish-German and German learners of English. *International Journal of Bilingualism.* doi:10.1177/1367006917752523.

Hopper, P. (1987). Emergent grammar. In J. Aske, N. Beery, L. Michaelis, & H. Filip (Eds.), *Proceedings of the Thirteenth Annual Meeting of the Berkeley Linguistics Society* (pp. 139–157). Berkeley: Berkeley Linguistics Society.

Hornberger, N. H. (1991). Extending enrichment bilingual education: Revisiting typologies and redirecting policy. In O. García (Ed.), *Bilingual education* (pp. 215–234). Amsterdam: John Benjamins.

Hornberger, N. H. (2007). Continua of biliteracy. In A. Creese, P. Martin, & N. H. Hornberger (Eds.), *Encyclopedia of language and education. Vol. 9: Ecology of language* (pp. 275–290). Berlin: Springer.

Hudson Kam, C. L., & Newport, E. (2005). Regularizing unpredictable variation: The roles of adult and child learners in language formation and change. *Language Learning and Development, 1*, 151–195.

Huguet, À. & Llurda, E. (2001). Language attitudes of school children in two Catalan/Spanish bilingual communities. *International Journal of Bilingual Education and Bilingualism, 4*(4), 267–282.

Hui, B. (2010). Backward transfer from L3 French to L2 English production of relative clauses by L1 Cantonese speakers in Hong Kong. *Hong Kong Journal of Applied Linguistics, 12*(2), 45–60.

Imaz Aguirre, A., & García Mayo, M. P. (2017). Transfer effects in the acquisition of double object constructions in English as an L3. In T. Angelovska & A. Hahn (Eds.),

L3 syntactic transfer: Models, new developments and implications. Amsterdam: John Benjamins.

Ionin, T., Grolla, E., Santos, H., & Montrul, S. (2015). Interpretation of NPs in generic and existential contexts in L3 Brazilian Portuguese. *Linguistic Approaches to Bilingualism, 5,* 215–251.

Ivanova, I., & Costa, A. (2008). Does bilingualism hamper lexical access in speech production? *Acta Psychologica, 127*(2), 277–288.

Iverson, M. (2009a). Competing SLA hypotheses assessed: Comparing heritage and successive Spanish bilinguals of L3 Brazilian Portuguese. In A. Pires & J. Rothman (Eds.), *Minimalist Inquiries into Child and Adult Language Acquisition: Case Studies across Portuguese* (pp. 221–244). Berlin: Mouton De Gruyter.

Iverson, M. (2009b). N-drop at the initial state of L3 Portuguese: Comparing simultaneous and additive bilinguals of English/Spanish. In A. Pires & J. Rothman (Eds.), *Minimalist inquiries into child and adult language acquisition: Case studies across Portuguese* (pp. 221–244). Berlin: Mouton de Gruyter.

Iverson, M. (2010). Informing the age of acquisition debate: L3 as a litmus test. *International Review of Applied Linguistics in Language Teaching (IRAL), 48*(2–3), 221–243.

Iverson, M. (2012). *Advanced language attrition of Spanish in contact with Brazilian Portuguese.* Unpublished PhD dissertation, University of Iowa.

Iverson, M., & Miller, D. (2017). Language attrition and maintenance. *Linguistic Approaches to Bilingualism, 7*(6), 704–708.

Izzo, G., Cenni, I., & De Smet, J. (2017). Third language acquisition and its consequences for foreign language didactics: The case of Italian in Flanders. In M. van Spaandonk, M. McCracken, K. Maes, L. De Wachter, J. Heeren, & D. Speelman (Eds.), *Proceedings Van Schools tot Scriptie III: Een colloquium over universitair taalvaardigheidsonderwijs* (pp. 61–72). Leiden: University of Leiden.

Jackendoff, R. (1997). *The architecture of the language faculty.* Cambridge, MA: MIT Press.

Jacob, G., & Felser, C. (2016). Reanalysis and semantic persistence in native and non-native garden-path recovery. *Quarterly Journal of Experimental Psychology, 69*(5), 907–925.

Jacobs, A. M. (2000). Five questions about cognitive models and some answers from three models of reading. In A. Kenney, R. Radach, D. Heller, & J. Pynte (Eds.), *Reading as a perceptual process* (pp. 721–732). Oxford: Elsevier.

Jacobs, K., & Cross, A. (2001). The seventh generation of Kahnawà:ke: Phoenix or dinosaur. In D. Christian & F. Genesee (Eds.), *Bilingual education* (pp. 109–121). Alexandria: TESOL.

Jaeggli, O., & Safir, K. (1989). *The Null Subject Parameter.* London: Kluwer Academic Publishers.

Jaensch, C. (2008). L3 acquisition of articles in German by native Japanese speakers. In R. Slabakova (Ed.), *Proceedings of the 9th Generative Approaches to Second Language Acquisition Conference (GASLA 2007)* (pp. 81–89). Somerville, MA: Cascadilla Proceedings Project.

Jaensch, C. (2012). L3 Acquisition of German: Do some learners have it easier? In J. Cabrelli Amaro, S. Flynn, & J. Rothman (Eds.), *Third language acquisition in adulthood* (pp. 165–193). Amsterdam: John Benjamins.

Jared, D., & Kroll, J. F. (2001). Do bilinguals activate phonological representations in one or both of their languages when naming words? *Journal of Memory and Language, 44*(1), 2–31.

Jarvis, S. (1998). *Conceptual transfer in the interlingual lexicon.* Bloomington: Indiana University Linguistics Club.

Jarvis, S. (2000). Methodological rigor in the study of transfer: Identifying L1 influence in the interlanguage lexicon. *Language Learning, 50*(2), 245–309.

Jarvis, S. (2002). Topic continuity in L2 English article use. *Studies in Second Language Acquisition, 24*(3), 387–418.

Jarvis, S. (2016). Clarifying the scope of conceptual transfer. *Language Learning, 66*(3), 608–635.

Jarvis, S., O'Malley, M., Jing, L., Zhang, J., Hill, J., Chan, C., & Sevostyanova, N. (2013). Cognitive foundations of crosslinguistic influence. In J. W. Schwieter (Ed.), *Innovative research and practices in second language acquisition and bilingualism* (pp. 287–308). Amsterdam: John Benjamins.

Jarvis, S., & Pavlenko, A. (Eds.) (2008). *Crosslinguistic influence in language and cognition.* Oxford: Routledge.

Jegerski, J. (2012). The processing of temporary subject-object ambiguities in native and near-native Mexican Spanish. *Bilingualism: Language and Cognition, 15*(4), 721–735.

Jegerski, J. (2014). Self-paced reading. In J. Jegerski & B. VanPatten (Eds.), *Research methods in second language psycholinguistics* (pp. 20–49). New York, US: Routledge.

Jegerski, J. (2015). The processing of case in near-native Spanish. *Second Language Research, 31*(3), 281–307.

Jegerski, J., Keating, G. D., & VanPatten, B. (2016). On-line relative clause attachment strategy in heritage speakers of Spanish. *International Journal of Bilingualism, 20*(3), 254–268.

Jegerski, J., VanPatten, B., & Keating, G. D. (2016). Relative clause attachment preferences in early and late bilinguals. In D. Pascual y Cabo (Ed.), *Advances in Spanish as a heritage language* (pp. 81–98). Amsterdam: John Benjamins.

Jenkins, J. (2009). English as a lingua franca: Interpretations and attitudes. *World Englishes, 28*(2), 200–207.

Jenkins, J. (2015). Repositioning English and multilingualism in English as a lingua franca. *Englishes in Practice, 2*(3), 49–05.

Jessen, A., & Felser, C. (2018). Reanalysing object gaps during non-native sentence processing: Evidence from ERPs. *Second Language Research.* doi:10.1177/0267658317753030.

Jessner, U. (1999). Metalinguistic awareness in multilinguals: Cognitive aspects of third language learning. *Language Awareness, 8*(3–4), 201–209.

Jessner, U. (2008). A DST model of multilingualism and the role of metalinguistic awareness. *The Modern Language Journal, 92*(2), 270–283.

Jin, F. (2009). *Third language acquisition of Norwegian objects: Interlanguage transfer or L1 influence?* In Y. I. Leung (Ed.), *Third language acquisition and Universal Grammar* (144–161). Bristol: Multilingual Matters.

Johnson, J., & Newport, E. (1989). Critical period effects in second language learning: The influence of maturational state on the acquisition of English as a second language. *Cognitive Psychology, 21,* 60–99.

Johnson, R. K., & Swain, M. (1997). *Immersion education: International perspectives.* Cambridge: Cambridge University Press.

Johnstone, R. (2006). Characteristics of immersion programs. In O. García & C. Baker (Eds.), *Bilingual education* (pp. 19–32). Clevedon: Multilingual Matters.

Jones, M. A. (1996). *Foundations of French syntax.* Cambridge: Cambridge University Press.

Jongbloed-Faber, L., van de Velde, H., van der Meer, C., & Klinkenberg, E. (2016). Language use of Frisian bilingual teenagers on social media. *Treballs de Sociolingüística Catalana, 26,* 27–54.

Juffs, A. (2005). The influence of first language on the processing of wh-movement in English as a second language. *Second Language Research, 21*(2), 121–151.

Juffs, A., & Harrington, M. (2011). Aspects of working memory in second language learning and teaching. *Language Teaching, 44*(2), 137–166.

Kaan, E. (2014). Predictive sentence processing in L2 and L1: What is different? *Linguistic Approaches to Bilingualism, 4*(2), 257–282.

Kamiyama, T. (2007). Acquisition of French vowels by Japanese-speaking learners: Close and close-mid rounded vowels. Paper presented at the *L3 Phonology Satellite Workshop of ICPhS XVI.* University of Freiburg, Germany.

Kania, U. (2016). Why don't you just learn it from the input? A usage-based corpus study on the acquisition of conventionalized indirect speech acts in English and German. In L. Ortega, A. E. Tyler, H. I. Park, & M. Uno (Eds.), *The usage-based study of language learning and multilingualism* (pp. 37–54). Washington, DC: Georgetown University Press.

Kecskés, I., & Papp, T. (2000). *Foreign language and mother tongue.* Hillsdale: Erlbaum.

Kellerman, E. (1983). Now you see it, now you don't. In S. Gass & L. Selinker (Eds.), *Language transfer in language learning* (pp. 112–34). Rowley, MA: Newbury House.

Kim, K. H. S., Relkin, N. R., Lee, K.-M., & Hirsch, J. (1997). Distinct cortical areas associated with native and second languages. *Nature, 388,* 171–174.

Kirsner, K., Smith, M. C., Lockhart, R. S., King, M. L., & Jain, M. (1984). The bilingual lexicon: Language-specific units in an integrated network. *Journal of Verbal Learning and Verbal Behavior, 23*(4), 519–539.

Klein, E. C. (1995). Second vs. third language acquisition: Is there a difference? *Language Learning, 45*(2), 419–65.

Klein, W. (1998). The contribution of second language acquisition research. *Language Learning, 48*(4), 527–549.

Kong, S. (2015). L3 initial state: Typological primacy driven, L2 factor determined, or L1 feature oriented? *Taiwan Journal of Linguistics, 13*(2), 79–116.

Kopečková, R. (2014). Cross-linguistic influence in child L3 instructed phonological acquisition. In L. Aronin & M. Pawlak (Eds.), *Essential topics in applied linguistics and multilingualism. Studies in honor of David Singleton* (pp. 205–224). Cham: Springer.

Kopečková, R. (2015). Differences in the perception of English vowel sounds by child L2 and L3 learners. In U. Gut, R. Fuchs, & E.-M. Wunder (Eds.), *Universal or diverse paths to English phonology* (pp. 71–90). Berlin: Mouton de Gruyter.

Koster, J. (1975). Dutch as an SOV language. *Linguistic Analysis, 1,* 111–136.

Kramsch, C. (Ed.) (2002). *Language acquisition and language socialization: Ecological perspectives.* London: Continuum.

Krashen, S. (1981). *Second language acquisition and second language learning.* Oxford: Pergamon.

Kroll, J. F. (2008). Juggling two languages in one mind. *Psychological Science Agenda, 22*(1). Retrieved from https://www.apa.org/science/about/psa/2008/01/kroll

Kroll, J. F., & Bialystok, E. (2013). Understanding the consequences of bilingualism for language processing and cognition. *Journal of Cognitive Psychology, 25*(5), 497–514.

Kroll, J. F., Bobb, S. C., & Wodniecka, Z. (2006). Language selectivity is the exception, not the rule: Arguments against a fixed locus of language selection in bilingual speech. *Bilingualism: Language and Cognition, 9,* 119–135.

Kroll, J. F, Dussias, P., Bogulski, C., & Valdés Kroff, J. (2012). Juggling two languages in one mind: What bilinguals tell us about language processing and its consequences for cognition. In B. Ross (Ed.), *The psychology of learning and motivation* (pp. 229–262). San Diego, CA: Academic Press.

Kroll, J. F., & Stewart, E. (1994). Category interference in translation and picture naming: Evidence for asymmetric connections between bilingual memory representations. *Journal of Memory and Language, 33*(2), 149–174.

Kroll, J. F., & Tokowicz, N. (2001). The development of conceptual representation for words in a second language. In J. Nicol (Ed.), *One mind, two languages: Bilingual language processing* (pp. 49–71). Malden: Blackwell Publishing.

Kroll, J. F., & Tokowicz, N. (2005). Models of bilingual representation and processing: looking back and to the future. In J. F. Kroll & A. de Groot (Eds.), *Handbook of bilingualism: Psycholinguistic approaches* (pp. 531–553). New York: Oxford University Press.

Kroll, J. F., van Hell, J. G., Tokowicz, N., & Green, D. W. (2010). The Revised Hierarchical Model: A critical review and assessment. *Bilingualism: Language and Cognition, 13*(3), 373–381.

Kulundary, V., & Gabriele, A. (2012). Examining the role of L2 syntactic development in L3 acquisition. In J. Cabrelli Amaro, S. Flynn, & J. Rothman (Eds.), *Third language acquisition in adulthood* (pp. 195–222). Amsterdam: John Benjamins.

Kupisch, T., & Rothman, J. (2018). Terminology matters! Why difference is not incompleteness and how early child bilinguals are heritage speakers. *International Journal of Bilingualism, 22*(5), 564–582.

Labov, W. (1966). *The social stratification of English in New York City.* Washington, DC: Center for Applied Linguistics.

Labov, W. (1994). *Principles of linguistic change: Internal factors.* Oxford: Blackwell.

Labov, W. (2001). *Principles of linguistic change: Social factors.* Oxford: Blackwell.

Lago, S., Gračanin-Yuksek, M., Şafak, D. F., Demir, O., Kırkıcı, B., & Felser, C. (2018). Straight from the horse's mouth: Agreement attraction effects with Turkish possessors. *Linguistic Approaches to Bilingualism.* doi:10.1075/lab.17019.lag.

Lago, S., Stutter García, A., & Felser, C. (2018). The role of native and non-native grammars in the comprehension of possessive pronouns. *Second Language Research*. Retrieved from https://journals.sagepub.com/doi/abs/10.1177/0267658318770491

Laka, I. (2018). OVO: Originating Variation from Order. Keynote address at the *Transdisciplinary Approaches to Language Variation* workshop. UiT The Arctic University of Norway, Tromsø, Norway.

Lakoff, R. (1975). *Language and woman's place*. New York: Harper & Row.

Lambert, W. E. (1973). Culture and language as factors in learning and education. Paper Presented at the *Annual Symposium on Cultural Factors in Learning*. Washington, DC.

Lambert, W. E., & Tucker, G. R. (1972). *Bilingual education of children: The St. Lambert experiment*. Rowley, MA: Newbury House.

Landa, A. (2009). De la presión psicolingüística a la convergencia estructural. *Oihenar*, *23*, 349–370.

Langacker, R. W. (1987). *Foundations of cognitive grammar. Vol. 1: Theoretical prerequisites*. Stanford: Stanford University Press.

Lardiere, D. (1998a). Dissociating syntax from morphology in a divergent L2 end-state grammar. *Second Language Research*, *14*(4), 359–375.

Lardiere, D. (1998b). Parameter resetting in morphology: Evidence from compounding. In M.-L. Beck (Ed.), *Morphology and its interfaces in second language knowledge* (pp. 283–306). Amsterdam/Philadelphia: John Benjamins.

Lardiere, D. (2007). *Ultimate attainment in second language acquisition: A case study*. New York: Routledge.

Lardiere, D. (2009). Some thoughts on the contrastive analysis of features in second language acquisition. *Second Language Research*, *25*(2), 173–227.

Larrañaga, P., & Guijarro-Fuentes, P. (2012). Clitics in L1 bilingual acquisition. *First Language*, *32*, 151–175.

Larsen-Freeman, D. (1997). Chaos/complexity science and second language acquisition. *Applied Linguistics*, *18*(2), 141–165.

Larsen-Freeman, D. (2002). Language acquisition and language use from a chaos/complexity theory perspective. In C. Kramsch (Ed.), *Language acquisition and language socialization: Ecological perspectives* (pp. 33–46). London: Continuum.

Larsen-Freeman, D., & Cameron, L. (2008). *Complex systems and applied linguistics*. Oxford: Oxford University Press.

Lasagabaster, D. (1998). The Threshold Hypothesis applied to three languages in contact at school. *International Journal of Bilingual Education and Bilingualism*, *1*(2), 119–133.

Lasagabaster, D. (2001). The learning of English in Finland. INTERFACE. *Journal of Applied Linguistics*, *16*, 27–44.

Lasagabaster, D., & Huguet, À. (Eds.) (2007). *Multilingualism in European bilingual contexts: Language use and attitudes*. Clevedon: Multilingual Matters.

Lasnik, H., & Lidz, J. L. (2016). The argument from the poverty of the stimulus. In I. Roberts (Ed.), *The Oxford handbook of Universal Grammar* (pp. 221–248). Oxford: Oxford University Press.

Lauro, J., & Schwartz, A. I. (2017). Bilingual non-selective lexical access in sentence contexts: A meta-analytic review. *Journal of Memory and Language*, *92*, 217–233.

Lechner, S., & Kohlberger, M. (2014). Phonetic transfer onto L3 English in subtractive bilinguals. Paper presented at the *SLE 2014 Workshop on Advances in the Investigation of L3 Phonological Acquisition*. Adam Mickiewicz University, Poznań, Poland.

Lemhöfer, K., & Dijkstra, T. (2004). Recognizing cognates and interlingual homographs: Effects of code similarity in language-specific and generalized lexical decision. *Memory & Cognition*, *32*(4), 533–550.

Lemhöfer, K., Dijkstra, T., & Michel, M. (2004). Three languages, one ECHO: Cognate effects in trilingual word recognition. *Language and Cognitive Processes*, *19*(5), 585–611.

Lenneberg, E. (1967). *The biological foundations of language*. New York: Wiley.

Leung, C. (2011). Language teaching and language assessment. In R. Wodak, B. Johnstone, & P. E. Kerswill (Eds.), *The SAGE handbook of sociolinguistics* (pp. 545–564). New York: SAGE Publications.

Leung, Y. I. (1998). Transfer between interlanguages. In A. Greenhill, M. Hughes, H. Littlefield, & H. Walsh (Eds.), *Proceedings of the 22nd Boston University Conference on Language Development* (pp. 477–487). Somerville, MA: Cascadilla Press.

Leung, Y. I. (2001). The initial state of L3A: Full transfer and failed features? In C. Higgins & H. Nguyen (Eds.), *The past, present and future of second language research: Selected proceedings of the 2000 Second Language Research Forum* (pp. 55–75). Somerville, MA: Cascadilla Press.

Leung, Y. I. (2002). *Functional categories in second and third language acquisition: A cross-linguistic study of the acquisition of English and French by Chinese and Vietnamese speakers*. Unpublished PhD dissertation, McGill University.

Leung, Y. I. (2003). Failed features versus full transfer full access in the acquisition of a third language: Evidence from tense and agreement. In J. M. Liceras, H. Zobl, & H. Goodluck (Eds.), *Proceedings of the 6th Generative Approaches to Second Language Acquisition Conference (GASLA 2002)* (pp. 199–207). Somerville, MA: Cascadilla Proceedings Project.

Leung, Y. I. (2005a). L2 vs. L3 initial state: A comparative study of the acquisition of French DPs by Vietnamese monolinguals and Cantonese–English bilinguals. *Bilingualism: Language and Cognition*, *8*(1), 39–61.

Leung, Y. I. (2005b). Second vs. third language acquisition of tense and agreement in French by Vietnamese monolinguals and Cantonese-English bilinguals. In J. Cohen, K. T. McAlister, K. Rolstad, & J. MacSwan (Eds.), *ISB4: Proceedings of the 4th International Symposium on Bilingualism* (pp. 1344–1352). Somerville, MA: Cascadilla Press.

Leung, Y. I. (2006). Full transfer vs. partial transfer in L2 and L3 acquisition. In R. Slabakova, S. Montrul, & P. Prévost (Eds.), *Inquiries in linguistic development: In honor of Lydia White* (pp. 157–187). Amsterdam: John Benjamins.

Leung, Y. I. (2007a). Second language (L2) English and third language (L3) French article acquisition by native speakers of Cantonese. *International Journal of Multilingualism*, *4*(2), 117–149.

Leung, Y. I. (2007b). Third language acquisition: Why it is interesting to generative linguists. *Second Language Research*, *23*(1), 95–114.

Leung, Y. I. (2008). The verbal functional domain in L2A and L3A. Tense and agreement in Cantonese-English-French Interlanguage. In J. M. Liceras, H. Zobl, & H. Goodluck (Eds.), *The role of formal features in second language acquisition* (pp. 379–403). Mahwah: Erlbaum.

Levelt, W. J. M. (1989). *Speaking: From intention to articulation.* Cambridge, MA: MIT Press.

Levelt, W. J. M., Roelofs, A., & Meyer, A. S. (1999). A theory of lexical access in speech production. *Behavioral and Brain Sciences, 22*(1), 1–38.

Levinson, S. C. (2001). Covariation between spatial language and cognition, and its implications for language learning. In M. Bowerman & S. C. Levinson (Eds.), *Language acquisition and conceptual development* (pp. 566–588). Cambridge: Cambridge University Press.

Lewis, S., & Phillips, C. (2015). Aligning grammatical theories and language processing Models. *Journal of Psycholinguistic Research, 44*(1), 27–46.

Libben, M. R., & Titone, D. A. (2009). Bilingual lexical access in context: Evidence from eye movements during reading. *Journal of Experimental Psychology: Learning, Memory, and Cognition, 35*(2), 381–390.

Lijewska, A., Ziegler, M., & Olko, S. (2018). L2 primes L1 – translation priming in LDT and semantic categorisation with unbalanced bilinguals. *International Journal of Bilingual Education and Bilingualism, 21*(6), 744–759.

Lindqvist, C. (2009). The use of the L1 and the L2 in French L3: Examining cross-linguistic lexemes in multilingual learners' oral production. *International Journal of Multilingualism, 6*(3), 281–297.

Lindqvist, C., & Falk, Y. (2014). When Germans begin to learn Swedish: Which is the transfer source for function words, content words and syntax? *EUROSLA Yearbook, 14*, 225–239.

Linford, B., Long, A., Solon, M., & Geeslin, K. L. (2016). Measuring lexical frequency: Comparison groups and subject expression in L2 Spanish. In L. Ortega, A. E. Tyler, H. I. Park, & M. Uno (Eds.), *The usage-based study of language learning and multilingualism* (pp. 137–153). Washington, DC: Georgetown University Press.

Liu, H., & Cao, F. (2016). L1 and L2 processing in the bilingual brain: A meta-analysis of neuroimaging studies. *Brain and Language, 159*, 60–73.

Llama, R. (2017). *Cross-linguistic syntactic, lexical and phonetic influence in the acquisition of L3 Spanish.* Unpublished PhD dissertation, University of Ottawa.

Llama, R., Cardoso, W., & Collins, L. (2010). The influence of language distance and language status on the acquisition of L3 phonology. *International Journal of Multilingualism, 7*(1), 39–57.

Llama, R., & López-Morelos, L. P. (2016). VOT production by Spanish heritage speakers in a trilingual context. *International Journal of Multilingualism, 13*(4), 444–458.

Llinàs-Grau, M., & Puig-Mayenco, E. (2016). Regressive transfer from German to non-native English: The case of that-deletion. In *On the move: Glancing backwards to build a future in English studies* (p. 281–287). Bilbao: Servicio de Publicaciones Universidad de Deusto.

Llisterri, J., & Poch-Olivé, D. (1987). Phonetic interference in bilingual's learning of a third language. In *Proceedings of the XIth International Congress of*

Phonetic Sciences. (Vol. 5, pp. 134–147). Tallinn: Academy of Sciences of the Estonian SSR.

Lloyd-Smith, A., Gyllstad, H., & Kupisch, T. (2017). Transfer into L3 English: Global accent in German-dominant heritage speakers of Turkish. *Linguistic Approaches to Bilingualism, 7*(2), 131–163.

Long, M. (2005). Problems with supposed counter-evidence to the Critical Period Hypothesis. *International Review of Applied Linguistics in Language Teaching (IRAL), 43*(4), 287–317.

Long, M. (2007). *Problems in SLA.* Mahwah, USA: Lawrence Erlbaum Associates.

Louriz, N. (2007). Alignment in L3 phonology. *Langues et Linguistique, 18/19*, 129–160.

Lowie, W. (2012). Dynamic Systems Theory Approaches to second language acquisition. In C. A. Chapelle (Ed.), *The encyclopedia of applied linguistics.* London: Blackwell.

Lozano, C. (2003). *Universal Grammar and focus constraints: The acquisition of pronouns and word order in non-native Spanish.* Unpublished PhD dissertation, University of Essex.

Lüdi, G., & Py, B. (2009). To be or not to be . . . a plurilingual speaker. *International Journal of Multilingualism, 6*(2), 154–167.

Lupker, S. J., & Pexman, P. M. (2010). Making things difficult in lexical decision: The impact of pseudohomophones and transposed-letter nonwords on frequency and semantic priming effects. *Journal of Experimental Psychology: Learning, Memory, and Cognition, 36*(5), 1267–1289.

Mackey, W. F. (1970). A typology of bilingual education. *Foreign Language Annals, 3*, 596–608.

MacWhinney, B. (1987). The Competition Model. In B. MacWhinney (Ed.), *Mechanisms of language acquisition* (pp. 249–308). Hillsdale: Erlbaum.

MacWhinney, B. (2000). *The CHILDES project: Tools for analyzing talk.* Mahwah, NJ: Lawrence Erlbaum Associates.

MacWhinney, B. (2001). The Competition Model: The input, the context, and the brain. In P. Robinson (Ed.), *Cognition and second language instruction* (pp. 69–90). Cambridge: Cambridge University Press.

MacWhinney, B. (2005). A unified model of language acquisition. In J. F. Kroll & A. de Groot (Eds.), *Handbook of bilingualism: Psycholinguistic approaches* (pp. 49–67). New York, USA: Oxford University Press.

MacWhinney, B. (2012). The logic of the Unified Model. In S. Gass & A. Mackey (Eds.), *The Routledge handbook of second language acquisition* (pp. 211–227). London: Routledge.

Mägiste, E. (1979). The competing language systems of the multilingual: A developmental study of decoding and encoding processes. *Journal of Verbal Learning and Verbal Behavior, 18*(1), 79–89.

Mägiste, E. (1986). Selected issues in second and third language learning. In J. Vaid (Ed.), *language processing in bilinguals: Psycholinguistic and neuropsychological perspectives* (pp. 97–122). Hillsdale: Erlbaum.

Mahon, B. Z., Costa, A., Peterson, R., Vargas, K. A. & Caramazza, A. (2007). Lexical selection is not by competition: A reinterpretation of semantic interference and facilitation effects in the picture-word interference paradigm. *Journal of Experimental Psychology. Learning, Memory, and Cognition, 33*(3), 503–535.

Marian, V., & Shook, A. (2012). The cognitive benefits of being bilingual. *Cerebrum: The Dana Forum on Brain Science, 13,* 1–13.

Marijuan, S., Lago, S., & Sanz, C. (2016). Can English-Spanish emerging bilinguals use agreement morphology to overcome word order bias? In L. Ortega, A. E. Tyler, H. I. Park, & M. Uno (Eds.), *The usage-based study of language learning and multilingualism* (pp. 189–210). Washington, DC: Georgetown University Press.

Marslen-Wilson, W. D. (2001). Access to lexical representations: Cross-linguistic issues. *Language and Cognitive Processes, 16*(5–6), 699–708.

Martins, A. M. (2006). Emphatic affirmation and polarity: Contrasting European Portuguese with Brazilian Portuguese, Spanish, Catalan and Galician. In J. Doetjes & P. González (Eds.), *Romance languages and linguistic theory 2004* (pp. 197–223). Amsterdam: John Benjamins.

Masgoret, A.-M., & Gardner, R. C. (2003). Attitudes, motivation, and second language learning: A meta-analysis of studies conducted by Gardner and associates. *Language Learning, 53*(S1), 167–210.

Matthews, S., Cheung, S. C., & Tsang, W. L. (2014). Anti-transfer effects in third language acquisition. Paper presented at the *9th International Conference on Third Language Acquisition and Multilingualism.* Uppsala University, Sweden.

May, S. (2008). Bilingual/immersion education: What the research tells us. In J. Cummins & N. H. Hornberger (Eds.), *The encyclopedia of language and education.* *(Vol. 5,* pp. 19–34). New York: Springer.

McClelland, J. L., & Rumelhart, D. E. (1981). An Interactive Activation model of context effects in letter perception: Part 1. An account of basic findings. *Psychological Review, 88*(5), 375–407.

McDonald, J. L. (2006). Beyond the critical period: Processing-based explanations for poor grammaticality judgment performance by late second language learners. *Journal of Memory and Language, 55*(3), 381–401.

Meisel, J. (1997). The acquisition of the syntax of negation in French and German: Contrasting first and second language development. *Second Language Research, 13* (3), 227–263.

Meisel, J. (2011). *First and second language acquisition.* Cambridge: Cambridge University Press.

Mesthrie, R. (2011a). Introduction: The sociolinguistic enterprise. In R. Mesthrie (Ed.), *The Cambridge handbook of sociolinguistics* (pp. 1–14). Cambridge: Cambridge University Press.

Mesthrie, R. (Ed.) (2011b). *The Cambridge handbook of sociolinguistics. Cambridge Handbooks in Language and Linguistics.* Cambridge: Cambridge University Press.

Mettewie, L., & Janssens, R. (2007). Language use and language attitudes in Brussels. In D. Lasagabaster & À. Huguet (Eds.), *Multilingualism in European bilingual contexts: Language use and attitudes* (pp. 117–143). Clevedon: Multilingual Matters.

Meuter, R. F. I. (2005). Language selection in bilinguals: mechanisms and processes. In J. F. Kroll & A. M. B. de Groot (Eds.), *Handbook of bilingualism: Psycholinguistic approaches* (pp. 349–370). New York: Oxford University Press.

Meyer, D. E., & Rudy, M. G. (1974). Bilingual word recognition: Organization and retrieval of alternative lexical codes. Paper presented to the *Eastern Psychological Association*. Philadelphia, PA.

Milroy, L., & Gordon, M. (2003). *Sociolinguistics: Method and interpretation*. Oxford: Blackwell.

Missaglia, F. (2010). The acquisition of L3 English vowels by infant German–Italian bilinguals. *International Journal of Multilingualism, 7*(1), 58–74.

Mollaie, A., Jabbari, A. A., & Rezaie, M. J. (2016). The acquisition of French (L3) wh-question by Persian (L1) learners of English (L2) as a foreign language: Optionality theory. *International Journal of English Linguistics, 6*(7), 36–47.

Montalbetti, M. (1984). *After binding. On the interpretation of pronouns*. Unpublished PhD dissertation, Massachusetts Institute of Technology.

Montalbetti, M. (1986). How *pro* is it? In O. Jaeggli & C. Silva-Corvalán (Eds.), *Studies in Romance linguistics* (pp. 137–152). Dordrecht: Foris.

Montrul, S. (2008). *Incomplete acquisition in bilingualism: Re-examining the age factor*. Amsterdam: John Benjamins.

Montrul, S., Dias, R., & Santos, H. (2011). Clitics and object expression in the L3 acquisition of Brazilian Portuguese: Structural similarity matters for transfer. *Second Language Research, 27*(1), 21–58.

Morgan-Short, K., Sanz, C., & Ullman, M. T. (2010). Second language acquisition of gender agreement in explicit and implicit training conditions: An event-related potential study. *Language Learning, 60*(1), 154–193.

Morgenstern, A., Beaupoil-Hourdel, P., Blondel, M., & Boutet, D. (2016). A multimodal approach to the development of negation in signed and spoken languages: four case studies. In L. Ortega, A. E. Tyler, H. I. Park, & M. Uno (Eds.), *The usage-based study of language learning and multilingualism* (pp. 15–36). Washington, DC: Georgetown University Press.

Morton, J. B., & Harper, S. N. (2007). What did Simon say? Revisiting the bilingual advantage. *Developmental Science, 10*(6), 719–726.

Munarriz-Ibarrola, A., Parafita Couto, M. C., & Vanden Wyngaerd, E. (Eds.) (2018). Special issue – Methodologies for intra-sentential code-switching research. *Linguistic Approaches to Bilingualism, 8*(1), 1–4.

Munnich, E., & Landau, B. (2010). Developmental decline in the acquisition of spatial language. *Language Learning and Development, 6*(1), 32–59.

Mykhaylyk, R., Mitrofanova, N., Rodina, Y., & Westergaard, M. (2015). The Linguistic Proximity Model: The case of verb-second revisited. In E. Grillo & K. Jepson (Eds.), *Proceedings of the 39th Boston University Conference on Language Development*. Somerville, MA: Cascadilla Proceedings Project.

Na Ranong, S., & Leung, Y. I. (2009). Null objects in L1 Thai–L2 English–L3 Chinese: An empiricist take on a theoretical problem. In Y.-K. I. Leung (Ed.), *Third language acquisition and Universal Grammar* (pp. 162–191). Bristol: Multilingual Matters.

Nair, V. K. K., Biedermann, B., & Nickels, L. (2017). Effect of socio-economic status on cognitive control in non-literate bilingual speakers. *Bilingualism: Language and Cognition, 20*(5), 999–1009.

Nakayama, M., Sears, C. R., Hino, Y., & Lupker, S. J. (2013). Masked translation priming with Japanese–English bilinguals: Interactions between cognate status, target frequency and L2 proficiency. *Journal of Cognitive Psychology, 25*(8), 949–981.

Nicoladis, E. (2018). Simultaneous Child Bilingualism. In D. Miller, F. Bayram, L. Serratrice, & J. Rothman (Eds.), *Bilingual cognition and language: The state of the science across its subfields* (pp. 81–102). Amsterdam, NL: John Benjamins.

Nicoladis, E., & Genesee, F. (1997). Language development in preschool bilingual children. *Journal of Speech-Language Pathology and Audiology, 21*(4), 258–270.

Norris, J., & Ortega, L. (2000). Effectiveness of L2 instruction: A research synthesis and quantitative meta-analysis. *Language Learning, 50*, 417–528.

Nosek, B. A., Ebersole, C. R., DeHaven, A. C., & Mellor, D. T. (2018). The preregistration revolution. *Proceedings of the National Academy of Sciences (PNAS), 115* (11), 2600–2606.

Odlin, T. (1989). *Language transfer: Cross-linguistic influence in language learning.* Cambridge: Cambridge University Press.

Odlin, T. (2008). Cross-linguistic Influence. In C. Doughty & M. Long (Eds.), *The handbook of second language acquisition* (pp. 436–486). Oxford: Blackwell.

Odlin, T. (2012). Cross-linguistic influence in second language acquisition. In C. A. Chapelle (Ed.), *The encyclopedia of applied linguistics.* London: Blackwell.

Odlin, T., & Jarvis, S. (2004). Same source, different outcomes: A study of Swedish influence on the acquisition of English in Finland. *International Journal of Multilingualism, 1*(2), 123–140.

O'Grady, W. (2005). *How children learn language.* Cambridge: Cambridge University Press.

O'Grady, W. (2008). The emergentist program. *Lingua, 118*(4), 447–464.

O'Grady, W. (2013). The illusion of language acquisition. *Linguistic Approaches to Bilingualism, 3*(3), 253–285.

Onishi, H. (2016). The effects of L2 experience on L3 perception. *International Journal of Multilingualism, 13*(4), 459–475.

Ortega, L. (2011). *Second language acquisition.* London: Routledge.

Ortega, L. (2013). SLA for the 21st century: Disciplinary progress, transdisciplinary relevance, and the bi/multilingual turn. *Language Learning, 63*(S1), 1–24.

Ortega, L. (2016). *Multi-competence in second language acquisition: Inroads into the mainstream?* In V. Cook & L. Wei (Eds.), *The Cambridge handbook of linguistic multi-competence* (pp. 50–76). Cambridge: Cambridge University Press.

Ortega, L., Tyler, A. E., Park, H. I., & Uno, M. (Eds.) (2016). *The usage-based study of language learning and multilingualism.* Washington, DC: Georgetown University Press.

Ortiz de Urbina, J. (1989). *Parameters in the grammar of Basque: A GG approach to Basque syntax.* Dordrecht, NL: Foris.

Ostler, N. (2011). Language maintenance, shift, and endangerment. In R. Mesthrie (Ed.), *The Cambridge handbook of sociolinguistics* (pp. 315–334). Cambridge: Cambridge University Press.

Özçelik, Ö. (2013). Selectivity in L3 transfer: Effects of typological and linguistic similarity in the L3 Turkish of Uzbek-Russian bilinguals. Paper presented at the *36th Conference of Generative Linguistics in the Old World (GLOW 36)*. Lund, Sweden.

Özçelik, Ö. (2016). An antisymmetric analysis of Turkish relative clauses: Implications from prosody. *Turkic Languages, 3,* 87–99.

Paap, K. R., Johnson, H. A., & Sawi, O. (2015). Bilingual advantages in executive functioning either do not exist or are restricted to very specific and undetermined circumstances. *Cortex, 69,* 265–278.

Pajak, B., Fine, A. B., Kleinschmidt, D. F., & Jaeger, T. F. (2016). Learning additional languages as hierarchical probabilistic inference: Insights from first language processing. *Language Learning, 66*(4), 900–944.

Paradis, M. (1978). Bilingual linguistic memory: Neurolinguistic considerations. Paper presented at the *Annual Meeting of the Linguistic Society of America*. Boston, MA.

Paradis, M. (1980). Language and thought in bilinguals. *LACUS Forum, 6,* 420–431.

Paradis, M. (1981). Neurolinguistic organization of a bilingual's two languages. *LACUS Forum, 7,* 486–494.

Paradis, M. (2004). *A neurolinguistic theory of bilingualism.* Amsterdam: John Benjamins.

Paradis, M. (2009). *Declarative and procedural determinants of second languages.* Amsterdam: John Benjamins.

Park, M. (2016). *Third language acquisition among early bilinguals.* Unpublished PhD dissertation, National University of Singapore.

Parma, A. (2017). Cross-linguistic transfer of object clitic structure: A case of L3 Brazilian Portuguese. *Languages, 2*(3), 14.

Pascual y Cabo, D., & Rothman, J. (2012). The (il)logical problem of heritage speaker bilingualism and incomplete acquisition. *Applied Linguistics, 33*(4), 1–7.

Pavlenko, A., Blackledge, A., Piller, I., & Teutsch-Dwyer, M. (Eds.) (2001). *Multilingualism, second language learning, and gender.* Berlin: Mouton de Gruyter.

Pearson, B. Z., Fernández, S. C., & Oller, D. K. (1993). Lexical development in bilingual infants and toddlers: Comparison to monolingual norms. *Language Learning, 43*(1), 93–120.

Peeters, D., Dijkstra, T., & Grainger, J. (2013). The representation and processing of identical cognates by late bilinguals: RT and ERP effects. *Journal of Memory and Language, 68*(4), 315–332.

Penfield, W., & Roberts, L. (1959). *Speech and brain mechanisms.* Princeton, NJ: Princeton University Press.

Perani, D., & Abutalebi, J. (2005). The neural basis of first and second language processing. *Current Opinion in Neurobiology, 15*(2), 202–206.

Perek, F., & Goldberg, A. E. (2017). Linguistic generalization on the basis of function and constraints on the basis of statistical preemption. *Cognition, 168,* 276–293.

Pérez-Leroux, A. T., & Glass, W. R. (1999). Null anaphora in Spanish second language acquisition: Probabilistic versus generative approaches. *Second Language Research, 15*, 220–249.

Pienemann, M. (2005). Discussing processability theory. In M. Pienemann (Ed.), *Cross-linguistic aspects of processability theory* (pp. 61–83). Amsterdam: John Benjamins.

Pienemann, M., Lenzing, A., & Keßler, J.-U. (2016). Transfer at the initial state. In J.-U. Keßler, A. Lenzing, & M. Liebner (Eds.), *Developing, modelling and assessing second languages* (pp. 79–98). Amsterdam: John Benjamins.

Piller, I., & Pavlenko, A. (2004). Bilingualism and gender. In T. K. Bhatia & W. C. Ritchie (Eds.), *The handbook of bilingualism* (pp. 489–511). Oxford: Blackwell.

Piller, I., & Pavlenko, A. (2009). Language, gender, and globalization. In V. Cook & L. Wei (Eds.), *Contemporary applied linguistics. Vol. 2: Linguistics for the real world* (pp. 10–27). London: Continuum.

Piller, I., & Takahashi, K. (2006). A Passion for English: Desire and the language market. In A. Pavlenko (Ed.), *Bilingual minds: Emotional experience, expression, and representation* (pp. 59–83). Clevedon: Multilingual Matters.

Pinker, S. (1994). *The language instinct.* New York: William Morrow and Company.

Pires, A., & Rothman, J. (2009). Disentangling sources of incomplete acquisition: An explanation for competence divergence across heritage grammars. *International Journal of Bilingualism, 13*(2), 211–238.

Piroth, H. (2003). Final devoicing and syllabification in German consonant clusters: A phonetic investigation. In M. J. Solé, D. Recasens, & J. Romero (Eds.), *Proceedings of the 15th International Congress of Phonetic Sciences* (pp. 2749–2752). Barcelona: UAB Press.

Pliatsikas, C. (2019). Multilingualism and brain plasticity. In J. W. Schwieter (Ed.), *The handbook of the neuroscience of multilingualism (pp. 230–251).* Oxford: Wiley-Blackwell.

Pliatsikas, C., DeLuca, V., Moschopoulou, E., & Saddy, J. D. (2017). Immersive bilingualism reshapes the core of the brain. *Brain Structure and Function, 222*(4), 1785–1795.

Pliatsikas, C., Johnstone, T., & Marinis, T. (2014). FMRI evidence for the involvement of the procedural memory system in morphological processing of a second language. *PLoS ONE, 9*(5), e97298.

Pliatsikas, C., Johnstone, T., & Marinis, T. (2017). An fMRI study on the processing of long-distance wh-movement in a second language. *Glossa: A Journal of General Linguistics, 2*(1), 101.

Plonsky, L., & Kim, Y. (2016). Task-based learner production: A substantive and methodological review. *Annual Review of Applied Linguistics, 36*, 73–97.

Plonsky, L., & Oswald, F. (2012). How to do a meta-analysis. In A. Mackey & S. Gass (Eds.), *Research methods in second language acquisition: A practical guide* (pp. 275–295). London: Basil Blackwell.

Plonsky, L., & Oswald, F. (2014). How big is "big"? Interpreting effect sizes in L2 research. *Language Learning, 64*(4), 878–912.

Polinsky, M. (2015). When L1 becomes an L3: Do heritage speakers make better L3 learners? *Bilingualism: Language and Cognition, 18*(2), 163–178.

Portocarrero, J. S., Burright, R. G., & Donovick, P. J. (2007). Vocabulary and verbal fluency of bilingual and monolingual college students. *Archives of Clinical Neuropsychology, 22*(3), 415–422.

Postman, L. (1962). Transfer of training as a function of experimental paradigm and degree of first-list learning. *Journal of Verbal Learning and Verbal Behavior, 1*(2), 109–118.

Potowski, K., & Rothman, J. (Eds.) (2008). *Bilingual youth: Spanish in English-speaking societies*. Amsterdam: John Benjamins.

Prévost, P., & White, L. (2000). Missing surface inflection or impairment in second language acquisition? Evidence from tense and agreement. *Second Language Research, 16*(2), 103–133.

Puig-Mayenco, E., González Alonso, J., & Rothman, J. (2018). A systematic review of transfer studies in third language acquisition. *Second Language Research*. doi:10.1177/0267658318809147.

Puig-Mayenco, E., & Marsden, H. (2018). Polarity-item anything in L3 English: Where does transfer come from when the L1 is Catalan and the L2 is Spanish? *Second Language Research, 34*(4), 487–515.

Puig-Mayenco, E., Miller, D., & Rothman, J. (2018). Language dominance and transfer selection in L3 acquisition: Evidence from sentential negation and negative quantifiers in L3 English. In J. Cho, M. Iverson, T. Judy, T. Leal, & E. Shimanskaya (Eds.), *Meaning and structure in second language acquisition: In honor of Roumyana Slabakova* (229–260). Amsterdam: John Benjamins.

Puig-Mayenco, E., & Rothman, J. (in press). Low proficiency does not mean ab initio: Actual exposure matters for L3 transfer studies. *Language Acquisition*.

Pullum, G. K., & Scholz, B. C. (2002). Empirical assessment of stimulus poverty arguments. *The Linguistic Review, 19*, 9–50.

Putnam, M., & Sánchez, L. (2013). What's so incomplete about incomplete acquisition? A prolegomenon to modeling heritage language grammars. *Linguistic Approaches to Bilingualism, 3*(4), 542–561.

Quirk, R., Greenbaum, S., Leech, J., & Scartvik, J. (1972). *A grammar of contemporary English*. New York: Seminar Press.

Radford, A. (2012). *Analyzing English sentences*. Cambridge: Cambridge University Press.

Ringbom, H. (1986). Crosslinguistic influence and the foreign language process. In E. Kellerman & M. Sharwood-Smith (Eds.), *Crosslinguistic influence in second language acquisition* (pp. 150–162). New York: Pergamon Institute of English.

Ringbom, H. (1987). *The role of the first language in foreign language learning*. Clevedon: Multilingual Matters.

Ringbom, H. (2001). Lexical transfer in L3 production. In J. Cenoz, B. Hufeisen, & U. Jessner (Eds.), *Cross-linguistic influence in third language acquisition: Psycholinguistic perspectives* (pp. 59–68). Clevedon: Multilingual Matters.

Ringbom, H. (2007). *Cross-linguistic similarity in foreign language learning*. Clevedon: Multilingual Matters.

Ringbom, H., & Jarvis, S. (2009). The importance of cross-linguistic similarity in foreign language learning. In M. Long & C. J. Doughty (Eds.), *The handbook of language teaching* (pp. 106–118). West Sussex: Wiley-Blackwell.

Rivers, W. M. (1979). Learning a sixth language: An adult learner's daily diary. *The Canadian Modern Language Review, 36*, 67–82.

Rizzi, L. (1982). *Issues in Italian syntax*. Dordrecht: Foris.

Roberts, L., González Alonso, J., Pliatsikas, C. & Rothman, J. (2018). Evidence from neurolinguistic methodologies: Can it actually inform linguistic/language acquisition theories and translate to evidence-based applications? *Second Language Research, 34* (1), 125–143.

Robinson, P. (2010). Implicit artificial grammar and incidental natural second language learning: How comparable are they? *Language Learning, 60*(S2), 245–263.

Roeper, T. (1999). Universal bilingualism. *Bilingualism: Language and Cognition, 2*, 169–186.

Roessingh, H. (2004). Effective high school ESL programs: A synthesis and meta-analysis. *Canadian Modern Language Review, 60*, 611–636.

Romaine, S. (1994). *Language in society: An introduction to sociolinguistics*. Oxford: Oxford University Press.

Romaine, S. (1995). *Bilingualism* (2nd ed.). Oxford: Blackwell.

Rosselli, M., Ardila, A., Araujo, K., Weekes, V. A., Caracciolo, V., Padilla, M., & Ostrosky-Solis, F. (2000). Verbal fluency and repetition skills in healthy older Spanish-English bilinguals. *Applied Neuropsychology, 7*(1), 17–24.

Rothman, J. (2007a). Heritage speaker competence differences, language change, and input type: Inflected infinitives in Heritage Brazilian Portuguese. *International Journal of Bilingualism, 11*(4), 359–389.

Rothman, J. (2007b). Sometimes they use it, sometimes they don't: An epistemological discussion of L2 morphological production and its use as a competence measurement. *Applied Linguistics, 28*(4), 609–614.

Rothman, J. (2008a). Aspect selection in adult L2 Spanish and the Competing Systems Hypothesis: When pedagogical and linguistic rules conflict. *Languages in Contrast, 8* (1), 74–106.

Rothman, J. (2008b). Linguistic epistemology and the notion of monolingualism. *Sociolinguistic Studies, 2*(3), 441–457.

Rothman, J. (2008c). Why all counter-evidence to the critical period hypothesis in second language acquisition is not equal or problematic. *Language and Linguistics Compass, 2*(6), 1063–1088.

Rothman, J. (2009a). Pragmatic deficits with syntactic consequences? L2 pronominal subjects and the syntax–pragmatics interface. *Journal of Pragmatics, 41*, 951–973.

Rothman, J. (2009b). Understanding the nature and outcomes of early bilingualism: Romance languages as heritage languages. *International Journal of Bilingualism, 13* (2), 155–163.

Rothman, J. (2010). On the typological economy of syntactic transfer: Word order and relative clause high/low attachment preference in L3 Brazilian Portuguese. *International Review of Applied Linguistics in Language Teaching (IRAL), 48*(2–3), 245–273.

Rothman, J. (2011). L3 syntactic transfer selectivity and typological determinacy: The Typological Primacy Model. *Second Language Research, 27*, 107–127.

Rothman, J. (2013). Cognitive economy, non-redundancy and typological primacy in L3 acquisition: Evidence from initial stages of L3 Romance. In S. Baauw, F. Dirjkoningen, & M. Pinto (Eds.), *Romance languages and linguistic theory 2011* (pp. 217–247). Amsterdam: John Benjamins.

Rothman, J. (2015). Linguistic and cognitive motivations for the Typological Primacy Model (TPM) of third language (L3) transfer: Timing of acquisition and proficiency considered. *Bilingualism: Language and Cognition, 18*(2), 179–190.

Rothman, J., Alemán Bañón, J., & González Alonso, J. (2015). Neurolinguistic measures of typological effects in multilingual transfer: Introducing an ERP methodology. *Frontiers in Psychology, 6*, 1087. doi:10.3389/fpsyg.2015.01087.

Rothman, J., & Cabrelli Amaro, J. (2010). What variables condition syntactic transfer? A look at the L3 initial State. *Second Language Research, 26*, 189–218.

Rothman, J., Cabrelli Amaro, J., & de Bot, K. (2013). Third language acquisition. In J. Herschensohn & M. Young-Scholten (Eds.), *The Cambridge handbook of second language acquisition* (pp. 372–393). Cambridge: Cambridge University Press.

Rothman, J. & Chomsky, N. (2018). Towards eliminating arbitrary stipulations related to parameters: Linguistic innateness and the variational model. *Linguistic Approaches to Bilingualism, 8*(6), 764–769.

Rothman, J., & Guijarro-Fuentes, P. (2010). Input quality matters: Some comments on input type and age-effects in adult SLA. *Applied Linguistics, 31*(2), 301–306.

Rothman, J., & Iverson, M. (2008). Poverty-of-the-stimulus and SLA epistemology: Considering L2 knowledge of aspectual phrasal semantics. *Language Acquisition, 15* (4), 270–314.

Rothman, J., & Iverson, M. (2013). Islands and objects in L2 Spanish. *Studies in Second Language Acquisition, 35*(4), 589–618.

Rothman, J., Iverson, M., & Judy, T. (2011). Some notes on the generative study of L3 acquisition. *Second Language Research, 27*(1), 5–19.

Rothman, J., & Slabakova, R. (2018). The generative approach to SLA and its place in modern second language studies. *Studies in Second Language Acquisition, 40*(2), 417–442.

Rothman, J., & Treffers-Daller, J. (2014). A prolegomenon to the construct of the native speaker: Heritage speaker bilinguals are natives too! *Applied Linguistics, 35*(1), 93–98.

Rothman, J., & VanPatten, B. (2013). On multiplicity and mutual exclusivity: The case for different SLA theories. In M. P. García Mayo, M. J. Gutiérrez Mangado, & M. Martínez-Adrián (Eds.), *Contemporary approaches to second language acquisition* (pp. 243–256). Amsterdam: John Benjamins.

Rüschemeyer, S.-A., Zysset, S., & Friederici, A. D. (2006). Native and non-native reading of sentences: An fMRI experiment. *NeuroImage, 31*(1), 354–365.

Safont Jordà, M. P. (2003). Metapragmatic awareness and pragmatic production of third language learners of English: A focus on request acts realizations. *International Journal of Bilingualism, 7*(1), 43–68.

Safont Jordà, M. P. (2005). *Third language learners: Pragmatic production and awareness.* Clevedon: Multilingual Matters.

Safont Jordà, M. P. (2007). Language use and language attitudes in the Valencian community. In D. Lasagabaster & À. Huguet (Eds.), *Multilingualism in European bilingual contexts: Language use and attitudes* (pp. 90–116). Clevedon: Multilingual Matters.

Sagarra, N. (2012). Working memory in second language acquisition. In C. A. Chapelle (Ed.), *The encyclopedia of applied linguistics*. London: Blackwell.

Sánchez, L., & Bardel, C. (2017). Transfer from the L2 in third language learning: A study on L2 proficiency. In T. Angelovska & A. Hahn (Eds.), *L3 syntactic transfer: Models, new developments and implications* (pp. 223–250). Amsterdam: John Benjamins.

Sánchez-Casas, R. & García-Albea, J. E. (2005). The representation of cognate and noncognate words in bilingual memory: Can cognate status be characterized as a special kind of morphological relation? In J. F. Kroll and A. M. B. De Groot (Eds.), *Handbook of bilingualism: Psycholinguistic approaches* (pp. 226–250). New York: Oxford University Press.

Sandoval, T. C., Gollan, T. H., Ferreira, V. S., & Salmon, D. P. (2010). What causes the bilingual disadvantage in verbal fluency? The dual-task analogy. *Bilingualism: Language and Cognition, 13*(2), 231–252.

Santos, A., Gorter, D., & Cenoz, J. (2017). Communicative anxiety in the second and third language. *International Journal of Multilingualism, 14*(1), 23–37.

Santos, H. (2013). *Cross-linguistic influence in the acquisition of Portuguese as a third language.* Unpublished PhD dissertation, University of Illinois at Urbana Champaign.

Sanz, C. (2000). Bilingual education enhances third language acquisition: Evidence from Catalonia. *Applied Psycholinguistics, 21*(1), 23–44.

Sanz, C., & Lado, B. (2008). Third language acquisition research methods. In K. A. King & N. H. Hornberger (Eds.), *Encyclopedia of language and education. Vol. X: Research methods in language and education* (pp. 113–135). New York: Springer.

Sanz, C., Park, H. I., & Lado, B. (2015). A functional approach to cross-linguistic influence in *ab initio* L3 acquisition. *Bilingualism: Language and Cognition, 18*(2), 236–251.

Saussure, F. (1916). *Cours de linguistique générale.* (Trans. C. Bally & A. Sechehaye). Paris: Payot.

Schiffman, H. F. (1998). Diglossia as a sociolinguistic situation. In F. Coulmas (Ed.), *The handbook of sociolinguistics* (pp. 205–216). Oxford: Blackwell Publishing Ltd.

Schilling, N. (2011). Language, gender, and sexuality. In R. Mesthrie (Ed.), *The Cambridge handbook of sociolinguistics* (pp. 218–237). Cambridge: Cambridge University Press.

Schmid, M. S. (2011). *Language attrition.* Cambridge: Cambridge University Press.

Schmid, M. S. (2013a). First language attrition: State of the discipline and future directions. *Linguistic Approaches to Bilingualism, 3*(1), 94–115.

Schmid, M. S. (2013b). First language attrition. *Wiley Interdisciplinary Reviews: Cognitive Science, 4*(2), 117–123.

Schmid, M. S., & Köpke, B. (2017). The relevance of first language attrition to theories of bilingual development. *Linguistic Approaches to Bilingualism, 7*(6), 637–667.

Schmiedtová, B., von Stutterheim, C., & Carroll, M. (2011). Language-specific patterns in event construal of advanced second language speakers. In A. Pavlenko (Ed.), *Thinking and speaking in two languages* (pp. 112–141). Clevedon: Multilingual Matters.

Schneider, E. W. (2007). *Postcolonial English: Varieties around the world.* Cambridge: Cambridge University Press.

Schneider, E. W. (2011). Colonization, globalization, and the sociolinguistics of World Englishes. In R. Mesthrie (Ed.), *The Cambridge handbook of sociolinguistics* (pp. 335–354). Cambridge: Cambridge University Press.

Schwartz, A. I., & Kroll, J. F. (2006). Bilingual lexical activation in sentence context. *Journal of Memory and Language, 55*(2), 197–212.

Schwartz, B. (1993). On explicit and negative data effecting and affecting competence and linguistic behavior. *Studies in Second Language Acquisition, 15,* 147–163.

Schwartz, B. D. (1992). Testing between UG-based and problem-solving models of L2A: Developmental sequence data. *Language Acquisition, 2*(1), 1–19.

Schwartz, B. D. (1999). "Transfer" and L2 acquisition of syntax: Where are we now? ("Transfer": Maligned, realigned, reconsidered, redefined). In K. Oga & G. Poole (Eds.), *Newcastle and Durham Working Papers in Linguistics 5* (pp. 211–234). Newcastle upon Tyne: Newcastle University.

Schwartz, B., & Sprouse, R. (1994). Word order and nominative case in nonnative language acquisition: A longitudinal study of (L1 Turkish) German interlanguage. In T. Hoekstra & B. Schwartz (Eds.), *Language acquisition studies in generative grammar.* Amsterdam: John Benjamins.

Schwartz, B., & Sprouse, R. (1996). L2 cognitive states and the Full Transfer/Full Access model. *Second Language Research, 12*(1), 40–72.

Schwartz, B., & Sprouse, R. (2000). When syntactic theories evolve: Consequences for L2 acquisition research. In J. Archibald (Ed.), *Second language acquisition and linguistic theory* (pp. 156–186). Malden, MA: Blackwell.

Schwartz, B., & Sprouse, R. (2013). Generative approaches and the poverty of stimulus. In J. Herschensohn & M. Young-Scholten (Eds.), *The Cambridge handbook of second language acquisition* (pp. 137–158). Cambridge: Cambridge University Press.

Selinker, L. (1972). Interlanguage. *International Review of Applied Linguistics in Language Teaching (IRAL), 10,* 209–231.

Serratrice, L. (2013). Cross-linguistic influence in bilingual development: Determinants and mechanisms. *Linguistic Approaches to Bilingualism, 3*(1), 3–25.

Siemund, P., Schröter, S., & Rahbari, S. (2018). Learning English demonstrative pronouns on bilingual substrate: Evidence from German heritage speakers of Russian, Turkish and Vietnamese. In A. Bonnet & P. Siemund (Eds.), *Language education in multilingual classrooms* (pp. 381–405). Amsterdam: John Benjamins Publishing Company.

Singh, R., & Carroll, S. (1979). L1, L2 and L3. *Indian Journal of Applied Linguistics, 5,* 51–63.

Singleton, D. (1987). Mother and other tongue influence on learner French. *Studies in Second Language Acquisition, 9*(3), 327–345.

Singleton, D., & Little, D. (1991). The second language lexicon: Some evidence from university-level learners of French and German. *Second Language Research, 7*(1), 61–81.

Singleton, D., & O'Laire, M. (2006). Psychotypology and the "L2 factor" in cross lexical interaction: An analysis of English and Irish influence in learner French. In M. Björklund, C. Fant, & L. Forsma (Eds.), *Språk, lärande och utbildning i sikte* (pp. 191–205). Vasa, Faculty of Education: Åbo Akademi.

Sjöholm, K. (1976). A comparison of the test results in grammar and vocabulary between Finnish- and Swedish-speaking applicants for English 1974. In H. Ringbom & R. Palmberg (Eds.), *Errors made by Finns in the learning of English, AFTIL 5* (pp. 54–137). Åbo: Åbo Akademi.

Sjöholm, K. (1979). Do Finns and Swedish-speaking Finns use different strategies in the learning of English as a foreign language? In R. Palmberg (Ed.), *Perception and production of English: Papers on interlanguage, AFTIL 6* (pp. 89–119). Åbo: Åbo Akademi.

Skutnabb-Kangas, T. (2000). *Linguistic genocide in education or worldwide diversity and human rights?* Mahwah: Erlbaum.

Slabakova, R. (2001). *Telicity in the second language.* Amsterdam: John Benjamins Publishing Company.

Slabakova, R. (2006). Learnability in the L2 acquisition of semantics: A bidirectional study of a semantic parameter. *Second Language Research, 22*(4), 498–523.

Slabakova, R. (2015). Is there a firewall between declarative knowledge and procedural knowledge of functional morphology? A response to Paradis. *Foreign Language Teaching and Research, 47*, 1–5.

Slabakova, R. (2016). *Second language acquisition.* Oxford: Oxford University Press.

Slabakova, R. (2017). The Scalpel Model of third language acquisition. *International Journal of Bilingualism, 21*(6), 651–666.

Slabakova, R., & García Mayo, M. P. (2015). The L3 syntax-discourse interface. *Bilingualism: Language and Cognition, 18*(2), 208–226.

Slobin, D. J. (1991). Learning to think for speaking: Native language, cognition and rhetorical style. *Pragmatics, 1*(1), 7–25.

Snyder, W. (2007). *Child language: The parametric approach.* Oxford: Oxford University Press.

Soares, C., & Grosjean, F. (1984). Bilinguals in a monolingual and a bilingual speech mode: The effect on lexical access. *Memory & Cognition, 12*(4), 380–386.

Solin, D. (1989). The systematic misrepresentation of bilingual-crossed aphasia data and its consequences. *Brain and Language, 36*(1), 92–116.

Sorace, A. (2011). Pinning down the concept of "interface" in bilingualism. *Linguistic Approaches to Bilingualism, 1*(1), 1–33.

Sprouse, R. (2006). Full transfer and relexification: Second language acquisition and Creole genesis. In C. Lefebvre, L. White & C. Jourdan (Eds.). *L2 acquisition and creole genesis* (pp. 169–181). Amsterdam: John Benjamins.

Stadt, R., Hulk, A., & Sleeman, P. (2016). The influence of L2 English and immersion education on L3 French in the Netherlands. In J. Audring & S. Lestrade (Eds.), *Linguistics in the Netherlands* (pp. 152–165). Amsterdam: John Benjamins.

Stadt, R., Hulk, A., & Sleeman, P. (2018). Verb placement in L3 German and L3 French: The role of L2 English. Paper presented at the *Workshop on Modern Linguistics and Language Didactics*. University of Konstanz, Germany.

Stedje, A. (1977). Tredjespråksinterferens i fritt tal – en jämförande studie [Third language interference in spontaneous speech – a comparative study]. In R. Palmberg & H. Ringbom (Eds.), *Papers from the Conference on Contrasted Linguistics and Error Analysis, Stockholm & Åbo, 7–8 February* (pp. 141–158). Åbo: Åbo Akademi.

Stroop, J. R. (1935). Studies of interference in serial verbal reactions. *Journal of Experimental Psychology, 18*(6), 643–662.

Stroud, C., & Heugh, K. (2011). Language in education. In R. Mesthrie (Ed.), *The Cambridge handbook of sociolinguistics* (pp. 413–429). Cambridge: Cambridge University Press.

Sullivan, M. D., Poarch, G. J., & Bialystok, E. (2018). Why is lexical retrieval slower for bilinguals? Evidence from picture naming. *Bilingualism: Language and Cognition, 21*(3), 479–488.

Swain, M., & Lapkin, S. (1982). *Evaluating bilingual education: A Canadian case study*. Clevedon: Multilingual Matters.

Swain, M., Lapkin, S., Rowen, N., & Hart, D. (1990). The role of mother tongue literacy in third language learning. *Language, Culture and Curriculum, 3*(1), 65–81.

Sypiańska, J. (2016). Multilingual acquisition of vowels in L1 Polish, L2 Danish and L3 English. *International Journal of Multilingualism, 13*(4), 476–495.

Szubko-Sitarek, W. (2011). Cognate facilitation effects in trilingual word recognition. *Studies in Second Language Learning and Teaching, 1*(2), 189–208.

Tagliamonte, S. A. (2006). *Analysing sociolinguistic variation*. Cambridge: Cambridge University Press.

Tagliamonte, S. A. (2011). *Variationist sociolinguistics: Change, observation, interpretation*. Oxford: Wiley-Blackwell.

Takahashi, K. (2013). *Language learning, gender and desire: Japanese women on the move*. Bristol: Multilingual Matters.

Talbot, M. (2010). *Language and gender* (2nd ed.). Cambridge: Polity Press.

Tammelin-Laine, T., & Martin, M. (2016). Negative constructions in nonliterate learners' spoken L2 Finnish. In L. Ortega, A. E. Tyler, H. I. Park, & M. Uno (Eds.), *The usage-based study of language learning and multilingualism* (pp. 75–90). Washington, DC: Georgetown University Press.

Tannen, D. (1994). *Gender and discourse*. Oxford: Oxford University Press.

Tanner, D., Nicol, J., & Brehm, L. (2014). The time-course of feature interface in agreement comprehension: Multiple mechanisms and asymmetrical attraction. *Journal of Memory and Language, 76*, 195–215.

Tavakol, M., & Jabbari, M. (2014). Cross-linguistic influence in third language (L3) and fourth language (L4) acquisition of the syntactic licensing of subject pronouns and object verb property: A case study. *International Journal of Research Studies in Language Learning, 3*(7), 29–42.

Thierry, G., & Wu, Y. J. (2007). Brain potentials reveal unconscious translation during foreign-language comprehension. *Proceedings of the National Academy of Sciences (PNAS), 104*(30), 12530–12535.

Thomas, J. (1988). The role played by metalinguistic awareness in second and third language learning. *Journal of Multilingual and Multicultural Development, 9*(3), 235–246.

Thorne, B., & Henley, N. (Eds.) (1975). *Language and sex: Difference and dominance.* Rowley, MA: Newbury House.

Tily, H. J., Frank, M. C., & Jaeger, T. F. (2011). The learnability of constructed languages reflects typological patterns. In L. Carlson, C. Hoelscher, & T. F. Shipley (Eds.), *Proceedings of the 33rd Annual Conference of the Cognitive Science Society* (pp. 1364–1369). Boston, MA: Cognitive Science Society.

Tollefson, J. W. (2011). Language planning and language policy. In R. Mesthrie (Ed.), *The Cambridge handbook of sociolinguistics* (pp. 357–376). Cambridge: Cambridge University Press.

Tomasello, M. (2003). *Constructing a language: A usage-based theory of language acquisition.* Cambridge, MA: Harvard University Press.

Tremblay, M. (2007). L2 influence on L3 pronunciation: Native-like VOT in the L3 Japanese of English-French bilinguals. Paper presented at the *L3 Phonology Satellite Workshop of International Congress of Phonetic Sciences XVI.* Freiburg, Germany.

Tsang, W. I. (2009). The L3 acquisition of Cantonese reflexives. In Y. I. Leung (Ed.), *Third language acquisition and Universal Grammar* (pp. 192–219). Bristol: Multilingual Matters.

Tsang, W. L. (2016). Acquisition of English number agreement: L1 Cantonese-L2 English-L3 French versus L1 Cantonese-L2 English speakers. *International Journal of Bilingualism, 20*(5), 611–635.

Tsimpli, I. M., & Dimitrakopoulou, M. (2007). The Interpretability Hypothesis: Evidence from wh-interrogatives in second language acquisition. *Second Language Research, 23*(2), 215–242.

Tsimpli, I., & Sorace, A. (2006). Differentiating interfaces: L2 performance in syntax-semantics and syntax-discourse phenomena. In D. Bamman, T. Magnitskaia, & C. Zaller (Eds.), *Proceedings of the 30th Annual Boston University Conference on Language Development* (pp. 653–664). Somerville: Cascadilla Press.

Unsworth, S. (2007). L1 and L2 acquisition between sentence and discourse: Comparing production and comprehension in child Dutch. *Lingua, 117,* 1930–1958.

Ushioda, E. (2016). Language learning motivation through a small lens: A research agenda. *Language Teaching, 49*(4), 564–577.

Ushioda, E., & Dörnyei, Z. (2012). Motivation. In S. Gass & A. Mackey (Eds.), *The Routledge handbook of second language acquisition* (pp. 396–409). Abingdon: Routledge.

Vainikka, A., & Young-Scholten, M. (1996). The early stages in adult L2 syntax: Additional evidence from Romance speakers. *Second Language Research, 12*(2), 140–176.

Valian, V. (2014). Arguing about innateness. *Journal of Child Language, 41*(S1), 78–92.

Van Assche, E., Duyck, W., & Hartsuiker, R. (2012). Bilingual word recognition in a sentence context. *Frontiers in Psychology, 3,* 174. doi:10.3389/fpsyg.2012.00174.

Van Assche, E., Duyck, W., Hartsuiker, R. J., & Diependaele, K. (2009). Does bilingualism change native-language reading? Cognate effects in a sentence context. *Psychological Science, 20*(8), 923–927.

Vandergrift, L. (2005). Relationships among motivation orientations, metacognitive awareness and proficiency in L2 listening. *Applied Linguistics, 26*(1), 70–89.

Van Hell, J. G., & Dijkstra, T. (2002). Foreign language knowledge can influence native language performance in exclusively native contexts. *Psychonomic Bulletin & Review, 9*(4), 780–789.

Van Heuven, W. J. B., Dijkstra, T., & Grainger, J. (1998). Orthographic neighborhood effects in bilingual word recognition. *Journal of Memory and Language, 39*(3), 458–483.

Van Heuven, W. J. B., Dijkstra, T., Grainger, J., & Schriefers, H. (2001). Shared neighborhood effects in masked orthographic priming. *Psychonomic Bulletin & Review, 8*(1), 96–101.

VanPatten, B., & Smith, M. (2015). Aptitude as grammatical sensitivity and the initial stages of learning Japanese as a L2. *Studies in Second Language Acquisition, 37*(1), 135–165.

VanPatten, B., & Williams, J. (Eds.) (2015). *Theories in second language acquisition*. Mahwah: Erlbaum.

Varley, R., & Siegal, M. (2000). Evidence for cognition without grammar from causal reasoning and "theory of mind" in an agrammatic aphasic patient. *Current Biology, 10*(12), 723–726.

Vikner, S. (1995). *Verb movement and expletive subjects in the Germanic languages*. New York: Oxford University Press.

Vildomec, V. (1963). *Multilingualism*. Leiden: A. W. Sythoff.

Villegas, Á. (2014). *The role of L2 English immersion in the processing of L1 Spanish sentence complement/relative clause ambiguities*. Unpublished PhD dissertation, Pennsylvania State University.

Wang, X., & Forster, K. (2010). Masked translation priming with semantic categorization: Testing the Sense Model. *Bilingualism: Language and Cognition, 13*(3), 327–340.

Wei, L. (2013). Codeswitching. In R. Bayley, R. Cameron, & C. Lucas (Eds.), *Oxford handbook of sociolinguistics* (pp. 360–378). Oxford: Oxford University Press.

Wei, L. (2018). Translanguaging as a practical theory of language. *Applied Linguistics, 39*(1), 9–30.

Weinreich, U. (1953). *Languages in contact, findings and problems*. New York, NY: Linguistic Circle of New York.

Wen, Y., & van Heuven, W. J. B. (2017). Non-cognate translation priming in masked priming lexical decision experiments: A meta-analysis. *Psychonomic Bulletin & Review, 24*(3), 879–886.

Westergaard, M. (2007). English as a mixed V2 grammar: Synchronic word order inconsistencies from the perspective of first language acquisition. *Poznan Studies in Contemporary Linguistics, 43*(2), 107–131.

Westergaard, M. (2017). Micro-variation in multilingual situations. Keynote address at the *14th Generative Approaches to Second Language Acquisition Conference (GASLA 14)*. University of Southampton, UK.

Westergaard, M., Mitrofanova, N., Mykhaylyk, R., & Rodina, Y. (2017). Crosslinguistic influence in the acquisition of a third language: The Linguistic Proximity Model. *International Journal of Bilingualism, 21*(6), 666–682.

White, L. (2003a). Fossilization in steady state L2 grammars: Persistent problems with inflectional morphology. *Bilingualism: Language and Cognition, 6*(2), 129–141.

White, L. (2003b). *Second language acquisition and Universal Grammar.* Cambridge: Cambridge University Press.

White, L. (2018). Formal linguistics and second language acquisition. In D. Miller, F. Bayram, L. Serratrice, & J. Rothman (Eds.), *Bilingual cognition and language: The state of the science across its subfields* (pp. 57–77). Amsterdam: John Benjamins.

White, L., Valenzuela, E., Kozlowska-Macgregor, M., & Leung, Y. I. (2004). Gender and number agreement in nonnative Spanish. *Applied Psycholinguistics, 25*, 105–133.

Whong, M., Gil, K.-H., & Marsden, H. (Eds.) (2013). *Universal Grammar and the second language classroom.* Dordrecht: Springer.

Whong, M., Gil, K.-H., & Marsden, H. (2014). Beyond paradigm: The "what" and the "how" of classroom research. *Second Language Research, 30*(4), 551–568.

Williams, S., & Hammarberg, B. (1998). Language switches in L3 production: Implications for a polyglot speaking model. *Applied Linguistics, 19*(3), 295–333.

Wodak, R., & Benke, G. (1998). Gender as a sociolinguistic variable: New perspectives on variation studies. In F. Coulmas (Ed.), *The handbook of sociolinguistics* (pp. 127–150). Oxford: Blackwell Publishing Ltd.

Wodak, R., Johnstone, B., & Kerswill, P. E. (Eds.) (2011). *The SAGE handbook of sociolinguistics.* New York: SAGE Publications.

Wolff, H. E. (2000). Pre-school child multilingualism and its educational implications in the African context. *PRAESA – Occasional Papers, 4*, 3–25.

Wong, K. C. (2011). Chi squared test versus Fisher's exact test. *Hong Kong Medical Journal, 17*(5), 427.

Wrembel, M. (2009). The impact of voice quality resetting on the perception of a foreign accent in third language acquisition. In A. S. Rauber, M. A. Watkins, & B. O. Baptista (Eds.), *Recent research in second language phonetics/phonology: Perception and production* (pp. 291–307). Cambridge: Cambridge Scholars Press.

Wrembel, M. (2010). L2-accented speech in L3 production. *International Journal of Multilingualism, 7*(1), 75–90.

Wrembel, M. (2011). Cross-linguistic influence in third language acquisition of voice onset time. In W.-S. Lee & E. Zee (Eds.), *Proceedings of the 17th International Congress of Phonetic Sciences* (pp. 17–21). Hong Kong: City University of Hong Kong.

Wrembel, M. (2012a). Foreign accent ratings in third language acquisition: The case of L3 French. In E. Waniek-Klimczak & L. Shockey (Eds.), *Teaching and researching English accents in native and non-native speakers* (pp. 29–45). Berlin: Springer-Verlag.

Wrembel, M. (2012b). Foreign accentedness in third language acquisition: The case of L3 English. In J. Cabrelli Amaro, S. Flynn, & J. Rothman (Eds.), *Third language acquisition in adulthood* (pp. 281–309). Amsterdam: John Benjamins.

Wrembel, M. (2015). *In search of a new perspective: Cross-linguistic influence in the acquisition of third language phonology.* Poznań: Wydawnictwo Naukowe UAM.

Wrembel, M., & Cabrelli Amaro, J. (Eds.) (2016). Special Issue – Advances in the investigation of L3 phonological acquisition. *International Journal of Multilingualism, 13*(4).

Wulff, S., & Ellis, N. C. (2018). Usage-based approaches to second language acquisition. In D. Miller, F. Bayram, L. Serratrice, & J. Rothman (Eds.), *Bilingual cognition and language: The state of the science across its subfields* (pp. 37–56). Amsterdam: John Benjamins.

Wunder, E.-M. (2010). Phonological cross-linguistic influence in third or additional language acquisition. In K. Dziubalska-Kołaczyk, M. Wrembel, & M. Kul (Eds.), *New sounds 2010: Proceedings of the 6th International Symposium on the Acquisition of Second Language Speech* (pp. 566–571). Poznań: Adam Mickiewicz University.

Xia, V., & Andrews, S. (2015). Masked translation priming asymmetry in Chinese-English bilinguals: Making sense of the Sense Model. *The Quarterly Journal of Experimental Psychology, 68*(2), 294–325.

Yang, C. (2016). *The price of linguistic productivity.* Cambridge, MA: MIT Press.

Yang, C. (2018). Three equations: A formalist perspective on language acquisition. *Linguistic Approaches to Bilingualism, 8*(6), 665–706.

Yang, C., Crain, S., Berwick, R. C., Chomsky, N., & Bolhuis, J. J. (2017). The growth of language: Universal Grammar, experience, and principles of computation. *Neuroscience & Biobehavioral Reviews, 81*, 103–119.

Yang, C., & Montrul, S. (2017). Learning datives: The tolerance principle in monolingual and bilingual acquisition. *Second Language Research, 33*(1), 119–144.

Yang, X., Matthews, S., & Crosthwaite, P. (2016). Anti-transfer in L3A of Portuguese. Paper presented at the *10th International Conference on Third Language Acquisition and Multilingualism.* Vienna, Austria.

Ytsma, J. (2001). Towards a typology of trilingual primary education. *International Journal of Bilingual Education and Bilingualism, 4*(1), 11–22.

Ytsma, J. (2007). Language use and language attitudes in Friesland. In D. Lasagabaster & À. Huguet (Eds.), *Multilingualism in European bilingual contexts: Language use and attitudes* (pp. 144–163). Clevedon: Multilingual Matters.

Zobl, H. (1980). The formal and developmental selectivity of L1 influence on L2 acquisition. *Language Learning, 30*(1), 43–57.

Index

ab initio, 54, 55, 140, 141, 237, 240, 241, 242, 254
adult L2 acquisition, 1, 8, 9, 11, 12, 16, 228
attrition, 57, 59, 227, 252, 253

Basque, 44, 53, 54, 67, 68, 69, 70, 71, 72, 74, 77, 180, 181
bi-/multilingual education, 67, 68, 69, 70
Bilingual Interactive Activation model (BIA/BIA+), 85, 89, 90, 114
Brazilian Portuguese (BP), 12, 20, 21, 63, 109

child L3/L*n*, 247, 250, 251
cross-language effects (CLE), 24, 25, 26, 27, 99, 106, 111, 142, 156, 188, 245
codeswitching, 65, 77, 92, 102, 103, 104
cognate effects, 82, 83, 85, 95, 114
cognitive economy, 25, 157, 161, 163, 224, 225
Competition Model (CM), 53, 54, 55
conceptual transfer, 106
Continua of Multilingual Education, 68, 71
cortical representation, 79
critical period, 14, 15, 16, 17
  hypothesis, 14
cue hierarchy
  CM, 54, 55
  TPM, 161, 162, 163, 167, 180, 197, 202, 218

declarative knowledge, 127, 128
Declarative/Procedural Model, 127
differential object marking (DOM), 255
Differential Stability Hypothesis (DSH), 254
diglossia, 64, 67
domain-general, 7, 9, 14, 46, 49, 51, 52, 258
domain-specific, 7, 14, 46, 47, 51, 52
Dynamic Model of Multilingualism (DMM), 58, 59, 60
Dynamic Systems Theory (DST), 58, 59, 60

electroencephalography (EEG), 247, 258, 260
event-related potentials (ERP), 210, 258, 259, 260

falsifiability, 31, 119
  strongest falsificator, 37, 38, 183, 191, 199, 200, 205, 233, 235
Full Transfer/Full Access (FT/FA), 149, 150, 151, 186, 236

gender
  and language use, 65, 66
  grammatical, 10, 11, 13, 43, 177, 260
GenSLA, 49, 117, 118, 119, 120, 134, 135, 136, 150, 151, 156, 159
grammatical representations, 10, 11, 12, 41, 151, 156

hybrid transfer, 199, 200, 201, 203, 205, 220, 226, 228, 229, 230, 236, 240, 242, 251

immersion
  naturalistic, 13, 79
  programs, 68, 70, 72
initial state, 118, 120, 136, 149, 151, 159, 229
instrumental role, 104, 105, 106, 115

L1 grammar, 119, 127, 142, 151, 152, 159, 186
L2 grammar, 13, 15, 17, 50, 142
L3 grammar, 41, 154, 256
language subsystem, 60, 78, 113
language/speech modes, 59, 77
learning task, 14, 41, 50, 51, 53, 54, 61, 117, 189, 190, 200, 203, 221, 234, 236
lexical decision task (LDT), 81, 82, 83, 84, 86, 87, 88, 89, 90, 91, 114
lexical inventions, 103
lexical organization, 79, 81, 87, 89, 94, 95

319